P9-DFF-547

The Presidency of
RUTHERFORD B.
HAYES

AMERICAN PRESIDENCY SERIES

George Washington, Forrest McDonald
John Adams, Ralph Adams Brown
Thomas Jefferson, Forrest McDonald
John Quincy Adams, Mary W. M. Hargreaves
Martin Van Buren, Major L. Wilson
James K. Polk, Paul H. Bergeron
Zachary Taylor & Millard Fillmore, Elbert B. Smith
James Buchanan, Elbert B. Smith
Andrew Johnson, Albert Castel
Rutherford B. Hayes, Ari Hoogenboom
James A. Garfield & Chester A. Arthur, Justus D. Doenecke
Grover Cleveland, Richard E. Welch, Jr.
Benjamin Harrison, Homer E. Socolofsky & Allan B. Spetter
William McKinley, Lewis L. Gould
William Howard Taft, Paolo E. Coletta
Warren G. Harding, Eugene P. Trani & David L. Wilson
Herbert C. Hoover, Martin L. Fausold
Harry S. Truman, Donald R. McCoy
Dwight D. Eisenhower, Elmo Richardson
Lyndon B. Johnson, Vaughn Davis Bornet

The Presidency of

RUTHERFORD B. HAYES

Ari Hoogenboom

UNIVERSITY PRESS OF KANSAS

For Olive

© 1988 by the University Press of Kansas
All rights reserved

Published by the University Press of Kansas (Lawrence,
Kansas 66045), which was organized by the Kansas
Board of Regents and is operated and funded by Emporia
State University, Fort Hays State University,
Kansas State University, Pittsburg State University, the
University of Kansas, and Wichita State University

Library of Congress Cataloging-in-Publication Data

Hoogenboom, Ari Arthur, 1927–
The presidency of Rutherford B. Hayes / Ari Hoogenboom.
    p. cm.—(American presidency series)
    Bibliography: p.
    Includes index.
    ISBN 0-7006-0338-7 (alk. paper)
    1. United States—Politics and government—1877–1881.
    2. Hayes, Rutherford Birchard, 1822–1893.
        I. Title. II. Series.
        E681.H69 1988
    973.8'3'0924—dc19   88-5709
                CIP

British Library Cataloguing in Publication data is available.

Printed in the United States of America
10 9 8 7 6 5 4 3 2 1

The paper used in this publication meets the minimum requirements
of the American National Standard for Performance of Paper for
Printed Library Materials Z39.48–1984

CONTENTS

FOREWORD

The aim of the American Presidency Series is to present historians and the general reading public with interesting, scholarly assessments of the various presidential administrations. These interpretive surveys are intended to cover the broad ground between biographies, specialized monographs, and journalistic accounts. As such, each will be a comprehensive, synthetic work which will draw upon the best in pertinent secondary literature, yet leave room for the author's own analysis and interpretation.

Volumes in the series will present the data essential to understanding the administration under consideration. Particularly, each book will treat the then current problems facing the United States and its people and how the president and his associates felt about, thought about, and worked to cope with these problems. Attention will be given to how the office developed and operated during the president's tenure. Equally important will be consideration of the vital relationships between the president, his staff, the executive officers, Congress, foreign representatives, the judiciary, state officials, the public, political parties, the press, and influential private citizens. The series will also be concerned with how this unique American institution—the presidency—was viewed by the presidents, and with what results.

All this will be set, insofar as possible, in the context not only of contemporary politics but also of economics, international relations, law, morals, public administration, religion, and thought. Such a broad approach is necessary to understanding, for a presidential administration is more than the elected and appointed officers composing it, since its work so often reflects the major problems, anxieties, and glories of the nation. In short, the authors in this series will strive to recount and evaluate the record of each administration and to identify its distinctiveness and relationships to the past, its own time, and the future.

The General Editors

ACKNOWLEDGMENTS

I owe an enormous debt to Director Leslie H. Fishel, jr., and his staff, particularly Thomas A. Smith, Janice Haas, Roberta Hudson, James B. Snider, and Margaret Nicely, at the Hayes Presidential Center for their gracious hospitality and unfailing help during my numerous visits to their library. They have made it a marvelous place for a Gilded Age historian to work. I also appreciate the tolerance of the librarians at Brooklyn College for all of my importunities throughout the years I have worked on this book, and I want to express my gratitude to all connected with the New York Public Library, which invariably has the books and periodicals I cannot obtain elsewhere.

Fellow historians have helped me with their criticisms. Robert V. Bruce of Boston University read the sections on the Great Strike, and Jerome Sternstein of Brooklyn College read and criticized the entire manuscript. I am especially indebted to Donald R. McCoy, Clifford S. Griffin, and Homer E. Socolofsky, the general editors of the American Presidency Series of the University Press of Kansas, for their extensive suggestions.

My greatest debts are to members of my own family. My daughter Lynn, a historian who is a writer and editor for United Feature Syndicate, read the entire manuscript for content and edited it for style. My wife, Olive, apart from encouraging me, read and edited the manuscript at least five times. Her knowledge of the Hayes family and the Gilded Age and her sense of style have influenced every page of this book.

Ari Hoogenboom

Brooklyn, New York
January 1988

1

★ ★ ★ ★ ★

THE CAMPAIGN OF 1876

As the United States began its centennial year, the Republican party had little to celebrate. In the upcoming presidential election, it faced almost certain defeat. Its image had been tarnished by incumbent President Ulysses S. Grant's scandal-ridden administration and by the severe economic depression following the panic of 1873. For its new leader, the Republican party did not turn to a well-known political figure; instead, it nominated the relatively obscure governor of Ohio, Rutherford Birchard Hayes.

Like other Americans, Hayes went to Philadelphia during the presidential campaign to celebrate his country's hundredth birthday. During this celebration, he and other United States citizens took pride in their nation's growth. Population had multiplied from 2.5 million to 46.1 million, with nearly a million people living on the Pacific slope. Farms, in 1876, occupied roughly a quarter of the 1.9 billion acres of land in the continental United States. On those farms, 188 million acres were in cropland, which produced prodigious quantities of corn, wheat, cotton, tobacco, meat, and milk. In 1876, there were still three rural Americans for every one who lived in a city or town, but urban America was growing more rapidly than was the countryside.[1]

The growth of both industrial and urban America, as well as the settlement of the West, was helped by the world's most extensive railroad system. The United States in 1876 had 76,808 miles of track that linked most of its regions and created a national economy. Railroads, supplemented by water transportation on rivers, lakes, and canals, enabled Americans to exploit their enormous resources by transporting to urban centers the products of mines, forests, and fields. Railroads not only supplied factories with raw materials; they also distributed manufactured goods from coast to coast.

There were, in 1876, about a quarter of a million factories, employing about 2.5 million workers. Steel production, among many manufactures, grew spectacularly from 19,643 tons in 1867 to 533,191 tons in 1876 and was at the heart of an ongoing American industrial revolution. But in 1876, manufacturers, revealing the agricultural base on which they thrived, also milled flour, refined sugar, brewed beer, distilled liquor, rolled cigars, wove cloth, and made farm equipment. The winner of the 1876 presidential election would lead the world's fastest-growing nation into its second century.

Americans in 1876 worked hard. Men, women, and children labored from sunup to sundown on the farm, or they worked in factories for ten to twelve hours a day, six days a week. In steel mills, where the furnaces were continuously operated, the twelve-hour day, seven-day week was standard. Americans worked harder for longer hours but received more pay than did their European counterparts. Certain industries, notably textiles, primarily employed women and children. In one South Carolina textile plant, where each of 760 operators worked eleven hours daily, two-thirds were female and one-fifth were children between the ages of ten and fifteen. In many instances, these children supported their families.[2]

The work place was also dangerous, and coal mining was the most hazardous occupation. In the country's centennial year, 256 coal miners died, or 2.8 out of every thousand employed. Industrialism deprived many workers of their tools, skills, and bargaining power; but by bringing the workers together, it made labor unions inevitable. In 1876, however, unions, as well as workers, were suffering from an economic depression.

Despite depression, dangers, difficulties, and drudgery, the hope for better pay attracted most of the 169,986 immigrants who arrived in the United States during the centennial year. Most of these immigrants, 61 percent, came from northern and western Europe, while only 10 percent arrived from southern and eastern Europe. The typical wage-earning family in Massachusetts that year had five members, who collectively earned about $64 a month and spent approximately $35.50 on food, $10.00 on rent, $9.00 on clothing, $4.00 on fuel, and $4.00 on other expenses, leaving $1.50 to be saved or squandered. Poor immigrants, like some Scandinavians who had previously subsisted on dark bread, seized the opportunity to become Americans, to work hard, and to enjoy an ample and varied diet.

American society emphasized toil, but it provided educational opportunities that made upward social mobility a reality for some and a hope for many. Primary education was widespread; 65 percent of those from age five to age seventeen were enrolled in public schools. Absenteeism, however, was common; the average student was present for only 79 of the 133 days in the school year. Illiteracy in the general population was 20 percent and among blacks 80 percent in 1870. Only a tenth of blacks between the ages of five and nineteen were in school that year. Ten years later, however, more than a third of blacks in that age group were enrolled, and illiteracy among all blacks had dropped to 70 percent, while that of the general population had dropped to 17 percent. Beyond grade school, educational opportunities were limited. In 1876, only about 100,000 students attended public high school, with 20,448 of these students graduating that year, while approximately 90,000 students attended college, with 12,005 earning bachelor's degrees, 2,094 of whom were women.

By 1880, the highly literate American population had almost a thousand daily newspapers, with a combined circulation of 3.6 million, while publishers annually produced more than two thousand books. In 1876, the essayist Ralph Waldo Emerson and the poet Henry Wadsworth Longfellow were alive and beloved, although past their prime. Herman Melville, author of the greatest American novel, and Walt Whitman, the nation's most original poet, were still living but, unlike the other two, were not appreciated. William Dean Howells, the editor of the *Atlantic Monthly*, was a friend of Mark Twain's, was married to one of Hayes's cousins, and was a representative novelist of his day. A representative poet was James Russell Lowell, another of Howells's friends. Twain and Howells, who would embrace realism, represented the wave of the future, while Lowell and his idealistic friend George William Curtis, a popular author who as the political editor of *Harper's Weekly* would champion Hayes, remained in the romantic literary tradition.

In art, Howells's writing had its realistic counterpart in the portraits of Thomas Eakins, Twain's writing had its counterpart in the scenes of Winslow Homer, and Albert Bierstadt painted romantic landscapes of the West. Contemporary Americans did not appreciate Eakins, but Homer and Bierstadt achieved popularity. Art and commerce were combined in the architecture of Henry Hobson Richardson and in John A. Roebling's magnificent Brooklyn Bridge, then under construction.

The Philadelphia Centennial Exhibition celebrated the accomplishments and reflected the aspirations of the American people. At the center of the 1876 exhibition was the great Corliss engine, whose geared flywheel and two huge walking beams dominated Machinery Hall and symbolized the nation's technological growth. This massive steam engine powered thirteen acres of machines that spun cotton, printed newspapers, made shoes, pumped water, and performed other tasks. Calling the Corliss engine "an athlete of steel and iron," Howells said, "It is in these things of iron and steel that the national genius most freely speaks; by and by the inspired marbles, the breathing canvases, the great literature; for the present America is voluble in the strong metals and their infinite uses."[3]

The exhibition stressed technology and its mastery by American men and women. The new typewriter on which for fifty cents one could have a letter written; an electric lamp; and Alexander Graham Bell's telephone were demonstrated. A 6-horsepower steam engine in the Woman's Pavilion powered looms that wove cloth and a press that printed a weekly magazine, *The New Century for Women*. Women not only operated machines in the building; they also created or designed its exhibits, ranging from statuary to corsets.

The exhibition celebrated agriculture, patriotism, and art, as well as machinery. There were the Agricultural Hall and the memorable Horticultural Hall, cast in the Moorish style of the twelfth century. Banded in gay colors inside and out, with ornamental stairs leading to galleries painted blue and gold, it typified both the period's interest in new materials and its love of the exotic. The main art exhibition consisted of two and a half miles of picture-covered walls in Memorial Hall. Unfamiliar with nude art, staid Americans were shocked by paintings and statues from France and Italy but jammed the area to view them. Eakins's *The Gross Clinic*—which some critics judge to be the finest American painting of the nineteenth century—was exhibited in the medical section among trusses and artificial limbs, lest Dr. Samuel D. Gross's bloody scalpel and gory hand should overpower the viewers. Patriotism and popular tastes were served by a "plaster cast of George Washington riding heavenward on the back of an eagle."

A special celebration was planned for the Fourth of July at Philadelphia's Independence Square, where once again the Declaration of Independence was to be read. Americans could be proud of their nation, which Abraham Lincoln had described as "the last best hope of earth." It had survived the devastating Civil War, had rid itself of the scourge of slavery, and was the most daring democracy on the globe. Despite a troubling economic depression, the United States continued to be a land of opportunity.

While there was much to celebrate at Philadelphia on 4 July 1876, a protest staged during the festivities showed that American society was not ideal. Made bold by the success of the Woman's Pavilion, suffragists asked to present, but not read, their Declaration of Independence for Women. When their request was turned down, they planned a daring protest. Just after 150,000 people, including presidential candidate Hayes, had listened to the reading of the original Declaration of Independence, Susan B. Anthony, supported by four determined friends, briefly addressed the stunned crowd. She then read the suffragists' declaration while Bayard Taylor was simultaneously reading his "National Ode." Many of those who were present resented the turmoil, seeing little connection between the two declarations. But women could not vote and had difficulty in keeping property after marriage, and many of them were determined to strive for their rights.[4]

Women found it galling that they could not vote, when the Fifteenth Amendment (1870) declared that the right to vote could not be denied "on account of race, color, or previous condition of servitude." To reconstruct the Union on the principle of equality, to secure the civil rights of blacks, and to provide a mass base of voters for the Republican party in the South, Radical Republicans had pushed through that amendment as well as the Fourteenth Amendment (1868), which prevented states from depriving anyone of life, liberty, or property without due process of law.

Despite these amendments and despite laws designed to enforce the provisions of these amendments, white supremacists intimidated southern blacks at the polls. By 1876, blacks were losing the right to vote, particularly in states where they were close to or in a majority. The most violent, disgraceful election in United States history had occurred in the previous year, 1875, when scores of black men had been killed in Republican counties in Mississippi. The Republican Governor Adelbert Ames had begged the Grant administration for troops to carry out the provisions of the Enforcement Acts, which would compel obedience to the Fourteenth and Fifteenth amendments. The administration did not help and, through Attorney General Edwards Pierrepont, sent word that the public was "tired of these annual autumnal outbreaks in the South."

The Grant administration also feared that intervention in Mississippi might draw away enough votes to defeat Hayes in a close gubernatorial campaign in Ohio. Hayes managed to carry Ohio, but Democrats took Mississippi by thirty thousand votes, thus confirming that a sharply defined color line divided southern politics. There, the Republican party was overwhelmingly black, and its small white membership was depleted by threats of social ostracism. The Democrats encompassed virtually all whites, whether prewar Democrats or Whigs, secessionists or unionists, rabid racists or moderate ones.[5]

Mingling racism and partisanship, northern Democrats cheered southern white supremacists, but northern Republicans were divided. During the late 1860s and early 1870s, northern Republicans had overwhelmingly supported federal military intervention in the South to uphold the civil rights of blacks. By 1876 an increasing number of Republicans considered Radical Reconstruction, with its emphasis on coercion by the national government, a failed experiment. They doubted that the unwilling, economically dominant white majority in most southern states could be forced by the nation to accept racial political equality. Although nationalism had triumphed in the Civil War, the United States remained a federal union. By 1876, state and local officials reflected the prejudices of dominant elements in their society except in South Carolina, Louisiana, and Florida, where governments that reflected a Radical national ideal remained shakily in power.

Not only was the promise of the Declaration of Independence postponed and resisted for blacks and women, but the purity of American leaders, which George Washington personified, also seemed to be hopelessly lost. Many Americans would have agreed with Henry Adams's private observation that "the progress of evolution from President Washington to President Grant, was alone evidence enough to upset Darwin." Although the presidency rewarded him for his past military services, Grant had no experience in politics. In contrast to his conduct on the battlefield, he was unsure of himself in the White House. He was inconsistent in carrying out policies, and he was dependent on his aides for strategy and tactics. He exhibited an uncanny knack for dismissing strong, able advisors and for retaining sycophants and corruptionists.

The closing years of Grant's second administration were disastrous. Numerous earlier scandals during his presidency were eclipsed when Secretary of the Treasury Benjamin H. Bristow uncovered a whiskey ring that had defrauded the government of millions in internal-revenue taxes. Grant, who cried, "Let no guilty man escape," proceeded to put friends before principle and carefully made certain that his implicated private secretary, Orville E. Babcock, received no punishment. In 1876, when Bristow discovered that Secretary of War William Worth Belknap had sold traderships at Indian posts, Grant accepted Belknap's resignation with regret, thus frustrating congressional plans to impeach

6

Belknap. Bristow, in turn, earned Grant's enmity for having discovered corruption and became so uncomfortable that he resigned in June 1876.[6]

After a brief attempt, Grant also gave up trying to reform the civil service. The appointment in 1875 of the seasoned spoilsman Zachariah Chandler as secretary of the interior, when that department, especially the corrupt Indian Bureau, needed cleaning up, underscored Grant's abandonment of civil-service reform. Chandler began to collect political assessments (a percentage of a civil servant's salary, which was used to finance election campaigns), and a few weeks after taking office, he fired the experienced chief clerk of the Patent Office for refusing to pay an assessment.[7]

In the early 1870s, corruption on the state and local level was even more blatant than corruption on the national scene, but by 1876, outraged public opinion had caused some changes. In New York City at the beginning of the decade, the Democratic ring controlled by William M. Tweed stole millions of dollars from the city; and Republican James McManes, head of the corrupt gas ring, ruled Philadelphia. Both the New York and the Pennsylvania state legislatures were notorious. To pass bills, New York legislators, known as the Black Horse Cavalry, accepted bribes and practiced blackmail. In Pennsylvania the absence of a general incorporation law and the prevalence of special and local legislation made corruption easy. Legislators sold their votes to grant privileges to corporations, then blackmailed the same corporations by threatening to rescind their privileges.

When exposed, spectacular corruption often aroused public opinion and produced reform. New Yorkers, with Samuel Jones Tilden playing a key role, overthrew the Tweed ring in 1871 and in 1874 adopted a constitutional amendment designed to eliminate the bribing of public officers. Pennsylvania adopted a new constitution that limited special and local legislation in 1873 and adopted a general law of incorporation in 1874.[8]

Despite these limited reform moves, Americans in 1876 felt that their society had not lived up to its promise. Quite apart from the economic hard times, which were recognized as a serious though temporary condition, many Americans thought that their society was suffering from a general malaise brought on by a growing immorality. James Russell Lowell, in his poem "Tempora Mutantur," celebrated the character of "our sires: a hundred years ago" and contrasted it with the sleaziness of centennial America:

> With generous curve we draw the moral line:
> Our swindlers are permitted to resign;

Their guilt is wrapped in deferential names,
And twenty sympathize for one that blames.

Concerned and frustrated, reform-minded Americans agreed with Lowell, who in another poem, "The World's Fair, 1876," sarcastically suggested to America that if it were to display on Centennial Day its most obvious homemade invention, it would:

Show 'em your Civil Service, and explain
How all men's loss is everybody's gain; . . .
Show your State Legislatures; show your Rings;
And challenge Europe to produce such things
As high officials sitting half in sight
To share the plunder and to fix things right;
If that don't fetch her, why, you only need
To show your latest style in martyrs—Tweed:
She'll find it hard to hide her spiteful tears
At such advance in one poor hundred years.

In the spring of 1875, while economic depression and political disaster stalked the nation, Rutherford Birchard Hayes was, at the age of fifty-two, in semiretirement and at peace with himself and the world. His meteoric career, which had demonstrated his capacity to survive and win, seemed to be over, and his proverbial luck in war and politics, which had made him unusually self-confident, apparently had run out.[9]

Hayes was born on 4 October 1822 in Delaware, Ohio, to Sophia Birchard Hayes and the late Rutherford Hayes. The baby was so weak that his mother did not expect him to live. His parents, who were of old New England stock, had migrated to Ohio in 1817. His father had left his mother a farm, which she rented, some additional land, and a house in town, where she kept two lodgers. Her sorrow and her dependence on religion deepened when in January 1825 Hayes's brother Lorenzo, a sturdy nine year old, drowned while ice skating, leaving only Hayes, a puny two year old, and his four-year-old sister, Fanny. Because his understandably protective mother allowed him neither to do household chores nor to join other boys in sports until he was nine, Fanny was Rutherford's constant companion. They remained unusually close until her death, when Hayes was thirty-three. A friendly, cheerful child, Rutherford admired his mother's carefree younger bachelor brother, Sardis Birchard, who left the household when the boy was four but who returned for visits and acted as his surrogate father.

Although Hayes became an ardent advocate of public schools, he never attended one. After his mother taught him to read, spell, and write, his Uncle Sardis generously paid for his education. Hayes attended a private primary school and then was tutored by a local lawyer. When almost fourteen, he left home to attend Norwalk (Ohio) Academy and the next year attended Isaac Webb's Preparatory School in Middletown, Connecticut. In 1838, just after his sixteenth birthday, he entered Kenyon College in Gambier, Ohio, and in 1842 graduated at the head of his class. After studying law for a year with a Columbus, Ohio, lawyer, Hayes entered Harvard Law School and received his Bachelor of Laws degree in 1845. While at Harvard, he studied under Supreme Court Justice Joseph Story, an experience that confirmed Hayes's sympathy for the Whig party.

From 1845 to 1849, Hayes practiced law in Sardis Birchard's town of Upper Sandusky (later Fremont), Ohio. Restless and bored, Hayes, who was an ardent expansionist, planned in June 1847 to leave for the Mexican War. His plan was foiled by his sly uncle, who influenced his nephew's physicians to convince him that his health could not stand a southern climate.

Anxious to be on his own in a challenging city, Hayes broke away in January 1850 and began to practice law in Cincinnati. He soon achieved prominence, and on 30 December 1852 he married Lucy Ware Webb, a recent graduate of Wesleyan Female College. She was a devout Methodist and a reformer who had decided temperance and strong abolitionist beliefs. In contrast, Hayes, a lifelong "worshipper" of Ralph Waldo Emerson, neither experienced conversion nor joined a church. He regularly attended services, however, explaining to his son Webb: "Where the habit does not Christianize, it generally civilizes."[10]

Before his marriage, Hayes also showed little interest in reform. He was a man of reason, not emotion, a conservative who adhered to traditional values. His commitment to reason and justice enabled Lucy to make Hayes a moderate reformer but not a conventional Christian. Beginning in September 1853, he defended captured runaway slaves, and later, to prevent the spread of slavery into western territories, he joined the Republican party. Hayes entered politics, and from 1858 to 1861 he held his first public office as Cincinnati's city solicitor.

When the lower southern states seceded (1860/61), Hayes wanted to *"Let them go,"* but he was outraged when on 12 April 1861 their new Confederacy attacked Fort Sumter at Charleston, South Carolina. Encouraged by Lucy, he went off to war, preferring to *"be killed in the course of it than to live through and after it without taking any part in it."* On 27 June he was commissioned a major in the Twenty-third Ohio Volunteer

Infantry. Hayes served with conspicuous gallantry throughout the Civil War, was wounded four times, and emerged from the struggle a major general and a member-elect of Congress.[11]

Serving in Congress from 1865 to 1867, Hayes consistently supported Radical Republican Reconstruction measures and despised President Andrew Johnson. As chairman of the Joint Committee on the Library, Hayes worked hard to develop the Library of Congress into a great institution. Despite his congenial work with the library, he was unhappy in Congress and resigned to run successfully for governor of Ohio. Reelected in 1869, Hayes served from 1868 to 1872 and counted as his greatest achievements the ratification of the Fifteenth Amendment and the establishment of Ohio State University.[12]

While governor, Hayes remained loyal to the principles of Radical Reconstruction and to Johnson's successor, President Ulysses S. Grant. Despite his friendship with Liberal Republicans and his awareness that Grant was not as great a politician as he was a general, Hayes refused to join the 1872 revolt against the Republican party. To Hayes, Grant's shortcomings were insignificant when compared to those of the Democratic party, which was led and ruled "by New York City plunderers" and "the enemies of the recent amendments" guaranteeing blacks the vote. After leaving the governorship, Hayes returned to Cincinnati, attended the 1872 Republican National Convention, enthusiastically supported Grant's renomination, helped to write the Republican platform, and was defeated that fall when he ran for Congress, primarily to help Grant carry Ohio.[13]

When Grant won both Ohio and the election, observers thought he would reward Hayes with a cabinet appointment, perhaps secretary of the interior, but Grant merely offered to make Hayes assistant United States treasurer at Cincinnati. Hayes resolved to decline this inferior appointment, but before he could act, Ohio's Republican Senator John Sherman temporarily blocked the Senate's confirmation of the appointment, which compounded Hayes's annoyance. A month later, when the appointment came through, Hayes, who had decided "definitely, absolutely, positively" that he had had enough of the "bother" of politics, declined for "reasons chiefly of a private nature." With Lucy and their five children, he left Cincinnati in May 1873 and returned to Fremont, where his Uncle Sardis, whose health was failing, needed him. Sardis Birchard died in January 1874, leaving Hayes the bulk of his estate.[14]

In Fremont, Hayes engaged in local civic matters, managed his real-estate investments, studied the history of the Sandusky Valley, enjoyed his family, and, by March 1875, had gotten "a little too fat for comfort."

He rejoiced in Lucy, who, ten years his junior, was beautiful and basically in good health, despite semimonthly attacks of "sick" headaches. He was proud of his older children: twenty-one-year-old Birchard, who had recently graduated from Cornell and was studying law; nineteen-year-old Webb, who was attending Cornell; and sixteen-year-old Ruddy, a delicate lad, who had just entered Michigan State University.

Hayes was particularly delighted with his only daughter Fanny, aged seven, who was "a boy in climbing, swinging, and playing generally," and his youngest boy, Scott, who had recently turned four and been promoted into pants. The death of three additional sons during the first three years of their lives brought sorrow to the Hayeses, but they were by nature cheerful persons who lavished love and attention on their surviving children. At the age of fifty-two, Hayes was as excited over the first snowfall and the prospect of good sleighing as were Fanny and Scott.[15]

After Hayes retired, the Republican party fell into disarray. Ohio Democrats, led by William Allen, a crusty old campaigner, had captured the governorship from Hayes's successor in 1873, and in that same year the failure of the banking house of Jay Cooke & Co. precipitated a severe panic. The deepening economic depression enabled the Democrats in 1874 to win control of the next House of Representatives. It also threatened Hayes's fortune, which was tied up in real-estate investments, and although "one of the noble army of debtors," Hayes abhorred inflation. He cheered Grant's 1874 veto of a mild inflationary bill that possibly would have increased the combined value of the national bank notes and greenbacks in circulation by $64 million. He was most gratified in 1875 when Grant signed the Specie Resumption Act, which would return the United States to the gold standard on 1 January 1879 by redeeming greenback dollars, which in 1875 were worth less than gold dollars, with gold dollars. Hayes thought he would "be able to stick to Grant to the end."

Sticking was not easy. The scandals of Grant's second administration dismayed Hayes, who, despite his opposition to the Liberal Republicans in 1872, sounded like one of them in 1875. "I do not sympathise with a large share of the party leaders," he wrote in his diary. "I hate the corruptionists of whom [Benjamin F.] Butler is leader. I doubt the ultra measures relating to the South, and I am opposed to the course of Gen. Grant on the 3d term, the Civil Service, and the appointment of unfit men on partisan or personal grounds." From his

11

perspective outside politics, Hayes began to emphasize reconciliation, rather than radicalism, and to affirm his bent for civil-service reform.[16]

Desperate to reverse the decline of their party, Ohio Republicans turned to their best vote getter. Their caucus at Columbus on 25 March 1875 unanimously called on Hayes to run a third time for governor. While begging him to join the fray, fellow Republicans suggested that if he were elected governor, he would "stand well" for the presidency for the next year. "How wild!" Hayes exclaimed. "No body is out of the reach of that mania." Though flattered, he refused to run, but not so emphatically that his supporters abandoned his candidacy. By 31 May, Hayes, though still declining, resolved to heed his party's call, if it persisted. Hayes's friends and the party did persist, and on 2 June 1875 he accepted the gubernatorial nomination.[17]

"Now that I am in for it I rather like it," Hayes admitted. An instinctive vote getter, he proposed a counterattack. He planned to identify the Democratic party with slavery, rebellion, and repression, as well as repudiation, corruption, and Catholicism. Hayes emphasized that the Republicans were right about the "honest payment" of the national debt in gold and not in depreciated paper or silver money, were right about equal civil and political rights for all citizens, were right about destroying slavery, saving the Union, and making "this people one Nation," and were right about resisting Roman Catholic demands that public funds be diverted to parochial schools.

Although the Catholic question—or school question, as Hayes called it—extended beyond Ohio's borders, the national interest in the gubernatorial race focused on the currency issue, even though the governor of Ohio had nothing to do with the nation's money supply. While William Allen, whom the Democrats renominated, favored the inflationary greenback (soft currency), Hayes—though "up to" his "eyes in debt"—regarded the gold standard (hard, sound, or honest money) as both an economic and a moral issue.[18]

Hayes campaigned vigorously, but by late September, he feared he would be beaten, "perhaps badly," by "Hard Times and Plenty of Money to cure it." Hayes preferred success, but when he was back home on Election Day, he noted the perfect weather and his beautiful house and anticipated "defeat with very great equanimity." A loss would immediately return him to the "quiet life" at Spiegel Grove, while he knew a gubernatorial victory would disrupt and trouble his life until he either lost the presidential nomination in June 1876 or, if nominated, lost the election in November 1876. He could accept defeat at this point, because he believed that a Republican defeat in 1876 was "almost a certainty." When Hayes won by 5,544 votes, at least ten Ohio papers pushed his candidacy for the presidency, while George William Curtis, writing in *Harper's Weekly*, the nation's leading illustrated journal, thought the significance of Hayes's triumph was that when Republicans adopted reform, they bucked the Democratic trend and won.[19]

After Hayes was inaugurated as governor of Ohio on 10 January 1876, the campaign to nominate him for the presidency gained momentum. Senator John Sherman urged Ohio Republicans to send a united Hayes delegation to the national convention, and when Gen. Philip A. Sheridan wrote that "his ticket is *Hayes and Wheeler*," Hayes confessed to Lucy, "I am ashamed to say, Who is *Wheeler?*" While gratified, Hayes was passive, but not because he lacked self-confidence. On the contrary, he felt that the "good purposes, and the judgment experience and firmness I possess would enable me to execute the duties of the office well. I do not feel the least fear that I should fail!" He neither encouraged his supporters nor meddled with their efforts to organize on his behalf, because he recognized that "the whole talk . . . is on the score of availability," and he decided shrewdly to "let availability do the work."[20]

On 29 March 1876 the Ohio Republican Convention unanimously declared for Hayes. While he was pleased to report that "my usual serenity carries me along" and while he professed that he wanted to be out of the race, he added that he could not embarrass his supporters by dropping out. Although he played the reluctant candidate, Hayes wanted the nomination. In April he whipped into line an Ohio delegate to the national convention, who contemplated voting for James G. Blaine, with the query, "If I am to be voted for at all, and as long as I am to be voted for at all, may I not reasonably expect the solid vote of Ohio?"[21]

Hayes had other rivals besides Blaine of Maine, whose strength lay among the party faithful. They were Benjamin H. Bristow of Kentucky, whom reformers loved and Grant hated because Bristow had attacked corruption during Grant's administration while serving as secretary of the Treasury; Senator Roscoe Conkling of New York, the stalwart machine politician, who was running with the blessing of Grant, who had decided not to seek a third term; Senator Oliver P. Morton of Indiana, whose radicalism made him the hero of southern Republicans; and John F. Hartranft, the favorite son of Pennsylvania.

Although a reformer and a Bristow supporter, George William Curtis was attracted to Hayes's candidacy, should Bristow falter. Curtis asked Hayes's friend Judge William M. Dickson of Cincinnati if Hayes would have the strength to resist Conkling and Simon Cameron of

Pennsylvania should "their force" help to make him president. Dickson unequivocally and perceptively replied that Hayes "would not consciously nor unconsciously be any man's man" and that Hayes was "self poised and self reliant, unobtrusive and repelling intrusion." Dickson predicted that Hayes would distribute patronage "fairly" among Republican factions, selecting the best men from each division, and that he would greatly raise the qualifications of officeholders. Dickson concluded that Hayes "would not fully meet the wishes of the advanced reformers, but he would . . . perhaps do as much as the country would bear. I think his chief excellence is in his intuitive perception of what at the moment is practicably attainable." Upon seeing Dickson's evaluation, Hayes remarked, "You understand me so well."[22]

Despite their strengths, Hayes's rivals for the prize were handicapped. Blaine, the strongest candidate, appeared to have only a minor problem in the enmity of Conkling, whom he had earlier taunted with scathing accuracy for his vain, posturing, "turkey-gobbler strut." Blaine's candidacy, however, sustained a severe blow when his enemies leaked to the press the allegation that Blaine had received $64,000 from the Union Pacific Railroad—which, as Speaker of the House, he could help—for some nearly worthless Little Rock & Fort Smith Railroad bonds. Blaine denied the story and accused his accusers of having suppressed evidence that would have exonerated him. On 5 June he dramatically read to a packed Congress innocent portions from letters that had been used to incriminate him. Blaine's performance convinced his followers that he was innocent, but delegates who supported other candidates were reluctant to switch to Blaine should the convention become deadlocked. Feeling the strain that he was under, Blaine collapsed a few days later, but quickly recovered. Although sympathetic about Blaine's illness and admiring his pluck, Hayes, who was everyone's favorite vice-presidential candidate, ruled out running with Blaine. Hayes did not relish the job of defending a man who had a questionable record.[23]

Although free from scandal, the other candidates also had drawbacks. Morton was in questionable health, was too radical for moderates on Reconstruction, and was too strongly identified with Grant's administration for reformers; Bristow was too much of a reformer for the administration; Conkling, who was even more strongly identified with the administration than was Morton, was too much the machine politician for reformers; and Hartranft suffered because he had pardoned the financial tycoon Charles T. Yerkes and because he came from Pennsylvania, a one-party state that would automatically go Republican.

When the convention assembled in Cincinnati on 14 June 1876, the major candidates objected less to Hayes than to each other. Hayes's public record as a Radical Republican was impeccable, though by 1876 he had private doubts about "ultra measures"; he was reform-minded, but had staunchly supported Grant in 1872; he had valiantly supported the Union during the war; he had stood fearlessly for equal rights and sound money, and yet by nature he was a conciliator and a compromiser; and he could carry Ohio, which was essential in 1876 for a Republican victory. Holding the convention at Cincinnati, largely at the behest of Bristow and Morton supporters, because of its proximity to Kentucky and Indiana, helped Hayes. Cincinnati, the scene of his early triumphs, was teeming with his supporters, and in his kinsman Edward F. Noyes, leader of the Ohio delegation, Hayes had a first-rate manager.

The convention, however, was driven to near frenzy when Robert G. Ingersoll, in his nominating speech, declared: "Like an armed warrior, like a plumed knight, James G. Blaine marched down the halls of the American Congress and threw his shining lance full and fair against the brazen foreheads of the defamers of his country and the maligners of his honor." Blaine's supporters later contended that if the convention had proceeded that evening, their man would have won, but balloting was postponed until the next day. What Blaine won that evening was a dubious sobriquet, which hostile cartoonists would use mercilessly, caricaturing him as a less-than-heroic knight in armor with a broken plume on his helmet.[24]

Hayes's supporters were pleased about the balloting. With 379 votes necessary to win, Blaine, on the first ballot, had 285, Morton 125, Bristow 113, Conkling 99, Hayes 61, and Hartranft 58. Blaine's lead was impressive, but allegations of scandal lingered. Supporters of the major candidates hardly budged. After four ballots, Blaine gained 7 votes. On the fifth round of balloting, however, Michigan, where Hayes had 5 delegates, gave all of its 22 votes to Hayes, thus helping to raise his total to 104. On the sixth ballot, Hayes received only 9 additional votes, while Blaine picked up 22, raising the latter's total to 308.[25]

With Blaine gaining momentum, his opponents huddled. When the roll call reached Indiana on the seventh ballot, its chairman withdrew Morton's name, giving 25 votes to Hayes and 5 to Bristow, and "four to five thousand persons," according to the London *Times* correspondent, were "jumping, yelling, stamping, waving arms and hats as if suddenly stricken with raving madness." Though Iowa and Kansas stayed with Blaine, John Marshall Harlan, a future Supreme Court justice, speaking for Kentucky, withdrew Bristow from the race and cast 24 votes for Hayes. As the roll call continued, both Hayes and Blaine gained votes, but New York, abandoning Conkling though not his prejudices, cast 61 votes for Hayes and only 9 for Blaine. If Blaine could pick up the 58 votes of Pennsylvania, the state of his birth, he still would have a chance, but Hartranft's supporters divided almost evenly, giving Blaine 30 votes and Hayes 28. When the roll was completed, at 5:30 P.M., on 16 June, Hayes had 384 votes, thus winning the nomination by 5 votes, although 21 additional votes, cast for Bristow before his withdrawal, would probably have gone to Hayes.

At 6 P.M., Hayes wrote to his eldest son Birchard, "My hand is sore with shaking hands." Blaine graciously congratulated Hayes, and deeply touched, Hayes responded with equal graciousness. Each man had need for the other. When the convention selected Congressman William A. Wheeler of New York as its vice-presidential nominee, it achieved a balanced ticket that would run well in the crucial states of New York and Ohio.[26]

"I cannot help thinking," Curtis wrote to Hayes, "that your nomination at this juncture is as fortunate for the country as that of Mr. Lincoln in 1860." Curtis believed that Hayes would attract the "immense independent vote" in New York. "The general & joyful response of this state as well as of the country, is due, I am very sure to the feeling that while you are a party man and the candidate of the whole party, yet that your sympathies and purposes are for the purification and elevation of the tone of the government." Hayes was proud that he was "in no way conscious of fault in getting" the nomination, and he determined that "if elected I shall try to do precisely what is right."[27]

Two weeks later, on 27 June, the Democratic convention met in St. Louis, denounced Republican corruption and "financial imbecility and immorality," offered itself as the party of reform, and nominated on its second ballot its strongest candidate, Governor Samuel J. Tilden of New York. In 1876, Tilden boasted a considerable reputation as a reformer. After having helped smash New York City's corrupt Tweed ring, he had smashed the state's corrupt canal ring. Tilden's running mate, Thomas A. Hendricks of Indiana, strengthened the Democratic ticket. He was from an important, doubtful midwestern state, and in contrast to Tilden's hard-money views, he was a soft-money man. With the country suffering from hard times, with the corrupt record of the Grant administration, with Tilden's reputation as a reformer, with the Democrats' straddling of the money issue, and with white supremacists in the South intimidating black Republicans, it looked as though Tilden and Hendricks would defeat Hayes and Wheeler. William Henry Smith, manager of the Western Associated Press, warned Hayes: "We have before us a strong, dangerous enemy."[28]

As was the custom, neither Hayes nor Tilden participated in the campaign except for writing formal acceptances of their nominations. Tilden's letter approved the Democratic platform, elaborated on his hard-money views, and stressed his commitment to frugality and reform. Hayes's letter approved the Republican platform; stressed the need for civil-service reform; promised not to seek a second term, lest patronage be used to secure his reelection; and emphasized his commitments to nonsectarian public schools, to resume specie payments as scheduled in January 1879, and to honest and capable local government in the South, when the constitutional rights of all citizens were respected.

"The two parts I took thought about," Hayes wrote, "were the Civil Service, and the South. In the latter, I wanted to plainly talk of the rights of the colored man, and at the same time to say what I could for the interests and feelings of the well disposed white man." Hayes's call for a "thorough, radical, and complete" reform of the spoils system went beyond the platform's criticism of congressional interference with executive appointments and arrested the drift of reformers toward Tilden. Initially, Hayes had been inclined "to say very little" about reform, but by heeding the advice of the reformers George William Curtis, Carl Schurz, and Benjamin H. Bristow and of the shrewd Ohio politicians John Sherman, Charles Foster, and James A. Garfield, Hayes had, as he said, "hit the nail on the head . . . pretty hard."[29]

Republican reformers agreed. Curtis said to Hayes: "The tone and grasp of the letter are alike most striking, for they show unmistakably that it is not the work of a politician but of a very different person." Even those reformers who opposed the one-term principle because they realized that the civil service could not be reformed in four years and that Hayes would be as badly needed in 1881 as he was in 1877, liked his letter. Most of the Liberal Republican bolters of 1872 followed Schurz back to the Republican party. The Hayes people welcomed Schurz, not so much as a reformer, which he certainly was, but as an early practitioner of ethnic politics, since he reputedly could influence his fellow German-Americans, many of whom were strategically located in close states. Illustrating his knack of being politic while appearing not to be a politician, Hayes assured Grant that the one-term declaration was not a reflection on Grant's administration.[30]

After the publication of their letters, Governors Hayes and Tilden played the role that tradition assigned to them. Pretending to be above the sordid business of electioneering, they steadfastly administered their state governments, while awaiting the call of the people. Aloof by nature, Tilden played the role so convincingly that Democratic campaign managers thought he was indifferent to the outcome of the election. Hayes wrote encouragingly to friends, but he said little beyond his public letter. "On general principles," he told Garfield, "I think explanations and defenses are bad things." For a "taking" campaign biography, he shipped William Dean Howells a half-barrel of what Howells termed "glorious material." But Hayes warned: "Be careful not to commit me on religion, temperance, or free-trade. Silence is the only safety." Insulated from the people, except on two official visits to the Philadelphia Centennial Exhibition as governor of Ohio, Hayes, as expected, had little to do with managing his campaign.[31]

Because party organization was decentralized, a separate committee ran the campaign in each state. The Republican National Committee coordinated the overall effort and concentrated its money in doubtful, crucial states. Under the leadership of a masterful, energetic organizer, such as Matthew S. Quay would be in 1888, the National Committee could lead the party to victory, but in 1876 the committee was ineffective. It met in July to select a new chairman; and Hayes, who preferred the capable Edward F. Noyes of Ohio, professed that he was "entirely content" when the Grant and Blaine people chose Zachariah Chandler. A former senator from Michigan, Chandler was secretary of the interior and was identified "with Grant and Grantism."[32]

Chandler lent the Republican cause his unsavory reputation, but he failed to give the campaign his undivided attention. Stanley Matthews, a Kenyon College chum, even warned Hayes that Chandler was part of a plot to throw the election to Tilden. Chandler, who rarely communicated with Hayes, angered independents by levying time and money from civil servants for the campaign. The depression and the bleak prospects for a Republican victory in 1876 made it five times more difficult to raise money than in 1872. But in the end, the Republican National Committee spent approximately $200,000, or roughly what it had spent in the two previous presidential elections. A hefty proportion of that total was raised by assessing Washington civil servants 2 percent of their annual salary. An outraged Schurz threatened to quit the campaign and demanded that Hayes publicly oppose political assessments and that he try to fire Chandler. Privately, Hayes suggested that assessments "ought not to be allowed," and Schurz, who was too committed to Hayes to withdraw his support, kept his speaking appointments.[33]

As time progressed, it became obvious that civil-service reform was not "*the* issue" of the campaign and that Hayes no longer intended it to be. "WE MUST CHOOSE OUR OWN TOPICS," he wrote to Garfield; "*the danger of giving the Rebels the Government*, is the topic people are most interested in. Next *Tilden* and after that *Schools—one term*—etc. etc." Hayes relegated civil-service reform, if indeed the one-term idea could be considered part of it, to a poor fourth place, behind his opposition to giving public money to sectarian schools. This defection from reform was not a temporary aberration. Hayes later reiterated to Garfield that the "true issue" with the masses was "Shall the late rebels have the government?" Hayes even wrote to Schurz in a similar vein.[34]

By urging the Republicans to "wave the bloody shirt," Hayes rejected the southern-strategy advice of Charles Nordhoff of the *New York Herald*. Nordhoff suggested that Hayes confer *"quietly"* with "a few of the prominent old Whig leaders of the Southern states, . . . detach from the Democratic side down there the real Whig vote," and "without much trouble & with no embarrassing engagements, make sure of carrying Louisiana, North Carolina, Virginia & Arkansas." Nordhoff optimistically argued that "all wise & patriotic" southerners accepted the "later Constitutional Amendments," that federal intervention in local southern affairs would no longer be necessary, and that southern parties were already "re-arranging themselves . . . independent of the color line." In short, he concluded: "the darkies you'll have any how; the white Whigs are what you want to capture."[35]

Reformers, however, refused to "wave the bloody shirt" and were annoyed that it diverted attention from reform. When George Frisbie Hoar, a Republican congressman from Massachusetts, made a strong civil-service-reform speech, it attracted attention as "almost the only one of the kind . . . from any active Republican politician." The *New York Times* pointed out that the fundamental nature of civil-service reform entitled it to be one of the campaign's chief issues, and Charles Eliot Norton of Harvard College found in Cambridge "less & less faith that Hayes & Reform are synonymous."[36]

Despite reform leanings, Hayes agreed with Blaine, Morton, and Chandler that playing on passions growing out of the Civil War would increase the Republican vote in the North. With southern Democrats defying the Fourteenth and Fifteenth amendments and bloodying more than enough Republican shirts to rekindle war passions, Republicans did not fabricate the issue. In most of the South, Reconstruction had all but ended by 1876, and by upholding white supremacy, the Democratic party had eclipsed the Republican party with its commitment to the rights of blacks. Republicans still clung to power in South Carolina, Louisiana, and Florida. The twenty-eight hundred federal troops who were stationed in the eleven former Confederate states were largely symbolic, but they protected the Republican administrations from hostile Democrats. As the campaign progressed, the hope that Hayes would carry even those states grew slimmer.[37]

South Carolina had appeared to be safely Republican. Besides its large black population, Governor Daniel H. Chamberlain, a popular reform Republican whom the Democrats considered endorsing, was up for reelection. On 8 July, however, the white rifle clubs of Aiken and Edgefield counties invaded the predominantly black town of Hamburg, fought with its militia, took thirty captives, and later murdered five of them. Although most Democrats deplored the attack, they were angered when Chamberlain charged that the "Hamburg Massacre" was a political move by Democrats to prevent Republicans from voting. When he asked Grant for more troops, Democrats, fearing a return to "bayonet rule," turned on Chamberlain and nominated Wade Hampton III to oppose him.

Because Hampton wanted black votes, he ruled out a repetition of Mississippi's violent 1875 campaign, but he did not rule out the threat of violence. Red-shirted Democratic rifle clubs paraded, and armed Democrats demanded equal time at Republican rallies. At such a meeting, George D. Tillman—whose brother Ben later promised his constituents that he would stick his pitchfork into President Grover Cleveland's "old ribs"—pointed at Chamberlain and a fellow Republican and urged his followers to "hang em now." Though goaded to assassinate, the intruding Democrats were content to draw half a dozen pistols, scream the rebel yell, and call the governor a "God damn Son of a bitch." Although acts of violence were few in proportion to the threats of violence, the Republican campaign was paralyzed. Fearing that South Carolina would be lost if something were not done, Chamberlain renewed his plea for federal troops to protect black voters at the polls.[38]

While leading Louisiana Republicans had settled their differences by 1876, their earlier factionalism had left the party demoralized. In some parishes, the party even neglected to name local slates. As in South Carolina, Democrats sought to attract black voters and wished to avoid the "Mississippi plan" of murder and fraud, lest Republicans be given an excuse to throw out Democratic votes. During the spring and summer of 1876, Democrats organized mounted rifle clubs, but they usually refrained from actual violence. Despairing Republican leaders begged for more federal troops—particularly a black cavalry regiment— to guard the polls in black parishes: "It would so encourage the people that they would not be killed for voting the Rep[ublican]. ticket, they would turn out en-masse. Now they are depressed & very many have joined Democratic clubs." Adding to the uncertain outcome of the campaign, the racial composition of Louisiana was in doubt. The 1870 federal census reported an almost equal number of blacks and whites, but an 1875 state census by Republicans claimed that adult blacks outnumbered whites by twenty thousand.[39]

Whites were in a majority in Florida, but many were northern in background and Republican in politics, which placed that party on an even footing with the Democratic party as long as blacks had access to the polls. Early in the presidential campaign, there were two Republicans running for governor, each with a separate, competing slate of Hayes-Wheeler electors. Republican disaster was averted when the frantic national leadership convinced the independent slate to withdraw, but the campaign was seriously weakened. Democrats nominated a moderate transplanted Yankee, who appealed to disaffected Republicans. Relying more on economic coercion than on physical force, the Democrats distributed numbered ballots to their employees. To offset Democratic coercion, Republicans in Florida, as well as in South Carolina and Louisiana, planned to use their control of the election machinery.[40]

In the light of events in Mississippi in 1875 and in South Carolina in 1876, it is understandable that Hayes sought to rally Republicans around the flag. On 18 September he noted in his diary thirteen "watchwords" that "might be useful if well circulated." All thirteen rephrased the question, "Are you for the Rebellion, or are you for the Union?" If the bloody shirt could win the doubtful northern states of Indiana and New York, strong-arm Democratic tactics in the South would help the Republicans. But Republican prospects in Indiana, a hotbed of Greenback sentiment, appeared bleak. Gen. Judson Kilpatrick, whose cavalry had made Sherman's march to the sea a painful memory for many southerners, wrote to Hayes that a *"bloody shirt campaign, with money,"* would save Indiana, but a *"financial* campaign and no money and we are beaten."

Republicans poured $47,000, less than half the $100,000 that Morton requested, into Indiana and lost the October election by five thousand votes. As Hayes expected, Ohio went Republican by nine thousand votes, which would likely double for him in November. With Indiana slipping away, Republican strategists realized that they had to concentrate on New York and on salvaging southern states. While urging the Republican National Committee not to give up Indiana, where Republicans had a "fighting chance," Hayes declared: "The contest is now with the East." And he prudently suggested: "In the South, if we have a prospect to carry any states, we must look after North and South Carolina, Florida, Miss[issippi], and L[ouisian]a."[41]

21

Jolted by the October loss in Indiana, the Grant administration reinforced South Carolina, despite the federal commander's claim that he had enough men. The additional troops made the rifle clubs lie low, and a jubilant South Carolina Republican told Hayes he would carry the state by twenty thousand votes. The show of federal force, however, lost Hayes the support of some liberals, such as his friend Charles Nordhoff, whose dream of having Republicans capture the southern-white-Whig vote was destroyed. He warned Hayes that despite his "good intentions," if he "were elected on a coercion . . . policy," he might "be a mere prisoner" of the high-handed "Chandlers, Mortons, Logans, and Butlers."[42]

Above all, the October elections confirmed the importance of New York. The home of Tilden and Conkling, New York posed a problem for Republicans. Tilden was both a popular governor—he had been elected in 1874 by a plurality of fifty thousand votes—and a reformer. He was also a political leader who, as chairman of the Democratic State Committee from 1866 to 1874, had organized his party. Besides utilizing all available speakers, his "perfect system"—as Republicans fearfully dubbed it—learned each voter's political preference, bombarded likely converts with Democratic literature, which was sent out by state and city employees, and targeted special ethnic groups. The Democrats, however, were off to a slow start. The Civil War Governor Horatio Seymour, whom they had nominated again, was ailing, so he refused to run; and at the second convention, Tilden's nominee, State Controller Lucius Robinson, squeaked through. Nevertheless, by mid October, Tilden's system appeared to be running smoothly, and Republicans were "cowed."[43]

Relying on federal civil servants, especially in the New York Customhouse, Republicans knew how to organize the electorate. But the man who was in control of the New York machine was not enthusiastic about the campaign. Roscoe Conkling would have accepted his failure to get the nomination with better grace if Hayes had ignored civil-service reform in his acceptance letter. The reformers whom Hayes had pleased were loathed by Conkling, and at the New York State Republican Convention, they kept Conkling from nominating for governor his customhouse lieutenant Alonzo B. Cornell. Although Conkling had prevented reformers from naming William M. Evarts and although Conkling was reasonably pleased with the compromise nominee, Civil War Governor Edwin D. Morgan, the convention confirmed that Conkling was not in complete control. He did manage to keep Cornell as state chairman, but Cornell's task was to carry New York for Morgan and Hayes, the men who had frustrated his and Conkling's ambitions.

With Conkling sulking and Cornell "sour & disappointed," the New York campaign was not inspired. Hayes tried to flatter Conkling by inviting him to campaign in the West, but Conkling remained silent in the East.[44]

While Democrats had Tilden's perfect system, Republicans had the 1871 Federal Elections Act, also called the Enforcement Act. They had designed the elections law to prevent Democrats from repeating the Tweed ring's frauds of 1868, when the naturalization of thousands of recent immigrants enabled Seymour, the Democratic presidential nominee, to carry New York City by sixty thousand votes and the state by ten thousand. With Republicans claiming that forty thousand of the New York City votes were fraudulent, Congress in 1870 tightened the naturalization procedures, and the Enforcement Act of 1871 regulated elections in cities of more than twenty thousand. It was the urban Democratic vote that Republicans hoped to curtail, since all but ten of the sixty-eight cities affected in 1871 were in the North.

If two citizens from a congressional district petitioned a federal circuit court, alleging that frauds were about to be perpetrated, the court was required to appoint, for each polling place, a Republican supervisor and a Democratic supervisor to challenge and arrest illegal voters. The local United States marshal, a political appointee, could deputize as many marshals as he deemed necessary—all of whom could be of the same party—and both supervisors and marshals could be paid five dollars a day for ten days. In 1872, Congress extended the law to rural areas. During the campaign of 1876, the Grant administration spent over $291,000 for 11,501 deputy marshals and 4,863 supervisors, and of that sum, more than $80,000 was used to hire 2,300 deputy marshals and 1,144 supervisors to police the election in New York City.[45]

The chief supervisor of federal elections in that city was John I. Davenport, a "fanatic" Republican who commanded the formidable force paid for by the federal government. Davenport had the residence of each registered voter checked against especially prepared real-estate maps, mailed notices to registered voters who were listed at unlikely addresses, ran newspaper advertisements warning those whose letters came back marked "addressee unknown" not to vote, and threatened that if they did, he would swear out a warrant for their arrest. So complete were Davenport's preparations that he predicted there would not be a hundred fraudulent votes cast in New York City. On 6 November, Cornell confidently telegraphed Hayes, "Our electoral vote will be cast for you."[46]

Hayes lacked Cornell's confidence. "I still think," he noted on Election Day, 7 November 1876, "Democratic chances the best." Even though he did not believe that a Democratic victory would postpone an economic revival, he thought that a Democratic victory would be "a calamity." The civil service would deteriorate, and the South would "drift towards chaos." With no laws to decide a disputed election, Hayes feared a "contested result." He vowed to avert bloodshed and civil war, but "if forced to fight," Hayes had "no fears of failure from lack of courage or firmness."[47]

Receiving dispatches on the evening of Election Day, the Hayes family and a few friends became depressed when "Ohio was not doing as well as" they "had hoped." Feeling the disappointment keenly, Lucy "busied herself about refreshments . . . and soon disappeared . . . abed with a head ache." Though Hayes commanded his "usual composure and cheerfulness," he "never supposed there was a chance for Republican success" after he had learned that Tilden would probably carry New York City by fifty thousand votes. When Hayes joined Lucy after midnight, they consoled each other with the thought that their lives would be simpler. "Both of us," Hayes wrote, "felt more anxiety about the South—about the colored people especially than about anything else. . . . There the amendments will be nullified, disorder will continue, prosperity to both whites and colored people, will be pushed off for years." Nevertheless, they "soon fell into a refreshing sleep and the affair seemed over."[48]

2

★ ★ ★ ★ ★

THE DISPUTED ELECTION

The affair was not over. Zach Chandler, at the Republican National Committee's headquarters in the Fifth Avenue Hotel in New York City, received the same discouraging reports and, like Hayes and Lucy, retired early, although, unlike them, he found consolation in a bottle of whiskey. Ohio had remained Republican, but Tilden had carried New York, New Jersey, Connecticut, Indiana, and apparently the entire South, giving him a plurality of about 250,000 votes and, it seemed, 203 electoral votes. Only 185 votes were needed for victory. When Gen. Daniel E. Sickles stopped at Republican headquarters on his way home from an after-theater supper, only the chief clerk remained on duty. A Republican with a checkered past, Sickles as a pre–Civil War Democratic congressman had murdered the son of Francis Scott Key in Lafayette Square, across from the White House, for having seduced Sickles's wife. As a Union general in the Civil War, he had disregarded orders at Gettysburg and had lost many men as well as his own leg; and as Grant's minister to Spain, Sickles's liaison with the deposed queen of that country had given new meaning to the phrase "foreign affairs." For many reformers, Sickles personified what was wrong with the Grant administration.

Although Sickles's fear of a Democratic victory seemed to be confirmed by the election-night dispatches on Chandler's desk, Sickles found a glimmer of hope. Hayes could win if the far-western states (California, Nevada, and Oregon) went Republican and if the southern states that had Republican administrations could be saved. Over Chandler's signature, Sickles telegraphed Republican leaders in South Carolina, Louisiana, Florida, and Oregon: "With your state sure for Hayes, he is elected. Hold your state." At 3 A.M., Governor Daniel H. Chamberlain responded: "All right. South Carolina is for Hayes. Need more troops. Communication with interior cut off by mobs." At about 6 A.M., Sickles received an "encouraging" answer from Oregon, whereupon he again telegraphed "all four states, informing them that the enemy claimed each of them and enjoining vigilance and diligence." While Hayes and Chandler slept, convinced of defeat and without plans to contest it, Sickles had set events in motion that would plunge the nation into a crisis and bring victory to Hayes. Satisfied with his night's work, Sickles went home to sleep.[1]

Sickles was not alone in refusing to believe that Tilden had won. John C. Reid, the rabid Republican managing editor of the *New York Times* who had been a Civil War prisoner in Richmond's notorious Libby Prison, continued to monitor the returns at the *Times* office and refused to concede the election to Tilden. In its first edition of Wednesday 8 November, the *Times* proclaimed the election "Doubtful." Reid and his colleagues then coupled encouraging reports, probably inspired by Sickles's telegrams, from Oregon, South Carolina, Louisiana, and Florida with the indiscreet 3:45 A.M. query of Daniel Magone, New York State's Democratic chairman: "Please give your estimate of electoral votes secured for Tilden. Answer at once."

The apparent Democratic uncertainty encouraged the *Times* in its second edition to claim 181 votes for Hayes and victory should Florida, with its 4 votes, be carried by Republicans. Shortly after 6 A.M., Reid rushed to Republican headquarters to tell Zach Chandler how the *Times* had interpreted the dispatches, but Reid found only William E. Chandler, New Hampshire's man on the Republican National Committee and a former secretary of that organization.[2]

Together, William Chandler and Reid went to Zach Chandler's desk and read his dispatches, including several in a scrawl that Chandler recognized as Sickles's. Rousing Zach Chandler from his whiskey-induced stupor, they learned that he knew nothing about the dispatches, whose import he could hardly comprehend, but he told them to "do what you think necessary." William Chandler reported to Hayes, "I immediately telegraphed to Florida, Louisiana, South Carolina, Nevada & Oregon that all depended on them and that with them we were safe, to look out for Democratic frauds & to telegraph us when sure. . . . My dispatches got off at 6½ ahead of similar democratic dispatches, Reid & I believed." Chandler soon began to receive favorable answers, and when Republicans arrived at headquarters that

Wednesday morning, "it seemed," he reported, "as if the dead had been raised." By Wednesday evening, a sober, confident Zach Chandler claimed that Hayes had been elected "beyond a doubt."[3]

Hayes and Tilden remained detached from the turmoil surrounding the election. Although convinced of defeat on Wednesday morning, Hayes wrote a few days later that by afternoon "it dawned on us that with a few Republican States in the South to which we were fairly entitled, we would yet be victors." Fearing "fraud, violence and intimidation," Hayes expected Republicans to be deprived of the victory. Warning himself to be prepared "to accept the inevitable," he observed, "I do it with composure and cheerfulness."

Tilden spoke like a winner on Wednesday but quickly adjusted to the possibility of defeat. On Thursday he was satisfied with his course "whether he had been elected or not," and by Friday he thought that people would prevent any attempt by the "fiery zealots of the Republican Party . . . to count me out," but he did nothing to arouse the people. Although many Democrats urged him to show "nerve and resolution" and "rescue the country," Tilden, dilatory by nature, remained silent. His faith in law and the American political system encouraged him to postpone decisions when confronted by demands that he rally public opinion. Too principled and irresolute to fight, Tilden remained inactive.[4]

While Hayes and Tilden remained calm, the blustering of their followers caused apprehension and brought action. Gen. William T. Sherman, commanding the Army of the United States, on 18 November 1876 diverted four artillery companies, which were en route to New York, to the United States Arsenal in Washington. His "confidential" order insisted that "as little display as possible" accompany their arrival and that "great prudence" be employed in explaining "to the Commanding Officers, all matters that will enable them to understand the reasons for this change of destination."[5]

As Hayes had foretold, the law was murky, and the American political system malfunctioned in 1876. The day after the election, it was clear that there were 19 disputed electoral votes in South Carolina, Florida, and Louisiana. If awarded to Hayes, they would give him 185 electoral votes to Tilden's 184. The election was close enough in those states to be in doubt when Sickles and William E. Chandler sent their telegrams. Several days would elapse before tallies were available, and those tallies would not be official.

The "returning" (election) board in each disputed state was controlled by Republicans and would determine the outcome. These boards did not merely count ballots; the law empowered them to throw out fraudulent votes. Because the returning boards would determine whether Hayes or Tilden would be president, Democrats would press them to count the ballots cast and Republicans would urge them to throw out votes. To keep their opponents from perpetrating frauds, nationally prominent Republicans and Democrats rushed south to bolster or overwhelm members of returning boards.[6]

Nothing was settled by the unofficial tally of ballots. Hayes appeared to have carried South Carolina by 600 to 1,000 votes, but the Democrats had won the governorship by 1,100 votes, and other contests were close. Although Election Day was relatively calm, there was considerable fraud (South Carolina had no registration law), because more votes were cast than there were eligible voters. With Hayes ahead and a Republican returning board determining the final outcome, it was obvious that Hayes would secure South Carolina; therefore few visiting statesmen went there to buttress their partisans.

Florida's vote was so close that Hayes would carry the state by 43 votes, if the Baker County canvassing board were allowed to throw out the vote of two precincts. If these votes were counted, Tilden would carry Florida by 94 votes. With fraud rampant, it is impossible to determine who would have won a fair election. Repeaters, stuffed ballot boxes, and Democratic ballots that had been printed with the Republican symbol to trick illiterate voters were all utilized. Returns from remote areas were delayed, to be altered as needed. William E. Chandler supervised the struggle to save Florida for Hayes; he was aided by agents from the Justice, Treasury, and Post Office departments, as well as by Hayes's friend Edward F. Noyes.[7]

Holding Louisiana proved to be the greatest challenge facing Republicans. There had been little intimidation on Election Day, Republican factionalism had alienated some black voters, and Tilden unofficially carried the state by more than 6,300 votes, while Democrat Francis T. Nicholls defeated Stephen B. Packard for the governorship. Republicans argued that the Democrats had intimidated enough blacks, who constituted a majority of registered voters, to carry the state.

The Republican visiting statesmen, led by John Sherman, James A. Garfield, and former Congressman Charles B. Farwell, a wealthy Chicago merchant, collected evidence of "intimidation & violence" to justify tossing out enough Democratic votes to bring a Republican victory. Sherman assured Hayes that he should and would have the vote of Louisiana according to the letter and spirit of its laws. Hayes agreed that in a fair election he would have won at least forty southern electoral votes. "But," he cautioned, "we are not to allow our friends to defeat one outrage and fraud by another. There must be nothing crooked on our part."[8]

The returning boards began their deliberations in South Carolina, Louisiana, and Florida on 10, 16, and 27 November respectively. All five members of the South Carolina board were Republicans, and three of them were candidates in elections that the board would canvass. On 22 November the board announced that because of widespread fraud and intimidation, the votes in both Edgefield (where George Tillman had threatened Governor Chamberlain) and Laurens counties were invalid. This announcement ensured that the Republicans would carry not only the state for Hayes but also the legislature and the governorship. When the legislature met on 26 November, Republicans in the lower chamber refused to seat Democrats who claimed to have been elected from Edgefield and Laurens counties, whereupon all Democrats withdrew and set up a rival state government.[9]

In Louisiana, four Republicans composed the returning board. Although the law required them to do so, they did not appoint a Democrat as the fifth member. The board's chairman was J. Madison Wells, whom Gen. Philip Sheridan had described nine years earlier as "a political trickster and dishonest man," but John Sherman thought Wells "firm, judicious and as far as I can judge, thoroughly honest and conscientious."

Sheridan was right; Wells was trying to auction off the presidency. First, through an intermediary, he approached Henry Watterson, offering Louisiana's electoral vote to the Democrats for $250,000 ($100,000 each for the two white board members and $25,000 each for the two black members), but Watterson, who was the editor of the *Courier-Journal* (Louisville, Ky.), as well as a congressman, an advisor to Tilden, and at that moment a "visiting statesman" in New Orleans, was not interested. Next, Wells supposedly failed to extract money from the leaders of his own party (for giving the state to Hayes). Through another intermediary, he then offered Louisiana's vote to Tilden and Hewitt for $1 million, which was also refused. Finally, Tilden's nephew, Col. William T. Pelton, the acting secretary of the Democratic National Committee, negotiated with Wells for a sales price of $200,000, but the deal had not been completed when the board had to report in early December.

The enterprising Wells was unable to sell the election to the Democrats, but he probably did realize a profit by negotiating with his own party. Although the Republican visiting statesmen had faith in Wells and his colleagues, Charles B. Farwell was extremely confident about the outcome on 22 November. "The vote cast, illegal & legal combined as you are aware, is against us,'' Farwell wrote to Hayes's friend William Henry Smith, manager of the Western Associated Press, ''but I have no reason to-day to fear the result. I am in constant communication with those who *know,* and they assure me that all will be well.''

Farwell's confidence apparently resulted from expenditures that he made out of his own well-lined pocket. One year later, Smith urged Hayes to give Farwell a cordial welcome at the White House, reminding the president that Farwell was the first to reach New Orleans and thwart the Democrats, ''that in all delicate and important matters last year he was our right hand man,'' and that ''his wealth . . . supplied the means when no other could be reached.'' The result announced on 5 December was as Farwell had predicted. Specifically, the board threw out the votes cast in East Feliciana and Grant parishes and disallowed selected votes in twenty-two other parishes, totaling fifteen thousand votes, thirteen thousand of which were Democratic. Instead of losing Louisiana, Hayes and Packard carried it by more than three thousand votes.[10]

Florida's returning board had a Democratic member, but he was outvoted by the two Republicans. The state board restored the vote of two Democratic precincts that had been thrown out by a local returning board, thus putting Tilden ahead by ninety-four votes. But then its Republican members accepted challenges to large Democratic majorities at other points, and on 6 December it declared Hayes the victor by nine hundred votes and the state Republican ticket victorious by a narrower margin.[11]

While the Republican returning boards in South Carolina, Louisiana, and Florida were counting their partisans into office, a bizarre development in Oregon played into Democratic hands. Everyone agreed that Hayes had carried that state by more than a thousand votes. John W. Watts, however, was both the postmaster of Lafayette, Oregon, and a Republican elector on the ballot; and the Constitution forbade him as a federal officeholder to be an elector. Watts and Oregon Republicans, who were aware of the problem, assumed that if elected, he would resign his post-office position. When he was elected, he did resign, as did a Vermont elector who was also a postmaster. Oregon, however, had a Democratic governor, La Fayette Grover, who upon the urging of Abram S. Hewitt, the Democratic national chairman, planned to void the votes cast for Watts and give the certificate of appointment to a Tilden elector. Hewitt did not seriously believe that this lone Oregon vote would elect Tilden, but he realized that this maneuver would force the Republican-dominated Senate ''to go behind the certificate, and open the way [for the Democratic House of Representatives] to get into

[the] merits of all cases," particularly those of South Carolina, Florida, and Louisiana.[12]

The day that Congress required electors to cast their ballots in state capitals was 6 December. In thirty-four state capitals, the procedure was routine, but not in Salem, Columbia, Tallahassee, and New Orleans. In those four capitals, both the Republican and the Democratic electors met, voted, and forwarded their conflicting votes to Washington, with or without the certifying signature of their governor. After the balloting, Tilden had 184 votes, Hayes had 165, and both candidates claimed the remaining 20 votes.[13]

While the political campaign entered a phase that is unique in American history, Hayes and Tilden remained as aloof as they had before Election Day. Each of them thought he had won the election and continued to rely on the judgment of the leading politicians of his party. For Hayes, this policy worked. With Republicans controlling the federal government and key state administrations and with members of the Republican National Committee and congressmen energetically advancing their party's cause, Hayes remained in Ohio, observing his drift toward the presidency.[14]

Tilden was as passive as Hayes, but his inaction damaged his cause. His party was out of power in the disputed southern states, and apart from controlling the House of Representatives, it was out of power in the national government. If the in-party advantage of Republicans were to be neutralized, Democrats would have to rally public opinion to their side. But Tilden's indecision and timidity hampered Democratic leaders, who were inclined toward bold action. As a result, Democratic reactions to the crisis were poorly coordinated. In early December, Hewitt prepared an address for Tilden, "calling upon the people to assemble in their several places" on Jackson Day (the anniversary of the Battle of New Orleans, 8 January 1815) "to protest against the frauds." Fearing violence, Tilden struck out this passage and then decided not to make an address at all.

Rather than arouse the public, he helped to compile and analyze precedents for *The Presidential Counts*, published on 2 January 1877, which he thought would enable the Democrats to win a case in the courts or a debate in Congress. Leaving Tilden's home near Gramercy Park, disappointed Democrats reportedly wailed, "Oh, Tilden won't do anything; he's as cold as a damn clam." To the dismay of Hewitt, Watterson, and other Democrats, Tilden remained detached and uncommunicative while watching his drift away from the presidency.[15]

The Constitution provided that the votes of the electoral college be "directed to the President of the Senate" who "shall, in the Presence of the Senate and House of Representatives, open all the Certificates and the Votes shall then be counted." The Constitution, however, did not specify whether the presiding officer of the Senate or the combined House and Senate was to decide what to count when conflicting votes were forwarded to Washington. After the death of Vice-President Henry Wilson, the president of the Senate in 1876 was Thomas W. Ferry, a Michigan Republican who Postmaster Gen. James N. Tyner wished were a "more resolute man." The Republicans, particularly those close to Hayes, argued that Ferry should decide. Citing recent Republican precedents, the Democrats insisted that the combined House and Senate, which had a comfortable Democratic majority, should make the crucial decisions. Yet all but the blindest of partisans realized that some losers must side with the victors if the count were to proceed and that agreement could only be achieved through concessions and compromise.[16]

Given the decentralized and factional character of American parties, disaffected politicians were bound to surface. A few senators and representatives would be ready to sacrifice a national victory for regional, local, or factional advantages. The most conspicuous disaffected Republican was Senator Roscoe Conkling, the boss of New York, who liked neither Hayes's nomination nor his letter of acceptance and who had been silent during the campaign. A Democratic victory would discredit his party's reform wing and enhance his chances to dictate the 1880 Republican nominee. With Hayes leaning toward Conkling's New York enemies, Conkling's chances of patronage might be better from Tilden, especially if Tilden were aware of Conkling's good wishes. Speaking on 19 November to a hometown Democratic friend who relayed the word to Tilden, Conkling asked whether Democrats were going "to act upon the *good-boy* principle of submission" or whether they meant "to have it understood that Tilden has been elected and by the Eternal he shall be inaugurated?" Allied to Conkling were southern Republican senators who were afraid that as carpetbaggers they would be ignored under Hayes's policy of conciliation.[17]

Hayes was aware of Conkling's "lack of hearty support" during the campaign and, worse, of Conkling's view that Ferry should not decide what votes to count. From a Conkling emissary, Hayes learned in mid December that Conkling would support him on how the count should proceed, if Hayes would repudiate reformers Carl Schurz and George William Curtis and if he would not disturb Conkling's lieutenants in the

New York Customhouse. Hayes also learned that if he would continue to back the carpetbag Republican senators, they would remain loyal. But he made no commitments. He reiterated his pledge to "deal fairly and justly by all elements of the party" and the views he expressed in his acceptance letter that to achieve peace and prosperity "the Southern people must obey the new amendments, and give the colored men all their rights." Hayes's noncommittal attitude did not placate Conkling, and although Conkling's man tried to get Hayes to be more specific, he would not budge.[18]

Disaffected Democrats also surfaced. Tilden's inactivity and his drift away from the presidency made many members of his party anticipate defeat. Although all Democrats preferred a Tilden victory, some southerners explored what terms the Republicans might offer for their capitulation. These southerners wondered whether Republicans would concede the South to the Democrats (home rule), if they acquiesced to Hayes's election. Southern Democratic newspapermen and politicians met often in December with Hayes Republican newspapermen and politicians in an effort to reach an understanding.

Col. William H. Roberts, of the New Orleans *Times,* who was close to Mississippi Congressman L. Q. C. Lamar and was also familiar with the views of Wade Hampton of South Carolina and Senator John B. Gordon of Georgia, met with Hayes on 1 December. Roberts told Hayes that he would be president, assured him that southerners would neither "make trouble" nor "oppose an Administration which will favor an honest administration and honest officers in the South," and promised to "secure the colored people all of their rights." For his part, Hayes said his "letter of acceptance covered the whole ground." In that letter, he had promised that if the rights of all would be recognized by all, the federal government would promote southern efforts to obtain "honest and capable local government." Remembering in particular Hayes's idea that "the intelligence of any country ought to govern it," Roberts, to Hayes's embarrassment, leaked to the press his impression that a compromise that would place Hayes in the White House and Democrats in southern statehouses could be worked out.[19]

Other cracks appeared in the Democratic façade. On 7 December, William Henry Smith told Hayes that Col. Andrew J. Kellar, the editor of the *Memphis Avalanche* who was an independent Democrat, wished to build a conservative Republican party in the South that would "destroy the color line & save the poor colored people." After conferring with William H. Smith and with Richard Smith of the *Cincinnati Gazette,* Kellar left for Washington on 14 December to "enter zealously on the great work." Hayes was "very hopeful that much good will come from friendly relations'' with good men in the South, but he was unwilling to be committed to persons or policies beyond the implication of his acceptance letter.[20]

By the time that Kellar arrived in Washington, Garfield had already reported that ''the leading southern Democrats in Congress, especially those who were old Whigs, are saying that they have seen war enough, and don't care to follow the lead of their northern associates who . . . were 'invincible in peace and invisible in war.' '' Garfield told Hayes it would be advantageous for Republicans ''if in some discreet way,'' he were to tell these southern men that he planned to treat the South ''with kind consideration.'' For ''several Southern men,'' kind consideration meant more than home rule and patronage. Within a week, they told Garfield ''that in the matter of internal improvements they had been much better treated by Republicans than they were likely to be by the Democrats.''

Along with L. Q. C. Lamar, Garfield was a member of the Committee on the Pacific Railroad, which was considering a bill to subsidize the expansion of the Texas & Pacific Railroad. Many southern congressmen backed the bill, and the railroad's president, Thomas A. Scott, who was also president of the Pennsylvania Railroad, lobbied for the passage of the bill. While estimates of southern Democrats who might accept Hayes ran as high as fifty, Garfield told Hayes that ''if a third of that number, would come out for peace, and acquiescence in your election, it would do much to prevent immediate trouble, & to make your future work easier.'' Although Garfield thought these overtures were worth exploring, he privately doubted that they would amount to anything.

The overtures puzzled Garfield. These Democrats wanted him to outline in a speech the southern policy that Hayes would adopt if elected, but ''just what sort of assurances the South wants, is not quite so clear; for they are a little vague in their expressions.'' He was also uncertain about Hayes's attitude towards the South. He could remember no public utterance by Hayes, beyond his letter of acceptance, that was friendly to the South. Hayes did not elaborate on his southern policy, and he continued to rely on friends, unhampered by precise instructions, to represent him somewhat officially. ''I wish *you*,'' he told John Sherman, ''to feel authorized to speak in pretty decided terms for me whenever it seems advisable—to do this not by reason of specific authority to do it, but from your knowledge of my general methods of action.''[21]

In Washington, Kellar joined with Henry Van Ness Boynton, a correspondent for the *Cincinnati Gazette*, in exploring Democratic fissures. By the morning of 20 December, Boynton declared that Kellar had "given a decided impetus" toward securing thirty to thirty-six southern Democrats who "will vote 'no' upon every proposition . . . revolutionary in its tendency." They wanted Hayes to "publicly avow his views," but Boynton explained "that it would be nothing more than a repetition of his letter of acceptance." Boynton was obviously fishing for votes with the bait of home rule, rather than of internal improvements, especially because Garfield, who was privy to Kellar's and Boynton's explorations, had on that same day resisted an effort in committee "to push Scott's bill through."[22]

Later, on 20 December, Boynton wrote to William Henry Smith, outlining a scheme to attract the thirty to thirty-six votes wanted "for *practical* success." "West Tennessee, Arkansas, a large Kentucky element, Louisiana, Texas, Mississippi *and Tom Scott* want help for the Texas Pacific Road," but Republican-party policy was opposed to subsidies. If Hayes, however, would support aid, "within proper bounds, and properly secured," for the Texas & Pacific Railroad and if "Tom Scott and the prominent representatives of the States I have named could *know* this, Scott with his whole force would come here, and get those votes in spite of all human power, and all the howlings which blusterers North and South could put up." Joseph Medill of the *Chicago Tribune* and Boynton's boss, Richard Smith of the *Cincinnati Gazette*, as well as William Henry Smith, were willing to go along with the scheme. For Medill, support of a federal land grant for a railroad represented a reversal of editorial policy, but he reasoned that no price was "too high that will secure protection to the lives of the poor negroes and peace to the south."[23]

Boynton wrote on 26 December that he wanted Hayes's general approval for a land grant to the Texas & Pacific Railroad without his saying "anything in favor of the Southern *road now.*" Boynton would then "tell Scott privately what the policy of Governor Hayes is to be" and in effect would unleash Scott and his presumably powerful lobby to persuade southern Democrats to oppose any move toward "revolution." Hayes, the *Chicago Tribune*, and the *Cincinnati Gazette* could wait until Hayes's first annual message to advocate the land grant. Expecting that "a new era of cordial co-operation on the part of the South" would then be in place, Boynton thought it would be easy to secure the land grant.[24]

Having had several contacts with southern Democrats, Garfield had faith in Boynton's plan. On 3 January 1877, after working with Lamar on Pacific-railroad committee business, he discussed "the political situation" with his fellow Ohio Republican Congressman Charles Foster and

with Hayes's friend James M. Comly of the *Ohio State Journal* (Columbus), at whose home the conference between Hayes and Roberts had
taken place. Comly said to Hayes: "Both Garfield and Foster intimated
regret that the Republican party was so squarely committed against
further subsidies as to prevent them from advocating the building of the
Texas Pacific Rail Road by the help of Congress. They thought a large
following might be gained for the Republican party in the South by
favoring this road, and both asserted that Texas might be made a
Republican State by advocating the road."[25]

The plans of Kellar, Boynton, and Smith inspired little faith in
Hayes. He did decide, however, to "urge a liberal policy towards the
South especially in affording facilities for education, and encouraging
business and emigration, by internal improvements of a National
character" in his Inaugural Address, which he hoped would "enable us
to divide the whites, and thus take the first step to obliterate the color
line." But Hayes was skeptical about a scheme that combined railroad
lobbyists and southern Democrats. "I am not a believer in the trust-
worthiness of the forces you hope to rally," he said to William Henry
Smith. "After we are in, I believe a wise and liberal policy can
accomplish a great deal. But we must rely on our own strength to secure
our rights." A bit taken aback, Smith countered: "There can be no harm
in furthering a great cause in searching for latent patriotism in the
South." In any event, Smith assured Hayes that he would pursue "the
Southern matter . . . on my own responsibility." In the same vein,
Hayes wrote to Schurz: "I look for nothing of value growing out of
Southern conservative tendencies in this Congress. Whatever the caucus decides to do will be done, and the influence referred to is too small
to control the large House majority."[26]

Republican as well as Democratic solidarity continued to be endangered. Conkling kept insisting that "the House has an equal voice in
the Count." In addition, southern Republican carpetbag senators—who
tended to follow Conkling's lead and owed their seats to Grant's
support—feared that Hayes would defer to reformers such as Benjamin
H. Bristow. If "Bristow is to run Hayes' Administration," Senator
George E. Spencer of Alabama declared on 22 December, "we want
Tilden." Contrasting their power in the Senate with their collapsing
political organizations, carpetbaggers wished to salvage as much as
possible. The carpetbaggers hoped for "consideration & patronage"
from Hayes, but Hayes supporters feared that if the carpetbaggers
thought they were to be abandoned, they would sell out in much the
same manner that southern Democrats had contemplated salvaging
concessions from a Tilden defeat. Conflicting reports, particularly about

Conkling, unsettled seasoned observers. "The times are strange," William E. Chandler concluded; "it will not do to neglect any rumor; nor to give ready credence to any."[27]

Conkling's doubts that Ferry could decide which votes to count was shared by many Republicans. Senator George F. Edmunds of Vermont thought the Supreme Court should decide; and Schurz, despite his friendship for Hayes, agreed. Hayes felt obliged to admit that there was some merit in that proposal, but he did nothing to advance it, preferring, as Schurz put it, to drift. Some Republicans even favored a new election, particularly in Louisiana. Jacob Dolson Cox of Ohio typified the widespread belief among moderate and reform Republicans that it would be almost fatal if Hayes were inaugurated "by fraudulent returns."[28]

While his lieutenants tried to rally their congressional colleagues, Hayes sought to conciliate Grant. Possibly influenced by Conkling, Grant in early December had told his cabinet and even Democratic National Chairman Hewitt that he believed Tilden had carried Louisiana. Realizing that Grant's opposition or even indifference would ruin his chances for the presidency, Hayes wrote a friendly letter to Grant just before Christmas. The letter touched Grant. Although Hayes delicately declined Grant's invitation to meet in Philadelphia, Comly visited Washington on 4 January and assured Grant of Hayes's staunch friendship. Comly insisted that there was not a chance in a million that Hayes would appoint Bristow, whom Grant despised, to a cabinet position. *"At this point in the conversation,"* Comly reported to Hayes, *"he drew the friendly cigars from his pocket,"* and a confidential talk ensued.[29]

On 5 January 1877, the very day that Hayes recorded his determination to support internal improvements for the South in order to split the Democrats, his Ohio lieutenants met in Washington to prevent his Republican support from eroding. Sherman told Attorney General Alphonso Taft, as well as Garfield, former Governor William Dennison, and Comly, that Conkling would "break with the party on the Presidential question," but no one knew how many senators he would carry with him. Dennison said he would talk to some of the southern Republicans, but Sherman blurted out: "I'll be damned if I do that. I can't talk with those fellows—don't know how to get at them." Taft, however, explained with a wink that since becoming head of the Department of Justice, he "had occasionally found it in his power to be serviceable to the Republicans of the South" (carpetbag regimes were dependent on Justice Department support) and that he might be able to influence them. A few days later, about twenty senators, congressmen, and cabinet members met at Sherman's home to "consult on the political situation." By 14 January, Garfield had been "appointed as one of six of Hayes's friends to confer with doubtful Senators, and confirm their courage."[30]

Although they tried, Hayes's friends could not hold their party to the extreme and dubious constitutional position that both houses of Congress should silently observe Senator Ferry decide what votes to count. George W. McCrary, an Iowa Republican, introduced a resolution that called for a special committee to settle the crisis. This had passed the House by mid December, and the Senate enacted a similar resolution, introduced by Edmunds, to set up a cooperating committee. Ardent Hayes supporters were outraged that the Democratic Speaker Samuel J. Randall appointed moderate Republicans, rather than one of them, to the House committee and were dismayed that Ferry, who did not want the responsibility of deciding the election, appointed Roscoe Conkling to the Senate committee.

Hayes men were in no mood for compromise. Richard Smith warned that a "compromise will cheat us out of our rights and if we shall be so cheated Congressmen who favor it may as well order their political coffins." Conkling's announcement in the Senate committee that he thought Tilden had carried Louisiana and Florida was enough to convince Garfield that appointing the compromise committee was a mistake. On 10 January, Edmunds and McCrary proposed to their committees that a commission independent of Congress be appointed to resolve the dispute. Both men proposed that members of the Supreme Court should serve, but Edmunds wished to include senators and representatives on his proposed commission.[31]

When the committees began to meet jointly on 12 January, they agreed on a commission but not on the composition of it. The Democrats ruled out Chief Justice Morrison R. Waite, a partisan Republican who had been a close friend of Hayes's Uncle Sardis Birchard; they also rejected the Republican proposal to choose the justices by lot. Tilden insisted that he would not "raffle" for the presidency, and Hayes agreed. Both committees then accepted a formulation by Edmunds, which was close to what the Democrats had proposed. He suggested that the Democratic justices Nathan Clifford and Stephen J. Field and the Republican justices Samuel F. Miller and William Strong would select the fifth judge, presumably David Davis, a political independent. In addition, five senators and five representatives, of whom five would be Republicans and five Democrats, would bring the membership of the proposed commission to fifteen. Both sides also agreed that the commission would decide whether to investigate official returns and that the commission's decisions would be final because they could be overturned only if the Republican Senate and the Democratic House would concur.[32]

Although the Electoral Commission bill originated with moderate Republicans, it proved palatable to Democrats, and it gained wide acceptance. To be sure, uncompromising Democrats, largely from the South, opposed it; but Tilden accepted it, even though he did not like it, and most Democrats supported it as their best chance for victory. Garfield observed that outside of Congress, businessmen, whether Democratic or Republican, were "clamorously in favor of it." Republican supporters ranged from reformers such as Carl Schurz to his archenemy, President Grant. Grant's tendency to support Conkling was buttressed by the strong support that Secretary of State Hamilton Fish gave to the commission bill, and together they lined up Republican support.[33]

It was in the Hayes camp that support for the measure was lacking. Hayes called it a "surrender, at least in part, of our case" that the vice-president alone could count the votes and declare the winner. Hayes argued the exalted, self-serving principle that by creating the commission, Congress had usurped presidential authority. Garfield agreed that the bill was unconstitutional, "a surrender of a certainty for an uncertainty," an eastern measure that sacrificed western interests; and he predicted that henceforth Congress, not the people, would determine presidential elections. Newspapermen, who had been maneuvering to gain southern support for Hayes by striving to convince him to advocate subsidies for Tom Scott's Texas & Pacific Railroad, were the most disappointed by the Electoral Commission bill, which renewed southern Democrats' hope for a Tilden victory. "The truth is we have had blunder upon blunder at Washington," William Henry Smith wailed. Spawned by the crisis, land-grant negotiations languished in the more relaxed atmosphere that followed the publication of the proposed bill.[34]

It was absurd for Hayes supporters to speak of giving up a certainty. Among them, Charles Foster realized their position was untenable. He asked Hayes: "Have we a case to surrender? We have a half dozen men in the Senate who I know are disposed to make merchandise of this position. Just where they will land no one can tell. This element with Conkling, Edmunds and others to hide behind, may play the devil with us before we get through." With the Senate dubious about the proposition that Ferry could count Hayes in and with the House opposed to it, Foster and many moderate Republicans were willing to accept the commission and its decision. "The overwhelming reason controlling men," he told Hayes, "is that whoever is elected should go in with the best possible title as can be given him." Foster apparently convinced Hayes. After it had passed Congress, he wrote: "I trust the measure will turn out well. It is a great relief to me. Defeat in this way after a full and public hearing before this Commission is not mortifying in any degree, and success will be in all respects more satisfactory."[35]

Everyone had assumed that Judge David Davis would be the key member of the Electoral Commission. But while the joint committee was drawing up the Electoral Commission bill, Davis became the Greenback candidate for senator from Illinois. After that state's legislature had deadlocked for two weeks, the Democrats threw their support to Davis and elected him on 25 January, the day before the Electoral Commission Act passed both houses. Tilden and Hewitt had nothing to do with Davis's victory, but apparently Tilden's nephew, Col. William T. Pelton, whose lack of ethics was matched by an absence of judgment, engineered it. While Republicans were elated by the news, which helped to reconcile the Hayes men to the Electoral Commission Act, and while most Democrats were aghast, Pelton was pleased. He and his cohorts believed that they had an understanding with Davis. They were wrong. Davis refused to serve on the commission, because he was beholden to the Democrats for his forthcoming Senate seat. His place was taken by Justice Joseph P. Bradley, a Republican from New Jersey.

The selection of Bradley gave the Republicans an eight to seven majority on the commission. Bradley's position was difficult. His fourteen colleagues were expected to be partisan, but Congress had intended that his chair be occupied by an unbiased justice. Several members of the joint committee that had created the commission served on it, but Hayes's friends were thankful that Conkling, who thought its duties "inconvenient if not distasteful," refused. They also rejoiced that Oliver P. Morton and Garfield, both of whom had uncompromisingly opposed the creation of the commission, were on that tribunal. Selecting Garfield, who as a visiting statesman had committed himself to Hayes's side of the Louisiana question, which had to come before the commission, emphasized the political, rather than the judicial, character of the commission.[36]

On 1 February, in compliance with the Electoral Commission Act, Congress assembled in joint session for the count. Beginning with Alabama, the count proceeded quickly until Congress referred the disputed returns from Florida to the Electoral Commission and then recessed. The commission assembled an hour later in the Capitol's Old Senate Chamber, where the Supreme Court regularly met, and on 2 February began to hear arguments. The justices, who had discarded their robes, occupied the center of the bench, with the senators on their right and the congressmen on their left. Counsel for the Democrats included Charles O'Conor and William C. Whitney of New York and Jeremiah S. Black of Pennsylvania; and counsel for the Republicans included William M. Evarts of New York and two of Hayes's personal friends from Ohio, Stanley Matthews and Samuel Shellabarger.

The crucial question was whether or not the commission should investigate the returns that had been certified by the governor and the secretary of state. The Democrats argued that testimony taken by both the Senate and the House proved that Tilden had carried Florida and that a partisan returning board and governor had defrauded Tilden of his electoral votes. That view had been upheld by the Florida Supreme Court on 14 December, when, reversing the decision of the returning board, the court had allowed the Democrats on 1 January 1877 to take over the state government. For the Republicans, Evarts argued against considering evidence that would challenge the official returns because reexamining the vote on the county and local levels would be an endless task, and a decision had to be reached by 4 March. O'Conor's final argument claimed "that we present the best legal title to Florida's electoral votes. That we have the moral right is the common sentiment of all mankind. It will be the judgment of posterity."[37]

On Tuesday, 6 February, the commission began to deliberate. By 2:13 P.M. the next day, when Justice Bradley spoke, fourteen members had spoken, and, as expected, each had argued for his own party. Garfield wrote in his diary: "All were intent because B[radley]. held the casting vote. It was a curious study to watch the faces as he read. All were making a manifest effort to appear unconcerned. It was ten minutes before it became evident that he was against the authority to hear extrinsic evidence. His opinion was clear and strong." At 3:00 P.M. on 7 February the commission, by a vote of eight to seven, decided not to investigate the official Florida returns, and two days later, by the same partisan vote, awarded Florida to Hayes.

Bradley's opinion and the Florida decision heartened Republicans and discouraged Democrats. William E. Chandler, who commanded Florida's Republican visiting statesmen, rejoiced that Hayes's victory "now seems absolutely certain." He went on to reflect: "I should hate to think that this work we have been doing before and since the election, has been only keeping a political party in power. I must believe that it has a higher purpose—that of protecting the colored man and saving the nation from great peril." Hayes, with his friends "very confident of success," began to jot down points to stress in his Inaugural Address, while Tilden, realizing that the strict party vote prophesied his defeat, showed even less inclination to lead his party. He and his friend John Bigelow began to plan a European trip.[38]

Angry and stubborn, the rudderless Democrats fought on. Possibly, they could win Louisiana; if not, they might delay the count and extract concessions from the Republicans. Above all, southern Democrats wanted home rule—that is, white-supremacy state governments—and if Tilden, who would certainly accede to their wishes, were not elected, they wanted a commitment from Hayes. A minority of southern Democrats were also anxious to secure federal support for railroad construction. Yet the Democrats showed restraint in their delaying tactics. After losing Florida, they did not withdraw from the commission, and although they postponed the count by recessing the House until Monday, they did not prevent the count, as some hotheads wished them to do. After their overwhelming support for the Electoral Commission Act, Democrats felt constrained to abide by its results.

The threat of a Democratic filibuster revived Kellar and Boynton, fueled their hopes, and fired their imaginations. Boynton predicted: "The plan we were at work upon before the compromise bill was passed will work beautifully and effectively in case the hot-headed democrats attempt to defeat Hayes by delay. Of course it will be a splendid thing to have the democrats submit quietly, but it would be a much better thing to have them start a filibustering scheme, and have thirty-five or forty of their party refuse to carry it on." Kellar reported—Boynton also heard from a different source—"that if filibustering attempts are not made, it will be because the democrats now *know* that it will not be safe for them to rely upon a very considerable number of Southern democrats."[39]

Ferry proceeded counting until he reached Louisiana, with its conflicting returns, which on the afternoon of 12 February were referred to the commission. Because the unofficial early returns in Louisiana gave the Democrats a large majority, because the Louisiana returning board was disreputable and did not have a Democratic member, and because Republican frauds could best be documented in Louisiana, the Democrats could make their strongest case for Louisiana's votes, if the commission would go behind the returns and hear evidence. From a technically legal standpoint, however, the Democratic case in Louisiana was no different from the one in Florida.

After hearing extensive arguments, the commission took eleven hours on Friday 16 February to decide the Louisiana issue. The crucial vote belonged to Bradley, the eighth speaker. Garfield suffered "the most nervous strain and anxiety'' since he fought at Chickamauga: ''We had no hint of the conclusion to be reached until Bradley was twenty minutes into his speech. The suspense was painful, and the efforts of members to appear unconcerned gave strong proof of the intensity of the feeling. I could hear, or fancied I could hear, the watches of members ticking in their pockets. When Bradley reached a proposition that made his result evident, there was a long breath of relief, up or down, but actual relief to all from the long suspense.'' A series of eight-to-seven votes gave Louisiana to Hayes.[40]

After the decision about Louisiana, neither Hayes nor the Democrats had much doubt about the ultimate result. There was a remote possibility that Conkling and some carpetbag senators might defect, but it was almost certain that the Senate would agree with the commission and that Louisiana would be counted for Hayes. The Democrats, in their frustration, tried to harass the Republicans by delaying the count with recesses, but in their caucus on 17 February the Democrats decided not to obstruct the process. That decision, which caused great elation among the Republicans, was particularly gratifying to Boynton and Kellar, who felt responsible for the outcome, because only one southerner voted for a filibuster. Boynton could not distinguish between the effects of the ''purely political'' negotiations concerning home rule that Kellar conducted and the economic negotiations of the ''Scott forces'' concerning a land grant for the Texas & Pacific Railroad. ''Both worked earnestly,'' and both ''contributed much'' to the result.

The southern Democrats, however, emphasized that they would obstruct the count if the Republicans did not specifically commit themselves to home rule. But Hayes shrewdly remained noncommittal beyond the statement in his acceptance letter, and he assured the black leader Frederick Douglass that he would not sacrifice black rights for the support of white southerners, that he would uphold ''the 13th, 14th and 15th amendments.'' On the other hand, his lieutenant Stanley Matthews assured Edward A. Burke of Louisiana that Hayes did not like carpetbag rule. Burke was the personal representative of ''Governor'' Francis T. Nicholls, the head of a rival Democratic government, like the Wade Hampton government in South Carolina. At a subsequent meeting on Sunday evening, 18 February, Burke also wanted assurances that strong Republican leaders such as Garfield, Sherman, Morton, and Blaine would not oppose home rule. When Matthews could not give any assurances, Burke threatened that Louisiana's congressmen would lead a filibuster to prevent Hayes's inauguration.[41]

Burke's threat to filibuster, which he made a day after the decision not to obstruct the count, emphasizes the strategy of southern Democrats. They would gain concessions, particularly in Louisiana and South Carolina, if they could convince Republicans that to complete the count and to elect Hayes their support was essential. Mingled with the threats were hints that political and economic concessions would not only cause southern Democrats of substance to acquiesce in Hayes's election but could even win their allegiance to the Republican party. Charles Foster on 15 February heard from Charles Nordhoff of the *New York Herald* that the southern Democrats would cheerfully accept Hayes as president. Nordhoff held out the prospect of forming "a real and honest Republican party in the South," based on old Whigs, "but only on condition that the carpet-bag leaders are dropped entirely." He estimated that the appointment of two southerners of Whig extraction in Hayes's cabinet would attract Democrats of that persuasion to the Republicans.[42]

On the same day that Nordhoff and Foster conferred, Grenville M. Dodge, the builder of the Union Pacific Railroad and a lobbyist for the Texas & Pacific Railroad, wrote Hayes that with "proper action," the Republicans "ought to have and to hold North and South Carolina, Florida, Alabama, Mississippi and Louisiana, and should be able to get a strong and permanent footing in Texas . . . without . . . abandoning any of our friends, white or black, who are now there." Dodge was too optimistic. Federal support for southern railroad construction—which is what Dodge meant by "proper action"—might gratify southern Democrats, but they insisted that their cooperation in Hayes's election—to say nothing of converting to Republicanism—could only be secured by the abandonment of the Republican governments in Louisiana and South Carolina.[43]

Although some reform-minded Republicans, such as Joseph Medill of the *Chicago Tribune*, were willing to abandon Governor-elect Stephen B. Packard of Louisiana and Governor Daniel H. Chamberlain in South Carolina, others were not. Even William Henry Smith, despite orchestrating the Kellar and Boynton negotiations, exclaimed on 19 February: "You cannot dismiss those gentlemen with a wave of the hand" for "mere party expediency." Foster, who also wished to attract southern Democrats, told Hayes on 16 February that he "did not see how you could throw Packard overboard." Sherman, whose opinion Hayes valued, wrote to him on 18 February, "I see no way but the recognition of the Packard government followed by the utmost liberality to the South."[44]

Indeed, the Republicans needed the crucial but wavering carpetbag support on Monday, 19 February, when the Senate considered the commission's decision about Louisiana. Southern Republicans had become so disturbed by the negotiations with southern conservatives that they were threatening to support Tilden unless Hayes would promise them a cabinet position. For leadership, they looked to Conkling, who also had a rule-or-ruin streak in his soul and appeared to be willing to see Hayes defeated, if it would enhance his power within the Republican party. The Democrats' last hope was that Conkling and his southern allies would object to the commission's decision about Louisiana, but on 19 February, Conkling was conspicuously absent. Carpetbag senators were whipped into line—after all, if Tilden were to win they would be certain of oblivion; the Senate approved the Louisiana decision; and the Democrats despaired of victory.[45]

With defeat certain, delay and the threat of chaos after 4 March were the Democrats' only bargaining chips to win Republican acquiescence to home rule. They were dangerous chips to play, because the American people, especially those connected with business, did not want chaos. After winning Louisiana with the support of southern Republican senators, Republicans would have to be badly frightened before they would abandon the carpetbaggers. Having forced a recess on 17 February and again on Monday, 19 February, House Democrats caucused anew on Monday night. At that caucus, Speaker Samuel J. Randall accused southern Democrats of bargaining with Hayes, whom he predicted would, if elected, revive bayonet rule and ruin them. Randall proposed a radical scheme: to recess day after day and force the Senate to accept a bill naming Secretary of State Hamilton Fish acting president until a new election could be held. The caucus could not agree, and the noncooperative, yet nonobstructive, policy that Democrats had adopted remained in place.

Southern Democrats tried to use Randall's speech to extract concessions from the Hayes men. Kellar and several southern Democrats called on Foster, who represented Hayes's district. "The Southern people who had agreed to stand by us in carrying out the Electoral law in good faith," Foster reported to Hayes, "were seized with a fright, if not a panic." They spoke about Randall's violent speech and asked for assurances that Hayes would end bayonet rule. After consulting with Matthews, Garfield, and Evarts, Foster planned to make a conciliatory and reassuring speech the next day. Kellar, Smith reported to Hayes, was disheartened and felt cut down. He feared that northern Democrats would be able to whip into line the southern Whigs and the Union Democrats. Kellar urged that Hayes say something and that he reassure the South by promising to appoint Kellar's friend Senator David M. Key of Tennessee to the cabinet. Hayes, however, resolutely kept his peace.[46]

Kellar's fears were not realized. The count reached Oregon on Wednesday, and by Friday, 23 February, Bradley strongly supported the Hayes elector; and the commission, by an eight-to-seven vote, awarded Oregon's three votes to Hayes. "A few days ago," Boynton reported on Thursday, "the struggle to break the democrats on the floor, to filibuster, seemed so desperate . . . that some means of *convincing* the leaders in our movement seemed . . . necessary," but that crisis had passed. It was no longer necessary for Hayes to say something. Boynton exulted: "Gen. Dodge has had the whole of Scott's force at work, and that with the purely political part will, *I feel confident*, defeat the desperate men. It is still difficult for me to judge which of these two forces has been the most potent element in the long fight."[47]

Ironically, on the very day that Boynton was so confident of victory over the filibusterers, an editorial in the *Ohio State Journal* defended Louisiana's carpetbag regime and urged Grant to uphold it with troops. Because Hayes's friend Comly edited the *Journal*, Hayes was thought to have inspired the article, which seemed to confirm Randall's prophecy that Hayes would revive bayonet rule and ruin the southern Democrats who had supported him. Neither Hayes nor Comly, who was ill, had anything to do with the article; but it did revive the filibuster movement and led southerners to demand further assurances that Hayes would not restore bayonet rule.[48]

With little more than a week remaining before the inauguration, both parties pursued erratic courses, sowing anxiety and confusion. Charles Foster's promise to southerners in Congress that "the flag shall float over States, not provinces, over freemen, and not subjects," for example, was followed by the hostile, bayonet-rule article in the *Ohio State Journal*, which reflected the views of many powerful Republicans. On the other hand, northern and southern Democrats, responding to shifting moods of ambition, fear, and frustration, drifted in and out of the filibuster movement. When Speaker Randall wished to prevent the count and force a new election, southerners held back, but five days later, on Saturday, 24 February, he and his northern cohorts prevented the filibusterers, reinforced at that time by southerners, from adjourning the House until Oregon had been counted for Hayes. The count, Keith I. Polakoff has observed, proceeded "fast enough to make certain it could be completed by March 4, yet slowly enough to lend credence to intimations that it might not be. No gambler ever presented a more inscrutable poker face than did these leaders of the white South."

Republicans had to decide whether the filibuster movement was a bluff or a genuine effort to stop the count. Would the arrangements of Boynton and Kellar, the assurances of Matthews and Foster, and the pressure of northeastern business interests suffice; or were more specific concessions to southern Democrats required if Hayes were to be inaugurated on schedule? While aware of the "fierce" struggle among House Democrats, Sherman and Garfield thought the count would be completed on time, but other Republican leaders felt "great anxiety."[49]

Ulysses S. Grant took the filibuster threat seriously and moved to resolve the crisis. On Monday morning, 26 February, he told Burke that the Nicholls government "should stand in Louisiana," that public opinion opposed the use of troops to uphold a state government, and that he had avoided action because he did not wish to embarrass Hayes. Later that morning, Burke told Sherman, Matthews, and Dennison that if they wanted him to call off the filibuster, they should tell Grant that the immediate withdrawal of troops upholding the carpetbag government would not embarrass Hayes. Sherman claimed that Grant would not agree, but Burke showed them a dispatch to Nicholls that Grant had approved. Sherman, Matthews, and Dennison had no choice but to agree to see Grant and to assure Burke that Hayes would follow Grant's policy.

Sherman insisted on two additional concessions. He wanted assurances that the Nicholls government would protect the rights of blacks and Republicans and that it would delay the election of a "long term" senator until 10 March, by which date William Pitt Kellogg, who had been elected by the carpetbag legislature, would presumably be seated, thus helping to retain the shaky Republican control of the Senate. The meeting broke up with an agreement to meet again that evening at Matthews's rooms at Wormley's Hotel.[50]

The significance of the meeting at Wormley's Hotel has often been exaggerated. Five Ohio Republicans—Sherman, Matthews, Dennison, Foster, and Garfield—met with three Louisiana Democrats—Burke and Congressmen E. John Ellis and William M. Levy—as well as Congressman Henry Watterson of Kentucky, who supposedly looked after South Carolina's interests but was there primarily because Matthews, who was his uncle, had invited him. Garfield opposed committing Hayes and making a "political bargain." Since the count on that Monday had reached South Carolina, Garfield was optimistic, did not think Burke could turn "the filibuster on or off at will," and thought a bargain was not necessary. Boynton, who was not present, agreed on that same day that there were "no signs of Southern men going back on us" and added: "Some of our men have a chronic panic." Like

Boynton, Garfield may have had confidence in the Kellar-Boynton arrangements, or he may have read the conflicting Democratic signals as signs of confusion, or he may have been influenced by both. In any event, perceiving at 11 P.M. that Matthews did not like his remarks, Garfield went home. The other participants remained and agreed to the bargain they had outlined that morning.[51]

Not only has the impact of the meeting at Wormley's Hotel been exaggerated, but the negotiations of Kellar and Boynton and the lobbying of Scott and Dodge have also been overstressed. Had there been no conference at Wormley's and no Texas & Pacific lobby, the count would have been completed on time. An analysis of electoral-count roll calls by Michael Les Benedict reveals that while region had little to do with Democratic support of or opposition to the filibuster, Democrats from the Northeast more consistently opposed the filibuster than did those from the South and the border states. Furthermore, southern Democrats who supported federal subsidies for internal improvements were no more likely to oppose the filibuster than were those who were prone to starve projects such as the Texas & Pacific. Most Democrats were not prepared to delay the count beyond 4 March, lest public opinion turn on them and provoke a new wave of Reconstruction legislation.

Democrats did prolong the crisis to extract concessions for the South, and their "bluff game" achieved a modest success. Hayes had consistently called for honest and capable local governments in the South, coupled with the recognition of the rights of all blacks and whites. Keeping his options open, he had not advocated the abandoning of Republican regimes in Louisiana and South Carolina. Sherman, Foster, Matthews, and Dennison, however, had committed him to sustaining the Democratic Nicholls government in Louisiana, as long as the civil rights of blacks were respected—a position that Grant regarded as inevitable and that he had taken steps to implement.[52]

On Tuesday, 27 February, it appeared that the count would proceed smoothly. The Electoral Commission met at ten that morning and adjourned at seven that night, with the South Carolina case being settled for Hayes by the usual eight-to-seven vote. Watterson read into the *Congressional Record* Grant's views supporting the Nicholls government in Louisiana and opposing the use of troops to maintain Republican Governor Packard. Burke worked to get the Democratic caucus in New Orleans to agree to respect the constitutional rights of blacks and Republicans and to delay the election of a long-term senator. Matthews saw Grant, who agreed to rescind—as soon as the count had been completed—his orders to the troops in Louisiana to preserve the status quo. Matthews also joined with Foster to sign a statement saying that Hayes would allow the people of "South Carolina and Louisiana the right to conduct their own affairs in their own way, subject only to the Constitution of the United States and the laws made in pursuance thereof." Not only were the Wormley's Hotel conference pieces falling into place, but Boynton, Kellar, and Dodge also claimed that their "force" was "strong and solid."[53]

They were too optimistic; the count did not go smoothly. On Wednesday 28 February, according to Garfield, "the Democrats filibustered with all their might to prevent the completion of the count." Hard-core filibusterers, numbering about sixty, were bolstered by other Democrats, including Hewitt, who challenged a Republican elector from Vermont and forced the House to adjourn. Hewitt later claimed that he had acted to gain time so that Burke could win recognition for the Nicholls government and added that neither he nor Randall would have let the filibuster prevent the completion of the count.[54]

The House session that opened at 10 A.M., Thursday, 1 March, was one of the longest and stormiest in history. The struggle over Vermont continued for thirteen hours. Filibusterers made dilatory motions to recess, to reconsider, and to call the roll; and Randall's refusals to entertain their motions added to the pandemonium. George M. Beebe of New York, for example, sprang up on his desk and screamed "with all his voice." While the uproar was continuing, Louisiana's Democratic congressmen met with Grant to persuade him to withdraw the troops immediately, but Grant refused until the count had been completed. Grant did warn Governor Packard that public opinion no longer supported the use of troops to maintain his government, and he told Burke that if the count were finished that evening, Nicholls "would be in peaceful possession tomorrow."

Having extracted all that he could from the filibuster, Burke called it aimless. Levy returned to the House to announce: "The people of Louisiana have solemn, earnest, and, I believe, truthful assurances from prominent members of the Republican party, high in the confidence of Mr. Hayes, . . . that he will not use the federal authority or the Army to force upon those States governments not of their choice. . . . This, too, is the opinion of President Grant." Perhaps because it was Grant's move or because winning the presidency was so important, Republican leaders who had supported Radical Reconstruction did not object to abandoning the carpetbag regimes.

Fifty-seven bitter and disorderly filibusterers prolonged the struggle until 3:38 A.M. The Senate then assembled in the House chamber, Wisconsin was counted for Hayes, and at 4:10 A.M. on 2 March 1877,

Ferry announced that Hayes and Wheeler had 185 votes to 184 votes for Tilden and Hendricks. "Wherefore, I do declare that Rutherford B. Hayes of Ohio, having received a majority of the whole number of votes is duly elected President of the United States for four years commencing on the 4th day of March, 1877."[55]

3

★ ★ ★ ★ ★

A NEW SOUTHERN POLICY

Shortly after Thomas Ferry had made his dramatic announcement, Hayes awoke to the good news at Marysville, Pennsylvania. He was traveling with Lucy and a small party in two special railroad cars, thoughtfully provided by Tom Scott. At about 9:30 A.M. on 2 March they arrived in Washington. After breakfast with John and Margaret Sherman, Hayes, accompanied by Sherman, called on President Grant. With the help of Secretary of State Hamilton Fish, Grant persuaded Hayes to be privately sworn in at the White House on Saturday evening, 3 March, thus avoiding an interregnum, because the formal inauguration was scheduled for Monday, 5 March. Moving on to the Capitol with Sherman, Hayes was pleased that the "colored hack drivers and others cheered lustily." At the Capitol, he went to the vice-president's room, where he met many senators and representatives of both parties.[1]

Hayes had his Inaugural Address prepared, but his cabinet was not complete. Because the electoral count had preoccupied everyone, fewer people than usual had pressed him for cabinet appointments. Back in January, he had consulted with some of his friends and his running mate William A. Wheeler, an unusually considerate act, but none of these men were close to the powerful party leaders. Hayes's decision not to offer cabinet positions to those with whom he had competed for the nomination, to their satellites, or to members of Grant's cabinet was shrewd. James G. Blaine, Benjamin H. Bristow, Roscoe Conkling, their lieutenants, or Secretary of War James Donald Cameron would have caused him grief. On the other hand, not conferring with powerful

51

Republican leaders in Washington, as Sherman had suggested, earned Hayes their hostility.[2]

After winning Louisiana in mid February, Hayes realized that cabinet making was "now in order." He resolved to ask John Sherman to take the Treasury Department and William M. Evarts, a superb lawyer who had experience in foreign affairs, to take the State Department. Hayes had wanted Evarts to head that department even before Evarts had argued Hayes's case before the Electoral Commission. Before leaving Columbus for Washington, Hayes had decided on two daring appointments. He asked Carl Schurz, who had campaigned for Hayes when he ran for governor as well as during the recent campaign, to serve as secretary of the interior. The Interior Department needed to be reformed, and Schurz would do that job, but he was despised by Republican-party regulars. Just four years earlier, he had led the Liberal Republican revolt and had supported Horace Greeley in an attempt to deny Grant a second term. Hayes also decided, in keeping with Kellar's negotiations, to appoint a southern Democrat to the cabinet, and he thought Confederate Gen. Joseph E. Johnston would make a fine secretary of war.[3]

In Washington, senators and representatives besieged Hayes with cabinet suggestions, while he sought reactions to his own ideas. The daring appointment of Johnston proved too impolitic to attempt. Blaine, whose opinion Hayes sought, said it would "harm everybody and help nobody"; Blaine countered by suggesting his man, William P. Frye, for the cabinet. "Blaine," Hayes reported, "seemed to claim it, as a condition of good relations with me," but Hayes steadfastly refused. Besides Blaine, Hayes had already offended Conkling by appointing Evarts, a New York rival who had reform leanings. The president-elect next defied powerful Pennsylvania and Illinois Republicans by refusing to give the War Department to either Cameron or John A. Logan, who had just lost his Senate seat to David Davis. Hayes gave the War Department to George W. McCrary of Iowa, who helped to originate the Electoral Commission Act and was a friend of railroad lobbyist Grenville Dodge. For his southern Democrat, Hayes named as postmaster general Kellar's friend David M. Key of Tennessee. William Henry Smith optimistically predicted that Key's appointment would "make the political break desired in the South; that the conservative men there in the State of Tennessee, Arkansas, Mississippi & Texas will follow him and support your administration."[4]

Hayes did gratify his friend Oliver P. Morton, who, though a presidential aspirant, was ill and would die within the year, by appointing Richard W. Thompson of Indiana as navy secretary. As attorney general, Hayes appointed Judge Charles Devens of the Massachusetts Supreme Court; this pleased Devens's law partner, Senator George F. Hoar, as well as Wheeler, who had recommended Devens. Although Hayes had resolved not to take care of anybody, every cabinet appointment rewarded someone who had helped make him president, and three of his appointments—those of Evarts, Schurz, and Key—were bound to provoke opposition among Republican leaders in the Senate.[5]

On Monday, 5 March, in front of the East Portico of the Capitol before thirty thousand spectators, the inaugural ceremony took place. After diplomats, Supreme Court justices, senators, and representatives were seated, Hayes and Grant appeared arm in arm and proceeded to the front platform, from which Hayes delivered his address. For the most part, he reiterated his letter of acceptance. He discussed five subjects: the South, civil-service reform, the currency question, foreign affairs, and the recent disputed election.[6]

It was clear to Hayes that the South should have "wise, honest, and peaceful local self-government." But he insisted that such a government must guard "the interests of both races carefully and equally" and that it must accept and obey the whole Constitution. Hayes also recognized that the federal government was morally obligated "to employ its constitutional power and influence to establish the rights of the people it has emancipated." He reasoned that the political unrest and poverty afflicting the South could "only be removed or remedied by the united and harmonious efforts of both races," and he urged that party ties and racial prejudices be surrendered, erasing the color line in politics. There was scant comfort in the address for Tom Scott, Grenville Dodge, and other backers of the Texas & Pacific Railroad. Despite Hayes's intentions on 5 January, he did not mention liberal internal improvements for the South; he merely said that it deserved the considerate care of the federal government, limited by constitutional restraints and economic prudence.

Hayes thought the schoolhouse, not the railroad, would save the South. The "improvement of the intellectual and moral condition of the people," he maintained, was the basis of prosperity. Insisting that "universal suffrage should rest upon universal education," he emphatically called for "liberal and permanent provision . . . for the support of free schools by the State governments, and, if need be, supplemented by legitimate aid from national authority."

Hayes's call for a "thorough, radical, and complete" reform of the civil service proved to be the most memorable part of his address. He wished to "return to the principles and practices of the founders of the Government," who had not allowed members of Congress to dictate civil-service appointments, who had not made appointments merely to reward partisan service, and who had retained public officers as long as their character and work remained satisfactory. Hayes realized that even while he owed his election to the "zealous labors of a political party," he should remember "that he serves his party best who serves the country best." Hayes had coined an oft-quoted aphorism. Convinced that much of the abuse of the civil service had resulted from the attempts of presidents to succeed themselves, he proposed a constitutional amendment that would limit a president to one six-year term.

The third domestic problem that concerned Hayes was the currency question. Noting the depression in commerce and manufacturing, which had prevailed since September 1873, Hayes judged that the fluctuating and uncertain value of irredeemable paper currency was "one of the greatest obstacles to a return to prosperous times." He pronounced: "The only safe paper currency is one which rests upon a coin basis and is at all times and promptly convertible into coin." Accordingly, Hayes called for congressional legislation to implement an early resumption of specie payments, a policy he thought was dictated by wisdom, self-interest, and public opinion.

Like many who have experienced the horror of war, Hayes was devoted to peace. To preserve peace with other nations, he wished to observe "our traditional rule of noninterference in the affairs of foreign nations" and to follow the policy, inaugurated by Grant, "of submitting to arbitration grave questions in dispute between ourselves and foreign powers." Hayes realized that the Democrats were unhappy with his election, but the fact that the two political parties had arbitrated the disputed election "under the forms of law," Hayes insisted, was reason for rejoicing. He was pleased also that the American people, who enjoyed the widest suffrage on earth, had given the world its first example of a great nation's peacefully settling a disputed election. Hayes again indicated his forthcoming southern policy by asking the people to help him secure prosperity, justice, and peace for all within "a union depending not upon the constraint of force, but upon the loving devotion of a free people."

Reactions to Hayes's address were mixed, but reformers were pleased. "There have been few inaugural addresses superior . . . in mingled wisdom, force, and moderation of statement," George William Curtis editorialized in *Harper's Weekly*. Edwin L. Godkin, editor of the *Nation*, thought the address "a clear, modest, and sensible document, which promises nothing which reasonable men may not hope to see performed, and leaves nothing untouched of which mention was desirable."[7]

That Hayes pleased reformers should come as no surprise, since he utilized advice from Carl Schurz. Schurz told Hayes to stick by his acceptance letter and specifically urged him "to soften party passions" growing out of the disputed election; to call for a southern policy that would discourage railroad subsidies, eliminate misgovernment, end race and party prejudices, and protect the rights of all; to call for the resumption of specie payments, for civil-service reform, and for a foreign policy stressing noninterference and arbitration; and finally to promise to serve only one term. So pervasive was Schurz's influence on the Inaugural Address that Hayes's most quotable line, "He serves his party best who serves the country best," was an improvement on Schurz's "You will serve that party best by serving the public interest best."[8]

For partisan Republican leaders in Congress, the emphasis of the address on conciliation and reform failed to strike a responsive chord. Even the reform-minded Garfield said nothing in his diary about the address, but he did record that after delivering it, Hayes took the oath of office from Sardis Birchard's friend Chief Justice Morrison R. Waite and then kissed the Bible "somewhere" in the first eleven verses of Psalm 118. Perhaps Hayes's kiss landed on verse 6: "The Lord is on my side; I will not fear: what can man do unto me?" The charmed life that Hayes had led as a soldier and as a politician, surviving battles and winning elections, did little to diminish his quiet self-confidence.

After the inauguration, the presidential party rode to the White House for a lunch planned by Julia Grant. The Inaugural Address apparently was not uppermost in people's minds. "There were," Garfield noted, "many indications of relief and joy that no accident had occurred on the route for there were apprehensions of assassination." Indeed, in Louisiana a Democrat had shot and wounded Stephen B. Packard, the Republican governor, and some months earlier, a bullet had been fired into Hayes's home in Columbus. After lunch, Rutherford and Lucy Hayes went to the carriage steps to bid the Grants farewell, as they left the White House.

With little time to plan celebrations and with little desire to provoke violence, the victors staged no inaugural parade that afternoon and no inaugural ball that evening, but Rutherford and Lucy Hayes attended a reception at Willard's Hotel, where jubilant Republicans celebrated into the night. "In the evening," *Harper's Weekly* reported, "the streets of Washington were so thronged with people that it was difficult to move about except with the general mass. All the public buildings and many private houses were brilliantly illuminated. Bands were playing, rockets flying, and cannon firing. Pennsylvania Avenue from end to end was one sea of light. . . . An immense torchlight procession ended the ceremonies."[9]

On Tuesday, the party was over. Smarting over his failure to push Frye into the cabinet, Blaine virtually defied Hayes to abandon the Packard government, which remained in place, since Grant's order to remove the troops had not been delivered. Blaine's speech delighted the Republican carpetbag senators but disturbed moderate Republicans, who feared that Blaine and Hayes were on a collision course.

On Wednesday, when Hayes submitted his cabinet selections to the Senate for confirmation, a majority of Blaine's colleagues joined him in harassing Hayes. Simon Cameron immediately objected to Evarts, whom he and Conkling disliked, and Blaine moved successfully that the nomination be referred to the Committee on Foreign Relations. In an unprecedented action, the Senate then referred all the nominations to committee, including that of Sherman, a member of the Senate, and vigorously denounced Evarts, Key, and, especially, Schurz. Rejoicing over Republican dissension, the Democrats caucused but decided not to help defeat Hayes's nominees. Hayes believed that southern Senators John B. Gordon, L. Q. C. Lamar, and Benjamin H. Hill were responsible for his Democratic support, and in truth, they would have aided their worst enemies by defeating the Hayes nominees.[10]

Hayes stood firm, and by Thursday the Senate began to back down. It confirmed Sherman after an hour's debate, apparently because his uncertain fate held up senatorial committee assignments. Sherman immediately began to lobby among his former colleagues for his fellow appointees, and the angry reaction of newspapers and constituents to the senators' obstructive acts began to be felt in Washington. Letters, telegrams, newspaper editorials, and resolutions, approved by meetings of substantial Republicans in New York, Philadelphia, and other cities, soon convinced most senators that the nominations should be confirmed.

On Saturday, 10 March, the six remaining nominees were reported favorably from committee and were promptly confirmed. The Senate voted unanimously for McCrary, Devens, and Thompson, and only two senators objected to Evarts, Key, and Schurz. Chagrined at his defeat and unwilling to work with Evarts, Simon Cameron, chairman of the Foreign Relations Committee, resigned from the Senate and had the pliable Pennsylvania Legislature name his son James Donald Cameron to succeed him. Hayes had won his first skirmish. A few leading Republicans, relying on the politics of organization, had been outflanked by a new president, relying on the politics of reform and the force of public opinion.

Hayes's Inaugural Address and his cabinet appointees inspired many Americans. "We must have a higher and improved civil service, and we must have honest administration at the South—and a *united* country. I have never felt such hope as I feel now," exclaimed Edward L. Pierce, the friend and biographer of Charles Sumner. Support from the educated and cultivated elite who thought of itself as "the best people" pleased Hayes. He was particularly gratified by the short note he received from James Russell Lowell, Henry Wadsworth Longfellow, Charles W. Eliot, Francis James Child, and Charles Eliot Norton: "The course of the President is what we expected and heartily approve."[11]

Hayes faced a knotty problem and a huge task. He had to decide which of two conflicting governments he would support in both Louisiana and South Carolina, and with the Senate ready to adjourn in two weeks, he had to appoint approximately a thousand officials for it to confirm. Preoccupied with his southern policy, Hayes realized that he could not make good appointments "in such a hurry," so he sensibly decided to fill only the vacant offices while the Senate was in session and to allow the other officials to remain "until he could take his time."[12]

Hayes also realized that his southern policy required careful consideration. Small detachments of federal troops, who were upholding Republican administrations, guarded the capitals of Louisiana and South Carolina; but much of each of those states was controlled by rival Democratic governments. To make Republican governments viable in those states, Hayes would have to use more troops. With the nation's meager 25,000-man army scattered in small detachments, primarily in the West, few troops were available; and by refusing to appropriate funds for the army beyond 1 July 1877, the Democrats threatened to disband it before they would allow troops to be employed in the South. Hayes's private thoughts, his public statements, and the commitments made in his name during the count indicated that he would withdraw the troops and accept home rule, if responsible white southerners promised to allow both black and white Republicans to participate freely in politics. Hayes also hoped to reestablish the prewar political alliance among former Whigs.

Despite his desire "to put aside the bayonet," Hayes did not immediately adopt a liberal policy toward the late rebels. When prominent Republicans such as Blaine were reluctant to abandon Packard and Chamberlain and were skeptical that a liberal southern policy would protect the rights of blacks, Hayes paused. Indeed, Packard's claim to have carried Louisiana was stronger than Hayes's claim to its electoral votes. Abandoning Packard would be an admission, in effect, that Tilden had deserved Louisiana and the election. Even Hayes's most staunch supporters—John Sherman, Charles Foster, William Henry Smith—had been reluctant in February to toss Packard and Chamberlain aside. Quick action might further inflame the Senate and endanger appointments, while delay, preferably until after the Senate had confirmed his appointees and had adjourned, would dissipate hostility. Delay would also enable Hayes to rethink this important policy change, while preparing the public for it. He could consider suggestions, including the holding of new elections and the calling of a constitutional convention, as well as the maintaining, increasing, or withdrawing of troops. He could seek guidance in and out of government.[13]

Hayes, however, would get no guidance from his staff. Unlike presidents a century later, he had few staff members and no offices such as the National Security Council or the Office of Management and Budget to study issues and problems and to offer counsel and advice. Hayes's small staff of nine, which was headed by a private secretary, performed prosaic tasks, such as receiving visitors, sorting incoming correspondence, assembling files on potential appointees to office, answering routine mail, and copying letters and papers that Hayes, who usually did not dictate to the stenographer on his staff, had written out. The Hayes White House ignored the newly invented typewriter, and although it boasted a telephone, there were so few elsewhere that it was seldom used. The center of communications in the White House was its busy telegraph office.

Hayes perceived that he needed a strong advisor as private secretary, but unfortunately neither William Henry Smith nor Judge Manning F. Force of Cincinnati would accept what they regarded as an inferior position. Hayes then resorted to his loyal friend William K. Rogers, who had failed in the ministry, law, and business and who at the White House would not get on well with either the press or the public. Hayes later noted that Rogers was "easily duped; trusts all men who profess friendship"; and lacked "a sense of duty and responsibility." But perhaps the most damning thing Hayes said about Rogers was that he "thinks well of almost anything I do." Of great help to Hayes was his twenty-one-year-old son Webb, who often served quite successfully as his father's unofficial secretary. With no staff to screen the swarms of applicants or to propose policy alternatives, Hayes, like his predecessors, had to rely on congressmen for advice on appointments and on his cabinet or friends for advice on policy.[14]

Hayes, however, would not allow congressmen to dictate appointments, would not slavishly follow the opinion of his cabinet, and would preside over a unified administration. Although he had been a Whig and was trying to revive and realign southern Whigs, he moved away from the Whig ideal of a weak president who would be subservient to Congress, deferential to his cabinet, and would allow virtual autonomy to heads of departments.

Hayes's immediate predecessors embraced or enhanced the Whig approach to the presidency. Abraham Lincoln deferred to Congress in appointments and in other political matters, did not meet often with his cabinet, and gave its members a free hand in running their departments. Andrew Johnson's inept opposition to Congress brought the Tenure of Office Act, which increased congressional power over cabinet members and the executive departments. Grant's attitude that the presidency was a reward—a semiretirement to be enjoyed—when coupled with his political ignorance, created a weak and passive president who was easily influenced and manipulated by friends, congressmen, and cabinet members.

Hayes admired Washington's integrity and Lincoln's commitment to equality of opportunity, but he identified with John Quincy Adams in his struggles with Congress, his patronage policies, and his desire to use national power to foster education. Hayes, however, was a much better politician than Adams. By working hard at being president and by fighting a number of battles with Congress, Hayes would reverse the ascendancy of Congress, the independence of cabinet members, and the decline of the presidency.[15]

Hayes trusted his cabinet members, valued their counsel, and maintained cordial relations with them. The cabinet was largely his creation, not that of congressional leaders, and he believed that its members would not sacrifice the goals of his administration. In crises, Hayes met with his cabinet daily and, in ordinary times, on Tuesdays and Thursdays from 12 to 2 P.M. Everything from minor appointments to major policies was discussed at these informal and usually harmonious meetings. But Hayes made the decisions, and on occasion he imposed his will upon reluctant department heads, including Sherman, Evarts, and Schurz, who were the strongest cabinet members. Each week, during a Sunday-afternoon drive, Hayes discussed various matters with Sherman, who proved to be the most valuable member of Hayes's cabinet. Sherman was experienced in financial matters, knowledgeable in politics, and expert in the art of cajoling senators. The able Evarts and the conscientious Schurz were excellent advisors, but they were mixed blessings, because regular Republicans disliked their political independence. The remaining cabinet members were able, but Key was hated by those Republicans who wanted to wave the bloody shirt, and Thompson embarrassed Hayes and had to leave in the final two months of his administration.[16]

The cabinet proved to be stable as well as competent, with its few changes coming late in Hayes's administration. In addition to Thompson, in December 1879, Hayes replaced George W. McCrary, whom he had named as a federal circuit judge, with Alexander Ramsey of Minnesota, and in August 1880 he replaced Key, whom he had made a federal district judge, with another Tennessean, Horace Maynard, who, in contrast to Key, was a Radical Republican. In short, Hayes relied on the cabinet to help him fashion a new southern policy.

At the cabinet meeting of 20 March, Hayes brought up the "Louisiana troubles" and found that except for Devens, the cabinet members agreed with him that the states themselves should settle contested state elections and that military force should not be used to uphold Packard's government. Even Devens was not decidedly for intervention. Practical and political considerations, rather than constitutional or moral ones, helped Hayes to make up his mind, and his views were perhaps more appropriate for foreign than for domestic policy. Like Grant, he thought the people opposed the use of federal forces to uphold one state government against a rival state government. If "the de jure Gov-[ernmen]t in a State" had been overthrown, Hayes believed "the de facto Gov[ernmen]'t must be recognized."

Hayes, who earlier had been an ultraradical supporter of the military occupation of the South, believed that superior force had failed the blacks. He thought that the few troops who were upholding Republican governments in Louisiana and South Carolina were counterproductive. He believed that only "peaceful methods" could "restore harmony and good feeling between Sections and races" and achieve "safety and prosperity for the colored people." He wanted "to make one government out of two in each State," and with the help of his cabinet, he decided to send a commission to Louisiana to work peacefully toward that goal.[17]

From a bleak situation, Hayes was trying to salvage something lasting for blacks and the Republican party. As long as the election had been in doubt, he had received optimistic reports that conservative southern Democrats, either Whig or Unionist in background, would acquiesce in his election, might help Republicans organize the House of Representatives with Garfield as Speaker, and might come over to the Republican party, if he were to withdraw federal support from the carpetbag-scalawag Packard and Chamberlain governments. These reports contrasted the poverty, ignorance, and corruption of the Packard regime, in particular, with "the capital, the intelligence, the virtue" of the conservative Democrats who, the reports insisted, were committed to the constitutional rights of blacks.

These correspondents stressed that the color line in southern politics could be abolished and that a viable two-party system could again flourish in the South. They argued that if the political color line were not obliterated, the white Democratic party would inevitably triumph over the black Republican party and that the "safety, the very existence of the political rights" of blacks, would be jeopardized. By that line of reasoning, getting rid of the carpetbaggers would benefit southern blacks.

The reports promised that the Republican party in the South could be reconstituted with wealthy, intelligent, virtuous, and conservative southern whites at its head, that instead of having the shakiest of footholds in only two states, it could carry at least five or six of the former Confederate states. To work that transformation, Jacob Dolson Cox urged Hayes "to choose men for federal office whose reputations shall command the confidence of all classes" and "to moderate the new kindled ambition of the colored people to fill places which neither their experience nor their knowledge of business or of the laws fits them for."[18]

In February 1877, Hayes told Cox that he shared his views on "the Southern Question . . . precisely." Hayes wanted blacks to enjoy their constitutional rights, yet he believed that "the intelligence of any country ought to govern it." Attracted to a policy that would woo conservative southerners, Hayes became willing, if need be, to abandon white carpetbaggers and scalawags. He rationalized that their corrupt course had forfeited their claims on the Republican party and the federal government for protection and that their leadership of the Republican party perpetuated the color line in politics. Indeed, as early as 4 October 1876, Hayes, along with the reformer Wayne MacVeagh, hoped that "by conciliating southern whites on the basis of obedience to law and equal rights . . . we may divide the southern whites, and so protect the colored people."

Although Hayes obviously wished to moderate the role that blacks would play in a Republican party led by southern conservatives, he did not want to stifle the ambitions of blacks. He consistently argued that they deserved support. He urged education to enable intelligent blacks to participate in governing the South. Both an elitist and a democrat, Hayes believed that all black males should vote and that educated blacks, such as Frederick Douglass, whom he appointed to the lucrative post of marshal of the District of Columbia, should be officers of the government. Appropriately for a man who favored civil-service reform, Hayes believed that the meritorious should govern, but he also believed that through public education everyone should have access to public office.[19]

After his inauguration, Hayes continued to receive reports disparaging the remaining carpetbag regimes and praising southern conservatives. These reports insisted that if local control and federal patronage were steered to southern conservatives, they would support the administration. On 10 March, Hayes was optimistic that enough southern Democrats would defect to elect Garfield Speaker of the House. From Richmond, Alexander H. H. Stuart, a distinguished prewar Whig, said that the administration would have "the sympathy & co-operation of the Whigs of the South" if it would "save the constitution from violation, & see that the officers of government discharge their duties with honesty & fidelity!" Although Hayes differed from Stuart in perceiving how the Constitution was violated in the South, Hayes was no doubt pleased by the promise of southern Whig support from such an influential source.[20]

Further confirmation that the administration was making political headway in the South came from office seekers in Petersburg and Lynchburg, Virginia. Their objective, however, was patronage, and office seekers frequently buttressed their applications with distorted analyses of the local political situation, while claiming that their appointment would strengthen the administration. Not only did the spoils system provide the civil service with inadequate public officers; it also provided political leaders, who had to make decisions, with misinformation concerning the people's reactions to party and public policies.[21]

For an outside opinion, Hayes turned to Judge William M. Dickson, a valued friend, who reassured Hayes that his southern policy was both "right" and "inevitable," since the "bayonet policy . . . *no longer protects.*" To be successful, "it must be maintained with a high hand. . . . The country will not *now* sustain that." Dickson also saw that there was an opportunity to protect the blacks by dividing the white vote through appealing "to the better sentiment [in the] South"; and should this overture fail and should blacks be abused, Dickson predicted, with monumental inaccuracy, that "the country will be prepared for repressive measures." He cautioned Hayes, however, not to "drive off the old anti-slavery sentiment" by pushing Chamberlain and Packard "out through the back door, as if they were culprits . . . and Hampton & Nicholls must not come in . . . *As Conquerors*—but through terms." Dickson wanted Hayes to appoint a commission, which would command the confidence of the old antislavery men, to help Chamberlain and Packard work out a satisfactory solution with their adversaries.[22]

The idea of a commission dismayed southerners who had been willing to see Hayes inaugurated in exchange for a Democratic administration in Louisiana. It appeared to them that he had yielded to the Radical Republicans and would renege on the conciliatory words in his Inaugural Address and on the assurances of Sherman, Matthews, Foster, Dennison, and Grant. Fearing that Hayes was about to change his southern policy, L. Q. C. Lamar of Mississippi urged him to "*do* as you *said* you would do." Randall, the Democratic candidate for Speaker of the House, thought the commission was a ploy to frighten southern Democrats into helping the Republicans organize the House, but the commission also worried people such as Smith and Kellar, who were trying to attract southerners to the Republican party.[23]

There was no cause for alarm. The crucial step in the rapprochement of old southern and northern Whigs was the withdrawal of troops, and Hayes was not about to use troops to protect Packard and Chamberlain. In late March, Hayes continued to receive optimistic predictions from the South, and Kellar expected Senators Augustus H. Garland of Arkansas and Ben Hill of Georgia to lead a southern administration party. In exchange for their support, they wanted patronage, and William Henry Smith urged Hayes to forget civil-service reform and give them offices. Smith asked him to let Key "so organize things in the South as to give you the control of the House." Hayes apparently agreed that Key could use patronage to secure the House of Representatives. "The political outlook," Kellar rejoiced, "is bright and full of hope. I am certain the end will be a complete victory for Hayes over the evil and disreputable elements in both parties."[24]

With the drive for southern support promising success, the governing days of Chamberlain and Packard were numbered. Chamberlain was the first to go. South Carolina was less agitated than Louisiana, and Hayes thought that a quick resolution of the dispute in South Carolina might guide the commission in Louisiana. A discussion with his cabinet on 22 March confirmed his intention to remove the troops and not to appoint a commission for South Carolina. Later that month, Hayes conferred with the rival South Carolina governors. Carrying his carpetbag, Chamberlain traveled anonymously to Washington, while Hampton responded to brass bands and fireworks along his triumphant way, with speeches demanding that there be no commission, no compromise, and no troops. Even though Chamberlain knew that his situation was hopeless and even though he admitted that without federal troops he could not maintain his government, he refused to resign.

In contrast, Hampton and Hayes struck a bargain. Hampton promised to preserve the peace in South Carolina, to recognize the constitutional rights of blacks as well as whites, and to aid in organizing the House of Representatives with Garfield as Speaker. Hayes, in turn, promised to withdraw the troops from the statehouse. He gave the order on 3 April, the troops left on 10 April, and Chamberlain ordered that the statehouse keys be given to Hampton, whose government moved in on 11 April 1877.[25]

It would take longer for the Louisiana commission to finesse the abandonment of Packard. William Henry Smith urged Hayes to hurry the commission to Louisiana and warned him that if it should uphold Packard or be slow in recommending his removal, the dream of a southern administration party would not be realized. In a conspiratorial tone, Smith advised Hayes: "I have confidence in an informal (uninstructed) commission of practical men to pioneer the way for the official committee. Such men as Richard Smith, Medill & Kellar, could drop down at once, quietly get to the bottom & controlling news sources could keep the public in ignorance until the way should be cleared."[26]

Hayes quickly appointed the Louisiana Commission and expected from it a prompt report in support of his southern policy. The commission was chaired by Charles B. Lawrence of Illinois; its other members were Joseph R. Hawley of Connecticut, John M. Harlan of Kentucky, John C. Brown, a former governor of Tennessee, and Wayne MacVeagh of Pennsylvania. Although the commissioners represented a geographical and political mix, none of them were conspicuous upholders of Radical Republican governments in southern states. While all seemed to be inclined toward Hayes's southern policy, MacVeagh's views "almost precisely" matched those of the president.[27]

For the administration, Evarts instructed the commission not to determine who won the recent state election but to concentrate on securing the acknowledgment within Louisiana of one government. If the people of Louisiana should refuse to accept all the branches of one government, then the commission should work for the recognition of a single legislature, since "the legislative power when undisputed, is quite competent" to resolve "conflicts in the coordinate branches of the Government."

Hayes also wanted to know whether the people of Louisiana would maintain the constitutional rights of all of its citizens, as he intended they should. By telling the commission that Hayes hoped to learn that the "great body of the people of Louisiana" would aid and not resist upholding everyone's constitutional rights, Evarts was specifying the information that Hayes desired. The instructions also emphasized that while Hayes had the right to intervene militarily to protect a state against domestic violence, he did not believe he had the power to determine or influence disputed elections. Evarts explained that Hayes wanted the commission to move with dispatch and that Hayes confidently hoped its "report will enable him promptly to execute a purpose he has so much at heart."[28]

Lest the point of these published instructions be missed, Evarts's "Second Instructions to Louisiana Commission" bluntly stated that it was Hayes's "purpose to remove the troops from the State House," but he did not want their removal to be "the occasion or opportunity of any outbreak of violence." Hayes left open the possibility of future intervention should affairs in Louisiana and his constitutional duty demand such action. Along with this threat, Hayes again hoped that the people of Louisiana would not thwart his earnest desire to end "even an apparent military interference."[29]

The commission arrived in New Orleans on 5 April. On that same day, Packard, upset by its instructions, urged Hayes to have the commission determine who should legally govern Louisiana, but Hayes's resolve was probably strengthened by the receipt of a petition signed by hundreds of local citizens, ranging from bishops to bankers, urging that the troops supporting Packard be returned to their barracks. The petition emphasized Packard's lack of power beyond the statehouse and concluded: "If local self-government is given us, we pledge ourselves for the loyalty of Louisiana to the Union, for the protection of life and property and civil rights of all her citizens, and for the equal benefit of her laws, without distinction of race, color, or previous condition." Hayes could not have phrased a pledge more pleasing to his ears.[30]

In truth, Packard's authority, although it was recognized by the state supreme court, did not extend much beyond the four New Orleans streets surrounding the St. Louis Hotel, in which the statehouse was located. Nevertheless, he refused to compromise. Most of the district judges and the parish (county) officers recognized Nicholls, whose regime, aware that the nation was watching, qualified 240 blacks, who had been elected to various positions, and appointed to state offices 21 other blacks. Running a de facto government from the New Orleans Odd Fellows Hall and encouraged by signs in Washington and South Carolina, the Nicholls forces conceded nothing. They were further strengthened on 6 April, the commission's second day in New Orleans, when, at a mass meeting, several thousand Nicholls supporters pledged: "Never to submit to the pretended Packard Government; never to pay it a dollar of taxes; never to acknowledge its authority; but to resist it at every point and in every way."

Because compromise was impossible, the commission tried to create a legislature in which both houses would have a quorum of members that both the Republicans and the Democrats could acknowledge were entitled to their seats. In theory, the Packard and Nicholls legislatures were to woo and win over the members of the other's legislature that had clearly been elected until a legislature would emerge that would have an uncontested quorum. The commission remained officially neutral, but it counted on New Orleans businessmen "bulldozing" the politicians into a settlement.[31]

The commission was above purchasing politicians, but Andrew J. Kellar was not. He was on the spot, "earnestly engaged in doing what is practical to solve the political troubles in this unfortunate State." Kellar told William Henry Smith: "You thoroughly understand that many things necessary to be done, but which the Commission cannot do, must be accomplished in order to reach results that will be accepted by public opinion." Working primarily through Cotton Exchange members, Kellar on 12 April was "somewhat confident" of securing that week a legislature of "members whose election is conceded on all sides" and which, "of course," would recognize Nicholls.

Kellar broke Louisiana law in winning over the requisite six Republican legislators, but he rationalized: "The corrupt government in existence, made laws to perpetrate bad government, and a change for reform, must of necessity violate the letter of bad laws enacted for corrupt uses. This is civil revolution, but it is the only remedy of relief." To reward and hold on to the defectors, Kellar called for a reorganization of the New Orleans Customhouse to "disband the political loafers in both parties . . . who hover about the Custom House like flies around an empty sugar barrel. The results in a political sense will be to unite the supporters of Gov. Nicholls and the friends of the Administration."[32]

Kellar was so encouraged that he no longer wrote off Louisiana in his larger scheme of organizing an administration party in the South. He told Webb Hayes that under Nicholls, party lines would "not only be obliterated but the party names themselves will be abolished," that "intelligent" whites and "industrious" blacks would "unite and support the Administration." Hayes's southern policy, he insisted, would "accomplish every thing he has at heart. The results of the war, as secured in the Constitutional amendments, will be extended in practical legislation and enforced by public opinion in Louisiana, much beyond my expectation.''[33]

The Reconstruction era rapidly ended. From Hayes's perspective, the timing seemed excellent, since delay prepared northern Republicans for Packard's ouster but apparently did not lose Hayes his potential allies among Nicholls's supporters. On Tuesday, 17 April, the United States Senate adjourned, leaving the most vocal critics of Hayes's southern policy without a forum. By Thursday, 19 April, enough Republicans had been induced to join the Nicholls legislature to give it a quorum, and the commission wired Hayes that a legal legislature existed and that the troops supporting Packard could be withdrawn.

That day, the commission had received from Nicholls resolutions by his legislature that fully accepted the Civil War amendments and pledged "the promotion of kindly relations between the white and colored citizens." Claiming that he had "earnestly sought to obliterate the color line in politics, and consolidate the people on a basis of equal rights and common interests," Nicholls pledged the full and equal protection of the rights of all persons, promised an equal system of tax-supported public education open to all "without regard to race or color," and expressed the wish to foster immigration to hasten Louisiana's economic development. Virtually repeating Hayes's prescription to cure the ills of southern society, these pledges were precisely the assurances that Hayes desired.

On Friday, 20 April, certain that disputes would "be settled by peaceful methods," Hayes directed that the detachment of troops protecting the Packard government "be withdrawn . . . on Tuesday next, the 24th of April, at 12 o'clock meridian." As the troops left for their barracks on schedule, crowds cheered, bells rang, and cannons roared. The next day, the Democrats took over the statehouse. Packard, whose legislature had already been dissolved, made no resistance. A brave man who had barely recovered from the effects of an assassin's bullet, he yielded to superior force. "I am," he exclaimed, "wholly discouraged by the fact that, one by one, the Republican State Governments of the South have been forced to succumb to force, fraud, or policy."[34]

Most Democrats and many Republicans did not share Kellar's vision of future southern politics. Guarding against attempts to split their solid white support in the South, Democrats argued that Hayes deserved no credit for having done what the Democrats had forced him to do. Far from accepting black participation in the political process (the Civil War amendments), they set their sights on new goals, such as the repeal of federal election laws, which would facilitate efforts to disfranchise black voters. Southern Republicans, both black and white, agreed with Packard. Amos T. Akerman of Georgia, who had been Grant's attorney general, observed that Hayes's course amounted to combating "lawlessness by letting the lawless have their own way." Kellar's idea that the "colored voter & laborer will be better protected than under former governments" was emphatically contradicted by a South Carolinian who exclaimed to Hayes: "I am a unprotected freedman. . . . O God Save the Colored People." Rather than anticipate an influx of Whiggish whites, southern Republicans feared that their party would wither away.

Some northern Republicans thought that Hayes's course was impolitic and wrong. Among former abolitionists, Wendell Phillips was furious, and William Lloyd Garrison thought Hayes had made a cowardly compromise with the "incorrigible enemies of equal rights and legitimate government." Abandoning Packard disturbed Charles B. Farwell of Chicago for personal as well as political reasons, since Hayes had reneged on promises that Farwell, as the first visiting statesman to reach New Orleans, had made to Packard. And Benjamin F. Wade, a friend who had seconded Hayes's nomination, consistently adhered to his Radical views and felt "deceived, betrayed, and humiliated" by Hayes's southern policy.[35]

Although most northern Republicans supported Hayes's move, their enthusiasm for it varied. Hayes's own representative, Charles Foster, exclaimed: "How rejoiced I am at the extremely happy undoing of the South Carolina & Louisiana muddle. Here & there a republican may be found who takes the Ben Wade view of the situation, but, generally speaking, the people of both parties are rejoiced to know that your policy has been a success, and that a genuine peace is to again grow up between the north & south." Favoring local self-government, believing in the supremacy of civil over military authority, and yearning for peace, northern Republicans were willing to try Hayes's southern policy. If his strategy could break the color line, win some whites to the Republican party, and protect the rights of blacks, the cause of civil rights would be advanced throughout the South.

More cautious and self-centered, Garfield thought that Hayes might succeed, if southern Democratic supporters of Hayes's policy would "give him an administration House" with Garfield as Speaker. "If not," Garfield predicted that northern Republicans would turn on Hayes and would "not tolerate a continuance of his Southern Scheme." If Hayes's strategy were to fail and if white-supremacy governments were to emerge in South Carolina and Louisiana, as they had in the rest of the South, the precarious foothold in those states would be lost. And if it were lost, it would be almost impossible to utilize the military to protect the rights of black voters and to rebuild a strong black-based Republican party.[36]

Feeling that his present course was correct, Hayes was guardedly optimistic about the future. With northerners tired of Reconstruction, with Democrats in control of the House of Representatives and refusing to make military appropriations, and with the Republican party in disarray in the South, Hayes saw that his choice was not whether the troops should be withdrawn but when they should be withdrawn. Using that tenuous military presence as a bargaining chip, he extracted pledges from the Hampton and Nicholls governments to reject white supremacy. He did not share completely the unbounded optimism of Kellar, who proclaimed that a new era of racial justice and political reorganization was at hand. Hayes hoped that South Carolina and Louisiana would faithfully observe, as they had pledged, the Reconstruction amendments and "that the colored people shall have equal rights to labor, to education, and to the privileges of citizenship. I am confident this is a good work." But he concluded, "Time will tell."[37]

During the summer and fall of 1877, Hayes, who traveled a good deal as president, toured New England, Ohio, and the South. Everywhere he went he preached reconciliation. In June he received an honorary Doctor of Laws degree from Harvard and, at a banquet in his honor, was touched by Oliver Wendell Holmes's poem, which hailed Hayes as a "Healer of Strife!" When in Ohio, Hayes took a side trip to Richmond, Indiana, to visit Oliver P. Morton, his Radical Republican ally who was terminally ill. Deeply moved by the imminent loss of his friend, Hayes kissed Morton on the forehead. Morton was also touched; he rallied and published on 23 October a vigorous letter urging Republicans not to abandon Hayes because of his conciliatory southern policy and his efforts to reform the civil service. Moving on to the South, Hayes held out the olive branch, but he consistently stressed that obeying the amendments was a prerequisite of reconciliation.

The South apparently accepted Hayes's terms, and his tour, which Governor Wade Hampton of South Carolina joined at Louisville, Kentucky, was a triumph. At Atlanta, Hayes addressed a mixed audience of Democrats and Republicans, whites and blacks. He aroused "immense enthusiasm and cheering for several minutes," when he told the blacks in the audience that he believed that their "rights and interests would be safer if this great mass of intelligent white men were let alone by the general Government." The crowd cheered, although not so enthusiastically, when Hayes reiterated his basic proposition that the Constitution and all of its amendments be "fully and fairly obeyed and enforced."[38]

Hayes was enormously encouraged by his southern trip. He wrote in his diary: "Received everywhere heartily. The country is again one and united! I am very happy to be able to feel that the course taken has turned out so well." Hayes was similarly encouraged a month later by a trip to Richmond, Virginia, and again that autumn when he was nominated to the Board of Trustees of the Peabody Education Fund by its southern members and then was elected by the unanimous board. George Peabody had endowed that fund with $3.4 million to combat illiteracy among southern blacks and whites, and Hayes, with his abiding faith in education and his hopes for racial harmony in the South, was the fund's most devoted trustee as long as he lived. Hayes's journey south and his election to the Peabody board convinced him that his southern policy was both wise and working. He believed that the war wounds had been healed, that white southerners had accepted the Reconstruction amendments safeguarding black lives, rights, and property, and that conservative Democrats would ignore color and sectional lines in politics and would move over to the Republican party.[39]

Hayes was wrong. The war wounds were not healed, white southerners had applauded the amendments because they thought it likely that they would be neither enforced nor obeyed, and conservative southern Democrats did not join the Republican party, which steadily shrank until its members were a mere handful of officeholders. A more cynical person than Hayes would not have expected southerners to be rapidly converted to civil and political rights for blacks. He failed to perceive the pervasiveness and the viciousness of racial prejudice in southern politics and society. Substituting reason and patriotism for the coercion that had failed in the past and was unfeasible in the present, Hayes tried to persuade white southerners to obey and enforce the Reconstruction amendments. For a brief season, he believed he had succeeded.[40]

Although heartened by his southern tour, Hayes was confronted by the harsh realities of politics when the special session of the Forty-fifth Congress began on 15 October 1877. He had gratified the reformers but had offended the organization men in his party; he had conciliated, but not converted, southern Democrats, and in the process had alienated many Republicans. Hayes called the special session because the previous Congress, after agreeing to his election, had adjourned on 3 March 1877 without having appropriated funds for the army, which had gone without pay since 30 June. Having originally called Congress to meet in

May, Hayes had postponed the special session until October 1877 in the hopes that Republicans who were opposed to his southern policy would calm down and that southern Democrats would align themselves with his administration. His hopes did not materialize. The Republicans were more divided than the Democrats, who solidly backed Samuel J. Randall and elected him Speaker of the House. Although Garfield received every Republican vote cast, five protectionist, inflationist Republican congressmen from Pennsylvania abstained from voting.[41]

Hayes persisted in his belief that his southern policy was working, but in January 1878 his faith was strained. The Nicholls government in Louisiana arrested Thomas C. Anderson, the acting collector of the Port of New Orleans, on felony charges of having altered Vernon Parish election returns while he was a member of the recent returning board. Imprisoned, tried, and convicted, Anderson, by early February, was being held without bail for sentencing. Outraged, Secretary of the Treasury Sherman told Hayes that ''this proceeding tends to show that this spirit of conciliation is not mutual, and cannot be successful.'' Because Sherman had been a visiting statesman in Louisiana, the case threatened his integrity as well as his authority as Anderson's superior officer. He claimed that the attorney general who had prosecuted Anderson was an officer of the White League, ''the chief instrument in the massacres and political murders in that state,'' that the judge was a defaulter, and that the jury was packed to convict Anderson.[42]

Anderson was sentenced to two years in the penitentiary, but the Hayes administration protested, so the Louisiana Supreme Court set aside the verdict and released him in March. When the Nicholls government later dropped the charges against three other members of the returning board, Hayes unrealistically concluded: ''For the first time the better classes have overruled the violent. Pacification begins to tell.'' He seemed to have forgotten that it was the Nicholls administration, supposedly representing the best public opinion, that had indicted Anderson.[43]

Reconciliation became even more unlikely later that spring. On 17 May 1878 the House of Representatives, dominated by Democrats, adopted the resolution of Clarkson N. Potter of New York to investigate the ''alleged false and fraudulent'' elections in Louisiana and Florida. Looking toward the campaigns of 1878 and 1880, the Democrats wished to identify the Republicans with fraud, and the more ardent spirits among the Democrats anticipated revelations on which to base a challenge in the courts to Hayes's title to the presidency.

Hayes was not overly concerned about the charges of fraud. Personally, he had nothing to hide. Although William Henry Smith told

Hayes that men such as Henry Van Ness Boynton and Charles B. Farwell possessed information that could be embarrassing, neither was slated to testify, and Hayes thought the witnesses the Democrats had lined up would "merely raise dust." Hayes, however, equated any effort that was made to unseat him through the courts with "another rebellion" and vowed that he would go to war rather than submit to an attempt to remove him by means other than the constitutional process of impeachment.[44]

The Potter resolution imposed unity on squabbling Republicans, produced division among Democrats, and thoroughly aroused the public. While some Democrats wished to unseat Hayes, others merely wanted to identify the Republicans with fraud, and a few, such as Alexander H. Stephens, the former vice-president of the Confederacy, denounced the Potter resolution as "most unwise, most unfortunate, and most mischievous." The eleven-member Potter committee, which Speaker Randall stacked with Hayes's enemies, speedily got under way, but its hearings in early June did the Republicans little harm. Unimpressive testimony, coupled with the firmness of Hayes and public opinion in his favor, undermined rabid Democrats who wished to unseat Hayes through a judicial process. On 14 June, moderate Democrats joined Republicans in overwhelmingly passing two resolutions denying that Congress, the courts, or any tribunal could reverse the declaration by the Forty-fourth Congress that Hayes and Wheeler were elected. "As to the Potter investigation," Sherman wrote in late June, "the general impression here is that it is fizzling out."[45]

Hayes's hope that southerners would respect the civil rights of blacks was shaken by the campaign of 1878. In early October, Joseph H. Rainey, a black congressman from South Carolina whom Hayes regarded highly, told Hayes that in Sumter and in other South Carolina counties, "the Whites are resorting to intimidation and violence to prevent the colored people from organising for the elections." After the election, Hayes candidly noted that despite solemn pledges to uphold the constitutional rights of all their citizens, South Carolina and Louisiana, by legislation, fraud, intimidation, and "violence of the most atrocious character," had prevented blacks from voting.

The civil rights of blacks were violated elsewhere in the South, and the Democratic party triumphed. In Texas, for example, the *Galveston News* reported that at Marshall, Democrats had "bulldozed the usual Republican majority of the county" from 1,500 votes down to 150. Finding themselves still defeated, the Democrats had taken armed possession of the ballot boxes and had appointed a "committee of citizens" to count the votes. The Democratic candidates were all declared elected, sworn in at once, installed, and supported by "an armed mob that garrisons the town."

Attempts by the administration to end the widespread violence that was depriving southern blacks of their civil rights failed. Federal marshals in November arrested twenty-two South Carolinians for having intimidated blacks, but legal maneuvering and all-white juries prevented convictions. Neither Hampton nor Nicholls kept his promise to respect the civil rights of blacks. Despite Hayes's hope, his conciliatory policy had neither split white southerners nor stopped their drive to disfranchise blacks. Nor did the Democrats to whom Key awarded patronage lead an exodus to the Republican party. *"I am reluctantly forced to admit,"* Hayes reputedly told the *National Republican* (Washington) on 13 November 1878, *"that the experiment was a failure."*[46]

In his annual message to Congress on 2 December, Hayes concentrated on "Southern outrages." He suggested that the victors in these dubious elections should not be seated, vowed that he would use his authority to bring offenders to justice, and asked Congress for more money to implement the 1870 and 1871 acts to enforce the Fourteenth and Fifteenth amendments. Hayes was convinced that the peace and prosperity of the states and the nation required "the maintenance in full vigor of the manly methods of free speech, free press, and free suffrage."

Yet on Christmas Day, a few weeks later, Hayes enumerated among the administration's "main ideas more acceptable than ever" his belief that his southern policy was "safely vindicated." Although his own comments on the recent election contradicted this stubbornly optimistic view, Hayes continued to hope that a better sort of politician would obliterate the color line in southern politics. That unrealistic hope was born of his realistic belief that a two-party system in the South was the only way to protect the civil rights of blacks. But "the better sort of politician" remained with the party for which the outrages were committed. Worse, those outrages had not harmed Democrats at the polls in the rest of the nation. Already in control of the House of Representatives, the Democrats would control the new Senate, and they would ignore Hayes's plea for money to enforce the election laws.[47]

The possibility of a party realignment disappeared in 1879. In January and February of that year, the Potter investigation was confounding its Democratic authors. During the previous October the *New York Tribune* deciphered and published dispatches that revealed that Tilden's nephew, Col. William T. Pelton, from his base in Tilden's home, had attempted to bribe the Florida and South Carolina canvassing boards. These revelations forced the Democrats to agree in January to widen the Potter investigation to include the cipher dispatches. The testimony of Pelton, who admitted that he had tried to buy the presidency for his uncle, and the testimony of Tilden, who even after having squelched a South Carolina bribery attempt had allowed his nephew to remain in his household, where he continued his negotiations, destroyed Democratic hopes of sweeping into the White House in 1880 on the issue of "the great fraud."[48]

On 3 March 1879 the Forty-fifth Congress adjourned without having appropriated funds to keep the army and the civil service functioning during the fiscal year beginning 1 July 1879. Lest government work cease on that day, Hayes immediately called the Forty-sixth Congress to meet in special session on 18 March 1879. Congress had not acted because the Republican Senate would not pass appropriation bills to which the Democratic House had attached provisions, called riders, that would have altered the election laws and other legislation; and the Democrats had refused to pass the appropriation bills without the riders. These votes, which were taken in the waning days of the Forty-fifth Congress, followed strict party lines, aroused passions, and unified the divisive elements in both parties. Blaine, Conkling, and Hayes men rallied around their party's standard, just as northern and southern Democrats, with or without Whig antecedents or hard- or soft-money proclivities, united in this partisan struggle.

The Democrats controlled the incoming Congress and had repeal in their grasp. The laws that they hated so much dated from the Civil War and Reconstruction era; these laws not only prevented former Confederates from serving as jurors in a federal court but also prevented fraud, intimidation, and violence at the polls. Specifically, the election laws— also known as the Force or Enforcement Acts—permitted federal troops to keep peace at the polls and authorized the federal courts to appoint and pay supervisors of congressional elections and their deputy marshals "in any city or town having upward of twenty thousand inhabitants . . . or . . . in any county or parish, in any congressional district."[49]

The Democrats believed that the repeal of the election laws would bring them the presidency in 1880, because all Democrats would unite to secure the local control of elections. A struggle against the election laws would also help the Democrats to forget the Potter investigation, which, rather than damaging Hayes, had destroyed hope for Tilden's renomination. Most important of all, the elimination of the election laws would help the Democrats by ending both the federal protection that these laws gave to southern black voters, who were virtually all

Republicans, and the federal supervision of congressional elections in cities of more than twenty thousand, which were usually controlled by Democrats. Getting rid of the federal presence in city elections would eliminate deputy marshals, who were paid by the federal government, and would unleash the Tammany tiger and other urban political machines.

Although the Democrats emphasized that they were struggling for the freedom of elections, the Republicans thought the Democrats' objectives were less idealistic. Judge William Johnston of Cincinnati wrote to Hayes: "The practical object of the 'so-called' Democrats is very plain. They want to kill with impunity so many negroes as may be necessary to frighten the survivors from the polls in the South; and . . . to stuff the ballot-boxes of New York after the manner of 1868." Hayes had managed to win in 1876 without New York, but with Florida, Louisiana, South Carolina, and the rest of the South in Democratic hands, the Republicans would have to carry New York to win the presidency in the foreseeable future. They could not let the election laws, particularly those relating to northern cities, be repealed.

Hayes was determined to veto any attempt to halt the federal supervision of national elections. He predicted that the Democrats would "stop the wheels . . . of government if I do not yield my convictions in favor of the election laws. It will be a severe, perhaps a long contest. I do not fear it—I do not even dread it. The people will not allow this Revolutionary course to triumph."[50]

In late April, after considerable debate, Congress passed, by a strict party vote, an army appropriations bill with a rider that would have prevented federal troops from keeping peace at the polls. Hayes unhesitatingly vetoed this legislation. He almost always wrote his own state papers, but he typically consulted his cabinet, mulled the issues over in his mind, and tried out his ideas in his diary. In his veto message of 29 April, Hayes forcefully argued that every citizen has the right "to cast one unintimidated ballot and to have his ballot honestly counted." The federal government, Hayes continued, has the power to enforce this right, and it did so by adopting the election laws, which unquestionably prevented fraud and violence. To be effective, the federal civil authorities, acting under those laws, must, when necessary, be able to ask the United States Army to keep the peace at the polls.

Hayes also attacked the abuse of attaching riders to appropriations bills. He damned as "radical, dangerous, and unconstitutional" the principle that the House could, by withholding appropriations, force the Senate and the president to agree to any legislation that the House saw fit to attach to an appropriations bill. That doctrine, Hayes warned, would consolidate "unchecked and despotic power in the House" and would shatter the balance of power. The Republican reaction to Hayes's veto was ecstatic, and in a strictly party vote on 1 May, it was sustained by the House.[51]

Changing their tactics, the Democrats in early May pushed through Congress a separate bill prohibiting federal troops from keeping peace at the polls unless state authorities asked them to do so. Hayes vetoed this measure on 12 May. It would, he insisted, suspend or annul the election laws by allowing state authorities, when threatened by domestic violence, to call upon federal troops "to maintain the conduct of a State election" while forbidding federal authorities to call on the army or navy "to maintain the conduct of a national election against the same local violence that would overthrow it." In Hayes's judgment, this bill would, "in spirit and tendency," amount to state supremacy over national authority. Sitting at his desk in the House of Representatives, Garfield wrote to Hayes: "The message has just been read; and I know the House so well as an index of the public mind that I cannot be mistaken when I tell you, that no speech or paper ever emanated from your hand that will strike so deep into the heart and minds of the American people, and live so long in their gratitude as this noble and masterly paper of today." On 13 May the House failed to muster the two-thirds majority necessary to override the veto, so the bill fell.[52]

While deliberating over army appropriations, Congress also considered an $18-million legislative, executive, and judicial appropriations bill to which the Democrats had added several clauses repealing the election laws. Again, by a strictly party vote, Congress adopted the bill, and on 29 May, Hayes again protected the election laws with his veto power. Normally an affable, placid man, Hayes, when aroused, became a steely adversary. He showed no signs of backing down; indeed, he relished his battle with Congress. Hayes's veto of this civil appropriations bill, like his other vetoes in the battle of the riders, was his own production. Apart from opposing riders on appropriation bills in principle, Hayes attacked this particular rider because, by depriving federal marshals and supervisors of their authority, it would destroy the federal government's control over congressional elections. As Hayes observed, the supervisors would remain and observe, but they would neither be protected nor have power to punish those who were violating the law. In addition, Hayes argued that the election laws were both constitutional and necessary, as the 1868 frauds in New York City had demonstrated. The people, he asserted, "do not think that a free election means freedom from the wholesome restraints of law." The House again failed to muster the requisite two-thirds majority to override Hayes's veto, so the bill fell.[53]

The Democrats were in a quandary. It was clear that Hayes's vetoes were strengthening him and his party. He had struck a responsive chord among Republicans and had helped them to prepare for the 1880 presidential campaign. Their reaction to Hayes's vetoes revealed that the war issues were not dead, that the Democratic party was still the "champion of state sovereignty as against the Union," that the "life of the *Nation* as a nation is again at issue." The Democrats had woefully miscalculated. Their desire to pose as the defenders of liberty by eliminating federal interference with elections had been frustrated by Hayes's vetoes, which hammered home the message that the federal government had the right and the obligation to prevent fraud and intimidation at the polls and implied that fraud and intimidation were what the Democrats had in mind.[54]

While Hayes was elated and confidently awaited the future, the Democrats caucused in early June to find a way out of their predicament. Having unwittingly united and strengthened the Republicans, the Democrats wished to retreat without suffering more damage. They decided to pass the major appropriations bills but hoped to salvage something from the battle of the riders. By mid June, Congress had passed an Army Appropriations bill and a Legislative, Executive, and Judicial Appropriations bill without political restrictions, both of which Hayes signed. The Democrats excluded "certain judicial expenses" from the civil appropriations bill and added to the army bill a face-saving but meaningless clause that would prevent the army from policing the polls. The clause was meaningless because civil authorities, rather than the army, regularly policed the polls, and these officials would continue to call on the army when it was needed to keep the peace.

When the Democrats placed judicial expenses, including the payment of deputy marshals and supervisors of elections, in a supplemental judicial appropriations bill that included riders, Hayes vetoed it on 23 June 1879. It excluded the "payment of general or special deputy marshals for service on election day," which in effect would "prevent any adequate control by the United States over the national elections." As usual, the Republican minority in Congress sustained Hayes's veto.[55]

This fourth veto of an appropriations bill that session cheered Republicans and threw Democrats into confusion. Hard-line Democrats could not force an adjournment without making further appropriations, because seventeen of their party had defected. After several caucuses and probably some consultations with Hayes, the Democrats passed a judicial expenses bill that contained no appropriation for marshals and that included riders providing for nonpartisan juries and repealing the test oath for jurors. Hayes, who had no objection to these provisions concerning federal jurors, declared, "This bill I shall approve"; but he also resolved to veto a companion appropriations bill for federal marshals, "with its objectionable rider." The rider in that bill, which was adopted by Congress on 28 June, attempted once again to prevent the compensation of marshals and their deputies while they were enforcing the election laws. Reiterating the position that he had taken on the judicial bill a week earlier, Hayes vetoed the federal-marshal bill on 30 June. The House sustained his veto, and on the following day, as the new fiscal year began, Congress adjourned without having appropriated the $600,000 for marshals.[56]

While Hayes savored his victory over Congress, he knew that his southern policy had failed. Conciliation had not realigned southern politics, the color line was even more sharply drawn, and rather than obey the Reconstruction amendments, the Democrats had united to deprive blacks of the ballot. With the Republicans rallying around him, Hayes experienced "one of the *ups* of political life. . . . The great newspapers, and the little, have been equally profuse of flattery. Of course it will not last. But I think I have the confidence of the Country. When the [New York] Tribune can say 'The President has the Courtesy of a Chesterfield and the firmness of a Jackson,'(!) I must be prepared for the reactionary counterblast."[57]

4

★ ★ ★ ★ ★

LABOR AND
CURRENCY PROBLEMS

Routine governmental tasks absorbed Hayes between April 1877, when his southern policy was in place, and July, when unprecedented rioting and bloodshed shattered the nation's peace. The Great Strike, the closest the United States has come to a general strike, was under way on the nation's major rail systems. For several days, Hayes had little else on his mind but determining how he should respond to the strike that was gripping the northeastern quarter of the country. There were precedents for both intervention and nonintervention.

In July 1877 the economy was still suffering from the depression that followed the panic of 1873. To offset falling income, railroads, between 1873 and 1876, cut operating expenses, including wages, by 18 percent; but in the same years they increased capital stock and bonded indebtedness by 16 percent. Seventy-six railroads failed in 1876, and all railroads were fighting for the shrinking volume of freight and passengers. Competition was particularly fierce among the five trunk lines— the bankrupt Grand Trunk of Canada, the New York Central, the Erie, the Pennsylvania, and the Baltimore & Ohio (B & O)—that linked the Northeast with the Midwest. In 1876 it cost eighteen cents, instead of the usual fifty cents, to ship one hundred pounds of farm products from Chicago to New York, and a passenger making that trip on the New York Central paid only thirteen dollars. Little improvement came in 1877. From January 1876 to early summer 1877, the stock of the B & O had fallen from $191 to $79, that of the Pennsylvania, from $56 to $32, and that of the well-managed New York Central, from $117 to $90.

To escape bankruptcy, railroad managers realized that they had "to earn more and to spend less." After negotiating all spring, four trunk-line roads, in "a very harmonious meeting" held on 8 June, agreed to pool westbound freight out of New York. Early negotiations went so well that in March the railroads doubled the rates on their westbound freight. The rate war was over, and the roads were hopeful that their earnings would improve.

To spend less, particularly on wages, cooperation among the railroads was again crucial. Although the managers denied that they had arranged to take turns cutting wages, the trunk lines behaved as if they had made that agreement. The giant Pennsylvania was first. It announced on 24 May that on 1 June all employees who were earning more than a dollar a day would take a 10 percent cut in wages. The men had already sustained a 20 percent wage cut. They worked twelve-hour shifts; they were often idle without pay; their tasks, particularly those of brakemen, were dangerous; and layovers frequently forced them to spend days away from home at their own expense. Still, the Pennsylvania's employees accepted the additional cut. Most brakemen and many conductors wanted to strike, but the engineers, without whose support a strike could not succeed, believed President Tom Scott's explanations and therefore refused to walk out.

Other railroads followed the Pennsylvania's lead. The Lehigh Valley also instituted a 10 percent cut on 1 June; the Lackawanna did so on 15 June; and on 1 July the New York Central, the Erie, the Michigan Central, the Lake Shore, the Union Pacific, and a host of other roads cut wages. The New York Central's act was particularly harsh. Its pay scale was already low, and that year it had earned more than 10 percent on its capital investment. Although there were protests, there were no strikes.[1]

Using the Pennsylvania's formula, the B & O scheduled its pay cut for Monday, 16 July. The B & O's financial condition was weak, but rather than reduce its usual 10 percent stock dividend, as banker Junius S. Morgan advised, President John W. Garrett called for a 10 percent wage cut on grounds of financial necessity. Morale among B & O employees was low. They had sustained a wage cut eight months earlier; their work had become more difficult because cars had been added to trains, while crews had been reduced; and they had not been paid since May. On 16 July, Garrett was prepared for trouble in Baltimore. The police dispersed strikers, whom Garrett then fired, while strikebreakers kept the trains going.

As Garrett was keeping trains rolling in Baltimore, B & O employees were stopping freight trains in Martinsburg, West Virginia. In that railroad town, strikers, supported by townspeople, were not hindered either by the local police or by a militia company, although one striker was fatally wounded. With rail traffic clogged at Martinsburg and with the strike spreading, Garrett urged Henry M. Mathews, the governor of West Virginia, to ask Hayes to disperse "the rioters" with federal troops. "The loss of an hour," he warned on 17 July, "would most seriously affect us and imperil vast interests." Mathews thought that the state militia could protect strikebreakers at Martinsburg, but its commander there insisted that such an attempt "would precipitate a bloody conflict, with the odds largely against our small force," so he called for at least two hundred United States Marines. Although no additional violence had occurred since the morning of 17 July and although Mathews had not fully utilized the resources at his command, he professed impotence on 18 July and asked Hayes to send two hundred to three hundred troops to protect "the law abiding people" and to maintain the "supremacy of the law." Garrett urged Hayes to act immediately lest "this difficulty" spread.[2]

Like other political leaders, Hayes thought the strikers had no right to prevent nonstrikers or strikebreakers from working. Fifteen months earlier, when governor of Ohio, he had ordered the state militia to protect the property rights of coal operators and the "right to work" of strikebreakers. Hayes had distinguished between the average decent miner and the "criminals" who led them, and he boasted to Garfield, who approved Hayes's course, that "we shall crush out the law breakers if the courts and juries do not fail."[3]

While prompt to put down "rioters," Hayes sympathized with individual workers, distrusted plutocrats, and was not a champion of railroad interests. He thought that a day's toil of "eight hours, should never be exceeded," that "colossal fortunes . . . threaten alike good government and our liberties," that railroads should be regulated, and that their stock watering and rate discrimination should be stopped. Hayes would intervene in a strike, not to break it, but to keep the peace, and then only when local or state authorities could convince him that they had exhausted their resources. Cherishing the values of an earlier, simpler age, Hayes cared for neither the labor agitator nor the railroad mogul, but his commitment to maintain the peace and an individual's right to work played into the hands of railroad managers.[4]

The success of his "prompt, decided policy" in dealing with striking miners in Ohio influenced Hayes more than the twenty-four occasions over the past dozen years when federal troops, at the behest of Republican governors, had quelled disturbances in the South. Nevertheless, Hayes was loath to intervene in West Virginia, and he wired for a full statement of facts. His skepticism vanished when Mathews responded that available state troops were scarce and that if immediate action were not taken, ''much property may be destroyed and . . . lives lost.'' At 3:50 P.M. on 18 July, Hayes ordered, through the War Department, every available man at the Washington Arsenal and at Fort McHenry in Baltimore to Martinsburg via the B & O, which charged the federal government for the men's fares. Hayes had responded to what appeared to be a local problem, but realizing Garrett's worst fears, it suddenly developed into the nation's most spectacular, pervasive, and violent strike. Its spread graphically illustrated that by 1877 the economy was nationwide in scope and that many of the social problems it engendered were beyond the capacity of state government to solve.

The army that Hayes called upon in 1877 had twenty-five thousand men scattered throughout the nation. Although its top brass, Generals William T. Sherman and Philip Sheridan, were great commanders, their army was a mere shadow of the Grand Army of the Republic. The peacetime army's primary tasks were subduing Native Americans, not strikers, and maintaining order on frontiers, not in railroad centers. That summer, the army was at war with the Nez Perce Indians in the Pacific Northwest and also, pending the solution of border problems, was facing Mexican army units along the Rio Grande.

The army also had incurred the wrath of the Democratic lawmakers, who had worked to reduce its effectiveness, since it had implemented Radical Reconstruction in the South. With the Democratic House refusing to pass an army appropriation bill, the army had been without money since 1 July. While bankers had moved to advance funds to pay the officers, no provision had been made for the enlisted men, whose pay was already in arrears. The 312 men of the Second United States Artillery who were sent to Martinsburg from Washington and Baltimore were tough and efficient, even though they had not been paid for seven months. When they reached Martinsburg on the morning of 19 July, it was calm, and fortunately it would remain calm.[5]

Hayes's prompt action, however, did not prevent the strike from spreading along the B & O, where workers in other industries were also suffering from hard times. ''The working people everywhere are with us,'' declared a striker in Baltimore. ''They know what it is to bring up a family on ninety cents a day, to live on beans and corn meal week in and week out, to run in debt at the stores until you cannot get trusted any longer, to see the wife breaking down under the privation and distress, and the children growing sharp and fierce like wolves day after day because they don't get enough to eat.'' Striking railroad workers were soon joined and outnumbered by unemployed boatmen on the Chesapeake & Ohio Canal, coal miners, ironworkers and steel-workers, factory employees, tramps, and numerous boys from fourteen to eighteen years of age.

On Friday, 20 July, rioting erupted in Baltimore, where there was great "distress and suffering among the laboring classes." Members of a mob, few of whom were railroad strikers, stoned units of the Maryland militia as they marched to the B & O depot to entrain for Cumberland, Maryland, where another mob had paralyzed train traffic. The troops opened fire, killing ten men and boys and wounding others. An ugly crowd of fifteen thousand gathered outside the depot, while the militia, police, railroad officials, the mayor, and Governor John Lee Carroll were inside. The mob burned passenger cars and part of the passenger platform, rioters attacked firemen, police attacked rioters, pistol shots were exchanged, and Carroll wired Hayes for federal troops. Having stayed up all Friday night to receive dispatches from Baltimore, Hayes promptly ordered the commandant of Fort McHenry to report to Carroll with all his available men, and on Saturday, Hayes asked Gen. Winfield Scott Hancock, the commander of the military division of the Atlantic, to take charge of a situation that seemed to be getting out of hand. But after Carroll had wired Hayes, Baltimore began to calm down. By Sunday, the five hundred United States soldiers and marines in that city were not needed.[6]

While Baltimore was calm that Sunday morning, Pittsburgh was burning. There, Pennsylvania Railroad freight trains had been stopped, and people also had been killed. To cut labor costs by eliminating fifty or sixty conductors and brakemen, Robert Pitcairn, the superintendent of the Pennsylvania's Pittsburgh division, ordered that, starting on the preceding Thursday, 19 July, all eastbound through freight trains would be doubleheaders—longer trains pulled by two locomotives.

His timing was bad. Emboldened by news from Martinsburg, the workers refused to take the doubleheaders out of the freight yard and refused to let anyone else take them out. "It's a question of bread or blood," a defiant flagman exclaimed, "and we're going to resist." The freight trains did not move, and a growing crowd blocked the switch near Twenty-eighth Street, which led to the main track. Within a few hours, railroad strikers were joined by numerous mill workers, tramps, and boys. After a minor scuffle at the switch, ten policemen got one freight train through that afternoon; but it proved to be the last freight to leave Pittsburgh for several days, even though passenger trains remained on schedule.[7]

The Trainmen's Union demanded that the Pennsylvania run no more doubleheaders, restore the June wage cut, rehire dismissed strikers, and abolish pay grades; but Alexander J. Cassatt, the vice-president of the Pennsylvania, refused to negotiate. He insisted that public authorities clear the track so that strikebreakers could take out the doubleheaders. Because neither the Pittsburgh police nor the sheriff of Allegheny County were able to disperse the crowd that was blocking the track, Adj. Gen. James W. Latta—acting in the absence of Governor John F. Hartranft, who was junketing about the West at Tom Scott's expense—called in local members of the Pennsylvania National Guard. Even before the guardsmen began to fraternize with the crowd, state and railroad officials realized that these men would not shoot their neighbors, so Latta ordered in the First Division of the Pennsylvania National Guard from Philadelphia.

The Philadelphia militiamen arrived on Saturday afternoon, 21 July, on two trains that had been pelted with rocks in Harrisburg, Altoona, and Johnstown. The Pittsburgh crowd would not disperse until ten to twenty of its number had been killed by the Philadelphians. The slaughter cleared the track, but after the violence, no strikebreakers would take out a doubleheader. After the troops had retired to a nearby roundhouse, the angry crowd set fire to some freight cars, looted others, and by 8 A.M. Sunday morning, had burned the Philadelphians out of the roundhouse. Snipers killed five militiamen and wounded others as these state troops retreated and abandoned Pittsburgh to the mob.

That Sunday, 22 July, the mob looted and burned railroad property. Adjutant General Latta did not order any additional National Guard troops to Pittsburgh. The feeble police department could not stop either the arson or the looting, and rioters would not let firemen turn their hoses on anything that belonged to the hated Pennsylvania Railroad. The mob did allow the firemen to fight fires that had spread to neighboring homes and businesses. Attempts by citizens to preserve the peace were fruitless, and business and religious leaders could not wring from the railroad any concessions that would detach the strikers from the mob, only a fraction of which was composed of strikers. By Sunday evening the riot had spent its force, but not before 104 locomotives, 2,152 railroad cars, and innumerable buildings had been destroyed. With the rioters tired, drunk, and running out of targets to burn and loot, the Pittsburgh police were able to stop further destruction.

Hayes monitored the spreading strike. Late Saturday, at his summer residence at the Soldiers Home, he learned about the bloodshed in Pittsburgh. On Sunday after attending church, he met with his cabinet and grimly read dispatches from Signal Corps sergeants who were stationed throughout the country as weather observers and were, in Robert V. Bruce's words, "tracking the social storm," which at that point was raging in Pittsburgh and was threatening Philadelphia.

Hartranft's absence troubled Hayes, who feared that federal action might prove both necessary and unconstitutional. Hayes took little comfort from Reconstruction legislation, which empowered presidents to quell civil disorders with federal troops. He took even less comfort from the fact that there were only three thousand troops in the Military Division of the Atlantic, so he delayed sending troops to Pennsylvania. That afternoon, Tom Scott urged Hayes to call for volunteers, as Lincoln had done in 1861, to put down disturbances along the railroads, which were highways of interstate commerce. Similar messages from Governor Hartranft and from Mayor William S. Stokley of Philadelphia indicated that Scott was orchestrating a drive for federal intervention.

Despite Scott's campaign, the Hayes administration did not break the Great Strike of 1877. On the surface, it would appear that Hayes would be friendly to railroad management and hostile to labor. After all, Tom Scott had lobbied for his election, and members of Hayes's cabinet were involved with railroads. Evarts's law firm did work for Vanderbilt's Lake Shore road, Thompson had asked Scott in 1873 for a job for his son, and McCrary was close to Grenville M. Dodge, who was in Scott's employ. Yet neither Hayes nor the men in his cabinet seemed anxious to do the bidding of the railroads, although they did wish to end the riots.

Although looting and burning had gone on all day Sunday in Pittsburgh, Hayes and his cabinet, after reassembling at 10 P.M. at Evarts's house, would not intervene without a proper invitation. While passing through Wyoming that evening, Governor Hartranft telegraphed Hayes "for troops to assist in quelling mobs." Because Hartranft's request failed to meet constitutional requirements, the Hayes administration did nothing for Pittsburgh beyond ordering fifty soldiers from Columbus, Ohio, to protect the Allegheny Arsenal. On the other hand, Hayes and his cabinet responded immediately to a direct and proper request for troops from Philadelphia's Mayor Stokley, whose police that evening were attacking and dispersing a mob. More significantly, the cabinet discussed, but rejected, Scott's plea that the federal government intervene on the side of railroad management. However beholden it might have been to Tom Scott, the Hayes administration restricted itself to keeping the peace, if requested to do so by a proper official in a proper manner. It responded to such a request by Hartranft on Monday, but it refused to supply men to operate the railroads or to break the strike.[8]

By Monday the administration's policy was clear. Before any request by a governor, army regulars would be ordered to a trouble spot to protect United States property—for example, arsenals and subtreasuries—"and by their presence to promote peace and order," but they were not to enforce state law until a formal request had been approved. Troops would be dispatched to prevent violence, but not to operate railroads.

Pretexts for intervention, particularly the obstruction of the mails, existed, but the Hayes administration did not seriously consider them. Except at Hornellsville, New York, strikers stopped only freight trains, waving through passenger trains and their mail cars. Vanderbilt and Scott refused to run trains made up only of mail cars, thus hoping to provoke federal intervention on the grounds that strikers were interfering with the mail. To keep Hayes from drawing that conclusion, a group of strikers in Erie, Pennsylvania, wired him on Tuesday: "The Lake Shore Company has refused to let U.S. mail east of here. We would be pleased if you would in some way direct them to proceed with mails and also passengers." Hayes simply accepted the lack of rail service, and Key sought alternative routes to get the mail through. A few strikers or rioters were convicted of obstructing the mails and were fined $40 to $100, but the administration made no attempt to restore train service.[9]

Violence in Pittsburgh inspired disturbances elsewhere. At Reading, Pennsylvania, arson and looting broke out on Sunday evening, 22 July, and culminated the next night, when the militia, the Easton Grays, killed six bystanders—apparently spectators, rather than rioters—while attempting to clear an obstruction from the railroad tracks. To restore peace, Hancock ordered a detachment of regulars to Reading. In Philadelphia on Monday the police dispersed a mob, and when a fire broke out on a freight train, four hundred police formed a hollow square to protect fire fighters while thousands watched. Although two firemen were severely burned by an exploding tank car, only six cars were destroyed, and the crowd did not get out of hand. That afternoon, 125 United States Marines arrived, and by the next afternoon they had been joined by 700 army regulars. With 1,400 armed and well-organized police backed by auxiliary forces, the federal troops were hardly needed.[10]

The strike spread to other railroads and to other states. At Hornellsville, New York, Erie Railroad strikers on Sunday, 22 July, even stopped passenger trains, and from Sunday to Tuesday, strikers in Buffalo halted traffic on the New York Central, as well as on the Erie, and clashed with the New York State militia and the Buffalo police. The strike also spread into Ohio, where trains were stopped; but there was no bloodshed, for generally the strikers were more in control there than mobs were. By Tuesday, 24 July, the strike had spread from the East throughout the Midwest and across the Mississippi River into Missouri and Iowa, but Hayes coolly noted that violence was diminishing and that United States troops were "every where respected."[11]

Although their presence did deter further violence, federal troops arrived too late to confront the enraged mobs. The War Department in Washington was the scene of frenzied activity, with troops being ordered one place, only to be intercepted and sent elsewhere. Although born of confusion, the constant movement of troops through rail centers had a beneficial effect. A few days later, Hancock remarked: "We have not made much noise, it is true, nor did we emblazon our numbers—and that silence led to an exaggeration of the strength of the force at our disposal at whatever point the troops appeared; the troops moved steadily with calmness and celerity." Had Hayes thrown all the available troops into Pittsburgh, they probably would have fared no better than did the Philadelphia militia, and the prestige of United States troops— which, given their scanty numbers, was crucial—would have been destroyed. Hayes did well to move with caution. Federal troops and the mob did not engage in a showdown.[12]

The calm of the administration contrasted with the hysteria of the press. The memory of the 1871 Paris Commune, with its killing of hostages and its own bloody suppression, was vivid; and major newspapers blamed the strike on a Communist conspiracy. On the Saturday after the Baltimore riot, the *National Republican* (Washington) called the strike "nothing less than communism in its worst form"; but Hayes, that paper reported the next day, "said he did not regard the present disorders as any evidence of the prevalence of a spirit of communism, since their attacks had not been primarily directed against property in general, but merely against that of the railroads with which the strikers had difficulties."

In 1877, Communists lacked numbers and influence in the United States. The First International, whose council Karl Marx had moved to the United States in 1872 to escape the influence of Russian anarchists, had expired in 1876; and the Marxist Workingmen's party, established that year, had only a few thousand members. It had nothing to do with the commencement of the Great Strike, but once the strike was under way, that party tried to make the most of it.[13]

The Workingmen's party played a small part in the violence that idled Chicago on Tuesday, Wednesday, and Thursday—24 to 26 July. On

Wednesday, with the stockyards, the packing houses, and factories shut down, mobs of strikers and adolescent toughs roved the streets; and clashes with the police resulted in three fatalities. That afternoon, Mayor Monroe Heath reluctantly called on Hayes, by way of Governor Shelby Cullom, for federal troops; but Hayes delayed his order until early Thursday morning, perhaps because he thought the two regiments of the Illinois National Guard that were on hand could keep the peace. That morning, it was the Chicago police, with support from the militia, who put down the rioters by repeatedly attacking them, as well as innocent bystanders, killing at least eighteen men and boys and wounding numerous others. By Thursday afternoon, when eight companies of federal troops had arrived and were at Mayor Heath's call, the mob had spent its force, and the troops were being used to guard property.[14]

The Workingmen's party played a more important role in St. Louis. A Sunday rally in East St. Louis, Illinois, which was dominated by party speakers, resulted in a decision to strike against six railroads at midnight. Compared to other cities, St. Louis was orderly. The Workingmen's party held well-attended rallies on Monday and Tuesday evenings, the latter of which culminated with the leaders warning against violence and calling a general strike for the eight-hour day and against employing children under fourteen.

Despite the relative calm, railroad management feared violence and begged Hayes for federal support. Anticipating trouble, six companies of United States infantry, under Col. Jefferson C. Davis, arrived in St. Louis on Tuesday afternoon. Lest anyone get the wrong impression, Davis carefully announced—as instructed by the War Department—that he and his men were there "to protect government and public property," not "to quell the strikers or run the trains." On Wednesday a crowd of white and black workers shut down factories, but with the Workingmen's party in control, there was no violence and little property damage.

Confronted by an orderly general strike, the St. Louis police did not interfere that day or on Thursday when five thousand men closed down additional factories. The Hayes administration remained aloof, even though a railroad manager wired it to "stamp out mob now rampant." Clearly enunciating Hayes's policy, Colonel Davis told local authorities that they had to "deal with these difficulties themselves & not call on me for aid until their whole resources are exhausted." Without federal help, on Friday the St. Louis police, aided by citizen militia, broke up the huge crowd outside the headquarters of the Workingmen's party. No shots were fired and no stones were thrown; but the strike leaders were arrested, which ensured the decline of the strike. All in all, the St. Louis experience was unique. Elsewhere the strike was a spontaneous, uncontrolled, violent mob action; but in St. Louis, socialist followers of Marx had organized and controlled a nonviolent strike.[15]

While the strike spread during the hot July week, the Hayes administration remained calm and cool. Although the cry for volunteers to suppress the strike was widespread among railroad and business leaders, Hayes and his cabinet withstood the pressure and avoided an action that many thought would have provoked a revolution. The ranking Democrat in the government, Speaker of the House Samuel J. Randall, agreed with Hayes, even though Randall regarded Hayes as a pretender to the presidency and persistently put his title in quotes. When Scott asked Randall to wire Hayes "to call out by proclamation a further force," Randall "abruptly and pointedly" said he "could not and would not do so."[16]

Even without a call for volunteers, the strike soon faltered. Railroad managers insisted that grievances would be discussed only after the men had come back to work. As early as Wednesday, some New York Central workers went back at Rochester and Syracuse, although those at Albany and Buffalo held out a bit longer; and the Erie strike ended at Hornellsville. By Thursday a combined force of militia and army regulars traversed the Pennsylvania Railroad from Philadelphia to Pittsburgh, opening up that road without opposition. The first doubleheader since the strike left Pittsburgh on Sunday, 29 July, and by Monday night the Pennsylvania had all the men back that it wanted. On the B & O, where it all began, the freight trains had started moving on Friday night. Despite pockets of resistance, the strike was over on Monday, 30 July. The only important person who thought the strike was not over was Tom Scott. "Please do not be misled," he begged Hayes on 31 July, "by any news of peaceable settlement of existing troubles, the removal of the military in all probability will be followed by renewed outbreaks." Hayes seems to have paid as much heed to this telegram as he had to Scott's earlier communications.[17]

Hayes avoided playing into Tom Scott's hands, but he did not avoid playing into those of three antilabor federal judges. United States Circuit Court Judge Thomas Drummond of Chicago and United States District Court Judges Samuel Hubbel Treat of Springfield, Illinois, and Walter Q. Gresham of Indianapolis held that strikers who obstructed bankrupt railroads that were in the custody of federal courts were in contempt of court. These judges did not distinguish between the public interest that their courts represented and the bankrupt railroad's interest that was represented by the court-appointed receivers. Indeed, they identified the federal courts and the public interest with the receivers, or railroad management, and tried to enforce their labor policies and break the strike.

Hayes, Evarts, Devens, and the rest of the cabinet accepted the judges' reasoning. On Thursday, with abundant signs that the crisis had eased, Hayes decided to send troops to Indiana to help Gresham's marshal keep the bankrupt railroads open. The administration urged the policies of Drummond and Gresham on federal judges in other strike-bound jurisdictions, and judges in Tennessee, Ohio, and Pennsylvania followed their lead. Drummond soon became the first federal judge to punish railroad strikers for contempt of court. Identifying the federal courts with railroad management in effect outlawed future strikes on bankrupt roads and was a precedent that had far-reaching significance for organized labor.[18]

Despite embracing the notions of Drummond, Treat, and Gresham, the administration was in most respects served well by its legalistic response to the strike. Observing proper procedures meant that federal troops neither provoked nor suppressed rioters and neither killed nor wounded anyone. By not calling up additional troops, by ignoring Tom Scott, and by not operating the railroads under a dubious interpretation of the Commerce Clause, the administration avoided a row over the constitutional powers of the president and avoided a confrontation between the strikers and federal forces.

Nevertheless, the Hayes administration shared the common bias against organized labor and strikes. It concluded that although workers had a right to strike, they could neither prevent others from working nor prevent a railroad, factory, or mine from operating. In the Great Strike, workers helped form the mobs that prevented strikebreakers from working, but management and public authorities seemed to assume that all strikers were physically obstructing strikebreakers from working. On that assumption, the police disturbed the peace by breaking up meetings of strikers as though they were rioting mobs obstructing strike-breakers. By equating striking and obstructing, the authorities placed state law—and where bankrupt railroads were involved, federal law—on management's side. Without seriously questioning this equation, the Hayes administration accepted it.

Hayes's moderate course, however, provoked railroadmen and conservatives. Grant, who, railroadmen regretted, was no longer in the White House, was critical of Hayes and argued that the strike "should have been put down with a strong hand and so summarily as to prevent a like occurrence for a generation." In some fashionable quarters, hostility to the strikers was virulent. In sermons on 22 and 29 July, the Reverend Henry Ward Beecher of Brooklyn, New York, condemned the strikers for "tyrannical opposition to all law and order," jeered at dollar-a-day workers with five children who were not willing to live on bread and water, and proclaimed that God intended "the great to be great and the little to be little" and that the poor must "reap the misfortunes of inferiority."

Nevertheless, moderation pleased most Americans, who thought railroads had brought the strike on themselves. Beecher was criticized by the *Commercial and Financial Chronicle* (New York) for lacking "either a wise head or a feeling heart," and the *New York World* called his words "suicidal" and "lunatic." While deploring violence, the *New York Times* recognized that because of the strike, the country had learned "of hardship, of suffering, of destitution to an extent for which it was unprepared." *Harper's Monthly* declared that it was the business of the government to prevent future disorders "by removing the discontent which is its cause." Several cabinet members agreed. On Tuesday, 31 July, in a cabinet discussion, Sherman, McCrary, and Evarts favored the federal regulation of railroads, and Sherman later spoke for it in Ohio.[19]

With the public sensing that railroad management was responsible for the appalling conditions that had led to the Great Strike, the railroads fell short of a total victory. It even appears that the workers gained more in the long run by fighting the wage cuts than they lost in the short run. Management was so burned by the strike that it attempted no further wage cuts and, from October 1877 to early 1880, restored the pay cuts that had precipitated the strike, and improved working conditions as well. In addition, railroad managers who were conspicuous during the Great Strike suffered a loss of prestige. The Great Strike also killed Tom Scott's lingering hope for a Texas & Pacific land grant. The strike, Charles Nordhoff cheerfully wrote to a friend, "finishes Tom Scott, and I shall not be sorry."[20]

Hayes wrote on 5 August: "The strikes have been put down by *force*, but now for the *real* remedy. Cant something [be] done by education of the strikers, by judicious control of the capitalists, by wise general policy to end or diminish the evil? The R.R. [railroad] strikers, as a rule are good men sober intelligent and industrious." Evarts suggested "that an attempt to probe and soothe the labor difficulties by means of a commission, under public instructions, would of itself do good and might promise really valuable results." Although Hayes claimed to be willing to do "anything . . . to remove the distress which afflicts laborers" and although other members of the administration were aware of "the grievances of the working people which are no doubt real," the investigation by a commission did not materialize. When the strike was blamed for the sluggish economy in early August, there was talk of coming to grips with its causes, but when the economy revived, the strike was all but forgotten.[21]

Despite his generous impulses, Hayes, as president, did not come to grips either with how to educate strikers or with how to control capitalists. He and his administration found no wise general policy to "diminish the evil," but a decade later he crystallized his view in language that makes him a precursor of the Progressive movement. Convinced "that the giant evil and danger in this country—the danger which transcends all others—is the vast wealth owned or controlled by a few persons," Hayes advocated federal legislation as the "true remedy" to eliminate "the rottenness of the present system." Governmental policy should "prevent the accumulation of vast fortunes; and monopolies, so dangerous in control, should be held firmly in the grip of the people." Hayes believed that with the Interstate Commerce Act of 1887 regulating the railroads, the government had taken the first step. He thought that act, though crude, was "one of the most beneficent in its results."[22]

The depression of the mid 1870s that led to wage cuts for railroad workers also brought demands for expansion of the currency. Three kinds of money existed in the post–Civil War United States: government-minted gold coins, notes issued by national banks, and greenbacks printed to help finance the war. The government, however, did not redeem its greenback dollars in gold, and their value declined, thus driving gold coin out of domestic circulation, while the influx of greenbacks into the wartime economy helped to double prices. National bank notes were limited to $300 million, were based on federal bonds that member banks purchased with greenbacks, and were redeemed in greenbacks, whose value they reflected.

After the war, the United States remained off the gold standard. The federal government left approximately $350 million in greenbacks circulating but refused to redeem them in gold at face value. The expanding postwar economy, however, with its agricultural and industrial growth, began to absorb the greenbacks, and as the money supply remained more or less constant, prices during the late 1860s began to decline toward prewar levels. This deflationary trend, with the worth of greenbacks appreciating, continued, and in January 1875, Congress passed the Resumption Act. It pledged to reduce the supply of greenbacks to $300 million and to redeem them with gold on 1 January 1879. It balanced its contraction of greenbacks with "free banking" by removing the $300-million limit on the issuance of national bank notes.

Two powerful groups—debtors and silver producers—challenged the move back to the gold standard. Debtors, who had to pay creditors in dollars worth more than those they had borrowed, were hurt by the deflation, which persisted into the 1890s. As farmers and businessmen expanded and borrowed, they competed for the limited supply of money, thus pushing up interest rates. The depression that followed the panic of 1873 accentuated the deflationary trend. Seeking to stabilize prices, debtors, particularly in the Midwest, urged that the circulation of greenbacks be expanded and that specie payments not be resumed as scheduled.

In the West, a second group urged that silver dollars again be minted. The coinage Act of 1873 had demonetized silver, but even before its passage, no silver dollars had been minted for decades, because the market value of silver had exceeded the government's sixteen-to-one ratio with gold. After 1873, increased production and the falling price of silver led to demands by the mining states that it be remonetized and coined at the old ratio. Aggrieved westerners believed that conspirators had committed the "Crime of 1873" when they had demonetized silver. In truth, governmental insiders, including Senator John Sherman, realizing that the price of silver would drop, had enacted the law to eliminate a threat to the gold standard. Aware that the free coinage of silver, like printing additional greenbacks, would inflate the currency, debtors in the South joined residents of mining states to push for free coinage.[23]

Hayes was a long-time supporter of hard money. He opposed inflation, whether it was achieved by circulating paper greenbacks that were not backed by gold or by coining silver dollars, whose intrinsic worth was less than that of gold dollars. He had welcomed the Resumption Act of January 1875, and his victory in the 1875 Ohio gubernatorial campaign was interpreted as a triumph for sound money. When the economic depression lingered and pressure mounted to repeal or weaken the Resumption Act, Hayes firmly urged those with whom he had influence to resist such efforts in Congress.

After taking office, Hayes and his administration, particularly Sherman, who had written the Resumption Act, began to build a gold reserve to meet the demands that 1 January 1879 might bring, and he continued his efforts to reduce the interest payments on the federal debt. Lot M. Morrill, treasury secretary under Grant, had arranged with New York and London bankers for a $135-million sale of bonds at 4.5 percent interest from 1 March to 1 July 1877. Though the syndicate profited by "a number of millions of dollars . . . without a particle of risk," the transaction was also good for the government, which used the proceeds to retire 6 percent bonds, thus reducing annual interest payments by more than $2 million. In July 1877, Sherman arranged for a $77-million sale of bonds with the same syndicate at 4 percent interest, using some of the funds to retire 6 percent bonds and the rest for a gold reserve for the resumption of specie payments.

After July, the Great Strike and agitation to remonetize silver undermined fiscal confidence, and few government bonds were sold during the rest of 1877. Suffering from depression and deflation, the West and the South pressed for the repeal of the Resumption Act and for the unlimited coinage of silver at the old sixteen-to-one ratio. By the summer of 1877, Ohio and Pennsylvania Republicans joined southern Democrats and western Republicans in demanding free silver, and rumors began to emanate from Washington that Hayes would sign a silver-coinage bill.[24]

During the special session of the Forty-fifth Congress, called to appropriate funds for the unpaid army, the House considered the questions of silver and resumption. On 5 November it overwhelmingly passed (164 to 34) a silver bill, presented by Democrat Richard P. ("Silver Dick") Bland of Missouri. Bland's bill, which the free-silver plank of the 1896 Democratic platform reiterated, called for the unlimited coinage of the old standard silver dollar of 412.5 troy grains. Given the temper of the times, it is not surprising that the silver bill passed the House, but that it should have passed by such a wide margin and without debate is noteworthy, as were its unexpected adherents. Among them were Ohio Republicans Charles Foster, who was Hayes's own congressman; Jacob Dolson Cox, a hero of civil-service reformers, most of whom strongly supported hard money; and William McKinley, who in 1896 would be the champion of the gold standard. On 23 November the House also voted, 133 to 120, to repeal the Resumption Act of 1875, but the president's close friends opposed the measure. A significant number of congressmen, responding to intense political pressure, voted both to remonetize silver and to resume payments in specie.

The Senate, however, disappointed the inflationists. During the special session, it ignored the repeal of the Resumption Act, and the Senate Finance Committee, headed by Iowa Republican William B. Allison, reported an amended silver bill which would require that at least 2 million and, at the discretion of the treasury secretary, up to 4 million silver dollars be coined monthly. The Senate failed to act upon this limited silver-coinage bill before the close of the special session.[25]

The Senate's inaction saved Hayes the trouble of vetoing a bill. His first annual message to Congress, on 3 December 1877, expressed his hostility to inflation. To Hayes, who since the panic of 1873 had been deeply in debt and would remain in debt throughout his presidency, the currency question was one of honesty and morality, not of personal or public economic advantage or political expediency. He believed that the speedy resumption of specie payments for greenbacks was a fiscal necessity. Returning to the gold standard would bring the country's system of exchange into harmony with that of the leading commercial nations. Even though resumption would entail difficulty and distress for some, Hayes believed the alternative would "end in serious disorder, dishonor, and disaster in the financial affairs of the Government and of the people." Hayes perceived that "the rich, the speculative, the operating, the money-dealing classes may not always feel the mischiefs of, or may find casual profits in, a variable currency, but the misfortunes of such a currency to those who are paid salaries or wages are inevitable and remediless."

Hayes ended the speculation on his attitude toward silver. He did not object to coining silver, but to keep it from driving gold from circulation and causing inflation, he insisted that the ratio between the two metals reflect their commercial value. He further emphasized that because market fluctuations made an absolute equality of the intrinsic value of gold and silver coins unattainable, silver coinage should be limited. And he finally asserted that the interest-bearing public debt—$729 million at 6 percent, $708 million at 5 percent, $200 million at 4.5 percent, and $75 million at 4 percent—should be paid in gold or its equivalent. To place this debt in perspective, the nation's income for the year ending 30 June 1877 was $269 million, and its expenditures were $239 million, leaving a $30 million surplus for the sinking fund to retire the debt.[26]

While Congress was more disposed to accept Hayes's views on resumption, it rejected his advice on silver. His close friend Senator Stanley Matthews proposed that the public debt be repaid in silver, which aroused "uneasiness" in financial circles and alarm among bondholders as far away as London. Members of Congress were determined to respond to the demands of their constituents, rather than to the falling prices of United States bonds. By February, it had become clear that while the "unlimited silver people" could not muster a two-thirds majority in Congress to override a veto, a bill providing for the coinage of a limited amount of silver would pass, despite a veto. Opponents of silver coinage consequently sought a compromise that would "avoid injury to the public credit."[27]

Hayes would not compromise. He wrote on 3 February: "It is now almost a certainty that the Silver bill will pass in such shape that I must withhold my signature." He reiterated that he would approve silver coinage if it guarded creditor rights but that he would veto any "measure which stains our credit." He insisted: "We must keep that untainted. We are a debtor nation. Low rates of interest on the vast indebtedness we must carry for many years is the important end to be kept in view. Expediency and justice both demand honest coinage." Hard-money men argued that in the United States, with its large public debt, the interest rates yielded by government bonds would regulate all interest rates. The 1875 Specie Resumption Act caused interest rates to fall because it gave investors confidence that the nation was rebuilding its depressed economy on the "bed-rock" of gold. But hard-money men feared that the silver bill, even as amended by Allison, would undermine the public credit, raise interest rates, and hurt debtors.[28]

The Senate, on 15 February, agreed to Allison's amendments to the Bland Free Silver bill, which limited the coinage of silver to between $2 and $4 million a month and called for an international bimetal convention. Of the twenty-one senators who constituted the hard-core opposition to silver coinage, fifteen represented New England, New York, and New Jersey; and sixteen of the twenty-two ardent supporters of free silver came from former slaveholding states. Most senators who represented the remainder of the country, from Pennsylvania to the Pacific, accepted a limited quantity of silver dollars. As expected, the House on 21 February approved the bill as amended by the Senate, although opponents from the northeastern seaboard, led by Abram S. Hewitt, tried to table the bill.

Despite the bill's limit on silver dollars, Hayes, after "some study and much anxious reflection," resolved to veto the bill, knowing that Congress would probably override his veto. On 26 February, Hayes sought the reaction of his cabinet to his veto message. Navy Secretary Thompson forthrightly opposed the veto, on both policy and constitutional grounds. He believed that the silver bill was wise, perceived that it was demanded almost unanimously by the people, and noted that it had been passed by more than two-thirds of both houses of Congress. Acknowledging that he was an old Whig and testifying that the old Whig doctrine was sound, Thompson emphasized that the veto was to be used, not for policy or for expediency, but only for "a violation of the Constitution, or haste or mistake."

Hayes countered Thompson by insisting that his veto was based on principle, not policy: "The faith of the nation was to be violated—the obligation of contracts was impaired by the law." But Thompson lectured Hayes that the Constitution denied states, but not Congress, the right to impair contracts; he further insisted "that no obligation was in fact impaired—that contracts were made in view of the right of Congress to alter the legal tender." Evarts rescued Hayes by repudiating the old Whig doctrine and embracing a modern twentieth-century concept of a powerful president who would not merely execute the laws. He argued that the Constitution made the president "part of the Law making power" and that it was within his rights to veto constitutional measures that he did not approve of.

The rest of the cabinet was moved more by morality and politics than by constitutional issues. Viewing the bill as "immoral and dangerous," Schurz, along with Devens and Key, unequivocally favored a veto. Though Sherman and McCrary supported a veto, they did equivocate. McCrary wanted the bill to pass over the veto, since he feared that a successful veto would bring into power the "Democrats with their worst elements in advance." Unhappy with the bill, yet fearing a veto, Sherman repeated the views of August Belmont, a prominent New York banker and Democratic politician, who preferred that "the bill should be approved, *bad* as he thinks it is."[29]

Although hard-money men "were stampeded at the critical moment" because they feared that a veto would produce "uncertainty and apprehension in business circles & strengthen greenback inflationists," Hayes vetoed the Bland-Allison bill on 28 February. Ignoring Thompson's views, he emphasized that it would impair the obligation of contracts both public and private and that it would injure the public credit. He argued that the market value of a 412.5-grain silver dollar was only 90 to 92 cents, as compared to the standard gold dollar, yet the Bland-Allison bill made it legal tender for existing debts. Hayes predicted that as soon as enough silver dollars were in circulation, taxes no longer would be paid in gold, and the government would be forced to breach "the public faith" by paying in silver both the principal and the interest of the public debt. Hayes doubted that the limited amount of silver dollars the bill authorized would be as valuable as gold dollars and concluded that "a currency worth less than it purports to be worth will in the end defraud not only creditors, but all who are engaged in legitimate business, and none more surely than those who are dependent on their daily labor for their daily bread."[30]

Not sharing the moral perceptions of Hayes and being more sensitive to political realities, Congress, with contemptuous haste, overrode his veto and made the Bland-Allison bill a law. The backbone of Hayes's support came from the Northeast (Blaine and Conkling both agreed with Hayes), where creditors had political clout and where the numerous national banks provided adequate currency and moderate interest rates. Further west, Garfield opposed the measure, but other Ohioans deserted Hayes. In the Senate, Stanley Matthews conspicuously supported the bill, and Jacob Dolson Cox, Charles Foster, Joseph Warren Keifer, and William McKinley joined the overwhelming majority in the House to override Hayes's veto.

Hayes minimized the effect of the Bland-Allison Act by coining only the $2 million monthly minimum and by keeping those silver dollars equal in value to gold dollars. Although he still castigated the act as "dishonest," he realized that it had sapped the strength of the inflationists. Trusting "that in fact no actual dishonesty will be permitted under it," he abandoned the dire prophecies of his veto message.

Furthermore, moderates, such as Jacob Dolson Cox and Murat Halstead, of the *Cincinnati Commercial*, had supported the Bland-Allison Act to prevent the repeal of the Resumption Act of 1875. A move toward that end had gathered impressive support in late 1877, but the Bland bill had shouldered it aside in January and February of 1878. With the passage of the Bland-Allison Act, several western senators who earlier had wished to repeal the Resumption Act were willing to delay that move until the effects of the Bland-Allison Act had become apparent.

In addition, Sherman's plans for resumption, his lucid explanation of them to Congress, and his success in carrying them out seemed to assure the return to payments in specie. In April he negotiated a loan at 4.5 percent with an international syndicate of bankers for $50 million in European gold to augment the $70 million worth of gold already in the United States Treasury. News of this contract virtually wiped out the premium on gold, and Hayes rejoiced that resumption of payments in specie was apparently secured. Finally, Hayes, who had a pragmatic streak, agreed to a bargain with the moderate soft-money men. He approved the Fort bill to keep $346 million in greenbacks in circulation—thus repealing the provision in the Resumption Act that would have reduced them to $300 million by January 1879—as long as the inflationists would agree to stop agitating for the repeal of resumption. With that agreement, there was certainty that payments in specie would be resumed. On 2 January 1879 (New Year's Day was a bank holiday), confidence in the nation's capacity to remain on the gold standard was so great that more gold was exchanged for convenient paper greenbacks than greenbacks for gold.[31]

Hayes's prediction that the resumption of payments in specie would "be followed by a healthful and enduring revival of business prosperity" came true. His third annual message to Congress, on 1 December 1879, boasted that resumption had particularly benefited foreign trade, because by making American currency equivalent to that of the commercial world, it had enabled Americans to compete on an equal basis with other nations. Increased foreign demand for the products of American farms and factories created a $59-million favorable balance of trade over the four and one half months from 1 July to 15 November. Foreign trade benefited both resumption and interest rates. Beginning in 1873, the United States generally, and during the Hayes administration invariably, enjoyed a favorable balance of trade and consistently imported gold. This influx of gold, primarily in payment for enormous exports of wheat, helped to moderate interest rates and facilitated the resumption of payments in specie.

Public credit, Hayes claimed, had also been improved by resumption, which enabled the government to sell at or above par value all the 4 percent bonds needed to refinance at lower interest rates as much of the national debt as the laws allowed. Since March 1877, funding the debt at lower interest rates had saved $14.3 million. Hayes asked Congress for legislation that would enable the government to issue 4 percent bonds to replace some $792 million in 5 and 6 percent bonds that would mature over the next two years, thus saving $11 million annually.

Prosperity, however, had not reconciled Hayes to silver dollars or greenbacks, even if they were redeemed in gold. He still thought that they threatened the gold standard. Against the advice of William Henry Smith, Evarts, and Thompson, Hayes urged Congress to authorize the secretary of the Treasury to suspend silver coinage since the market value of silver dollars was uniformly less than that of gold dollars. He raised the specter that if both gold and silver were coined without limit, it would be impossible to maintain them at par value and that silver would become the sole standard.

Having smitten the inflationists on the silver issue, Hayes turned to smite them on the greenback issue. He called for the "retirement from circulation of United States notes" as a step "toward a safe and stable currency," despite having approved legislation in the spring of 1878 that maintained the level of greenbacks at $346 million. It was his conviction that issuing paper money based wholly on the authority and credit of the government was a violation of sound financial principles and that it was unconstitutional, except in extreme emergencies.[32]

When Congress ignored these requests, Hayes repeated them a year later in his fourth annual message. With technical accuracy he called greenbacks in circulation a forced loan, levied by the government upon the people, and he again demanded that they be canceled to promote "the interest and security of the people." Once more he emphasized that the 412.5-grain silver dollar was not the equivalent of a gold dollar, and he asked Congress to stop minting it. This time, however, he coupled his request with a proposal that Congress author-ize the minting of a larger silver dollar that would be equivalent in value to the gold dollar. Hayes was facing up to the fact that the United States produced more silver than any other nation and that its people wanted silver to be one of the two precious metals furnishing "the coinage of the world."

Above all, Hayes was determined that the nation remain on the gold standard, and he fought to eliminate any threat to it. Congress, viewing the currency, not as a question of faith and morals, but as one of politics and economics, was content to ignore that issue, especially since business was booming. But Hayes believed that his hard-money policies sustained that boom, and the continued circulation of greenback and silver dollars made him uneasy. For him, it was an eternal verity of both economic and moral law that gold was the proper base for a nation's currency.[33]

5

★ ★ ★ ★ ★

THE FEDERAL BUREAUCRACY

In addition to securing the gold standard and obliterating the color line from southern politics, Hayes made improving the civil service his main objective. When he took office, the federal bureaucracy, especially the field service outside of Washington, was politicized by the spoils system. That system had fastened itself onto the civil service with the advent of democracy earlier in the nineteenth century. The widening of the suffrage coincided with the rapid growth of the population, the acquisition of new territories, the admission of new states, and the proliferation of elected officials; and this growth caused political parties to expand into huge mass-based organizations. These political parties brought a semblance of order to complex election machinery by nominating and supporting candidates for offices at all levels. Controlling the nominating process at local, state, and national conventions; campaigning; keeping track of voters; and getting them out on Election Day required a multitude of devoted party workers. For some of these workers, the triumph of their political heroes was sufficient reward, but many others hoped to secure a position in the civil service for their pains.

What was good for party organization was not always good for the bureaucracy. After the Civil War, the negative effects that the spoils system had on the civil service were obvious. Politicians, usually members of Congress, dictated appointments, and the civil servants whom these patrons sponsored often possessed neither the talent nor the motivation to perform adequately their public tasks. Nor was their tenure secure. A civil servant would almost certainly be removed if he ceased his political activities or if his patron lost his influence. Even if the civil servant's party remained in power, he might lose his position if his faction were eclipsed in an intraparty struggle. Morale was low as the fear of dismissal haunted governmental workers, and in an atmosphere of nervous tension, it was difficult to develop loyalty to an office or an agency.

The lack of professionalism in the civil service was matched by a lack of strong national feeling. A civil servant was loyal primarily to his patron—the politician with a local power base who had procured him his job. Not only did politicians expect field officers to electioneer, but with astounding frequency, administrators granted Washington civil servants paid leaves to campaign in their home districts. If a civil servant came from a state in which local and federal elections were held on different dates—a common occurrence—he was often granted two paid leaves.

Politicians gave civil servants their jobs, and the civil service gave the politician his strength. It provided a payroll for hacks and ward heelers; it was also a primary source of campaign funds. Local, state, and federal politicians usually assessed a civil servant from 2 to 7 percent of his yearly salary, and those who occupied potentially lucrative posts made heavy payments. If a civil servant did not respond to a letter that stated the sum due, he often received a second and even a third threatening letter. Lists of noncontributing governmental workers were circulated among department heads, and politicians frequently entered Washington departments to extract from reluctant civil servants "cash on the barrel" or the promise of it on the next payday.[1]

Attempts had previously been made to reform the civil service. Congressman Thomas A. Jenckes, a Rhode Island Republican, had introduced legislation in 1865 requiring that those who stood highest in an open competitive examination be appointed to the civil service. Though he had fought hard for his bill, which would have depoliticized and professionalized the civil service, it did not pass. During his brief congressional career, Hayes had supported the Jenckes bill. In 1871 a rider to an appropriations bill empowered the president to appoint a commission to prescribe rules for examining applicants for office. This commission, headed by George William Curtis, devised rules, but when Grant had ignored them in a conspicuous case in 1873, Curtis had resigned. His successor, Dorman B. Eaton, carried on with limited success until 1875, when Congress refused to appropriate funds for the commission. Eaton was still head of the moribund Grant Civil Service Commission when Hayes took office.[2]

While Hayes wished to reform the civil service, Schurz was his only cabinet advisor who was thoroughly committed to a nonpartisan career governmental service. Indeed, there was much about civil-service reform, as modeled on British and European efforts, that did not appeal to Americans. It smacked of elitism, with examinations that would favor the better educated, and it aimed for a stable bureaucracy. Civil-service reform ran counter to the egalitarian notions that the duties of governmental workers were simple enough for any intelligent person to master and that the public would be best served by rotating its workers, thus giving the service an infusion of fresh blood.

Underlying these objections was the fear that American democracy, specifically American political parties, could not function without a partisan civil service. In 1877, Great Britain, the preeminent model of civil-service reform, was emphatically not a democracy. Even a member of America's elite such as Hayes's Secretary of State William Maxwell Evarts, who was the nation's leading lawyer and whose grandfather had signed both the Declaration of Independence and the Constitution, recognized the connections between the spoils system, political parties, and the daring and unique American experiment in government of the people, by the people, and for the people. On 5 April 1877, Congressman James A. Garfield enjoyed dinner and a stimulating evening at the Evarts home. In the course of the conversation, Evarts asked, "In a Republic what political motive is an adequate substitute for patronage?" Dinner-party guests did not come up with the answer. Garfield, who also had proclivities toward reform, could only conclude, "This is the central difficulty that underlies the Civil Service."[3]

The civil service was a formidable organization, and its ability and zeal determined the effectiveness of laws and the quality of services. From its inception, the federal government has been the nation's largest single employer. Divided into seven departments and a few independent offices, this bureaucracy numbered during the Hayes administration approximately one hundred thousand persons, of whom about thirteen thousand were employed at headquarters in Washington. With an office in every village, the Post Office Department employed about half of the civil service, and over a third of all civil servants were unsalaried fourth-class postmasters. They were compensated by fees and, more significantly, by attracting patrons to their stores or newspapers. Next in size and in political importance was the Treasury Department, which had a large office in Washington, sizable customhouses in major port cities, and internal-revenue agents throughout the country. The somewhat smaller Department of the Interior was also politically significant because of the Land, Indian, and Pension bureaus. With the nation at peace, the War Department and the Navy Department in Washington were small, but together they employed approximately fifteen thousand mechanics and laborers in arsenals and navy yards. Finally, the smaller State Department and Justice Department controlled prestigious offices in missions abroad as well as the judiciary at home.[4]

There were vast differences among civil servants. They ranged from the minister to England to menial laborers in navy yards; from the well-compensated consul at Liverpool ($20,000 a year) to the fourth-class postmaster at Jones Cove, Tennessee ($2.37 a year); from policy-making assistant secretaries of departments to policy-implementing departmental clerks; from important officers appointed by the president with the advice and consent of the Senate to inferior offices appointed by the president alone or by heads of departments; from those two thousand to three thousand significant field officers, whose four-year terms made removal of them a simple matter of nonreappointment, to the remaining vast majority who served until they were removed; from Washington clerks, who tended to come from the District of Columbia and the Northeast, to field officers, who almost invariably were local residents; from the somewhat professionalized clerks at Washington, where a primitive personnel system existed, to the highly politicized customhouse employees; from field officers in one-party or modified one-party states, where their political activity would not appreciably affect the outcome of an election, to field officers in hotly contested districts and states, where their expertise in organizing the electorate was desperately needed; from the few highly skilled, experienced, essential officers who survived political changes and served the government for a lifetime to the victims of intraparty factionalism who measured their tenure in months.[5]

Varying functions gave each department its own organization and its personnel characteristics. While the bureaucracy could limp along with little direction from the top, it responded to active leadership. The condition in which members of Hayes's cabinet found their respective departments owed much to the previous incumbent. The new heads of these departments would, in turn, determine how well their departments would function and how much progress Hayes would make in reforming the civil service. Evarts, for example, did not have to overhaul the State Department, because it had largely escaped the deleterious effects of the spoils system. That department often demanded of its employees a familiarity with alien languages and cultures, with the traditions and usages of diplomacy, with history and international law—

in short, expertise that could not be acquired quickly. Furthermore, Evarts's predecessor, Hamilton Fish, had made certain, during his eight-year tenure, that the State Department was not a happy hunting ground for spoilsmen.

Evarts—who, like all cabinet members, earned $8,000 a year—had some experience in foreign affairs. During the Civil War the government had sent him on two missions to Great Britain to prevent the construction of vessels for the Confederates, and he was a United States counsel at the Geneva Arbitration of the Alabama Claims (1871/72). In the State Department, he had a staff that included three assistant secretaries of state ($3,500 a year), a chief clerk ($2,500), and five bureaus, each with its chief ($2,100) and a total of forty subordinate clerks (earning from $1,800 down to $900, the salary that the four women clerks received). From Evarts to the elevator conductor, the total staff numbered eighty-one. The key staff member in 1877 was the venerable Second Assistant Secretary of State William Hunter, who had served the department for forty-eight years and would remain nine more years. For a staff that was not, like those of most other departments, plagued by a rapid turnover, Hunter provided an additional measure of stability and supplied his rotating superiors with the benefits of his experience. Because of his mastery of several languages and his diligence and faithfulness, Hunter was exceedingly useful, but "his prodigious memory" provided "a veritable index to the Department," making him almost indispensable.[6]

Evarts made some appointments that brought experience and talent to the State Department. He appointed Alvey A. Adee as a clerk to draft state papers, and in 1878 made him chief of the Diplomatic Bureau, responsible for correspondence with legations. A Shakespearean scholar, a poet, an accomplished linguist, and a mathematician with broad scientific interests, Adee had recently spent eight years in Madrid as secretary of the legation and chargé d'affaires. His clearly written, intelligent dispatches, which covered a broad range of topics, commended him to his Washington superiors. Over the next forty-seven years, until his death in 1924, the State Department did not dispatch a single important paper abroad that had not been written or revised by Adee. Like Hunter, he guided inexperienced secretaries of state and often saved the United States from embarrassment. As his assistant secretary of state, Evarts appointed Frederick William Seward, who had served in the same capacity under Lincoln and Johnson while his father, William Henry Seward, had been secretary of state. When Frederick Seward resigned in 1879, Evarts replaced him with John Hay, who had been Lincoln's secretary before he had acquired diplomatic experience in Paris, Madrid, and Vienna and who would become an outstanding secretary of state under William McKinley and Theodore Roosevelt.[7]

Fortunately for Evarts, Fish had left him a smoothly running department and had disposed of the most troublesome diplomatic questions. What remained were difficulties with Mexico, over Texas-border raids by Mexican outlaws, and with China, over immigration to the United States. But the department that Fish left Evarts was an archaic one. Aware that William Hunter would not live forever, Fish had created the Bureau of Indexes and Archives to keep track of departmental papers. The staff was disciplined, and the work of copying dispatches was up to date. Yet the new Index Bureau and diligent clerks could not overcome difficulties imposed by an obsolete record-keeping system that had been designed early in the nineteenth century by John Quincy Adams. Correspondence was not filed by subject; instead, it was divided into diplomatic and consular categories, subdivided further, and bound chronologically by country. The Diplomatic Bureau arranged the world according to the alphabet. The same clerk handled the correspondence for Chile and for China. The filing system also had a miscellaneous category, which was divided into incoming and outgoing mail and was filed chronologically. With this system, making a brief or compiling information for Congress became a major undertaking. The State Department also failed to keep its diplomats abreast of world developments. Haphazard methods would, for example, leave United States ministers in Europe unaware of changes in United States Far-Eastern policy, even though their host countries had interests in the Far East.[8]

The foreign service was small. In 1877, twenty-three ministers—the rank of ambassador was still too pretentious for the United States—represented the Hayes administration abroad. Some, such as J. C. Bancroft Davis in Germany, George Perkins Marsh in Italy, and George Frederick Seward in China, were experienced diplomats. Others, such as poet James Russell Lowell in Spain and philanthropist John Welsh in Britain, were ornaments of American culture. Still others, such as John A. Bingham in Japan, John W. Foster in Mexico, and Horace Maynard in Turkey, were politicians whom Grant had rewarded and Hayes had not disturbed. There were also politicians whom Hayes had rewarded for helping him to the presidency. These included two visiting statesmen—former Congressman John A. Kasson of Iowa in Austria-Hungary and former Governor Edward F. Noyes of Ohio in France—and Hayes's friend James M. Comly of the *Ohio State Journal* in Hawaii.[9]

While Congress did not dictate diplomatic appointments, it did its best to determine who should represent the United States abroad.

Kasson, for example, owed his appointment not only to Hayes's gratitude but also to the strong endorsement given him by his colleagues in the Iowa congressional delegation and by six senators. Kasson's somewhat scandalous reputation—a decade earlier he had not denied having committed adultery when his wife sued for divorce—hurt his chances for a cabinet position, but the administration perceived that his reputation would do him no harm at the Hapsburg court in Vienna.[10]

An appointment to a prestigious mission could involve, as did that of John Welsh to London, pressure from Congress, wishes of the president, demands of politics, and the social and professional position of a candidate. To conciliate Pennsylvania's new senator, J. Donald Cameron, who was not retained as secretary of war, Hayes and Evarts informed him that Pennsylvania could have the British mission if its congressional delegation could agree on a candidate. Cameron embarrassed Hayes by suggesting his father, Simon Cameron, who had resigned from the Senate in protest to Hayes's appointments and to provide a place for his son. Not only was Simon Cameron hostile to the administration, but during his political career, which spanned five decades, he had earned a reputation for being corrupt. The day after Cameron suggested his father, a majority of the Pennsylvania delegation told Hayes that they had been coerced into favoring the appointment. When a delegation of Philadelphia businessmen proposed John Welsh as minister to England, Hayes nominated him, to the chagrin of both Camerons. Welsh had mercantile, banking, and railroad interests, was involved in philanthropic and civic enterprises, and was particularly acclaimed for having successfully managed the finances of Philadelphia's 1876 Centennial Exhibition.[11]

To be appointed secretary of a legation in a major capital usually delighted aspiring young men. Richard Henry Dana III was an exception. He rejected such a patronage plum, not because Evarts had awarded it to him on the grounds that he was the son of a friend, but because the post had no future. "Could the civil service reform be ensured for more than four years and were diplomacy a career in this country," young Dana wrote, "I should not hesitate to accept so high a start in so honorable a course, but, as it is, am I not right in saying that the position leads to no other?" It did not seem to occur to Dana that if reform principles governed personnel policies in the foreign service, Evarts could not have offered him the position.[12]

Distinct from the diplomatic service, the consular service was concerned primarily with the commercial interests of Americans. By 1877, there were more than two hundred consulates scattered throughout the world, often in countries where there was no other United States representative; and in busy port cities, these posts were eagerly sought. In addition, about four hundred consular agencies were serving areas that lacked enough business for a consulate. Foreigners were usually appointed to these posts, whose fees could not support an American abroad. The compensation of consuls ranged from fees alone to a maximum of $6,000 a year plus fees. At Liverpool, the famous one-armed veteran Lucius Fairchild earned more than $20,000 annually, but many posts offered little more than poverty in an exotic setting.

With three thousand employees and a complex organization in Washington, the Treasury Department contrasted sharply with the State Department. Although less in the public eye, Treasury Department employees played a more active role in the Republican party. While many Treasury Department positions called for special skills, numerous routine jobs were available for the party faithful. Some of these positions were filled by women, who usually did not participate in the hurly-burly of politics but who did owe their positions to political patrons. Women workers were often the widows or daughters of Civil War casualties, and while the Treasury Department often employed women in Washington, they were rarely hired in its field offices.

At the head of the Treasury Department was John Sherman, who was eager to succeed Hayes in the White House and who hoped to use treasury patronage to achieve that goal. Among prominent politicians, Sherman was the most qualified to become treasury secretary. He had chaired both the House Ways and Means Committee and the Senate Finance Committee, and for more than a decade and a half he had been the chief congressional architect of currency legislation.[13]

One of Sherman's assistant secretaries was Richard C. McCormick, who had been secretary of the Republican National Committee during the recent campaign. Sherman's other assistant secretary was Henry Flagg French of Concord, Massachusetts, who was the kind of appointee that civil-service reformers celebrated. He came from a distinguished family, and he practiced law in Boston and landscape gardening at his home in Concord. He also raised two distinguished sons, William M. R. French, who became director of the Art Institute of Chicago, and Daniel Chester French, who had already received national acclaim for his sculpture *The Minute Man*, which had been unveiled on 19 April 1875.[14]

The Treasury Department was divided into bureaus and offices in the categories of currency, taxes, expenditures, and miscellaneous functions. With approximately five hundred employees, the Bureau of

Printing and Engraving, under Edward McPherson, was one of the largest offices in Washington. Although he was a congressman from 1859 to 1863, McPherson is chiefly renowned as clerk of the House from 1863 to 1875, 1881 to 1883, and 1889 to 1891 and for his *Hand-book of Politics* (in effect the Republican campaign sourcebook), published biennially from 1868 to 1894. His knowledge of parliamentary law and politics was unsurpassed, and he proved to be indispensable to Republican Speakers of the House. Because the Republicans were no longer in control of the House in 1877, Hayes awarded McPherson the Bureau of Printing and Engraving at $4,500 a year.[15]

That bureau employed many highly skilled technicians, as well as numerous unskilled workers. It also employed many women, almost all of whom were restricted to less skilled work and earned less pay than males. This pattern was repeated throughout the public service. The eight engravers in the bureau earned up to $9.75 per diem, while their superintendent earned the princely salary of $16.00 per diem, which rivaled the salary of McPherson. Employees in the Printing Division, who numbered more than two hundred, were less handsomely paid. The superintendent received $8.50 per diem, 88 plate printers and 10 apprentices were on piece rates, and 97 women printer's assistants and apprentices earned $1.25 per diem. In some divisions, such as Examining or Numbering and Separating, nearly all employees were women, and they were supervised by women who earned $5.00 per diem. The salaries of bureau women ranged from $0.75 per diem for laborers to $1,200 per annum for three clerks in McPherson's office. While some of these salaries sound niggardly to modern ears, they were generous by 1877 standards, as were all governmental salaries.

The federal government also minted money. The director of the mint was Henry Richard Linderman. Since 1853 he had served almost continuously as an official at the mint, and his knowledge about procedures at the mint, market prices of bullion, and the theories of monetary standards was unsurpassed. It was Linderman who alerted Comptroller of the Currency John Jay Knox, Secretary of the Treasury George S. Boutwell, and Senate Finance Committee Chairman John Sherman that the falling market price of silver would soon make the 412.5-grain silver dollar inflationary. In February 1873, congressmen, who were largely unaware of that probability, passed the Coinage Act, which eliminated the coinage of silver dollars. Linderman, Boutwell, and Sherman had engineered what inflationists later called the "Crime of 1873." An admirer of the British, Linderman was convinced that their gold-based currency was the foundation for their prosperity, and he was anxious that the United States return to the gold standard.[16]

The federal mints and assay offices were located outside of Washington. In 1877 the largest mints, each of which had approximately 250 employees, were in Philadelphia and San Francisco. While many skilled tradesmen worked steadily at these mints, their superintendents were dispensable political appointees and were often replaced. The mint in Carson City, Nevada, had 85 employees, while the Denver and New Orleans mints in 1877 had only skeleton crews of 9 and 12 employees. In 1879, in response to the Bland-Allison Act, the New Orleans Mint went into full production with 115 employees. The only large assay office (55 employees) was located in New York, because gold was used in balancing foreign trade deficits; the United States during the Hayes administration enjoyed a favorable balance of trade, so it consistently imported gold.

The National Banking Act of 1863 created the Office of the Comptroller of the Currency to supervise the National Banking System. Specifically, the comptroller was to issue and regulate circulating notes for national banks. To insulate the office from presidential whims, Congress specified that the comptroller serve a five-year term and that the Senate agree both to the appointment and to any premature removal of that official. In addition, Congress insisted that the comptroller report annually and directly to it, thus by-passing the secretary of the Treasury.

In 1877 the comptroller was John Jay Knox, a bureaucrat who was the country's chief expert on banking. Aided by the 84 members of his office staff, half of whom were women, Knox exercised power without having fame. He had entered the Treasury Department during the Civil War and had become the comptroller in 1872, having served as deputy since 1867. With Linderman's help, Knox wrote the Coinage Act of 1873, he helped plan for the resumption of specie payments on 1 January 1879, and he negotiated with bankers for the sale of government bonds. While Knox was a firm believer in bank examinations to detect violations of the law, he was a passive administrator who believed in a free banking system, open to all who qualified. He rejoiced when Congress in 1875 removed the original $300-million limit on national bank notes in circulation. Recruited from the banking community, Knox provided an example that later regulators would follow by returning to it as president of a New York bank when he retired from governmental service in 1884.[17]

The Internal Revenue Office and the Customs Service, which were charged with collecting taxes, had large field services and were heavily involved with politics. Of federal receipts totaling $281 million in 1877, the Customs Service collected $131 million and the Internal Revenue Service, $119 million. Green Berry Raum, the commissioner of internal revenue from 1876 to 1883, presided over a Washington office of 172 employees, but his extensive field staff, with its legitimate compensation and its opportunities for illegitimate graft, enabled him to strengthen his party in every state. Spread throughout the country, collecting excise taxes on whiskey and tobacco and trying to prevent illicit distilling, were 126 collectors who earned from $2,125 to $4,500 annually; they were assisted by more than 2,700 deputy collectors, gaugers, storekeepers, inspectors, and agents, who were compensated by fees or by salaries ranging from $4 per diem to $2,000 annually.

The Customs Service, which was headed by a commissioner, was larger than the Internal Revenue Service. Customhouses, totaling 135, were positioned along the seacoast from Eastport, Maine, to Brownsville, Texas, and from Sitka, Alaska, to San Diego, California. They also spread along the Canadian and Mexican borders, and dotted the interior at major cities such as Cincinnati and minor ones such as Dubuque, Iowa. Of these customhouses, 84 had fewer than 10 employees, but 9 had more than 50 employees. The larger offices included New York (1,250), Boston (360), Philadelphia (223), Baltimore (210), San Francisco (210), New Orleans (175), Burlington, Vermont (65), and Chicago (51).

The Customs Service was both a base for partisan leaders and a haven for senior statesmen. Lot M. Morrill, the collector at Portland, Maine, had been a senator and was Grant's last secretary of the Treasury. Hayes offered Morrill the British ministry, but he felt that his health was too precarious for that post; in its place he accepted the lucrative ($6,000 a year) Portland Customhouse, which he held until his death in 1883. Hayes rewarded his newspaper friend William Henry Smith by making him collector of the port of Chicago. In the New Orleans Customhouse, J. Madison Wells, the purchasable presiding officer of Louisiana's returning board, retained his post as surveyor, at $4,500 a year.[18]

Chester A. Arthur, Roscoe Conkling's chief lieutenant, was, within the limits of the spoils system, a reasonably effective New York collector. Prior to 1874, Arthur's compensation, enhanced by moiety fees—from confiscated smuggled goods that were sold, with the proceeds being divided among the informer, the government, and the collector, the naval officer, and the surveyor of the port—ran as high as $56,000 a year. After those fees were eliminated, Arthur's salary was more modest ($12,000 in 1877, or $4,000 more than John Sherman earned as secretary of the Treasury). Among the employees of the New York Customhouse was Arthur's old Union College schoolmate, although not a particular friend, Silas W. Burt, the comptroller ($5,000 a year), who for several years had championed civil-service reform in that office. The tension between the ideas represented by Arthur and by Burt would mount during the Hayes administration.[19]

The government's accounting procedures involved several major treasury offices. The double-audit accounting system that Alexander Hamilton had devised was still in use. All accounts were first examined in one of six auditors' offices and were then forwarded for settlement to one of two comptrollers' offices or to the office of the commissioner of customs, who functioned as the comptroller for that service. The comptrollers, as well as the commissioner of customs, also heard appeals from those who objected to the audits of their accounts. All of these auditing offices had been relatively unscathed by the spoils system under Grant, and they remained that way throughout the Hayes administration.[20]

Although the offices of auditors and comptrollers varied in size, they handled the accounts of specific departments or bureaus. For example, the huge Sixth Auditor's Office, which had 166 clerks, 10 temporary clerks, and 35 ''assorters,'' handled Post Office Department accounts. Perhaps because of their special demand for accounting skills, these offices recruited a disproportionate number from north of the Potomac and Ohio rivers and east of the Mississippi. Of the 166 regularly appointed clerks in the Sixth Auditor's Office, 78 percent came from that northeastern quarter of the United States, where 56 percent of the population lived.

Along with the auditors, the treasurer and the register participated in the day-to-day business of the Treasury Department. The Register's Office kept the Treasury Department's records, preserving the vouchers of bills and validated documents. Less than half of that office's staff of 124 were male clerks who earned $1,200 to $1,800 a year, while the majority of workers were female copyists or counters who earned $900 a year. The treasurer was charged with recording the monies received and disbursed, storing the money paid into the Treasury, and seeing that no money left the government vaults without a proper warrant. Among governmental departments, the Treasurer's Office was unique in sepa-rately listing the 106 clerks, 11 messengers, and 13 laborers who were male and the 188 clerks, 2 messengers, and 30 laborers who were female; but like other governmental offices, the Treasurer's Office paid women employees less than it paid men.

Nine subtreasuries were located in major cities throughout the country. Of these, the New York Subtreasury, which received huge deposits from the local customhouse, was the largest; and the assistant treasurer who directed it earned $2,000 a year more than the treasurer of the United States. As a member of the New York Clearing House, the assistant treasurer at New York also had duties relating to the banking system. In contrast to New York, one of the smallest subtreasuries was located in Cincinnati; it was headed in 1877 by Alexander M. Stem at $4,500 a year. Four years earlier, Grant had offended Hayes by offering him that office.

The Treasury Department also housed functions that were not connected with collecting and dispensing revenue or with money and banking. One of these functions was overseeing the building and repairing of federal facilities throughout the nation, as well as granite cutting in Maine, Massachusetts, and Virginia. During the Hayes administration, these tasks were under Supervising Architect James G. Hill of Massachusetts, who was paid $4,500 a year. His office in Washington had six clerks, twenty-one draughtsmen, twenty-one "computers," seventeen copyists, and a large field staff. Since these positions, as well as similar ones, often required special expertise, the tenure of civil servants who executed them was usually secure.

Several of the Treasury Department's nonfiscal functions were associated with commerce. The Revenue Marine Service—forerunner of the United States Coast Guard—numbered approximately 220 officers (enlisted men were not enumerated), and the Life Saving Service employed about 160 men at various coastal stations. In 1877, these services were headed by Sumner Increase Kimball, an extraordinary public servant. He had served in the Maine legislature, and in 1861 the incoming Lincoln administration had appointed him to the Second Auditor's Office, where he had become chief clerk. In 1871, he had been made chief of the Revenue Marine and Life Saving Service. Recognizing Kimball's worth and his pioneering work in organizing the Life Saving Service, Hayes in 1878 made him superintendent of that service, a position that Kimball held until 1915. During his tenure, he made the United States Life Saving Service, which was among the first of such services supported by a national government, a model for other nations to follow.[21]

The federal government also assumed the medical care of merchant seamen. The modest Marine Hospital Service included 12 surgeons, 18 assistant surgeons, 7 hospital stewards, and 3 matrons. Lucy Hayes's brother, Dr. Joseph Webb, aspired to be its surgeon general; but Hayes, who was hostile to nepotism, refused to make the appointment, thus angering Webb and hurting Lucy. Striving to avoid marine disasters, the federal government, despite its aversion to intervening in the private sector, maintained a Steamboat Inspection Service. This service had about 130 inspectors who served at ports on America's coasts, rivers, and lakes. To operate and maintain beacons for navigators, the Light

House Service had approximately 950 lighthouse keepers and 180 inspectors and engineers, who were supervised by a distinguished Lighthouse Board, which in 1877 included Joseph Henry, the director of the Smithsonian Institution; Gen. John G. Barnard of the Corps of Engineers; and Comdr. George Dewey of the navy.[22]

The Coast Survey charted the United States coastline. Its head, Carlile Pollock Patterson, who was paid $6,000 a year, maintained its reputation for innovation, precision, and nepotism. Patterson, the son and brother of distinguished naval officers, was the brother-in-law of Adm. David Dixon Porter. The Coast Survey's reputation had been earned during the long tenure (1843-67) of its second superintendent, Alexander Dallas Bache. In 1877, there were still three Baches on the Coast Survey payroll. America's leading mathematician, Benjamin Peirce, directed its longitude determinations from 1852 to 1867, superintended the Coast Survey from 1867 to 1874, and then continued as "consulting geometer" at $4,000 a year while serving Harvard as Perkins Professor of Mathematics and Astronomy. In 1861, Peirce secured the appointment of his son Charles Sanders Peirce to the Coast Survey just two years after he had graduated from Harvard. In the thirty years that he remained with the Coast Survey, Charles S. Peirce conducted astronomical and mathematical investigations, established himself as the greatest formal logician of his time, and originated a philosophical position that he called pragmatism. The Washington office of the Coast Survey was run by Julius Erasmus Hilgard, a geodesist with an international reputation who was with the survey for forty years. While virtually all civil servants had been born in the United States, in this highly technical office employees had frequently been born abroad, especially in Germany, as was the case with Hilgard.[23]

The Treasury Department also employed statisticians. In 1876, aided by three clerks, Joseph Nimmo, Jr., began to compile *Annual Reports on the Internal Commerce of the United States* and to provide information on railroads for contemporary businessmen and subsequent scholars. One of the twenty-two clerks in the Statistics Office was Lester Frank Ward, a Civil War veteran who had secured his appointment in 1865. While employed in the Treasury Department, Ward had completed his formal education by attending night classes at Columbian College, later to be called George Washington University. In 1877 he argued in two articles in the *National Union* (Washington) that governmental statistics should be expanded and refined and that they should be used as a basis for "scientific lawmaking." Ward, a man of enormous talent who was a disciple of Darwin, was the pioneer of evolutionary sociology. He also was a linguist, a botanist, and a geologist—he later transferred to the Geological Survey. Cherishing humane and democratic values, he believed that people could plan human progress, that the human mind could affect the evolutionary process, that government should abolish poverty and be responsible for the people's welfare, and that democracy would evolve into "sociocracy." Ward formulated these ideas while he was in the Statistics Office, and he was writing his major work, *Dynamic Sociology* (1883), when Hayes was president.[24]

With Charles S. Peirce in the Coast Survey and Lester Frank Ward in the Statistics Office, the Treasury Department was employing two of the most original minds in the history of American thought. Despite the abuses of the spoils system, the civil service attracted some public servants of outstanding ability. By sponsoring the collection and discovery of useful information for commerce, agriculture, and industry, the United States government in the 1860s and 1870s was recruiting minds that in subsequent generations would gravitate toward the universities, as they developed into centers of scientific research and original thought.

The modest War Department and the small Navy Department were organized similarly. Secretary of War McCrary and Secretary of the Navy Thompson each had his own office and staff, and their departments were divided into bureaus that were headed by army and navy officers but were staffed by civil servants. In the War Department, the adjutant general, the quartermaster general, the paymaster general, the surgeon general, the inspector general, the chief of engineers, and the chief of ordnance presided over offices of varying sizes. The Adjutant General's Office, with approximately 220 clerks, for example, was quite large, while the Ordnance Department, whose chief was Brig. Gen. Stephen V. Benét, had only 12 clerks in Washington. The Ordnance Department at large, however, comprised the national armory at Springfield, Massachusetts, which had 44 civilian employees and 5 army supervisors, and several arsenals throughout the country, which employed about 600 men. Combined, the Navy Department's eight bureaus—Yards and Docks, Equipment and Recruiting, Navigation, Ordnance, Medicine and Surgery, Provisions and Clothing, Steam Engineering, and Construction and Repair—employed fewer than 40 clerks.

Neither Thompson nor McCrary was inclined to disturb key employees of his department. The eight chief clerks of the War Department and the nine chief clerks of the Navy Department were all in office in 1875, 1877, and 1879. There was little patronage in the Navy Department except just before elections, when navy-yard laborers, who were presumably more adept at building and repairing political machines than vessels, were employed on a per diem basis.

The Navy Department also administered the Naval Observatory, the Hydrographic Office, and the Nautical Almanac Office. The high level of technical competence in these offices was exemplified by the Naval Observatory's Simon Newcomb, who technically was not a civil employee but was a professor of mathematics in the United States Navy. When Newcomb was young, Joseph Henry of the Smithsonian Institution had secured him an appointment in the Coast Survey and had encouraged him to study mathematics. Impressed with Newcomb's progress, Henry and the head of the Coast Survey had secured his appointment in 1857 as a computer in the Nautical Almanac Office, then located in Cambridge, Massachusetts. Newcomb earned a B.S. degree at Harvard in 1858, published papers in astronomy, was commissioned a professor in the navy in 1861, and served in either the Nautical Almanac Office or the Naval Observatory until he retired in 1897.

More of a mathematical than an observational astronomer, Newcomb, through his numerous papers, had gained worldwide recognition by 1877. In September of that year, the Hayes administration appointed him superintendent of the *American Ephemeris and Nautical Almanac,* a governmental publication for navigators which contained accurate tables predicting the positions of heavenly bodies and the times of celestial phenomena. Newcomb moved the Nautical Almanac Office to Washington, eliminated inefficient personnel, and planned and started an "astonishing" program, which revised the fundamental data involved in the computation of the positions of celestial bodies.[25]

With four major and several minor offices, the Department of the Interior, under Schurz, was neither as complex as the Treasury Department nor as simple as the War and Navy departments. The Patent Office required technical competence, particularly among its 89 patent examiners, who were graded and paid from $1,400 to $3,000 per annum. These examiners were divided into specialties (textiles or steam engines, for example), and each year they issued about thirteen thousand patents, out of approximately twenty thousand applications.

The examiners were recruited from among the graduates of the nation's technical schools, and after being appointed as third assistant examiners, they were expected to become expert in the complicated field of patent law. Appointment and promotion on the basis of competitive examinations had been the rule in this demanding office even before the promulgation of civil-service rules by the Grant Civil Service Commission. Hayes and Schurz, given their commitment to civil-service reform, continued these enlightened personnel practices and even appointed their commissioner and assistant commissioner of patents from subordinate positions in the Patent Office. As might be expected given the specialization of the offices, fewer than one in five examiners came from west of the Mississippi and south of the Potomac and Ohio rivers. Even the Old Northwest was slighted; the vast majority of skilled Patent Office workers came from seaboard states north of the Potomac. Stable tenure was a problem, but not because spoils-minded politicians wished to substitute their cronies for incumbent examiners. Once the examiners had mastered the intricacies of patent law, they often took more lucrative private positions. Of 88 examiners in 1875, only 66, or 75 percent, were in office two years later. Almost 400 draughtsmen, clerks, copyists, laborers, and temporary employees facilitated the work of the examiners.[26]

While the Patent Office was one of the least politicized, the Pension Office aroused intense political interest. In 1877 it had not experienced the explosive growth that would make it in 1891 the world's largest executive bureau. That expansion resulted from the Arrears Act, which Hayes signed in January 1879. For those who were seeking pensions, it substituted bureaucratic procedures in place of special legislation, thus transferring a burden from Congress to the Pension Office. Also before that act, a pension began on the date of the application; after that act, a pension began on the day the pensioner had been honorably discharged. Inspired by the prospect of a back payment, which in some instances amounted to thousands of dollars, and a regular income, thousands of veterans became aware of service-related disabilities.

Late-nineteenth-century presidents liked to have their own man head this politically sensitive office, but throughout his administration Hayes, encouraged by Schurz, retained J. A. Bentley, who had been Grant's fifth commissioner of pensions. The growing volume of applicants, the pressure that Civil War veterans were applying, the badgering by congressmen, and the pestering by pension attorneys made the Pension Office difficult to administer. In office longer than most commissioners (six years), Bentley proved able, but the Grand Army of the Republic secured his removal when Hayes left office. During Hayes's term, Bentley presided over a staff of almost 350 in Washington, as well as 18 regional pension agents, whose fees were not to exceed $4,000 a year, plus $0.25 for each voucher paid. Pension agents were usually active politically and required senatorial confirmation. With Schurz inspecting efficiency reports periodically and adjusting salaries accordingly, the Washington staff worked diligently, but the system to determine legitimate claimants was faulty. Local physicians and officials had to examine and certify that applicants were disabled, and as an observer remarked in 1884, "The false swearing looks just as well as the true."[27]

Of all federal offices during the late nineteenth century, the General Land Office had the worst reputation for confusion, laxity, and fraud. The nation's land policy, which was enunciated in the Preemption Act of 1841 and in the Homestead Act of 1862, aimed at the settlement of the public lands in 160-acre plots by heads of families or single individuals over twenty-one years of age. Land speculators and corporations, however, worked to secure large tracts of choice farmland, stands of timber, and rich mineral deposits. With the rapid post–Civil War settlement of the West, the demands on this federal agency were so great that the expression "land office business" became synonymous with booming sales. In 1876 the Land Office, with 156 clerks at Washington, disposed of 6,524,326 acres of public land, and in 1880 it disposed of 14,792,372 acres—a 127 percent increase—with 195 clerks, an increase of less than 26 percent.

Congress complained that the General Land Office was inefficient, but the office was understaffed, and under Schurz its employees were overworked. Land Office Commissioner James A. Williamson was inexperienced, but his six principal subordinates were either already at their posts by 1875 or were promoted from within the Land Office. Specializing in certain areas, such as public lands, private lands, railroad lands, and surveys, Land Office clerks examined papers and decided cases. Their decisions were rarely reversed. The press of work ensured that reviews by superior officers were perfunctory. The office in 1877, for example, was six months behind in its correspondence, and Williamson noted that there was a "very large arrearage" in all of its work. Under his leadership, the Land Office clerks did their utmost to keep up with increased demands, working after hours and even on Sundays. With little success, he begged for more and better-trained help and for more space.

To make their decisions, General Land Office clerks acquired a substantial knowledge of land laws, judicial decisions, and administrative precedents; and this expertise set them apart from typical Washington clerks. The tenure problem in the Land Office was similar to that of the Patent Office. In 1881 the chief clerk of the Public Lands division complained: "Some of the best men employed during an administration of 20 years have left us and connected themselves with big corporations or firms, who wanted shrewd, capable, and experienced men; my division has been weakened and crippled during the last two or three years by the loss of five or six good men."

To survey public land and to convey it into private hands, the Land Office maintained a considerable field service. Surveyors general, who were paid from $2,000 to $3,000, presided over fifteen districts, all of which, with the exception of Florida, were located west of the Mississippi. The ninety regional land offices, each of which had a register in charge of the office and a receiver in charge of finances, were inadequately supervised. Regional officers, who were often careless and negligent, were confirmed by the Senate; and when their offices were busy, their jobs were lucrative. They were paid $500 per annum, plus 1 percent of the money entered at their office, 1 percent of the cash value of land entered at their office under the Homestead Act, and fees for military land warrants.[28]

While the General Land Office was known for its confusion, the Office of Indian Affairs was renowned for its corruption. The crucial work of the Indian service was performed by 69 field agents, not by the 50-member Washington staff. The Indian agents were appointed, with the advice and consent of the Senate, for four-year terms. In spite of large responsibilities and small staffs, these agents administered Indian reservations—some as large as Connecticut—and often cheated both the government and the Native Americans under their jurisdiction. Aided by approximately 750 employees—averaging about 11 per agency—but possessing little authority, the agents were expected to keep the peace and to help the Native Americans become law-abiding, economically productive people. A typical agency might hire from outside the reservation a farmer; a blacksmith; a carpenter; a teacher, who was occasionally a woman; and a miller and from the tribe itself, an interpreter; a herder; a teamster; and a laborer. Native American employees were yearly paid $400 or less.[29]

Along with his four major bureaus, Schurz administered several minor offices. Among these was the Bureau of Education, headed by John Eaton, whose staff of seventeen collected statistics and information on education for dissemination throughout the United States. Eaton shared with Hayes an ardent belief in free public schools, and he advocated federal aid to states that were developing school systems. Both Eaton and Hayes supported Senator Henry W. Blair's bill, which was first introduced in 1881, to distribute federal aid for education among the states on the basis of illiteracy. Designed to provide good public schools for blacks as well as whites, this bill passed the Senate three times but was always defeated in the House.[30]

The National Museum (the Smithsonian Institution) was under the direction of the distinguished zoologist Spencer Fullerton Baird, who was paid $2,700. He had a staff of thirteen to classify the specimens that he had encouraged army and navy officers and private individuals to collect for the museum. In 1879, Congress authorized the building of the "Castle," the most distinctive of the many buildings on the Mall in Washington that house the Smithsonian, one of the world's greatest museums. Baird also served, after 1871, as the unpaid head of the United States Commission of Fish and Fisheries, established the marine laboratory at Wood's Hole, Massachusetts, and fostered the protection and propagation of useful fish and ichthyological research.[31]

Rounding out the educational agencies of the Interior Department was the Geological Survey, established in 1878, with Clarence King at its head. Schurz's objective in appointing King, who had made surveys since 1865, was to coordinate long-established, overlapping surveys. In 1877, there were two Geographical and Geological Surveys of the Territories: one had a staff of seventeen, headed by United States Geologist Ferdinand V. Hayden at a salary of $4,500, and the other had a staff of nine, headed by John Wesley Powell at a salary of $3,150. In 1867, Hayden had surveyed the Dakota Badlands for the General Land Office, and in 1872 he had resigned as professor of geology at the University of Pennsylvania to conduct governmental surveys. Powell, who had lost his right arm at Shiloh, explored the Grand Canyon by boat in 1869 for the Smithsonian Institution and, as head of the Second Division of the Survey of the Territories, continued his western explorations during the 1870s. Under Schurz and King, Powell's division was given the subtitle Rocky Mountain Region to distinguish it from that of Hayden. As interested in the Native Americans as he was in their land, Powell became the director of the Bureau of Ethnology under the Smithsonian Institution in 1879, and the next year he succeeded King as director of the Geological Survey.[32]

The Census Office employed only one clerk in 1877, but by 1879 it was gearing up for the 1880 census. The superintendent of the census was Francis Amasa Walker, a professor of political economy and history at Yale University's Sheffield Scientific School. He had superintended the 1870 census and was chagrined that it was unreliable, particularly in the South. He had been handicapped by inadequate authority, derived from an 1850 law governing the census, and by the spoils system, which provided personnel who were not capable of enumerating precisely the nation's people and resources. In 1870, Congress had cut off Walker's compensation, and to enable him to continue his supervision of the 1870 census, Grant had made him commissioner of Indian affairs. Though Walker gave that office a mere fraction of his attention, he proved to be the most reform-minded of late-nineteenth-century heads of the Indian Bureau. In 1877, no longer in the Indian Bureau, he was still the unpaid superintendent of the census. He urged that the Census Office be placed on a permanent footing and that the machinery for the decennial count be continuously maintained. In 1879, Congress responded with a law that enabled Walker, who was at last paid $5,000, to set up a Washington Census Office with a staff of twenty and to select his own enumerators for the tenth census.[33]

At $6 per diem, nine highly qualified special field agents were also employed by the Census Office in 1879 to collect statistics on agriculture, fishing, mining, lumbering, railroading, manufacturing, and urban growth. George E. Waring, for example, collected social statistics about cities with the aid of a $1,400-a-year clerk. A sanitary engineer, Waring was planning a sewage system for Memphis, where 5,150 of its 40,000 population had died of yellow fever in 1878. From 1895 to 1898, he would serve New York City as street-cleaning commissioner and, by eliminating politics and inefficiency and by raising morale, would become the most renowned street-cleaning commissioner in history. With the full support of the Hayes administration and with a stellar group of assistants, Walker presented to the nation an outstanding census in twenty-two large volumes.[34]

The Office of the Auditor of Railroad Accounts, which was newly housed in the Interior Department, was also concerned with statistics. This office's chief objective was to keep track of the railroads' capacity to pay their debts to the government. Theophilus French, a former division chief in the Treasurer's Office, was the auditor of railroad accounts; he had a staff of five and a salary of $5,000. After considering information collected by French's office, Schurz advocated that the railroads owing money to the federal government establish sinking funds to pay their debts.[35]

Eight territorial governments were also Schurz's responsibility. Like the states, these territories had a large measure of self-government through their legislatures, but their governors, who were paid $2,600, and their secretaries, who were paid $1,800, were appointed by the president, with the advice and consent of the Senate, and were a part of the Department of the Interior. These offices, particularly the governorships, were often used to reward older statesmen, or senators and congressmen who had lost elections. Upon the urging of Lucy Hayes in particular, Hayes helped the impoverished John Charles Frémont, the first Republican presidential nominee, for whom Hayes's hometown was named, by appointing him territorial governor of Arizona.

The remainder of Schurz's responsibilities involved public buildings and District of Columbia affairs. Approximately 240 men, employed on a per diem basis, worked on the extension of the Capitol Building.

The painter Constantino Brumidi, who had been decorating the Capitol with symbolic figures, historic scenes, and portraits since 1855, was still employed at $10 a day, which was what Secretary of War Jefferson Davis had paid him during the Pierce administration. During Hayes's term this "Michelangelo of the Capitol" planned the Rotunda Frieze. Shortly before his death in 1880, Congress appropriated $30,000 for Brumidi, specifically for the frieze, a third of which he completed, but in effect for twenty-five years of underpaid work. The government also employed two inspectors of gas and meters, and it maintained in the District of Columbia the Columbia Hospital for Women and the Lying in Asylum, with a staff of seventeen, the Freedmen's Hospital, with a staff of thirty, and the Government Hospital for the Insane, with a staff of approximately two hundred.[36]

The Department of Justice, under Attorney General Charles Devens, who made virtually no changes in personnel, was a small, stable department. Aiding Devens was Solicitor General Samuel F. Phillips, who was paid $7,000; a law clerk; and 2 assistant attorneys general, who were paid $5,000. The assistant attorneys general also had 5 assistants to help them prepare court-of-claims cases. The solicitor of the Treasury was also part of the Justice Department, as were the legal officers detailed to the Interior, Navy, Post Office, and State departments and the Internal Revenue Service. Like Schurz, Devens had substantial responsibilities within the District of Columbia. He administered approximately 250 metropolitan police; the United States Jail, with a staff of 40; and the reform school, with 10 employees.

The judicial branch of the government, comprising approximately twenty-five thousand individuals, was linked in the selection process to the Justice Department. Its principal officers were appointed by the president, with the advice and consent of the Senate. Federal judgeships were for life and were among the most desirable governmental offices. The nine-member Supreme Court headed the system, with the chief justice earning $10,500 a year and associate justices $10,000. The Supreme Court also employed a clerk, who was compensated by fees, a marshal, and a reporter. The United States Court of Claims, composed of five justices, also sat at Washington and was assisted in its work by two clerks.

The nation was divided into nine judicial circuits, over each of which a Supreme Court judge presided. The nine circuits were subdivided into sixty-four districts. Each district had a circuit judge (salary, $6,000), a district judge (salary, $3,000 to $5,000), and a district attorney, a marshal, a clerk of the circuit court, a clerk of the district court, a register in bankruptcy, and several United States commissioners (all of whom were usually compensated by fees). Like the states, the District of Columbia had a five-justice supreme court and court officers. The most prominent of these officers was Frederick Douglass, who as marshal was handsomely compensated by fees.

Although it was a separate executive department in 1877, the Department of Agriculture was not accorded cabinet status. William G. LeDuc, Hayes's commissioner of agriculture, was a boyhood chum of John and William T. Sherman's and was a graduate of Hayes's alma mater, Kenyon College. LeDuc had lived in Minnesota, where he promoted its settlement and railroads. As commissioner of agriculture, he was responsible for an unsuccessful tea farm in South Carolina, but he also promoted research on the production of sugar from sorghum and beets and on the eradication of animal diseases and the collection of information by his small but distinguished staff of chemists, biologists, and statisticians.[37]

Like the Department of Agriculture, the Government Printing Office was independent from other executive departments. It was large, with approximately 850 employees in its printing division and 400 in its binding division. Wages ranged from 44 cents per hour for stereotypers and 40 cents for pressmen, compositors, and marblers to 12.5 cents for some apprentices.

When compared with other governmental agencies, the Post Office Department was gigantic, but almost all of its employees were located outside of Washington. Despite the size of his department, Postmaster General Key received the same compensation ($8,000) as other cabinet members. He had three assistant postmasters general, who were paid $3,500. First Assistant James N. Tyner had been second assistant until he had been named postmaster general in 1876 for the remainder of Grant's term. Upon Key's appointment, Tyner, who had corresponded with Hayes, stepped down, becoming the first assistant postmaster general, presumably to continue his task of strengthening the Republican party with judicious appointments of postmasters in the North and West, while Key concentrated on building an administration party among old Whigs and Union Democrats in the South. The second assistant postmaster general was Thomas J. Brady, who, like Tyner, was from Indiana, was very much into politics, and was a protégé of Oliver P. Morton's. Brady probably owed his 1876 appointment to Tyner. Among Brady's responsibilities were contracts for carrying mail in sparsely settled western states and territories on routes that were designated by three stars in governmental reports. Brady decided whether population growth required changes in those contracts, which were made for four-year periods. The third assistant postmaster general, A. D. Hazen, had been promoted to that position from chief of the Division of Postage Stamps.

In addition to the offices of Key and his three assistants in 1877, there were eight divisions in the Post Office Department: Money Orders, Foreign Mails, Postage Stamps, Free Delivery, Topography, Mail Depredations, the Dead Letter Office, and Disbursements. The heads of divisions tended to be promoted from within the department and to enjoy secure tenure. These divisions employed about 280 clerks, of whom all 54 clerks in the Dead Letter Office and 18 of the clerks in other divisions were women, who were paid $900. The Hayes administration overhauled the Post Office Department by eliminating the chiefs of Free Delivery, Topography, and Mail Depredations. Presumably these functions were acquired by the assistant postmasters general.

The post-office field service was gargantuan. The *Official Register* for 1877 lists roughly 38,000 postmasters, 5 percent of whom were women. These postmasters earned from $2 to the $8,000 a year earned by Thomas L. James, the New York City postmaster. For other major cities, compensation ranged from $2,700 for the Denver postmaster to $4,000, which was earned by the San Francisco, Chicago, Baltimore, Boston, St. Louis, Cincinnati, and Philadelphia postmasters. Tenure in these positions was not secure. Of the fifteen largest cities, the postmasters of only four remained in office from 1875 to 1879. In addition to postmasters, there were approximately 4,650 clerks employed in the nation's post offices. These clerks earned anywhere from $50 to $4,000 annually. The size of post-office staffs varied with the volume of business. Hannibal, Missouri, employed 5 clerks; Chicago, approximately 260; and New York City, about 700.

In addition, the Post Office Department employed approximately 2,800 letter carriers, more than 400 of whom were in New York City, compensating them $736.25 annually in towns and small cities, $831.25 in larger cities (recognizing the higher cost of living), and $926.25 in San Francisco. In rural areas, the department employed approximately 1,000 route agents, who were paid from $900 to $1,000. More than 1,000 railway post-office clerks, who earned from $1,000 to $1,300 a year, sorted mail in transit; and an army of contractors, which took up twenty-three pages of the 1877 *Official Register* and consisted of railroads, stage companies, and individuals, transported the mail.

For detective work, the Post Office Department employed more than two hundred special agents, who were paid from $100 to $1,600 yearly. But Anthony Comstock, the redoubtable ''roundsman of the

Lord," crusaded without compensation to rid the mails of obscene and fraudulent material. Comstock, who made no attempt to distinguish art from pornography, pursued cheats and artists with equal fervor. His zeal caused Hayes embarrassment and jeopardized the solid support that the president received from the Protestant press and clergy, largely because after his first state dinner he had banished wine and liquors from the White House.

In 1877, Comstock, using an alias, received publications from Ezra Hervey Heywood, the cofounder with his wife, Angela Fiducia Tilton, of the New England Free Love League. Comstock arrested Heywood at a meeting of the Boston Free Love League and, in June 1878, secured his conviction for mailing obscene matter. Fined $100 and sentenced to two years at hard labor, Heywood's plight provoked a protest meeting attended by six thousand at Faneuil Hall. Hayes's devotion to marriage and to his wife Lucy was unabashed and unshakable, and he had contempt for pornographers, but he pardoned Heywood. Although Hayes considered Heywood's writings objectionable, he found that they "were not obscene, lascivious, lewd, or corrupting in the criminal sense."[38]

Comstock soon gave Hayes a second opportunity to sort out his ideas on the pardoning power and obscenity. On 5 June 1879, Comstock obtained the conviction of De Robigne Mortimer Bennett for sending obscene matter through the mails. Earlier the purveyor of "Dr. Bennett's Quick Cure, Golden Liniment, Worm Lozenges, and Root and Plant Pills," Bennett had become during the 1870s the freethinking editor of the *Truthseeker*. His specific offense was to mail Ezra Heywood's pamphlet *Cupid's Yokes: Or, The Binding Forces of Conjugal Life*. Sentenced to thirteen months in the penitentiary and a fine of $300, Bennett applied to Hayes for a pardon, but Hayes refused because he thought that *Cupid's Yokes*, which contained many indecent passages "not required for the argument," amounted to "obscenity to make money." Furthermore, Hayes believed that the "pardoning power must not be used to nullify or repeal Statutes, nor to overrule the judgments of the Courts." Its use should be saved for "palpable mistakes, hasty decisions, newly discovered facts." Those instances were rare. In general, Hayes was determined that he and the one hundred thousand civil servants at his command would "see that the laws are executed."[39]

6

★ ★ ★ ★ ★

CIVIL-SERVICE REFORM

"Now for Civil Service Reform," Hayes exclaimed on 22 April 1877, having, for the moment, disposed of his southern problems. "Legislation must be prepared & Executive rules and Maxims. We must limit, and narrow the area of patronage—we must diminish the evils of office seeking—we must stop interference of federal officers with elections. We must be relieved of congressional dictation as to appointments." The next day, carrying out Hayes's orders, Secretary of the Treasury Sherman appointed John Jay, a reform-minded New York aristocrat, to head a commission to investigate the New York Customhouse. Sherman also appointed commissioners to investigate the Philadelphia, New Orleans, and San Francisco customhouses. Hayes had fired the first shot in what became the classic political battle to control and reform the New York Customhouse.[1]

With its threat to congressional patronage and party organization, civil-service reform was not a simple issue, and as always, Hayes moved with caution. His moderation, however, angered the civil-service reformers, while reform, even on a modest scale, infuriated the spoilsmen. The president's initial inclination to leave the civil service intact, since it was impossible to make a thousand good appointments during the first two weeks of his term, provoked opposition from reformers. They urged that the collectors of Boston, New York, and Philadelphia be removed, because these customs officials were both partisan and corrupt.[2]

In addition, the administration's new rules for clerical appointments in the Washington departments required that they be made at the lowest grade and that they be given to those who had passed a standard, noncompetitive examination. Reformers, who wanted appointments made on the basis of open competitive tests, as in the British system, were disappointed that the administration palmed off a variant of "pass examinations" as civil-service reform. For more than twenty years these noncompetitive tests had been required by law and had proved to be no obstacle for spoilsmen. William Grosvenor of the *New York Tribune* complained to Schurz on 26 March, "I am afraid the President is making haste *too* slowly," and two weeks later, a Philadelphian, after reading that Hayes had proposed as reform an eight-year term of office for civil servants, wrote Schurz in bitter disappointment, "The country has asked for bread & you have given them a stone." The eight-year term was not administration policy, although Hayes had a tendency to reappoint civil servants who had successfully completed one four-year term, but not those who had completed two terms.[3]

Reformers were encouraged when Schurz established a three-member board of inquiry to guide Interior Department appointments, promotions, and removals and when Hayes ordered that the New York Customhouse be investigated, but they perceived that most members of the administration distributed spoils according to their own predilections. Harboring political ambitions and heading a department whose patronage could make them a reality, Sherman, for example, eagerly used the spoils at his disposal.

It was the Post Office Department, however, that made the most obnoxious appointment in the early days of the new administration. In all probability, Thomas J. Brady, the second assistant postmaster general, named George H. Butler, a nephew of Congressman Benjamin F. Butler's, as a special agent to establish postal routes and offices in the Black Hills of Dakota, the scene of the nation's recent gold rush. George Butler had been consul general of Egypt in 1869, where his activities included selling vice-consulships, touring Egypt with dancing girls, and "a shooting affray in the streets of Alexandria." Joseph R. Hawley, the Connecticut Republican leader whom Hayes appointed to the Louisiana Commission, predicted that Butler's nomination would be regarded as perpetuating "the mysterious power which Benjamin F. Butler exerted over Gen. Grant's administration."[4]

Despite repeated urging by Schurz, Hayes—who, when pushed, was not easily moved—refused to revoke Butler's appointment until newspapers loudly echoed the protests. "It would be a joke," Whitelaw Reid of the *New York Tribune* wrote to Schurz, "if the fact should become public, that the Civil Service Reform champion in the Cabinet was unable to secure the dismissal of a person whose appointment compelled the friends of the Administration to hold their noses whenever its Civil Service reform was mentioned, until the *Tribune* lost all patience, and openly denounced the shameful act." Reid, who was close to Blaine, soon stopped pretending to favor civil-service reform and opened his columns to attacks on Schurz and reform.[5]

Hayes's caution, coupled with Sherman's attitude, particularly with respect to Jay's investigation of the New York Customhouse, made the administration's policy in regard to civil-service reform appear weak and vacillating. The Jay Commission's first report on 24 May suggested that 20 percent of the customhouse's 1,262 employees could be dispensed with and that subsequent reductions might be necessary. An atmosphere of laxness prevailed in the customhouse. Hours were from nine to four, but work rarely started before ten, and presumably lunch breaks were taken as well, so employees put in less than a six-hour day. The one rule that was strictly enforced was the paying of political assessments, which some employees recouped by "exacting or accepting from . . . merchants unlawful gratuities." After making these charges, the Jay Commission recommended "the emancipation of the service from partisan control."[6]

Sherman approved the Jay Commission's minor recommendations, but he asked Hayes to comment on the part pertaining to political appointments made "without due regard to efficiency," since administration policy was involved. Hayes's reply virtually reiterated the commission's recommendations:

> It is my wish that the collection of the revenues should be free from partisan control, and organized on a strictly business basis. . . . Party leaders should have no more influence in appointments than other equally respectable citizens. No assessment for political purposes, on officers or subordinates, should be allowed. No useless officer or employee should be retained. No officer should be required or permitted to take part in the management of political organizations, caucuses, conventions, or election campaigns.[7]

Sherman's instructions to Arthur watered down Hayes's forceful commands. While demanding that Arthur trim his force within a month, Sherman suggested, "in a government like ours, other things being equal, those [officers] will be preferred who sympathize with the party in power; but persons in office ought not to be expected to serve their party to the neglect of official duty." Sherman's letter did not mention political assessments, and far from removing Arthur as reformers had hoped, Sherman commended him for approving the Jay Commission's preliminary report. George William Curtis cleverly paraphrased Sherman's letter: "Mr. Collector, the President wishes the Custom-house to be taken out of politics. You will please do it in your own way, only—you will, of course, leave politics in."[8]

The caution of the administration and its contradictions disappointed reformers and caused them to fear for the future of civil-service reform. "For if," Horace White, a former editor of the *Chicago Tribune*, worried, "our enemies can say that, with an Administration of our kind & with a President who didn't want to be reelected, we could still do nothing, will they not convince the Country that reform is simply impracticable & that time should not be wasted upon it?"[9]

Hayes moved to satisfy the reformers. On 22 June 1877 he ordered that federal civil servants not "take part in the management of political organizations, caucuses, conventions, or election campaigns," and he prohibited political assessments. The president was again popular with reformers, and again politicians were disgruntled. The *Nation* called his order the "best thing he has yet done for politics" after ridding the south of carpetbaggers. Samuel Bowles, of the *Springfield* (Mass.) *Republican*, wrote Schurz: "The theory of civil service reform at Washington is beautiful, but the practice is often pretty bad. But the comfort is that . . . you have gone so far that you cannot go back."[10]

Hayes, however, had not committed himself irrevocably. To be sure, he wanted his order that forbade political activity by officeholders obeyed, yet he did not want it to destroy Republican party organizations. His caution and the efforts and advice of trusted friends made him search for a middle ground. Sherman continued to do his best to prevent a rupture between Hayes and Conkling over the New York Customhouse. By 5 July, Sherman reported from New York that "several arrangements of a minor character have been made . . . that I think will leave the Custom House here in an excellent condition," and he advised Hayes to inform "Collector Arthur . . . that he will not be disturbed during the continuance of his present [term of] office." William M. Dickson defended the spoils system, arguing that "party work is a necessary work" in a republic, that "politics must pay the politician," and he urged Hayes to "give us honest & capable men, but partizans. All else is the cry of Amateur literary politicians." Another friend, W. D. Bickham, the proprietor of the *Dayton* (Ohio) *Daily and Weekly Journal*, complained that Hayes's civil-service order, although necessary in cities such as Cincinnati, Cleveland, and Toledo, hampered party organizations in the country "tremendously" because "our most efficient campaign managers are usually officials and faithful officials at that."[11]

To the dismay of Curtis and his friend Charles Eliot Norton, Hayes, around 20 July, agreed with Sherman. Desiring "to make as few removals as possible," Hayes decided to retain Collectors Arthur of New York and W. A. Simmons of Boston as long as they cooperated with reform efforts. Norton told Hayes that they "must be removed" because they personified corruption for the people and "to retain them in office would be to weaken greatly your own power of good, & because, however unjustly, either your sincerity, or your good-sense would be suspected."[12]

The arrogance of Roscoe Conkling soon convinced Hayes that any reform of the New York Customhouse was impossible as long as it remained under Conkling's control. William Grosvenor told the administration in July that the paring of the customhouse staff, as required by the Jay Commission report, had been carried out with "outrageous partiality & knavery. . . . It was, and everybody here knows it, a most impudent avenging of Conkling & his crew, by ousting the men who had become distasteful." Worse, Naval Officer Alonzo Cornell refused to resign from the Republican National Committee despite Hayes's order forbidding officeholders to engage in political activities. (In the customs service, naval officers had nothing to do with the navy; they acted as a check upon collectors.)

Cornell's defiance assumed the proportions of a "national scandal" and turned into a test case, pitting the administration against the spoils senators, led by Conkling. The *Nation* insisted that Cornell must be removed, for if he could defy the president with impunity, the administration's civil-service policy would be broken. David A. Wells wrote to Schurz on 1 September: "I think there is a feeling that on civil service reform there is hesitation—perhaps timidity to go forward in the path commenced. I hope there will be no hesitation in meeting the defiance apparently shown by Cornell at New York."[13]

Hayes did not move against Arthur and Cornell until after 31 August, when the Jay Commission made its fourth and most elaborate report, which dealt with the appraiser's office. The commission estimated that the undervaluations and excessive damages allowed by New York appraisers cost the government up to a fourth of its rightful revenues. The commission appears to have exaggerated. The example it gave, of $3 to $5 million lost by undervaluing silk imports at $35 million, suggests that a tenth might have been a more accurate estimate.[14]

On 6 September, Hayes challenged Conkling by announcing that Arthur and Cornell would be replaced in a customhouse reorganization. Although Conkling was a conspicuous spoilsman, who dressed, postured, and strutted about like a dandy, he was less hostile to civil-service reform than were Grant's other spoilsmen friends. When suggesting appointments, Conkling usually kept the commonweal, as well as his machine, in mind. He was, nevertheless, a spoilsman, and his fief, the New York Customhouse, which collected 70 percent of the nation's customs revenue, was the most important federal office in the land. Striking a blow for reform there would have an enormous impact on reformers, and if reform had merit, it would also have a significant practical effect on governmental service.

Apart from reform considerations, Hayes had compelling political reasons for attacking Conkling's control of the New York Customhouse. Conkling had crossed Hayes repeatedly. Conkling had opposed Hayes's nomination; he had been conspicuously silent during the campaign; he had failed to deliver New York; he had hindered the Republican effort to "count" Hayes in; and he had, after the inauguration, referred to Hayes as "Rutherfraud." Conkling's main objective seems to have been to discredit the reform wing of the New York Republican party, which was led by Secretary of State Evarts. Evarts wished to form an administration party by fusing the reformers with the remnants of the old Reuben E. Fenton machine, which had been displaced by the Conkling organization. Evarts overcame Sherman's argument that appointments should be balanced between Evarts and Conkling supporters. The administration stood to gain doubly by attacking Conkling; reformers would be pleased, and a hostile faction that failed to deliver the vote in 1876 would be eliminated.[15]

On 26 September, with Cornell and other officeholders in attendance, Conkling launched a counterattack at the New York State Republican Convention in Rochester. As temporary chairman, Congressman Thomas C. Platt, a Conkling henchman, made a "violent and abusive attack" on the administration, and the platform, which Conkling wrote, ignored the Hayes administration and piously called for an ideal civil service. George William Curtis tried unsuccessfully to amend the platform with a resolution commending Hayes for his efforts to permanently pacify the South and to correct "evils and abuses in the Civil Service" and stressing that his title to the presidency was "as clear and perfect as that of George Washington." W. L. Sessions, a delegate from

Chautauqua County, reported: "In spirit & matter, Curtis made the finest speech I ever heard."

Conkling responded vehemently. He maintained that New York Republicans had the right to criticize Hayes, and he argued that a state convention was not called upon to approve or commend the administration. His speech is most memorable, however, for its vilification of reformers in general and Curtis in particular as "man-milliners, the dilettante and carpet knights of politics," who "forget that parties are not built up by deportment, or by ladies' magazines, or gush," and for its conclusion: "When Dr. Johnson defined patriotism as the last refuge of a scoundrel, he was unconscious of the then undeveloped capabilities and uses of the word Reform."

Conkling's speech and his manner of delivery made a profound impression on those who were present. "Had all the Gall & bitterness of Tophet been breathed into Conkling," Sessions remarked, "he could not have shown more than he did, toward Curtis & Hayes." "It was the saddest sight I ever knew," Curtis wrote, "that man glaring at me in a fury of hate, and storming his foolish blackguardism." Conkling carefully wrote out his speech for the press; "and therefore you do not get all the venom and no one can imagine the Mephistophelean leer and spite," Curtis remarked. Conkling's followers loved his performance, but his enemies rejoiced that he had "put himself frankly at the head of the malcontents" and, despite his temporary triumph, had sealed his fate.[16]

Undeterred by Conkling's bombast, Hayes determined on his fifty-fifth birthday—4 October 1877—to make improving the civil service a constant aim, and two weeks later, he noted that appointments had to be divorced "from Legislative control except the power of confirmation by the Senate." His nominations to the New York Customhouse, however, reveal that he was more in tune with Evarts, rather than with the civil-service reformers.

For collector, Hayes nominated Theodore Roosevelt, Sr.; for naval officer, L. Bradford Prince; and for surveyor, Edwin A. Merritt. None of the nominations reflected the preferences of reformers, who wanted Hayes to appoint revenue reformer David A. Wells as collector and to promote Deputy Surveyor James I. Benedict and Deputy Naval Officer Silas W. Burt, a prominent civil-service reformer. Roosevelt was acceptable, but Merritt years earlier had been a Fentonite naval officer, and Prince allegedly had received financial help from New York City's notorious Boss William M. Tweed and had consequently been friendly toward Tweed legislation. Nevertheless, reformers acquiesced in the New York nominations. Curtis explained to Burt: "The position of the

President is, for many reasons, very difficult. He cannot do all that he would. There must be many inconsistencies and many mistakes; but I think that we should not despair so long as the general tendencies of the administration are right." The Senate referred the customhouse nominations to its Committee on Commerce, chaired by Roscoe Conkling.[17]

Hayes made these nominations when his relations with Congress were at a low point. His independent course had offended leading members of his party. Specifically, they objected to Evarts, Schurz, and Key in the cabinet, to making the civil service nonpartisan, and most bitterly, to any attempt to "Deprive Congressmen of all control and share of the patronage of the Government." On 30 November 1877, Conkling won his first victory; the Commerce Committee unanimously voted, with three Democratic abstentions, to reject Hayes's nominations. Schurz observed: "The political situation seems extremely confused. The struggle for mastery in the Senate has re-inflamed party feeling to such an extent that men, who some time ago talked and acted very sensibly, are entirely off their balance. The administration, I am happy to say, takes things with great coolness, and I have no doubt, the real questions of the day will soon resume their place in the foreground again."[18]

The administration appeared to be in disarray. Tilden's wishful observation on 4 November—"This administration will be the greatest failure the Country ever saw"—was extreme, but even reformers were disheartened. In late October, Attorney General Devens had explained to officeholders that Hayes's order forbidding them to take "part in the management of political organizations, caucuses, conventions or election campaigns" did allow them "to vote and to express their views on public questions either orally or through the press." In short, they could campaign if it did not interfere with their duties. Collector Simmons of Boston provoked this explanation by blaming Hayes's order for keeping him and the customhouse personnel out of the 1877 Massachusetts campaign. The administration was anxious that Governor Alexander H. Rice, who was nominated by a convention that "cordially endorsed" Hayes, be reelected, and it needed the help of Simmons and the customhouse crowd in order to win. When Rice triumphed, Hayes rejoiced, but reformers were displeased with the president's drift away from reform.

Hayes's attempt to control the nominating power, which was the core of his struggle with Conkling, appeared ludicrous when Secretary of State Evarts asked the Pennsylvania and Illinois congressional delegations to nominate ministers to England and Germany. Pennsylvania named Simon Cameron, its venerable spoilsman boss, and Illinois suggested Robert G. Ingersoll, an enthusiastic supporter of James G. Blaine. The administration disappointed the politicians by not nominating their men, whom it considered unsuitable; and it peeved reformers by consulting spoilsmen. In addition, the administration's attempt to induce Collector Arthur to resign by offering him the Paris consulate further eroded the administration's reform position.[19]

Hayes's first annual message, which was forwarded to Congress on 3 December 1877, failed to rally either Congress or the public to his side. Undeterred by congressional dissatisfaction with his southern, monetary, and civil-service policies or by the hostility of many senators of his own party, Hayes, on 8 December, resubmitted his New York Customhouse nominations. To him, "Senatorial usurpation" was the problem, and he believed that "the claim of a single Senator to control all nominations in his State" was "preposterous" and would "fall of its own weight." He was convinced that the destruction of that claim was "the first and most important step in the effort to reform the Civil Service." Unconscious of the irony of using patronage to achieve civil-service reform, he wondered "whether I should not insist that all who receive important places should be on the right side of this vital question." Admitting that this step was "rather radical," he decided not to use it unless "the war goes on."[20]

Initially, Conkling defended Arthur and Cornell before the Senate on the plausible administrative grounds that their four-year terms had not expired and that they did not merit dismissal. But on 12 December 1877, when the crucial vote was taken in executive session, Conkling defeated Hayes by calling the nominations an attack on "the courtesy of the Senate" and "an attempt to degrade him personally." A struggle between the Conkling and Evarts factions of the New York Republican party had escalated into a battle between the president and the Senate over the power of appointment. Because the term of Surveyor Sharpe had expired, the Senate approved Merritt as Sharpe's successor, but rejected both Roosevelt and Prince. Only six Republicans—two of them from Massachusetts—joined with nineteen Democrats to support the president, while twenty-eight Republicans and three Democrats sided with Conkling. "The Senate is the citadel of the Spoils System," lamented Richard Henry Dana, Jr., the celebrated author of *Two Years before the Mast* and a distinguished maritime lawyer.[21]

Discouraged reformers blamed Hayes for Conkling's victory. If Hayes's "hands were clean," said Horace White, Conkling would have been defeated. Edward L. Pierce from Massachusetts wrote: "The *natural* friends of the administration are lukewarm, and the defeat of Roosevelt has added discouragement to discontent. Some things have gone wrong in Civil Service." Even Curtis, despite his closeness to Hayes, wrote in *Harper's Weekly* that Conkling had defeated the administration "with weapons which its own inconsistency had furnished." "We are somewhat adrift," Henry Cabot Lodge complained, "as to what civil service reform means in the Presidential mind & the reform element is sadly dispirited."[22]

The reformers judged Hayes hastily and unfairly. Like subsequent historians and many of his contemporaries, Hayes utilized the metaphor of war in conceptualizing his struggle with Conkling. For Hayes, that imagery was a source of strength. A seasoned, determined campaigner, not given to quick decisions but unshakable once his mind was made up, Hayes was confident that he would win. He observed in his diary on 13 December: "In the language of the press 'Senator Conkling has won a great victory over the Administration.'. . . But the end is not yet. I am right, and shall not give up the contest."[23]

Hayes did not give up, but he realized that a fresh assault would fail, since "the friends of a real reform are a minority." He reassured Curtis of his "loyalty to the minority in this contest. Loss of confidence in those who lose a fight, or even a skirmish, is common, but I hope it will not be, in this case, permanent." Indeed Hayes was planning to counterattack with a special civil-service-reform message to Congress, based on the responses of cabinet members to fourteen questions prepared by Dorman B. Eaton, the unpaid head of the Civil Service Commission that had been created during the Grant years. In addition, Hayes asked Curtis for his ideas, received a detailed argument against the intervention of senators and representatives in the appointing process from Senator George F. Edmunds of Vermont, and collected evidence from his friend Collector William Henry Smith of Chicago to the effect that appraisers in the New York Customhouse regularly undervalued goods, giving New York merchants an advantage over importers in Chicago and other cities and cheating the federal government of tariff revenue.[24]

Hayes, however, did not risk a counterattack in early 1878. Although Smith's evidence confirmed Hayes's judgment that he should fire Arthur and Cornell, Hayes bided his time, and despite his preparations, he sent no special reform message to Congress. Apart from supporting Schurz in his attack on a corrupt ring in the Indian Bureau, Hayes shied away from reform and tried to restore party harmony. Senators who voted to sustain Hayes in his struggle with Conkling also favored compromise and conciliation. Senator Henry L. Dawes of

Massachusetts felt that "civil-service reform, holy and noble as it was, must be postponed in order to resist the Solid South and the silver movement, and restore Harmony in the Party." Hayes's January nominations did not include the New York offices. In addition to putting aside his struggle with Conkling, Hayes invited Blaine to dinner at the White House.[25]

Even though Hayes did not press for civil-service reform during the spring of 1878, there was little harmony with Republican political leaders. After going down to self-righteous defeat over the Bland-Allison Act, Hayes reflected that he was "not liked as a President by the politicians in office, in the press or in Congress." Nevertheless, he believed that his policies were right, that his appointments were good, and that the people would sustain him. There was no nepotism in executive appointments, he maintained, nor were federal officeholders participating in political caucuses or running elections. Although he turned to congressmen for advice, he had resisted their dictation of appointments, and his administration made no removals except for cause. For its first year in office, he believed its record on appointments and removals was the best of any administration since that of John Quincy Adams.

Hayes's appointments were unusually good. Perhaps his finest appointment was that of John Marshall Harlan, of Kentucky, to the seat vacated by David Davis on the Supreme Court, despite pressure for another Illinois man. Over the next thirty-four years, Harlan sustained Hayes's judgment by interpreting the Constitution to extend the power of the federal government, to uphold the civil rights of individuals, and to curtail the monopolistic power of giant corporations.[26]

Superb appointments did little, however, to curb the hostility of the political leaders in Congress and of the party press. Although independent newspapers and the religious press were generally favorable to Hayes, most party papers, whether Republican or Democratic, were not supportive. Whitelaw Reid, who had converted the crusading *New York Tribune* into an organ for James G. Blaine, believed in March 1878 that Hayes had surrendered his leadership to Schurz and that the administration was "hopelessly impracticable and inconsistent." Reid claimed to know of "no human being of either party who pretends that the Administration thus far has been a success."[27]

By late March, Republican Senator Timothy O. Howe of Wisconsin, who thought that he, rather than Harlan, should have been appointed to the Supreme Court, exploded with a virulent speech attacking the administration. Edwin L. Godkin of the Nation called the speech a "trial-balloon" sent up by spoilsmen to test public reaction. Blaine also joined Howe's attack, but the results were disappointing to the spoils-men. Flooded by complimentary letters, Schurz commented, "If such men as Howe and Blaine would only go on a little while longer, they would succeed in making the administration positively popular." Hav-ing learned their lesson, the spoilsmen began to show restraint. A Republican congressional caucus in early April did not adopt a resolu-tion to condemn Hayes's order forbidding "federal office holders from managing the party politics of the Country." That such a resolution was proposed and that such restraint was considered news illustrate how estranged many Republicans were from the administration.[28]

Hayes had embraced enough civil-service reform to alienate the spoilsmen but not enough to satisfy the reformers. Jacob Dolson Cox said that the president "had utterly failed to accomplish anything in the way of Civil Service reform—and that he had pursued no system that could be defended by any class of politicians." Wayne MacVeagh—a Philadelphia reformer, a member of the 1877 Louisiana commission, and later, Garfield's attorney general—wrote to fellow reformer Charles Eliot Norton that Hayes was "genuinely noble and true-hearted,—only slow and patient and half-blind. But why should we complain of him when Mr. Evarts saddens everybody but his enemies day by day. It is enough to make ones heart break when he reflects what possibility of great glory was before us and to what distant future it seems to have receded."

Glory for reformers receded further when the administration again interpreted Hayes's civil-service order. The portion that particularly troubled the Republican campaign managers, since Attorney General Devens had pointed out that it did not prohibit civil servants from campaigning, was the section prohibiting political assessments. These provided a vital source of revenue and were thought by party regulars to be essential to victory. A modification of Hayes's order seemed neces-sary. In the spring of 1878, Hayes carefully explained that he saw no objection to federal officers making political contributions and that he himself intended to contribute, but that any employee who refused to contribute would not be removed. He insisted to Curtis that "the order issued last June stands without alteration," but Curtis agreed with Cox that Hayes "has broken up one system without establishing another."[29]

It was obvious that the administration had retreated. By the end of May, the Republican Congressional Campaign Committee issued its usual circular to officeholders, stipulating the amount they were to contribute and assuring "those who happen to be in Federal employ that there will be no objection in any official quarter to such voluntary contribution." Although Schurz later drew up a circular, which Hayes adopted for executive departments, emphasizing that noncontributing clerks would retain their positions, it was generally conceded that only Interior Department employees would take the circular seriously.[30]

Reformers were further disturbed that spring by the Potter Committee, which, while it failed to undermine Hayes's title to the presidency, revealed that he had rewarded with patronage members of Louisiana's returning board. Ben Butler exposed "the bastard character of Mr. Hayes' pretended reform" by his cross-examination of witnesses before the Potter committee. He forced Gen. T. C. H. Smith, the Treasury Department's former appointments clerk, to admit that "he had never made, or observed, or even heard of, an appointment for other than political reason."[31]

The sniping by reformers and the shelling from congressmen did not shake Hayes's confidence. He was certain that his modest reform efforts, which outraged the spoilsmen and disappointed the reformers, were on a scale that could succeed and would improve the public service. He was certain that his attempt to end the usurpation of executive power by the Senate was correct. He was a moderate reformer whose principles had been shaped by a realistic appraisal of what was possible. He was patient, and as long as conditions improved, he was willing to wait generations for a complete reformation. He would experiment with civil-service reform in a few offices, but he did not insist that appointments in the Treasury Department, under a responsible spoilsman such as Sherman, be any less political than Gen. T. C. H. Smith said that they were. While there were advances and retreats, Hayes pressed toward his goals. "The progress is no doubt slow," he wrote to Curtis, "but there is progress."[32]

After Congress had adjourned, Hayes, on 11 July 1878, revived the spirits of reformers by suspending Collector Arthur and Naval Officer Cornell from the New York Customhouse. Celebrating the victory, reformers could not foresee that it would make Arthur president of the United States and Cornell governor of New York. Thurlow Weed, an astute and ancient New York wirepuller, warned Evarts, whom insiders held responsible for these moves, that in removing these men before a good reason for their dismissal could be given, he "was preparing crowns for his victims." Hayes replaced Arthur with Surveyor Edwin A. Merritt and Cornell with Deputy Naval Officer Silas W. Burt. "This action," Charles Eliot Norton rejoiced, "puts a new face on affairs."[33]

Many people failed to see reform (some even detected vengeance) in the New York changes. One reformer called them a foul blow at Conkling, a view that Curtis called "mere craziness." The New York daily press disapproved of Hayes's action, and Curtis hoped that Hayes would be neither "amazed nor disheartened by the outcry." Merritt's appointment, however, did lend credence to the cynical charge that the administration was planning to destroy Conkling's power by reorganizing the New York Republican party around the spoils-minded followers of his predecessor, Reuben E. Fenton. In fact, Evarts frankly avowed to Hayes that "these changes are both useful to the public service and to the unity of the party." Evarts went on to accuse "the political management now displeasured" with bringing the party "to its low estate in New York" and with exposing "the supremacy of the Republican principles in the Government" to the perils of the Democrats. Thinking primarily in political terms, Evarts recognized that the new collector would be the political manager of the New York Republican party.

Hayes's appointment to fill Merritt's old place seemed to confirm that the president had removed Arthur and Cornell in order to build an administration machine. Following Evarts's counsel to keep politicians *"in expectancy,* rather than in spleen,'' Hayes at first did nothing. Then, although Curtis again urged that Deputy Surveyor Benedict be promoted to the position that Merritt had vacated, Hayes appointed Gen. Charles K. Graham. He was a Union veteran, a civil engineer, and a Fenton Republican who had no connections with either the customs service or reform.

Despite his disappointment, Curtis continued to suggest that worthy subordinates be promoted in the customhouse. He warned Hayes "that certain appointments, such as I have seen mentioned as probable, would be so apparently conclusive proof that the change is merely of one faction for another, that the result could only be disastrous." After speaking highly of Burt's appointment, Curtis asked why the same promotion policy could not be followed in naming a new appraiser. "Why name a politician from the outside? . . . The selection of gentlemen, for instance, known only as 'Fenton politicians' would be fatal to all possibility of explanation and defense."[34]

Hayes was rankled by the reform outcry that followed each of his appointments. He had previously written to Curtis: "We have only a per cent on our side—not enough to quarrel, or sulk about things. Let us get together. The harshest blows many crotchety reformers strike are against each other. Many of the blows are in sheer ignorance of facts." Responding to the charge of appointing a "Fenton politician," Hayes agreed that one set of party workers should not replace another but parried that he did not wish to "proscribe people who have been active in politics."

Hayes, for example, would keep in office Thomas L. James, New York City's Conklingite postmaster. Despite his friendship with Conkling, James was supported by reformers and businessmen for his efficient management of the post office. They agreed with Hayes that James was "a capital officer" and should not "be set aside merely for his opinions." James had outlined the reforms that he had instituted in the New York Post Office, and Curtis forwarded them to Hayes. James removed officers only for cause, he usually appointed Republicans, but he always insisted on fitness and integrity. He promoted on the basis of competitive examinations, he protected employees who did not pay political assessments, and he believed that he and his workers could do more for their party by giving their city "a good and efficient postal service than by controlling primaries and dictating nominations."[35]

With Merritt as acting collector, pending his confirmation, the New York Customhouse remained in politics. New York Congressman Anson G. McCook wrote to John Sherman after the 1878 election requesting the permanent suspension of an order to cut down customhouse personnel. Promulgated before the election, the order had been suspended during October and November. McCook complained that it would "seriously affect several of my best friends, who stood by me in the late campaign in which I was elected by over 5,000 majority." Sherman forwarded the letter to Hayes, commenting that it "presents fairly the claim of our Friend McCook that we must govern the New York Customs House so as to keep in those who help him whether their services are needed or not." Collector Merritt, Sherman added, "recommends the restorations proposed." Before closing, Sherman stated to the president, "I don't want to embarrass you with this but send it for your information."

William Henry Smith, the Chicago collector, was also in politics but not to the extent that he wished. He complained to Hayes that his celebrated civil-service order hampered efforts to strengthen the administration, because it prevented Smith from attending party conventions. The Illinois State Republican Convention of June 1878 had resulted in "a drawn battle between the friends of the Administration and its opponents. . . . Heretofore such gatherings have had a good many agents of the Executive, whereas this was without them and being deprived of them the platform is without the customary personal laudation of the President." Resolutions endorsing Hayes "in handsome and strong language" were prepared, but Smith claimed, "as Order No. 1 excluded me, there was no one sufficiently aggressive to carry them through."[36]

While Hayes condemned overt political activities by officeholders, he accepted less conspicuous politicking. Naval Officer Cornell's position on the Republican National Committee was unacceptable, while

Postmaster James's support for Arthur, Cornell, and Conkling was acceptable as long as James did not use his office against the administration. Hayes did not want officeholders to pack conventions or to finance campaigns unwillingly, but he did not object if they contributed their time and money voluntarily to elect their patrons. Hayes appointed his supporters to office, but he warned them not to remove subordinates except for "undoubted reasons," and he neither wished to tap their pay nor to dragoon them into electioneering. He wanted his officials "not to be chargeable with the sins we condemn."

Hayes was both a reformer and a practical politician. His letters to George William Curtis during the 1878 campaign emphasize his commitment to reform and his toleration of political dissent among efficient civil servants, while his correspondence with Evarts, Key, and William Henry Smith reveal a willingness to utilize appointments to secure support for the administration. Hayes's support of reform, combined with a recognition of the demands of practical politics, was reflected in his appointments to the New York Customhouse. Burt, whose appointment gratified reformers, would make the naval office politically neutral, while Collector Merritt and Surveyor Graham would strive to strengthen the administration, or the Evarts elements, in the New York Republican party.

Hayes and his friends used the post offices to build up their party. Through Webb Hayes, Collector Smith of Chicago posted the president on efforts to renominate "the only one of the three Congressmen from this section who stood by the Administration" and emphatically named the right man for the South Evanston post office. Hayes appointed postmasters as part of his program to attract southern Democrats to the Republican party. When Postmaster General Key had to urge Col. D. G. Potts, the postmaster of Petersburg, Virginia, to support the Republican incumbent for Congress, it was obvious that Hayes's southern strategy was not working and that the administration expected the postmasters whom it had appointed to support its candidates.[37]

As expected, when the Senate reconvened for its lame-duck session in December, Conkling opposed the confirmation of Merritt, Burt, and Graham. Hayes believed that while most senators would prefer to confirm, many would oppose it because of "Senatorial courtesy, the Senatorial prerogative, and the fear of Conkling's vengeance." But no matter what the Senate did, Hayes resolved, "In no event will the old incumbents be allowed to return to their former places, if I have power to prevent it, and as to that I am not in doubt."[38]

Conkling appeared to be as powerful as ever. In January 1879 the Republican caucus in the New York legislature nominated him for a third senatorial term. When his election by the Republican majority followed, the Speaker of the assembly lauded Conkling as the peer of Webster, Clay, and Calhoun. The *Nation* commented that Hayes supporters could "hardly have supposed that it was for this they 'harmonized' last summer." Their support of the New York Republican ticket had amounted to support for Conkling. On 15 January 1879, Sherman's charges of corruption against Arthur and Cornell, which were made in an executive session of the Senate, were, at Conkling's behest, kept secret; and on 24 January, Conkling's Commerce Committee advised the Senate to reject the Merritt, Burt, and Graham nominations.

Despite New York's endorsement of Conkling and despite the Commerce Committee's action, Hayes took the initiative. He submitted a letter to the Senate, stating the reasons for his New York appointments. Hayes maintained that the New York Customhouse, which collected two-thirds of the nation's customs revenue, was of national rather than local significance; yet Arthur and Cornell had "made the custom-house a center of partisan political management. The custom-house should be a business office. It should be conducted on business principles." Hayes had no hope that Arthur and Cornell would manage the customhouse similarly to the way that James administered the New York Post Office. They believed that if they were compelled to take the New York Customhouse out of politics, they would be forced, in Cornell's words, "to surrender their personal and political rights."[39]

On 3 February 1879 the administration finally defeated Conkling. The Senate confirmed the appointments of Merritt, Burt, and Graham. Most Republicans sided with Conkling, but, thanks to Sherman's "extraordinary personal efforts," which included pursuing senators to their lodgings, a minority combined with southern Democrats to support the administration. Southern Democrats had not been bitten by the reform bug, nor were they siding with Hayes primarily because of his southern policy. They gave him their support chiefly to keep alive the divisive struggle among the Republicans.

Conkling's clever defense of his men left the reformers shaken and, according to the *New York Times*, "created a profound sensation." Adopting the lofty reform "principle that efficiency and fidelity . . . constitute the sole title to retention in the public service," Conkling asserted that Arthur and Cornell had been efficient and faithful, while the Hayes administration had violated the principles of civil-service reform. Conkling presented a package of letters written to Arthur by Hayes and members of his cabinet, pushing their candidates for positions in the customhouse. For "manifest reasons," a son of Supreme Court Justice Joseph P. Bradley, who had cast the deciding vote on the electoral commission that had elected Hayes, was provided for in the New York Customhouse, and J. Q. Howard, the author of a Hayes campaign biography, was forced upon Arthur as a deputy collector. Conkling denounced, "as undignified, unprincipled, and in every way unworthy of a cabinet officer," Sherman's personal appeals to senators and the seventeen recent customhouse appointments that Sherman had made to secure the votes of these senators.

Already convinced that Hayes was being inconsistent, the *New York Times* took a dim view of the change: "The public service will hardly be elevated by the removal of one officer for being too much a politician to make way for another who has never been anything but a politician." The reformers, however, while they were pained by Conkling's revelations, regarded his defeat as a "great gain for the country—so great," the *Nation* added, "that we can well afford to disregard the motives of the disputants."[40]

Conkling's self-righteous indignation was absurd. Hayes had never pretended to be above recommending his political supporters for offices that they were qualified to fill, and in truth, after he had been burned, he had become less inclined to give offices as rewards. Even when Hayes did recommend friends, his reluctance to fire able civil servants to make way for them marks him as the least partisan president between John Quincy Adams and Theodore Roosevelt.[41]

Despite whatever favors Hayes and his cabinet may have requested in the past, Hayes had decided to make the New York Customhouse a showcase for reform. He instructed Merritt:

> My desire is that your office shall be conducted on strictly business principles. . . . In making appointments and removals of subordinates you should be perfectly independent of mere influence. Neither my recommendation, nor Secretary Sherman's, nor that of any member of Congress, or other influential persons should be specially regarded. . . . Let no man be put out merely because he is Mr. Arthur's friend, and no man put in merely because he is our friend.

Hayes also directed Naval Officer Burt, Collector Merritt, and Surveyor Graham to devise regulations that would be based on the Grant Civil Service Commission rules, with which Burt had experience.

Publication of Hayes's letter to Merritt brought praise from reformers, and this praise grew louder when the new rules were published.

These rules applied to all New York Customhouse and subtreasury appointees with the exception of those in a few offices of special trust. Appointments were made from the three candidates who had scored highest on a competitive examination, administered by one of three boards of examiners. New appointees could enter only at the lowest grade; higher vacancies were to be filled by promotions within the customhouse.[42]

Naval Officer Silas W. Burt, an early and ardent civil-service reformer, was the dynamic force behind the rules of the New York Customhouse. Although Collector Merritt was not opposed to competitive examinations, he believed that the experiment would be short-lived, and he asked Burt to enforce the rules. "If you can revive this corpse you are entitled to all the glory," Merritt assured Burt. It was Burt's idea to invite well-known citizens, particularly editors, to observe the examinations. Twelve citizens were invited to each examination, and Curtis attended them all to explain the proceedings. "The editors who attended," Burt later recalled, "were specially interested and their impressions, always favorable, were reflected in their papers." Editors who favored the spoils system invariably declined the invitations.[43]

Even though Merritt was not a convert to reform, the reformers acknowledged his success in administering the customhouse. The highly critical *New York Times* admitted in July that "after four months' experience, it is simple justice to say that the reform has been applied there in good faith, and with a degree of pertinacity, a patient attempt to make it successful, and an enlightened appreciation of its nature and its scope, which have been an agreeable disappointment to the doubt-ers."[44]

With reform working well in New York, Hayes in April 1879 ordered that the rules and regulations governing appointments and promotions in both the New York Post Office and the Customhouse be sent for consideration to postmasters and collectors in the nation's major offices. Wishing to be flexible, Hayes had his private secretary, William K. Rogers, add: "Any alteration or addition that you may deem advisable will be favorably considered."

Throughout the remainder of 1879, Sherman, Key, and Hayes received the reactions of postmasters and collectors to the New York rules. Hayes was behind this thrust for reform. During his term, he alone was responsible for the limited reform that was accomplished in federal offices outside of Washington. The heads and virtually all the employees of these offices were active in politics and were neither ready nor eager to change the habits of a lifetime. Nor were they ready to throw over, at the behest of a lame-duck administration, a spoils tradition that had been entrenched for half a century.

D. V. Bell, the collector of customs at Detroit, insisted on 5 May that the New York rules, which were designed for a huge operation, would be cumbersome, inconvenient, and disadvantageous in his small office. Bell recommended that no rules be adopted for his district. But when he was told that the Treasury Department wanted the rules carried into effect, he complied, sending the names of his examiners and his modified regulations. Given his attitude toward the competitive system, Bell's assurances that the rules would "be observed as closely as is practicable in this District" did not augur well for reform in Detroit. In Chicago, Collector William Henry Smith, Hayes's personal friend, promised that the New York rules would be examined and applied if "practicable," but he revealed his true attitude by losing his copy of the rules and by not taking action until after the fall elections.[45]

Other responses were more positive. Postmaster E. S. Tobey of Boston approved of the New York rules in general, but he suggested some changes tailored to his office, as did John Tyler, the collector of customs at Buffalo. Tyler's correspondence with the Treasury Department, as well as that of Collectors Bell and Smith, illustrates that the Hayes administration wanted the New York rules to be seriously considered. George N. Lamphere, chief of the Appointments Division in Sherman's office, did not take at face value Tyler's assertion that his proposed regulations in regard to appointments and promotions were in the spirit of civil-service reform. Lamphere ordered a comparison made which showed that Tyler had made no material changes. Lamphere, whom Sherman had promoted from assistant chief to chief of his division, was himself an example of civil-service-reform principles at work.

During the spring of 1879 the administration made some progress toward instituting reform in its major field offices. In June, Tyler nominated as inspector of customs at Buffalo the individual who stood first in a competitive examination of twenty candidates, and in New York, Merritt, after having been urged by Curtis, also nominated the man at the top of the list. The real challenge to reform, however, would come with the fall elections.[46]

As these elections approached, politicians tried to enlist the civil service in the campaigns, contrary to Hayes's desire. For those whose political lives were at stake, the commitment, if any, to a nonpartisan civil service evaporated. Party organizations depended on the public service for electioneering personnel. Typically, the state political boss was a senator in Washington, whose power depended on his political machine at home. The boss's lieutenants, who operated the machine, were the prominent collectors and postmasters, while their political minions were minor postmasters, marshals, weighers, and gaugers.

With his earlier order that civil servants refrain from political activities and with his introduction of the New York rules into the field service, Hayes took the first steps to convert a partisan civil service into a nonpolitical bureaucracy. Without congressional legislation, however, it was impossible for him to permanently reform the civil service. Reforming the bureaucracy was merely a policy of an administration that had less than two years remaining, and the leading candidates to succeed Hayes, namely Grant, Blaine, and Sherman, would mobilize the civil service for their own advantage.

During the summer of 1879 the lack of enthusiasm for reform became apparent. Even in the New York Customhouse, the administration's showcase, reform could not be taken for granted. On one occasion, when Merritt followed the advice of George William Curtis and appointed a candidate from among those who had placed highest on a competitive examination, he "chafed . . . under the apparent officiousness of one who is not in any official position." Having conceded a position to the reformers, Merritt proceeded to ignore the results of an examination and nominated as inspector W. H. Grace, who, Curtis complained to Hayes, "was convicted a year or two ago, of a flagrant assault upon Surveyor Sharpe." Sherman characteristically confirmed the nomination, but with Merritt away, the acting collector declined to administer the oath of office to Grace, since the appointment violated the rules.

"There could be no graver breach of good faith," wrote a distraught Curtis, "and as the whole value of the present effort is in its honesty, if such a thing as this is permitted, I should" advise that the scheme be abandoned, with "a frank declaration that, under existing circumstances, it is impracticable. The Collector certainly ought to be able to see that such a system as he has pledged himself to cannot be, at the same time observed and disregarded." Although Hayes could tolerate a less-than-ideal practice of civil-service reform elsewhere, he immediately told Sherman: "You know my earnest desire to keep the New York office above all criticism. Please deal judiciously and kindly, but with the utmost firmness in this and all such matters."[47]

There were compelling reasons why Hayes and everyone else were focusing their attention on New York. It was the seat of Roscoe Conkling, the most conspicuous spoilsman; it was the site of the most serious reform efforts; and it was the home of George William Curtis, the most indefatigable civil-service reformer. New York would also elect a governor in the fall of 1879. The Republicans would select a nominee for that post in early September, and neither the supporters of Conkling nor those of the administration, with the exception of reformers such as Curtis and Schurz, were averse to using the civil service to achieve victory. By late August the best candidate from the administration's standpoint was Sherman S. Rogers of Buffalo, while Conkling's man was Alonzo Cornell, whom Hayes had recently dismissed from the New York Customhouse. If Cornell were nominated, it was widely perceived that Conkling would be vindicated and Hayes would be rejected by the New York Republicans.

In their anxiety to defeat Conkling, the administration Republicans pressed Hayes to replace John Tyler at Buffalo (who, though he was friendly to Conkling, was one of the few collectors to have nominated an appointee on the basis of a competitive examination) with someone whom they believed would work for Rogers's victory over Cornell. In addition, Collector Merritt of New York told Hayes that if Hayes "would permit him to take some part [in the upcoming convention]—only the turning of his hand—he could secure the defeat of Cornell." Hayes refused to unleash Merritt or to replace Tyler, and he did not fire Conkling's lieutenant, Lewis F. Payne, a marshal who had flagrantly managed political conventions in defiance of Hayes's order. Hayes reasoned that the administration's "correct line of action" was to set an example for "the political conduct of Office holders." He told Curtis: "We have simply let New York politics alone. Of course we are deeply interested in the result, but we have not interfered to control it."

Dominated by officeholders who were loyal to Conkling, the 1879 New York State Republican Convention at Saratoga nominated Cornell for governor. Practical politicians in the administration blamed the outcome on civil-service reform. "With hands tied and the enemy free," William Henry Smith concluded, "defeat is inevitable." Reformers, however, drew the opposite conclusion. Angered and frustrated, Curtis forcefully told Hayes that his "correct line of action" had been a mistake. "The Convention was carried against us by deliberate disregard of your order. The adverse majority was Seven. The Erie and St. Lawrence delegations together number thirty, and both were 'fired' by office-holders" from Buffalo and Ogdensburg. "Should this conduct be disregarded by the Executive, the same means will secure the State Presidential Convention next year. The position of the Administration and its character require the summary removal of such offenders. No 'cause' can be more stringent than 'packing' caucuses and conventions.''

The introduction of reform at the New York Customhouse and Post Office and a reform-minded collector at Buffalo did not keep those offices out of politics. Curtis emphasized that heads of offices not only should obey the civil-service order but also should believe in its wisdom and should make their subordinates obey it. Curtis insisted: ''If Mr. Burt was the head of the whole Custom House, for instance, every subordinate would know that he erred at his peril. . . . I mean no reflection upon General Merritt. But as you also know, he acquiesces where Mr. Burt believes.'' And at the post office it was not enough for James to ''appoint only upon merit.'' He should also insist that officers who had been appointed under the spoils system conform to the new system, for ''If they find that they can sin with impunity they will sin eagerly.'' At Buffalo, ''if Mr. Tyler is content to sit in his office and be ignorant of what is done by his subordinates in this way and 'out of office hours' I should replace him with a Collector who would take care that they all did as he did.''[48]

The ensuing New York campaign embarrassed Hayes. Not only was Cornell running for governor, but Arthur was managing his campaign. Republican reformers, who were among Hayes's staunchest supporters, were planning to scratch Cornell's name from the Republican ballot and either to leave the space blank or to write in the Democratic nominee and incumbent, Governor Lucius Robinson. While independent Republicans could not stomach Cornell, Tammany Hall Democrats refused to support Robinson, a Tilden protégé; instead, they ran ''Honest'' John Kelly for governor. The administration was in a ludicrous position. As head of his party, Hayes could not and would not support a Democrat, whether a Tilden or a Tammany man; but having earlier declared Cornell unfit to serve in the New York Customhouse, Hayes could not consistently support him for governor.

Party loyalty and inconsistency triumphed, and the administration supported Conkling's nominee. Sherman, who was angling for the 1880 presidential nomination, was eager to place others in his debt, so despite his earlier attacks on Cornell, Sherman journeyed to New York to campaign for him. Even Hayes asked Schurz to permit Interior Department clerks to return to New York to vote. With administration support and a split Democratic ticket, Cornell was elected governor, despite the defection of reformers.[49]

The administration's course exasperated the reformers, but the reformers exasperated Hayes. ''The great embarrassment in dealing with my 'friends' (not you),'' Hayes wrote to reformer Wayne Mac-

Veagh, who was also spoilsman Simon Cameron's son-in-law, "is they are without experience in practical affairs—have never been responsible for results—are without training in actual government, or law making—are some hot and soon cold. You can't fight but one battle at a time—*two* at the most. This they don't know." Reformers did know that the "reform" administration's behavior in the New York election gave civil-service reform the "air of humbug" and destroyed the hope of further reform under it. Edward Cary, the editor of the *New York Times*, wrote: "I have little or no patience with Mr. Hayes. He is a victim of 'goody' rather than good intentions & his contributions to the pavement of the road to the infernal regions are vast & various."[50]

Despite his exasperation with reformers, Hayes devoted the largest section of his 1879 annual message to civil-service reform. At Hayes's request, Dorman B. Eaton, the chairman of the moribund Civil Service Commission, made a study of the British civil service and found that open competitive examinations, supervised by a commission, were used with advantage for the appointment of almost every subordinate public officer in Britain and India. Hayes submitted Eaton's study to Congress and asked Congress to decide whether British reform measures were adaptable "to our institutions and social life."

Having commended Eaton's study, Hayes analyzed the United States civil service. His experience as president had deepened his awareness of the evils of a partisan system of appointments. He was referring, not to policy-making positions, but to subordinate civil servants, whose duties were the same no matter which party triumphed at the polls. The power to appoint, he explained, "is not a perquisite, which may be used to aid a friend or reward a partisan, but is a trust to be exercised in the public interest." Any bestowal of offices "upon any theory which disregards personal merit is an act of injustice to the citizen," Hayes continued, as well as a breach of trust by the appointing power. While recognizing that a pure and efficient civil service was largely the president's responsibility, he insisted "that nothing adequate can be accomplished without co-operation on the part of Congress and considerate and intelligent support among the people."

Hayes reported that appointments based on competitive examinations in the Washington executive departments—especially in Schurz's Interior Department—and in a number of post offices and customhouses, most notably in New York City, were "salutary in a marked degree." He felt certain that a general and permanent application of these rules would benefit governmental service, and to implement this work he again requested an appropriation for the Civil Service Commission. An active commission, backed by Congress, could also perpetuate

his ban on political assessments and political activities by officeholders.[51]

Although legislation was needed to make reform stick, the problem,
Hayes acknowledged to Curtis, was that in Congress there were "no
champions of Civil Service reform." Those who "would *float* or *lean* that
way" needed "some earnest man to propose the bills, to make the
argument, and champion the cause as a hobby." Hayes still believed
that the first step should be "to regulate by law the conduct of members
of Congress with respect to what is called, and, unhappily, properly
called, patronage." Curtis agreed that "patronage and Congressional
interference" should be restricted, and he cheered Hayes with word
that Eaton's book on the British civil service, which Harper and Brothers
had just published, was arousing great interest, receiving elaborate
notices, and winning an excellent reception.[52]

Realizing the value of publicity and aware that he had struck a
telling blow for civil-service reform in New York, Hayes asked Eaton to
report on open competitive examinations for appointments and promotions in the New York Customhouse and Post Office. Eaton reported in
February 1881 that never before had so much time been given to proper
work and so little to partisan politics. Even though political activity had
not been entirely eliminated, economy, efficiency, and high morale
characterized the service in New York. Eaton's report demonstrated not
only that civil-service reform would eradicate political evils but also that
it was a workable and necessary bureaucratic innovation.[53]

7

★ ★ ★ ★ ★

THE NATIVE AMERICANS

Ten days after Hayes was nominated for president, the Sioux Nation annihilated George A. Custer and his command, and soon after Hayes occupied the White House, the Nez Perce War occurred. Hayes and Schurz, however, both held enlightened, although paternalistic, views on relations with Native Americans. They hoped that through education, especially vocational training, Native Americans would join the nation's producers by becoming farmers, herders, teamsters, and laborers; would own property; would become citizens, rather than wards of the state; and would participate fully in the political process. There was, however, a vast distance between the wishes of Hayes and Schurz and the realities of contacts between the white and the red inhabitants of the West. Native Americans were content with their own cultures, white settlers either coveted or occupied the lands of Native Americans, and the federal government sent them mixed signals through corrupt agents in the Indian Bureau and through the officers and men of the United States Army.

Indian policy and its administration had long troubled the federal government. Although many a westerner in 1877 thought of Native Americans as wild beasts and advocated that they be annihilated, the Grant administration instituted a "peace policy" that compelled Native Americans to settle on reservations, where federal agents administered governmental aid to them, while teaching them to become self-sufficient, educated Christian citizens. The army was responsible for controlling Native Americans who either had no treaties with the United States or were not on reservations—an estimated fifty-five thousand in 1872, but their number dwindled rapidly as transcontinental railroads penetrated the West. The army also dealt with serious Indian problems, whether they occurred on or off reservations. Since Congress refused to build new army posts at railroad junctions, the troops remained disadvantageously deployed in small detachments along old wagon roads.

Both the War Department and the Interior Department wanted to control the Office of Indian Affairs, which had been taken from the War Department and given to the Interior Department in 1849. In 1876, 1878, and 1880, congressional committees recommended that Indian affairs be returned to the War Department. But with the Hayes administration in general and Schurz in particular resisting this transfer, the drive lost momentum. Some of those who opposed the change feared that a return to War Department control would bring back the sporadic annihilation of Native Americans, while others claimed that soldiers were a disreputable lot and would debauch the Native Americans.[1]

Although the Interior Department did not debauch Native Americans, it did defraud them. The argument for turning Indian affairs back to the War Department was fueled in part by the corruption that honeycombed the Indian service. To counteract fraud, a number of expedients were adopted during Grant's administration. All contracts to provide services for Native Americans had to be approved both by the commissioner of Indian affairs and by the secretary of the interior. Inspectors, who were appointed for four-year terms by the president with the advice and consent of the Senate, were to visit each Indian superintendency and agency twice a year to inspect all business transactions. The Board of Indian Commissioners, which was composed of eight unpaid citizens appointed by the president, decided, along with the secretary of the interior, on how the annual appropriations for Indians would be spent; its members also visited reservations and investigated contracts, expenditures, and accounts. Rather than allowing western politicians to nominate Indian agents, as had his predecessors, Grant relied on major religious denominations (a practice that probably was unconstitutional and that discriminated against Roman Catholics). These innovations, which Hayes continued, resulted in fewer frauds and better agents but did not prevent an unjust, tragic war.[2]

The Nez Perce War, which broke out in June 1877, originated in a classic fashion. The ancient home of the bands that constituted the tribe was in the mountainous region surrounding the point at which Oregon, Washington, and Idaho meet. The Nez Perces deified their ancestral land—"the Earth is my mother"—and to exchange it for other land was like renouncing their religion. In 1855 the United States government had guaranteed this area to the Nez Perces, but in 1860, white intruders discovered gold in the heart of the region. Those who rushed to mine the gold and stayed to raise cattle and crops paid no heed to the fact that they were trespassers. Abetting the covetous settlers, Indian agents in 1863 bribed and coerced the chiefs of some Nez Perce bands to agree to a treaty that would remove the Nez Perces to a reservation at Lapwai, Idaho. Other Nez Perce bands did not agree, however, and remained on their land. One of these bands, which was led by Chief Joseph, stayed in the Wallowa Valley of northeastern Oregon and tried to live peaceably with its white neighbors. Many white settlers were fond of Joseph, a feeling that he reciprocated, but others were contemptuous of Indian rights and Indian lives and wanted to force the nontreaty Nez Perces onto the Lapwai Reservation.[3]

The Grant administration had vacillated and exacerbated matters. On 16 June 1873, Grant had pleased Joseph by ordering that his band could have part of the Wallowa Valley for a reservation, but a vigorous protest by white settlers, the governor, and the congressional delegation of Oregon had made Grant waver. After the Indian Bureau had reexamined the case, Grant, on 10 June 1875, rescinded his earlier order and, on 6 January 1877, decided that all Nez Perces were bound by the 1863 treaty and must move to the Lapwai Reservation.

The government's attitude had frustrated Joseph, who said: "I have been talking to the whites many years about the land in question, and it is strange they cannot understand me. The country they claim belonged to my father, and when he died it was given to me and my people, and I will not leave it until I am compelled to." Apparently, neither Hayes nor Schurz, when they took office in March, reconsidered the Indian Bureau's policy toward the nontreaty Nez Perces. While Schurz was learning the ropes of his new job, he did not interfere with the implementation of decisions made by the previous administration. Joseph and his fellow nontreaty Nez Perce chiefs, Looking Glass and White Bird, still hoped to reason with the Indian Bureau and the United States Army, but at a council with Gen. Oliver Otis Howard there was no reasoning. Haughty and adamant, Howard insisted on 14 May that if the Nez Perces did not move in thirty days, they would be forced off their ancestral land. Faced with the option of moving or fighting, Joseph and other nontreaty Nez Perce chiefs, with heavy hearts, agreed to move.[4]

These older, experienced men knew that they could not win a war against the United States Army, but their young braves were ready to fight to keep their homeland. The Nez Perces were aggrieved, not only by the imminent loss of their land but also by unpunished and unavenged murders of their people by white settlers. Nevertheless, Joseph and his younger brother Ollokot counseled peace and acceptance, and his band started to round up its thousands of cattle and horses, which were scattered throughout the Wallowa Valley, a six-months' job for which they had only thirty days. Abandoning some of their livestock to the settlers, Joseph's band crossed the Snake River into Idaho, losing many cattle, horses, and possessions in the swollen river. They pushed on to the Salmon River, where on 2 June they camped a few miles from the reservation with the other nontreaty Nez Perces, hoping to enjoy their last two weeks of freedom.

The camp was smoldering with resentment, and a young brave from White Bird's band, who had suffered taunts for two years, decided to avenge his father's murder. Disregarding his father's dying wish that his son not seek revenge, the brave set off with two friends. Unable to find the killer, on 13 June, they murdered four whites who were known for their hostility to Nez Perces. Moved by these killings, seventeen warriors—all but one of them from White Bird's band—joined the avenging braves on a two-day rampage, killing fourteen or fifteen settlers along the Salmon River. Although the settlers and Howard believed that Joseph was responsible for these atrocities, Joseph and Ollokot had been away on a hunting trip. When they returned, they tried to convince the nontreaty Nez Perces to remain in camp, wait for the army, explain what had happened, and thus save all but the guilty from punishment.

When Joseph's counsel was not heeded, he and his brother, along with their people, joined White Bird's band, which was already on the move. The addition of the Wallowa band strengthened those in flight, but Joseph still hoped that Howard would send emissaries and that a war would be averted. Joseph and White Bird moved their bands—of one hundred fifty men and a greater number of women and children—to a defensible position on White Bird Creek and awaited the army. Unfortunately, the Army's Capt. David Perry did not send any emissaries, did not seek any explanations, and did not ask the Nez Perces to give up the murderers before he attacked at dawn on 17 June 1877. Facing him were sixty or seventy Nez Perces, armed with bows and arrows, shotguns, old muskets, and a few modern rifles; the remaining men were too old, too sick, too afraid, or too drunk to fight. As Perry's ninety-nine-troop cavalry, supported by eleven citizen volunteers, swept down White Bird Canyon, one of the civilians fired at six Indians, carrying a white flag and hoping to arrange a peaceful parlay. The shot missed, but an elderly Nez Perce returned the fire, killing one of Perry's two buglers. A war had begun.

The Battle of White Bird was a disaster for Perry, and the war was a tragedy for the Nez Perces and for the United States. Fighting without a plan, the Native Americans made the most of Perry's overconfidence and soon divided his command into small details that were lucky if they escaped up the canyon. The out-manned and outgunned Nez Perces killed thirty-four of Perry's command and captured sixty-three rifles and numerous pistols, while only three of their warriors were wounded. The Nez Perce victory sent shock waves throughout the Pacific Northwest.

Howard called for reinforcements and then moved against Joseph at White Bird Canyon, but Joseph withdrew to a new position, across the Salmon River. The remarkable leadership of Joseph impressed Howard: "No general could have chosen a safer position, or one that would be more likely to puzzle and obstruct a pursuing foe." Howard's professional admiration for his adversary, which was publicized by the press, led to the erroneous portrayal of Joseph as an "Indian Napoleon." Admiration aside, Howard relentlessly pursued the Nez Perces, who were encumbered by their old and infirm, by women and children, and by their possessions and livestock, including about twenty-five to thirty-five hundred horses.[5]

A blunder by Howard had provided reinforcements for the fleeing Nez Perces. To prevent Looking Glass and his band from joining Joseph, Howard ordered Capt. Stephen C. Whipple and two cavalry companies armed with Gatling guns to arrest them. On the way to Looking Glass's village, Whipple picked up twenty civilian volunteers. Although Looking Glass and his band were nontreaty Nez Perces, they were on the reservation and had no intention of joining in the war. Their village was a prosperous settlement that had gardens and pastures. Whipple arrived early on Sunday morning, 1 July, and he demanded to see Looking Glass. But before Looking Glass could emerge from his tipi, a trigger-happy volunteer shot a Nez Perce, others joined in the firing, and the band of about forty braves and one hundred twenty women and children fled into the hills. Frustrated that they had allowed their quarry to escape, Whipple and his men burned the tipis, destroyed the crops, and stole the cattle and more than seven hundred horses. Whipple's actions infuriated Looking Glass and plunged him into a war that he had tried to avoid.

By early July, the Nez Perces were outfighting and, despite encumbrances, outmaneuvering the United States Army. According to the

Associated Press, Hayes's cabinet considered removing Howard, but because he won a victory at Clearwater, Idaho, on 11 to 12 July, he retained his command, only to blunder again. Not pressing his advantage, he allowed the Nez Perces, who had fled in confusion, to regroup and retreat in an orderly fashion.

Joseph was not another Napoleon in either a political or a military sense. While he led his band, he in no way ruled the Nez Perces; each band looked to its own chief, and each brave was individualistic and undisciplined. Pressure from Howard had forced the Nez Perces to cooperate with one another. While respected in war councils, Joseph had never been a war chief, and his opinion carried less weight than that of experienced war leaders, such as Ollokot and Looking Glass. Joseph's challenging task on the Nez Perces' long retreat was caring for the women, children, and old men. The outside world also credited Joseph with having restrained the Nez Perce warriors, who did not harm women or noncombatants and did not scalp or mutilate the bodies of their enemies. The Nez Perces' conduct, Alvin M. Josephy writes, "stemmed from their own group notions of right and wrong." From the time seventy-two years earlier when they had welcomed and fed the starving members of the Lewis and Clark expedition, they had befriended white Americans.[6]

Against Joseph's wishes, the Nez Perces agreed with Looking Glass and sought safety among the Crows in Montana. If that should fail, they planned to join Sitting Bull in the Old Woman's Country—Queen Victoria's Canada. Still hoping that his band might return to his beloved Wallowa Valley, Joseph wished to remain close to it, but he and his brother reluctantly accepted the leadership of Looking Glass. On 16 July, under Looking Glass's command, the "patriot" Nez Perces (200 men and 550 women and children), driving pack animals and a herd of more than two thousand horses, started toward Lolo Pass and moved through the Bitterroot Range into Montana. From there, they retreated south into southern Idaho, crossing the Continental Divide two times, then turned east again across the divide into Montana and Wyoming through Yellowstone Park, and then north into Montana across the Yellowstone River near Billings, past Lewistown, across the Missouri River, and past Bear Paw Mountain. There, near Canada and led by Joseph, they were cornered in October by four hundred men under Col. Nelson A. Miles.

On their 1,700-mile retreat, the Nez Perces were encumbered by their noncombatants and by their possessions. Although they proved again that Native Americans were better fighters than regular soldiers, the army was disciplined, coordinated, unencumbered, and well supplied with weapons and ammunition, food, and clothing. It could carry on a war in winter; the Nez Perces could not. The Nez Perces alarmed Governor Benjamin F. Potts of Montana, who telegraphed for the authority to raise five hundred volunteers; but the Hayes administration, having had enough of volunteers, assured him that the army did not need his help. The Nez Perce War, however, was not the primary concern of either the army or the administration during the summer of the Great Strike.[7]

Hayes, who wanted to be just, apparently did not understand that the government was illegally forcing the nontreaty Nez Perces off their land. He noted for Schurz that the Indians should lay down their arms, leave their lands, go to the reservation, "take *separate* titles" to land, and "give up the murderers." He thought that "a commission" should determine their guilt or innocence and that those who were found guilty should "be dealt with according to the law applicable to white men." Before the Battle of White Bird, Perry could have secured these objectives, if he had only asked.[8]

During their retreat, the Nez Perces staved off the pursuing detachments until Miles caught them at Bear Paw. After a five-day battle in which both sides suffered heavy losses, Howard reinforced Miles, and Joseph surrendered with the understanding, agreed to by Miles and Howard, that the prisoners could return to the Northwest. The prisoners included 87 men, 184 women, and 147 children, but more than 200 Nez Perces escaped to join Sitting Bull in Canada. Joseph, whose clothes were riddled with bullet holes, proudly but not defiantly gave his rifle to Miles and, through an interpreter, addressed his old adversary Howard:

> I am tired of fighting. Our chiefs are killed. . . . It is cold, and we have no blankets. The little children are freezing to death. . . . Hear me, my chiefs! I am tired. My heart is sick and sad. From where the sun now stands I will fight no more forever.[9]

The cost of this unjust and needless war was high. The retreating Nez Perces lost 65 men and 55 women and children; and the attacking whites lost 180 men. The United States government spent $1,873,410 to make dependent, albeit proud, paupers of the once-prosperous Nez Perces. To the dismay of Miles, who to his death remained an advocate of the Nez Perces, Generals Philip Sheridan and William T. Sherman refused to carry out Miles's promise to Joseph; instead, they ordered the Nez Perces to Indian Territory (present-day Oklahoma). Indeed, Sherman wanted to execute Joseph and the other Nez Perce leaders. In November 1877, Miles appealed to Sheridan to permit him to take a Nez

Perce delegation to Washington; but Sheridan refused, and William T. Sherman, Commissioner of Indian Affairs Ezra A. Hayt, Secretary of War McCrary, and Secretary of the Interior Schurz backed Sheridan's decision. Accustomed to the cool mountains of the Northwest, the Nez Perces suffered in the hot southern plains, and sixty-eight died during the first year of their captivity. Hayt did permit them to move to a better location on the Ponca Indian Reserve, but almost every child who was born there died.

Eloquent, wise, and humane, Joseph continued to struggle for the rights of the Nez Perces. He won the admiration of white Americans, but he could not win justice for his people. In January 1879, he was permitted to come to Washington, D.C., to plead for permission to return to the Northwest. Although Joseph spoke to a large gathering of distinguished officials, saw Hayes and Schurz, and published a stirring interview in the influential *North American Review*, Miles's pledge to him at Bear Paw Mountain was not honored. Indictments were still out in Idaho for the murders along the Salmon River, and both the War Department and the Interior Department feared trouble if the Nez Perce exiles were to return. Two years later, Miles asked Hayes to let them go back to Idaho, but Hayes did not respond.

Continued pressure by the Indian Rights Association and the Presbyterian Church brought some results. Twenty-nine old men, women, and orphans were allowed to go to the Lapwai Reservation in 1883. In 1884, Congress approved the return of all Nez Perces at the discretion of the secretary of the interior, and by May 1885 they were in the Northwest. A few Nez Perces were allowed to go to Lapwai, in Idaho, but most of them, including Joseph, were kept at Colville, Washington. In 1899 and again in 1900, Joseph was allowed to visit his beloved Wallowa Valley and the grave of his father, but although he was courteously received, the white settlers refused to sell him even a small piece of the land that had belonged to him and his forebears. He died at Colville in 1904.

The Nez Perce War underscored the inadequacies of the nation's policy toward Native Americans. While Joseph was retreating, Schurz sought guidance on how to reform the Indian Bureau; he shared his findings with Hayes. John B. Wolff, an ardent and humane, although paternal, advocate of the Native Americans, responded and claimed that if the Indian service were reconstructed on business principles, $10 million to $15 million would be saved annually, Indian wars would be averted, and within five years, most Native Americans would be self-supporting. Making them self-sufficient would have eliminated the contractors who supplied Native Americans but defrauded both them and the government. Wolff believed that the Board of Indian Commissioners, which had been created under Grant, did secure better Indian agents than those selected by the spoils system, but he thought that even better agents could be secured. "If the Indians are dealt by *justly*," Wolff insisted, "they will give us little trouble."[10]

Hoping to secure justice for Native Americans, Schurz tried to reform the Indian Bureau. In August 1877 the report of a board that he had appointed to investigate the bureau's Division of Accounts prompted him to reorganize the division and fire its chief, George W. Smith, a kinsman of Indian Commissioner John Q. Smith's. Schurz also appointed a board to inquire into the activities of the bureau's chief clerk, Samuel A. Galpin; and Schurz found Commissioner Smith's report of a recent tour of Indian agencies disappointing. Aware of Schurz's dissatisfaction and probably worried by the board's secret investigation of Galpin, its so-called star chamber proceedings, John Q. Smith resigned to become the consul at Montreal.

The board of inquiry's report, published on 8 January 1878, was devastating. It revealed that a ring within the bureau, which Chief Clerk Galpin had countenanced, had received gifts from Indian contractors and had allowed them to defraud both the Native Americans and the government. Schurz fired the ring members, but he was attacked by spoilsmen such as Senator Timothy O. Howe of Wisconsin and by Julius H. Seelye, the president of Amherst College, who believed that Galpin had been victimized. Even Garfield told Hayes that Schurz's treatment of John Q. Smith had been "outrageous and unjust." Rumors surfaced that Schurz would resign from the cabinet, but he was confident that he had Hayes's firm support. Ironically Smith's replacement, Ezra A. Hayt, who as a member of the Board of Indian Commissioners had earned a reputation as an opponent of frauds in the Indian Bureau, disappointed Schurz and Hayes, and they removed him when they learned that his son was involved with a disreputable Indian agent.[11]

Nevertheless, Indian affairs improved under Hayt, Schurz, and Hayes. The administration's investigations, appointments, and policies reduced frauds and violence. Its most important innovation occurred in 1878, when, following recommendations by Hayt and Schurz, Congress appropriated funds that enabled the agents to appoint Native American police. Before that date, agents had to call on the army to deal with serious crime. In 1883, after Hayes left office, the policy was expanded to include the appointment of Native American judges. By mixing Anglo-Saxon jurisprudence with Native American practices, policemen and judges were able to keep order on the reservations, and they proved to be effective agents of acculturation. E. M. Marble, who succeeded Hayt as commissioner of Indian affairs, declared that the appointment of Indian police "at first undertaken as an experiment, is now looked upon as a necessity." Schurz and Hayes had been flexible and perceptive enough to realize that the realities of reservation life demanded these local police.[12]

By the summer of 1878, after a hostile Congress adjourned and with a year's perspective on the Nez Perce War, Hayes groped for a civilized and practical policy toward Native Americans. His thinking was triggered by a July visit to the Wyoming Valley in Pennsylvania to commemorate the centennial of the Indians' massacre of pioneers during the American Revolution. Probably recalling his own parents, he admired "the men and women who encountered disease, and hardship, danger and suffering, to reclaim the wilderness and turn [it] into civilized homes." Although the pioneers had been dealing with Indians for nearly three centuries, Hayes concluded, the Indians were still the pioneers' "most dreaded danger."

Believing that William Penn had come closer to solving Indian problems than had other founders of colonies, Hayes resolved to "correct the errors of the past." He concluded that a successful Indian policy should be rooted in justice and good faith and that it should be liberal in providing for the "physical wants, for education in its widest sense, and for religious instruction and training" of the Indians. Hayes realized that such a program would be costly, but he knew that it would be a "wise economy." A believer in equal opportunity, he consistently urged the federal government to subsidize education for poor black, red, and white children, so that they might have a fair start in life.[13]

After the Nez Perce War there was little bloodshed during Hayes's term, but there was much friction between whites and Native Americans, between easterners and westerners, and between the Interior Department and the War Department. The Office of Indian Affairs was lodged in the Interior Department, but despite the Indian police, the army often had to enforce decisions that affected Native Americans. Further complications arose because westerners often ignored Indian rights, which easterners championed. A persistent problem that was faced by the Interior Department, War Department, and Native Americans was the encroachment of settlers into Indian Territory.

In late April 1879, Hayes, to dissuade "certain evil-disposed persons," proclaimed that anyone who attempted to settle in Indian Territory would be expelled from it. Enforcing the proclamation was not easy. Illegal settlers often claimed to be either half-breed Cherokees or citizens of the Cherokee Nation. That summer, Lt. Eugene Cushman of the Sixteenth Infantry asked for instructions concerning J. M. Bell, who insisted that the Department of the Interior had authorized him to settle near Shalokic Creek, Indian Territory, on land known as the Cherokee Outlet. Commissioner of Indian Affairs Hayt was incensed that Gen. John Pope endorsed Cushman's query with the claim that ''the Interior Department has in no way aided us, and we have no means of knowing if the statement as to the authority said to have been given to Bell, be true or not.'' Hayt insisted that ''Bell and his party never received any authority from this office to settle in the outlet,'' and in reply to Pope's endorsement, Hayt declared that his office had unfailingly responded to army requests.

Hayt proved cooperative. Cushman asked on 16 August 1879 about a certificate that had allegedly been granted by Lucien B. Bell, the agent of the Cherokee Nation, to John F. Jones, under which Jones claimed authority to reside in the Cherokee country; again Cushman asked for instructions on how to deal with white men who claimed to have authority from the Cherokee Nation to settle in the outlet. Ten days later, Cushman reported that persons named ''Eaton, Brash, Carey, Kennedy, Marshall and Ryan have been persistent intruders in the Cherokee outlet for the past six or seven years.'' Although they had been repeatedly notified that their intrusion was illegal, they continued to cultivate crops. Inspired by Cushman's queries, Hayt investigated and discovered that neither Lucien Bell nor the Cherokee Nation had authorized anyone to settle in its outlet.

Hayt recommended that the army use force if necessary to clear Cherokee lands of ''all persons who have settled, or may hereafter settle therein, except such as hold genuine permits from the Cherokee Nation for grazing purposes only, or who holding such grazing permits, violate them by cultivating the soil and establishing residence''; he also recommended that ''their crops and improvements be turned over to the Indians.'' Besides illustrating the well-known friction between the War and Interior departments and the fact that westerners persistently violated treaties guaranteeing Indian lands, Hayt's correspondence reveals that work by a conscientious army lieutenant could produce a careful investigation by the Office of Indian Affairs and could result in specific instructions to obtain some redress for Native Americans.[14]

Despite the efforts of Lieutenant Cushman and other army officers, the intruders persisted. When arrested, convicted, and fined, they had no money to pay their fines; and when released, they again settled in Indian Territory. False reports that Hayes had changed his mind led him on 12 February 1880 to reissue his April 1879 proclamation, reiterating his determination to prevent these incursions. When Capt. David L. Payne again led settlers into Indian Territory, Hayes insisted on prosecuting him. In the long run, the trespassers succeeded because they were already occupying much choice land when, in 1889, Congress opened Indian Territory to settlement. When it was admitted to the union in 1907, Oklahoma encompassed all of Indian Territory.[15]

In his last annual message to Congress in December 1880, Hayes was pleased to state that Indian affairs were "in a more hopeful condition now than ever before." Rather than having made war during the past year, the Indians had "made gratifying progress in agriculture, herding, and mechanical pursuits," as well as in the wagon freighting business. The organization of an Indian police force, Hayes reported, had helped to maintain law and order on reservations and had been a wholesome moral influence on the Native Americans themselves.

As Hayes desired, the Interior Department had increased the educational facilities for Indian children. Besides building new boarding schools at Indian agencies, it had increased the number of Indian pupils at Hampton Institute in Virginia, had established Indian schools at Carlisle, Pennsylvania, in 1879, and at Forest Grove, Oregon, in 1880, and had sent eastern Cherokee children to boarding schools in North Carolina. The pupils at these schools received an elementary English education, as well as instruction in housework, agriculture, and useful mechanical pursuits. While on an extended tour of the West in 1880, Hayes and Lucy took a 50-mile side trip to Forest Grove, to visit the small school there, and they "were much pleased" with what they observed. The Interior Department's "permanent civilization fund" paid for the education of all these children, but the fund was so reduced that Hayes asked Congress for a specific appropriation for these schools. He not only wanted them to survive; he also wanted them to expand.[16]

Two days after he had assured Congress about the hopeful state of Indian affairs, a troubled Hayes wrote in his diary, "A great and grievous wrong has been done to the Poncas." While Hayes was working on his upbeat annual message, Senator George F. Hoar of Massachusetts had informed him about a recent meeting in Worcester that had protested the removal of the Ponca Indians from their ancestral lands in northeastern Nebraska and southeastern Dakota Territory. Hoar urged the president to redress the wrong and to enable his administration "to take its place in history as the purest and freest from stain since the inauguration of Washington." When Hoar blamed Schurz, Hayes replied: *"I suppose General Schurz has been most shamefully treated in this affair,* but I may be mistaken. I will look into it carefully." Henry L. Dawes, the other Massachusetts senator, who was even more aroused, feared for the Poncas should they visit the Interior Department for redress. Hayes assured Dawes that "nothing unfair or inconsiderate" would be done to them if they were to call on Schurz. Hayes also reminded Dawes pointedly that "this is the first time that you have called my attention to the subject"; but he graciously added, "I would be glad to know what you would advise."

Because he had not had enough time to investigate the Ponca affair, Hayes did not mention it in his annual message, but a Boston protest meeting on 3 December kept the problem on his mind. Everyone agreed that the Poncas had been wronged, but Hayes wanted to know the details of the injury and how it might be redressed. With Dawes blaming Schurz and with Schurz claiming that Congress and Dawes, as a member of the Senate Committee on Indian Affairs, were at fault, Hayes determined to research the problem himself. To better understand its details, he studied congressional debates and reports of the commissioner of Indian affairs for the previous four years.[17]

Public meetings at Worcester and Boston underscored the failure of the administration to deal justly with Native Americans. Although relations with them had improved, both the formation and the execution of a workable policy troubled the Hayes administration. Along with Schurz, Hayes, upon entering office, had a limited understanding of the hardships caused by uprooting people and moving them hundreds of miles to Indian Territory. But both men learned and eventually stopped the removal policy. By 1879, Schurz prevented a Ute uprising in western Colorado from escalating by restraining the army, as well as the governor and the citizens of that state. Schurz saved part of their lands for the Utes, saw that they were compensated for land they had lost, and paved the way for individual ownership. While both of them pushed individualism and education for Native Americans, neither Hayes nor Schurz thought that the culture of Native Americans was worth preserving. They wished to save Native American lives, but they pressed for the annihilation of the Native Americans' way of life.[18]

Although Schurz ably defended his role in the Ponca affair, his review of the "salient points of the case" reveals the contradictions, neglect, and deceit in a policy that was legislated by Congress and administered by the Indian Bureau. The root of the problem lay in the treaty of 1868 between the United States and the Poncas' traditional enemies, the Sioux. This treaty gave them the 96,000-acre Ponca Reserve along the Missouri River, which had been guaranteed to the Poncas by 1858 and 1867 treaties. When the Poncas remained, the Sioux harassed them until the Poncas asked to be moved to the reservation of the Omahas, a kindred tribe in Nebraska. In 1874 and 1875 the commissioner of Indian affairs urged that the Poncas be granted their wish, but Congress did not act. In September 1875 the Ponca chiefs petitioned to be removed to Indian Territory, but they later insisted that they had misunderstood and really wished to live with the Omahas.

In 1876, Congress appropriated $25,000 for the removal of the Poncas to Indian Territory, if they would agree to relinquish their claims on their old reserve. In January 1877, Edward C. Kemble, an inspector in the Indian Bureau, cajoled them into sending chiefs to look for a possible new home in Indian Territory. He also reported to his superiors that the Poncas, at a council on 27 January 1877, had orally agreed to move to Indian Territory, but the chiefs had signed no document relinquishing their lands. Most of the Ponca chiefs who scouted Indian Territory for a new home found that territory and its people inhospitable. Footsore and weary after a forty-day walk, the Ponca chiefs abandoned their search and returned home. But a remnant of the Poncas found a suitable place on the Quapaw Reservation. Acting on Indian Bureau assurances, which were based on Kemble's report, Congress appropriated an additional $15,000 on 3 March 1877 to move the Poncas and to provide for the Sioux to take over Ponca lands.

As the Hayes administration took office, the Poncas were divided between a minority, who were willing to move to Indian Territory, and the majority, who were opposed to making that journey. The change of administration did not change the decision to move the Poncas any more than it changed the decision to move the Nez Perces. Schurz was able and energetic, but he was ill informed about the Poncas. He was new to the Interior Department, and for six months he gave his attention to learning its vast and complicated machinery. During that period of tutelage, he left the management of the bureaus to the bureau chiefs whom he had found in office, seldom interfering with their decisions. He did not doubt the judgment of Commissioner of Indian Affairs John Q. Smith, and he did not oppose Congress's decision to move the Sioux to the land of the Poncas and to move the Poncas to Indian Territory.

The Hayes administration was six weeks old when 175 Poncas departed for Indian Territory on 17 April. A month later the approach of four cavalry companies forced most of the 550 remaining Poncas to begin their trek. They made the journey from present-day South Dakota to Oklahoma "under great difficulties and hardships, occasioned by unprecedented storms and floods." When they arrived, disease swept their camp, killing many of them. Harassed by white adventurers, who hovered around them, rustling their cattle and smuggling whiskey into their camps, most of the Poncas did not like the Quapaw Reservation, and their chiefs requested permission to put their case before the authorities at Washington.

By the fall of 1877, when these Ponca chiefs arrived in Washington, Schurz had asserted control over his department, and he was willing to question earlier policies and practices. But he did not want the Poncas to return to their old reservation, since the Sioux were on that land. After having consulted William Welsh, a prominent Indian-rights advocate, Schurz made his decision. He approached the problem, not in terms of what he thought was right, but in terms of what he thought would be in the Poncas's best interest. If they returned, the Sioux would renew their attacks and might go to war against the Poncas. Schurz told the Poncas to search Indian Territory for a suitable tract as large as the 96,000 acres that they had left. He also assured them that they would be compensated for the log houses, furnishings, and implements that they had left in Dakota. In his 1877 annual report to Congress, Schurz listed the hardships that the Poncas had suffered, emphasized that they were a friendly, well-behaved tribe, "entitled to more than ordinary care at the hands of the Government," and recommended that a liberal provision be made to aid their resettlement.

Although Congress failed to respond to Schurz's request, the Poncas found lands more to their liking at the Salt Fork of the Arkansas River. In July 1878, they occupied their new reservation. The 1878 report of Commissioner Hayt reflected the changed attitude in the Indian Bureau. He spoke about the blunder in the 1868 Sioux Treaty and about the violation of the Ponca Treaty; he said that the government had wronged the Poncas and that restitution should be made. The Interior Department requested $140,000 to indemnify the Poncas for their losses and to enable them to gain title to their new reservation, but Congress did not act. In his 1879 report, Schurz reiterated that the Poncas had been wronged and insisted that his department had done all that it could do in the absence of legislation. Although he resubmitted the bill to indemnify the Poncas, Congress merely passed its routine appropriation.

The new Ponca lands along the Arkansas River and the Salt Fork proved to be better than the tribes' land in Dakota. As they became acclimated to their new surroundings, most Poncas were content with their location, but like the Nez Perce and all other Native Americans, they revered their ancestral lands. That land was so important that a minority of the Poncas decided to return to it. While pleading with Congress to indemnify the Poncas, Schurz insisted that none of them return to Dakota. Even though the Sioux had abandoned the Ponca lands and had become peaceful, he continued to adhere to his earlier decision. To justify his stubbornness, Schurz argued that the young Sioux might kill some Poncas and start a war and that if the Poncas were to leave their land in Indian Territory, lawless white incursions on that land would increase. By not reversing himself, Schurz had become as rigid a bureaucrat as Commissioner Smith, who in 1877 had refused to deviate from the course that removed the Poncas.[19]

Congress had ignored Schurz's earlier pleas, and probably no one would have noticed the difficulties of the Poncas, if it had not been for Standing Bear. This Ponca chief's desire to return to the home of his people was made urgent by the death of his grandchild. In early 1879, Standing Bear, carrying the remains of the child, set off with thirty-four followers. After enduring terrible hardships on a 600-mile winter journey, they were arrested by the army in northeastern Nebraska, where they had stopped to rest among the Omahas; they were to be sent back to Indian Territory. Their dramatic story attracted Thomas H. Tibbles of the *Omaha Herald*, who had been a militant abolitionist in "Bleeding Kansas" and an itinerant Methodist minister before he had become a journalist.

A man of action who would be the 1904 Populist candidate for vice-president, Tibbles helped to secure two of the best lawyers in Nebraska for Standing Bear and his band, who were soon freed on a writ of habeas corpus. On 30 April 1879, Judge Elmer S. Dundy of the federal district court ruled that the constitutional guarantee that no person shall be deprived of life, liberty, or property without due process of law applied to these Poncas and presumably to all Native Americans. Schurz, instead of risking his control over Indian tribes by appealing this ruling to the Supreme Court, ignored the ruling except as it applied to Standing Bear and his followers.

Flushed with victory, Tibbles planned for the American people to hear the Poncas' story. He arranged for Standing Bear and two gifted Omahas, Susette La Flesche and her brother Francis, to embark on a speaking tour. Susette's father was the head Omaha chief, Joseph La Flesche or Iron Eye, and her grandfather was a French trader. She had been educated in Elizabeth, New Jersey, and had taught at the government school on the Omaha Reservation. Her brother Francis would become a distinguished ethnologist. Along with her father, Susette had visited and helped the Poncas in Indian Territory, and she later publicized their misery. Before her eastern speaking tour, Susette adopted the Omaha name Bright Eyes; and she captured her audiences with her forceful eloquence and graceful dignity. She and Standing Bear aroused many Americans to the injustice that had been done to all uprooted Native Americans, but particularly to the Poncas. After hearing them, Helen Hunt Jackson began to do research for *A Century of Dishonor* (1881), her widely read indictment of United States Indian policy. Bright Eyes and Standing Bear also stirred Congress. Senator Henry L. Dawes introduced a bill, and after an investigation, the Senate Committee on Indian Affairs recommended on 31 May 1880 that the Poncas be allowed to return home.[20]

Resolutely setting his face against the rising tide of public opinion and senatorial displeasure, Schurz continued to frustrate any Ponca attempt to move back to the Missouri River. Defying the Interior Department, Bright Eyes and Tibbles, who would marry in 1881, did their best to induce the Poncas to leave Indian Territory. Letters from Bright Eyes kept alive the desire, particularly among young Poncas, to return to their old home, and those desires provoked unrest among the Poncas. In the summer of 1880, Tibbles went to Indian Territory to encourage the Poncas to assemble near the Nez Perce Reservation, where he had collected supplies, and then to depart for their old home. Nez Perce policemen arrested him on their reservation and turned him over to the Ponca Agency; and he was ''escorted to the State line and warned of the consequences should he return.'' Many Poncas did not fall in with the plans of Bright Eyes and Tibbles. Satisfied in their new home, these Poncas petitioned in October 1880 to relinquish their old land claims for title to their new reservation.[21]

Schurz's stubbornness in regard to the Poncas culminated in the November and December 1880 meetings in Worcester and Boston. Hayes decided that the situation required an investigation by a special commission. He consulted with Senator Hoar about its composition and agreed to allow the Ponca Relief Committee of Boston to appoint up to half of the commission, if the committee would pay the expenses of those whom it named. Hayes lamented that he was restricted to the army or the Interior Department for his own appointments, since he had no contingency fund to compensate commission members. He urged Hoar to persuade Congress to provide his successor with such a fund. ''With ten thousand dollars each year I could have done a great deal of good,'' Hayes declared. On 18 December 1880 he appointed to the commission Brigadier Generals George Crook and Nelson A. Miles; William Stickney, the secretary of the Board of Indian Commissioners; and Walter Allen of Newton, Massachusetts, the Boston committee's man. After conferring with the Poncas in Indian Territory and Dakota, where some remained, the commission suggested that all Poncas be granted their wish. The commission found that the 521 Poncas in Indian Territory wished to stay there, while the 150 Poncas in Dakota and Nebraska wanted to remain close to their ancestors.[22]

Hayes and Schurz agreed. In his annual report, Schurz had announced that the administration had abandoned the policy of removal unless the land that the Native Americans were occupying could not provide them a living. "I have found good reason very much to regret," Schurz confessed, the removal to Indian Territory of the Pawnees, the Northern Cheyennes, and the Poncas. Schurz drafted and Hayes revised the special message of 1 February 1881 to accompany the commission's report. Hayes requested that Congress compensate the Poncas, allow them to choose where they would live, and let them gain title to their land as individuals, but with the proviso that it be nontransferable ("inalienable") for a period of years, in order to protect them from scheming whites. "In short," Hayes declared, "nothing should be left undone to show the Indians that the Government of the United States regards their rights as equally sacred with those of its citizens."[23]

The "great and grievous wrong" that had been done to the Poncas, which had been publicized by Bright Eyes and Tibbles, enabled Hayes to reiterate four leading ideas that, he believed, Indian policy should embrace. First, young Indians of both sexes should receive an industrial and a general education, which would "enable them to be self-supporting and capable of self-protection in a civilized community." Second, Indians should be allotted land "in severalty, inalienable for a certain period." Third, Indians should receive "fair compensation for their lands not required for individual allotments, the amount to be invested, with suitable safeguards, for their benefit." Fourth, after meeting these prerequisites, Indians should become citizens of the United States.

Having considered the Indian problem in general, Hayes returned to the injustice that had been done to the Poncas. He was "deeply sensible" that as president, "when the wrong was consummated . . . , enough of the responsibility for that wrong justly attaches to me to make it my particular duty and earnest desire to do all I can to give to these injured people that measure of redress which is required alike by justice and by humanity." Unaware that his antagonist Schurz had had a hand in writing the message, Dawes wrote Hayes about his

> great gratification in the Ponca message just read to the Senate. Every word of it meets my hearty commendation, and is worthy of your high office and high character. In my opinion it

will pass into history as a great state paper, marking an epoch in our dealings with the weak and defenseless more conspicuous and grand than any other public expression from the head of the nation for many years.

Congress did appropriate $165,000 for the Poncas, as Schurz and Hayes had suggested. Although Dawes continued to attack Schurz, Dawes incorporated Schurz's and Hayes's ideas about land and citizenship for Native Americans into the Dawes Severalty Act of 1887.[24]

8

★ ★ ★ ★ ★

FOREIGN AFFAIRS

During the Hayes administration the United States had few problems with foreign governments and little inclination to become an imperialistic power. The few problems that the country had involved Mexican bandits, who ignored the border between the United States and Mexico; Californians, who ignored the Burlingame treaty and discriminated against Chinese residents of their state; and Ferdinand Marie de Lesseps, who ignored Hayes and plunged ahead with his plans to build a Panama Canal. There were hints of United States imperialism that would develop over the next two decades, but neither Hayes nor the American people embraced imperialism during his administration. Although Hayes believed that the United States had a special interest in any project to connect the Caribbean Sea with the Pacific Ocean, he was against the de Lesseps project because he perceived it as a French imperialist threat to Western Hemisphere republics, and although he wished to annex Canada, he favored annexation only if the Canadians would approve and if the United States would refrain from using "artificial stimulants" to achieve such a union.[1]

The paucity of United States arms during the Hayes administration demonstrates that the nation harbored no ambition to play an active imperialist role. Although Congress authorized an army of thirty thousand men, it appropriated funds for only twenty-five thousand, who were ineffectively scattered about the country; and it was content with a small obsolete navy. While the spoils system was less a problem for the armed forces than for the civil service, politicians hurt morale and efficiency by intervening to secure rapid promotions and choice assignments for their favorites. Congressman James A. Garfield, for example, fostered the careers of army friends, and politicians regularly badgered the Navy Department to secure shore assignments or Mediterranean cruises for officers who were not inclined to show the flag in remote parts of the globe. Secretary of the Navy Thompson, who had "been annoyed almost to death by these" requests from members of Congress, was "especially embarrassed" when Hayes detached several officers from ships, thus delaying their departure for the South Atlantic and angering Senator Dawes, because Thompson had refused to detach one of Dawes's constituents.[2]

Despite their limitations, the army and the navy were able to carry out the commands of the Hayes administration. The army was equal to its task on the Mexican border. For years, United States relations with Mexico had been strained by incursions made across the Rio Grande into Texas by bands of Mexican marauders, who rustled the cattle of American ranchers. Political instability made it difficult for Mexico to control its border. Benito Pablo Juárez, the leader of the liberal anti-clerical forces in Mexico, dominated that country before and after Archduke Maximilian of Austria had reigned as emperor from 1864 to 1867. After Maximilian was executed, Juárez was reelected president of Mexico and served from 1867 until his death in 1872. His liberal policies were continued by his successor, Sebastián Lerdo de Tejada.

On 20 November 1876, two weeks after the Hayes-Tilden election, Porfirio Díaz overthrew Lerdo de Tejada, and on 2 May 1877, two months after Hayes's inauguration, Díaz assumed the office of president. After he had consolidated his position, he wielded absolute power until he was overthrown in 1911. In 1877, however, neither Grant nor Hayes had any inkling that Mexico had embarked on a period of economic growth and political repression, and they had no indication that Díaz would be any more successful than his predecessors had been in preventing border incursions. On 1 June 1877, Hayes ordered Gen. Edward O. C. Ord to keep "lawless bands" from invading United States territory, even if his troops had to cross into Mexico to punish these outlaws. The Díaz regime protested Hayes's order and sent troops and a cabinet minister to the border to protect Mexico's sovereignty.

Díaz's protests were echoed in the United States, although many other Americans applauded Hayes's policy. In addition to criticizing the invasion of a neighbor with whom the United States was at peace, commentators feared more sinister designs. Critics speculated that the administration wished to provoke a war with Mexico in order to drive the recent abandonment of Republican regimes in South Carolina and Louisiana from public consciousness and to annex several Mexican states. This aggression would gratify the administration's new allies among white southern Democrats who, since the days of James K. Polk, had hoped for that territory. The administration denied that its motives extended beyond securing the nation's border; nevertheless, its enemies continued their criticism.

Smarting because Hayes had ignored his suggestions for appointments and unhappy with the administration's southern policy, James G. Blaine insisted that Hayes and Evarts had embarked on an adventurous course in Mexico. After having noted in a Fourth of July speech at Woodstock, Connecticut, that "we are kindly assured that in no event shall any Mexican territory be acquired or annexed to the United States," Blaine observed, "as in many cases of similar design and movement, the most important feature may be that which is specially disavowed." The implication that he had lied stung Hayes, who declared, "There is nothing secret or underhand in the Mexican policy." Neither he nor Evarts was duplicitous. They were merely protecting American citizens from raids by outlaws. Evarts characteristically quipped that being habitually truthful, he was able to conceal his diplomatic objectives from those who expected him to be deceptive.[3]

Although Hayes and Evarts were telling the truth, there was some basis for the speculations of Blaine and his cohorts. Gen. William S. Rosecrans wanted the Hayes administration to play a larger role in Mexican affairs and to "secure for our commercial and manufacturing interests, the lion share of the commerce of ten millions of people." Rosecrans was not only the original colonel of Hayes's Twenty-third Ohio Volunteers; he was also Andrew Johnson's minister to Mexico in 1868 and 1869 and was a promoter of mining and railroad interests in Mexico. The fact that Rosecrans was a Democrat did not diminish Hayes's admiration for his old commander, who wrote to Hayes, through Stanley Matthews, in the summer of 1877.

Rosecrans advocated the building of railroads through Mexico's populous and productive "table-lands," tying them to the United States rail system. While Rosecrans insisted that "our interest is to have Mexico develop under her own autonomy," he suggested that the best way for Mexico to raise desperately needed capital to fund its debt and put the country in a position to give "reasonable subventions and privileges" to the builders of railroads "would be to sell to the United States the sparsely settled states of Sonora, Chihuahua, Coahuila, Nuevo Leon and Tamaulipas and the Territory of Lower California." Rosecrans recognized that the Mexican constitution's prohibition against the sale or alienation of Mexican soil would have to be amended and that opposition by the Mexican "political class" to "Northern annexation" was "practically a monomania capable of overturning any government not backed by money, power and popularity." This opposition was heightened by "coarse and blunt" articles about annexation in American newspapers.

If annexing northern Mexico and building railroads in what remained of that country were desirable, "our government must take prompt and efficacious measures to assure the good will and popularity of the Díaz administration." Above all, Rosecrans feared that the border problems with Mexico might escalate into a war, which would be "not only a blunder but a crime against humanity." He believed it was the manifest destiny of the United States to consolidate "the family of Western Republics under our leadership," not by force but "whenever they see it [union with the United States] diminishes the expenses of maintaining governments and largely multiplies the benefits."[4]

Rosecrans's ideas combined old territorial with new economic ambitions, but they did not determine the administration's policy toward Mexico. Neither Hayes nor Díaz wished to buy or sell northern Mexico, and they were not willing to go to war over vexing border problems. Despite Díaz's bombastic talk, he agreed that Mexico would pursue outlaws jointly with Ord. In addition to pursuing Mexican cattle thieves, Ord also tried to prevent Mexican revolutionaries from using the United States as a base for raids on Mexico. On 22 July 1877, Ord arrested Gen. Mariano Escobedo and a handful of his followers, who were recruiting troops in Texas to overthrow Díaz and restore Lerdo de Tejada. After several months, these desultory revolutionary activities ceased to challenge Díaz, and on 9 April 1878 the Hayes administration recognized his regime.

Although Rosecrans had desired this move the previous summer, Hayes and Evarts had let "Mexico hang by the eyelids," because Díaz could not stop the border raids. A year later, noting that Díaz was trying to attract United States capital, Evarts commented sharply that Americans "will hesitate to embark in commercial enterprises in any region where life and property are insecure." By early 1880, Mexico had restored order on the border, and Hayes on 24 February revoked the 1 June 1877 order permitting Ord to follow outlaws into Mexico. Many years later, Woodrow Wilson's administration would confront a similar problem with a less satisfactory outcome.[5]

Peace on the southern border of the United States increased its exports to Mexico, which amounted to roughly $6 million per year during the 1870s, $11 million in 1881, and $15 million in 1882; border peace also led to rail connections between the two countries. Alluding to the September 1880 concessions by Mexico to two United States companies, Hayes announced in December that "several important enterprises of this character will soon be set on foot, which can not fail to contribute largely to the prosperity of both countries."[6]

Although peace prevailed along the northern border of the United States, fishing rights complicated American relations with Canada. The problem seemed to have been solved by the 1871 Treaty of Washington, but while the *Alabama* claims were arbitrated without delay at Geneva in 1872, the resolution of the fisheries question took much longer. For the next ten years, the treaty allowed Americans to fish in Canadian Atlantic waters and allowed British subjects to fish as far south as Delaware Bay, with both countries able to ship fish to each other duty free. Since the Canadians believed that the Americans had gotten the better part of the bargain, a commission was appointed to determine a cash compensation for the disadvantaged country. That commission finally met in June 1877 at Halifax, Nova Scotia; and in November, over the protests of the United States commissioner, it awarded Great Britain $5.5 million.

Convinced that entering the United States market was a great boon for Canadians, Americans were unhappy with the award. Although Congress appropriated the money, it asked Hayes to delay payment until he had ascertained that the award conformed with the requirements of the treaty. During the summer of 1878, Evarts protested to the British government that the award was excessive and argued that the commission's decision should have been unanimous. That autumn an eighty-page response from Lord Salisbury, England's secretary of state for foreign affairs, demolished Evarts's arguments, and Hayes approved the payment of the award.[7]

In February 1879, two weeks after Hayes's victory in the battle over the New York Customhouse, Congress passed a bill that would restrict Chinese immigration to the United States. The gold rush had attracted Chinese to California during the early 1850s. By 1860, they constituted more than 9 percent of that state's population. As the gold fields became exhausted, Chinese laborers drifted into other occupations, most notably railroad construction (from 1866 through 1869 the Central Pacific employed ten thousand Chinese workers), agriculture, and urban jobs in factories, laundries, and homes.

While the percentage of Chinese inhabitants in California declined to 7.5 percent in 1880, their percentage in the population of San

Francisco grew from 8 percent in 1860 to 26 percent in 1870 and to almost 30 percent by 1880. Before the completion of the transcontinental railroad, manufacturing had flourished in San Francisco because high shipping costs made East Coast goods expensive. By providing cheap transportation, the railroad made eastern goods competitive and forced San Francisco manufacturers to cut costs, which they did by importing cheap Chinese labor through Chinese merchants. The Contract Labor Law of 1864, which encouraged that practice, had been repealed in 1868, but the importation of contract labor was not outlawed specifically until Congress passed the Foran Act in 1885.[8]

White workers were hostile to Chinese workers, who in the 1870s constituted a quarter of the wage earners in California and an even higher percentage of those in San Francisco. In February 1867, hundreds of white workers attacked Chinese workers who were excavating for a San Francisco street railway and prevented them from taking construction jobs in the area. But Chinese laborers continued to work in factories, whose products faced tough national competition. The depression following the panic of 1873 made cheap Chinese labor more appealing to employers and more offensive to white laborers. Anticoolie clubs attracted white laborers and small manufacturers, who had difficulty meeting the competition of Chinese workers and the shops in which they worked.[9]

As early as the late 1860s, anti-Chinese politics was successful in the West, and by 1876 the national conventions of both parties adopted anti-Chinese planks. The Democratic plank was explicitly racist, while the Republican one, which called for a congressional investigation of the moral and material effects of the "immigration and importation of Mongolians," was implicitly racist. In October and November 1876 a joint congressional committee chaired by Oliver P. Morton, a champion of human rights, held public hearings in San Francisco on Chinese immigration. The majority report, which was issued early in 1877 but was ignored in the midst of the election controversy, called for the renegotiation of the 1868 Burlingame Treaty to eliminate its guarantee of unrestricted Chinese immigration. Morton's minority report, which appeared after his death, claimed that Chinese laborers benefited the West. It also noted that the hostility toward the Chinese was racially motivated, and it argued against restricting Chinese immigration. Emphatically a minority view, Morton's report was literally a dying gasp of abolitionist commitment to racial equality.[10]

The Great Strike of 1877 inspired anti-Chinese riots in San Francisco. That fall the Workingmen's party, led by Denis Kearney, a demagogue who wished to "stop the leprous Chinamen from landing," began to expand, and by early 1878 it was a major force in California politics. At the 1878 California Constitutional Convention, the Workingmen's party secured articles that prevented the Chinese, along with idiots, the insane, and criminals, from voting. It also prohibited the employment of Chinese or Mongolians on state or local public works or by any corporation operating under California law. Everyone realized that these articles were contrary to the United States Constitution and would be struck down by the federal courts, yet these provisions sent a message to Congress that a large segment of Californians favored unconstitutional acts against Chinese laborers.

Having received the message, the House, after an hour's debate, passed a bill that restricted immigration by limiting any incoming vessel to no more than fifteen Chinese passengers. Despite the hostility of a remnant of antislavery Republicans and of a bipartisan group that was sensitive to the country's international obligations, the measure also passed the Senate, with an additional provision that abrogated articles five and six of the Burlingame Treaty, which upheld voluntary immigration of Chinese and Americans to each other's country and protected them while they were living under the jurisdiction of the other nation.[11]

Outside of Congress, eastern reformers, such as George William Curtis, and the Protestant clergy, among whom Henry Ward Beecher was most prominent, opposed Chinese exclusion. It appears that Beecher had found in the Chinese the ideal laboring man who could live on bread and water. Beecher seemed to be alone in perceiving that the advocates of Chinese exclusion aimed "to break down industrial competition" and take "a step in the direction of *Socialism*." In New York on 21 February, Curtis found "so general and strong a protest against the Chinese bill as an act of bad faith, and so universal a hope of a veto, that I venture to add my most earnest wish that you may see the bill, as I do, as a most flagrant breach of the National faith. If Asiatic immigration be undesirable, this is certainly not the way to apply the remedy; and that the Republican party should be the first to shut the gates of America on mankind is amazing."[12]

On the other hand, the California Constitutional Convention, which was still in session, thanked Congress for having passed the fifteen-passenger bill, and a bipartisan Republican and Democratic rally in San Francisco, which excluded Kearney's Workingmen's party, urged Hayes to sign the bill into law. "Our Countrymen on the Pacific Coast," Hayes noted, "with great unanimity, and with the utmost earnestness desire a change in our relations with China."[13]

Despite the pressure, Hayes on 1 March vetoed the bill. He was bitterly denounced west of the Rocky Mountains and was even burned in effigy in one town. He had prepared his own veto message, but he adopted in its place a more detailed argument written by Evarts. Although virtually all state papers that Hayes signed were his own productions, he preferred Evarts's exposition of how this restrictive bill would affect the nation's relations with China, as well as its posture among the nations of the world.

Rather than stressing the idealistic racial equality argument, Hayes pragmatically argued that the fifteen-passenger bill contradicted and abrogated parts of the Burlingame Treaty that were advantageous to the United States. If signed into law, the bill, Hayes indicated, would amount to a "denunciation of the whole treaty." While Chinese immigrants would lose the advantages they had enjoyed under the treaty, so also would American merchants and missionaries working in China. "Fortunately," Hayes noted, Chinese migration to the West Coast was slowing down, and its "instant suppression," despite the urgency with which that demand had been made, was not required. The problem could be handled in the proper course of diplomatic negotiations.[14]

Hayes's private musings show how far he had strayed from Morton's ideological position:

> I am satisfied the present Chinese labor invasion—(it is not in any proper sense immigration—women and children do not come) is pernicious and should be discouraged. Our experience in dealing with the weaker races—the negroes and indians for example is not encouraging. We shall oppress the Chinamen, and their presence will make hoodlums or vagabonds of their oppressors. I therefore would consider with favor measures to discourage the Chinese from coming to our shores.

Hayes identified with the white Californians: "If we could put ourselves in their places it is absolutely certain that we should think and feel as they do. . . . We should at once devise appropriate measures to give them assurance of relief." He nevertheless would maintain the national faith and "stand for the sacred observance of treaties." Hayes observed that the vital articles of the Burlingame Treaty, which Congress wished to "abrogate without notice, without negotiation," were "of our own seeking, and it may be truthfully said of our own making." Hayes clearly believed that the West Coast exclusionists could secure "relief . . . long before there is any material increase of their present difficulties without any violation of the national faith, and without any real or substantial departure from our traditional policy on the subject of immigration."[15]

Hayes seemed to embrace exclusion because of the shortcomings of the white race. Although he shared the common assumption that other races were inferior to Caucasians, it was the vicious characteristics of the supposedly superior race, particularly its tendency to oppress, that Hayes feared. This fear of white oppressiveness was rooted in the dismal relations of black, red, and yellow peoples with whites during Hayes's lifetime, which could be amply illustrated by events that had taken place during his presidency: southern "bulldozers" who intimidated blacks; arrogant, thieving settlers who violated the rights of Native Americans to their ancestral lands; and rioters who murdered Chinese workers. Hayes had not abandoned the idea that the white race should be forced to live up to the equal-rights principle in the Declaration of Independence, whether dealing with blacks, Native Americans, or Chinese.

Native Americans and blacks had long been part of the American scene, while the Chinese were recent arrivals. They also, as Hayes stressed, were "without women—without wives and mothers." That fact had made him conclude that they could neither be assimilated nor admitted into the bosom of American society. Why Hayes thought that exclusion would not constitute a real or substantial departure from American immigration policy is difficult to understand, unless he saw a parallel—which he did not express—between prohibiting the importation of slaves from Africa after 1808 and of coolies from China after 1879.[16]

The veto, which Congress could not override, neither answered nor closed the Chinese question. For expert opinion, the administration turned to George Frederick Seward, the nephew of William H. Seward, Lincoln's secretary of state. Having served as a consul in China from 1861 to 1876 and as the minister to China since 1876, George F. Seward was, by March 1879, an old China hand. He was also in trouble. Two days after Hayes had vetoed the Chinese bill, the Democrats in the House of Representatives tried to impeach Seward for "high crimes and misdemeanors while in office." The allegations were that he had embezzled, bribed, and extorted while he was a consul, that he was an arbitrary administrator, and that while helping to build China's first railroad, he had defrauded the Chinese government. Although the Democrats regarded Seward as a "contumacious witness" and were angry because he did not produce his accounts, they failed to impeach him when the Republicans refused to vote and thus prevented a quorum.[17]

Despite his difficulties, Seward handed Evarts a confidential memorandum, dated 25 March 1879, on the Chinese question. To preserve good relations with China and at the same time to "allay the anxiety felt in this country regarding Chinese immigration," Seward suggested that both China and the United States investigate the extent of contract immigration and take steps to prevent it. Both nations should consider the problems that Chinese immigration were creating in the United States, estimate the prospects of further Chinese immigration, and if desirable, revise the Burlingame Treaty. Seward claimed that very little was known about contract immigration. He implied that while people believed that it existed, it was possibly not important; he also suggested that an investigation could set the question at rest. He seemed to equate all contract immigration with illegal involuntary immigration, and he assumed that a strengthened consular service, which would issue a certificate to each immigrant who attested to his voluntary status, would take care of the problem. He ignored the fact that voluntary contract labor, while it was no longer being encouraged by the federal government, was not illegal.

Seward continued: "I take it for granted that there is no person in the land who would be willing to consent to a large immigration of the Chinese. This is very decidedly my own sentiment, but I have no fear that we are to witness such a result." He emphasized that the proportion of Chinese to the whole California population was falling and "that the Chinese are not an emigrating people." Indeed, Seward believed that the question of Chinese immigration was settling itself "in a way which should be satisfactory to those who are opposed to it." Even if he had erred in his projection, Seward maintained that there was time to negotiate with the Chinese, to explain American political difficulties, and to learn what the estimated future migration of Chinese would be and how willing they were to accept limitations, if the United States should deem them necessary.

Seward had found the Chinese foreign office realistic and sophisticated. He predicted that Hayes's veto of the Chinese Immigration bill would favorably dispose the Chinese toward the administration and prepare the way for negotiations to revise the Burlingame Treaty. He believed that the Chinese would agree to a provision "against importations of laborers and of persons of the pauper and criminal classes" which would, since almost all Chinese immigrants were laborers, severely limit Chinese immigration. The result, he predicted, would "conserve all the interests . . . involved in our relations with China" and would imply "no departure from the traditions of the past." Like Hayes, Seward seems not to have regarded unrestricted immigration as an American tradition.

Seward did not wish to jeopardize American trade with China. Although he spoke about "a constantly increasing stream" of "our cotton goods and some of the products of our mines and of our soil" flowing into China, that trade was unimportant in 1879. Seward did not want the future prospects to be judged by recent statistics. Emphasizing the vast market, he predicted that "our people will avail of it if we do not cut off their opportunities." Having implemented United States Far Eastern policy since 1861, he found it clearly defined in 1879: "It has recognized the identity of all legitimate foreign interests in China and in Japan, and the wisdom of cooperation with other governments to advance those interests and to stand in the way of irregular procedure and selfish purposes on the part of any of them." American policy endeavored "to sustain and support both Empires alike in the name of one common humanity and of alliances which should be productive of continuously increasing advantages."[18]

Twenty years later, the Open Door notes of Secretary of State John Hay gave this policy its classic form. Although his notes echoed Britain's traditional if not current policy in China, they were basically a forceful restatement of America's longstanding Far Eastern policy, with which Hay was intimately acquainted. Eight months after Seward had written his memorandum, John Hay joined the Hayes administration as assistant secretary of state. Negotiations with China were under way, and Hay could not avoid being familiar with America's traditional desire to sustain and trade freely with the Chinese and Japanese empires. It was natural for Hay, twenty years later, to adopt quickly and without fuss the Open Door notes, since they did not depart from what Seward in 1879 had regarded as a well-defined United States policy.[19]

Initially, the Hayes administration did not take seriously the difficulties that Seward was having with the Democratic side of the House of Representatives. Hayes and Evarts sent him back to China to negotiate changes in the Burlingame Treaty. Evarts's instructions to Seward were largely based on his 25 March memorandum. Seward returned to China to open negotiations, but his troubles with the House continued. On 4 June 1879 the House took a step in the impeachment process by referring the charges against him to the Committee on the Judiciary. Although he was neither impeached nor tried, Seward was recalled on 27 December 1879. His evasive tactics, coupled with the unrelenting pressure applied by House Democrats, had undermined his usefulness.[20]

In place of Seward, Hayes in the spring of 1880 appointed James B. Angell, president of the University of Michigan. He had been recommended by Senator George F. Edmunds, whom Hayes had praised because he did not badger the administration with suggestions for collectorships and postmasterships. To a commission that would work with Angell, Hayes appointed John F. Swift, a California Republican who was renowned for his antimonopoly and anti-Chinese views, and William H. Trescot of South Carolina, a diplomatic historian who had had diplomatic experience. The objectives were the same as those outlined to Seward, but Evarts told the commission not to discuss the rights and privileges of the Chinese who had "already transferred to our territory." Those Chinese, Evarts insisted, had and would continue to have the guarantees and protection enjoyed by immigrants from other countries and by all Americans.

With Angell chairing the United States mission, negotiations proceeded smoothly and quickly. While Swift wished to exclude the Chinese, Angell and Trescot wanted to regulate and restrain their immigration. This more moderate course reflected the view of the Hayes administration, which wanted to curb the influx of Chinese but did not want to jeopardize the advantages of American merchants and missionaries in China. Working harmoniously, the Angell mission and the Chinese plenipotentiaries had agreed both on an immigration treaty and on a commerce treaty by 17 November 1880. Article 1 of the immigration treaty allowed the United States to regulate, limit, and suspend, but not to prohibit, the coming of Chinese laborers. The commerce treaty prohibited United States involvement in importing opium into China and Chinese involvement in importing opium into America. When these treaties were ratified in 1881, Hayes had left office. The next year, after attempting to suspend Chinese immigration for twenty years, Congress settled for a ten-year suspension.[21]

Except for the problems along the Mexican border and over Chinese immigrants, the administration had experienced few difficulties in its conduct of foreign affairs. In 1878, Hayes contributed to peace in South America by arbitrating a dispute between Argentina and Paraguay over the Chaco territory. He awarded that territory to Paraguay, and it gratefully changed the name of Villa Occidental in that region to Villa Hayes, and the department of which it was the capital was later named Presidente Hayes. But while Hayes was being honored by Paraguay, a proposal to build a Panama Canal was posing a new problem.[22]

In 1879, schemes to connect the Atlantic and the Pacific through Mexico, Nicaragua, or Panama revived dramatically. In May of that year, the Congres International d'Études du Canal Interoceanique met in Paris. Although 136 delegates from twenty-two countries attended the meeting (two naval officers, Daniel Ammen and Aniceto García Menocal, represented the United States), Ferdinand de Lesseps, the builder of the Suez Canal, dominated the proceedings. With little forethought, he proposed that a sea-level Panama Canal be constructed by 1892 for $240 million. Menocal, who had surveyed the route, realized that a sea-level Panama canal was impossible; he advocated a Nicaraguan canal with locks. Ignoring the opinions of the expert engineers who were present, the gathering caught de Lesseps's vision and enthusiastically endorsed his sea-level Panama proposal.[23]

De Lesseps immediately began to organize a private syndicate to build the canal. The decision of the international congress also led to counter proposals—one was by James B. Eads, one of the greatest engineers of the nineteenth century, for a ship railway across the Isthmus of Tehuantepec in Mexico—and provoked concern in the Hayes administration. It would have been uneasy about any non-American attempt to join the oceans across Central America but was doubly suspicious of a French project. Little more than a decade had elapsed since Napoleon III had tried to make Maximilian the emperor of Mexico. Evarts had been reluctant to send delegates to Paris, and Menocal and Ammen returned home full of doubts about de Lesseps's ill-conceived, grandiose dream. The congress had turned out to be a promotional gathering with scientific trappings that ignored technological problems. De Lesseps had little success in raising funds during the summer and fall of 1879; nevertheless, he remained optimistic, and in December he embarked for the New World. He and his entourage landed at Colón, Panama—then part of Colombia—on 30 December and commenced an inspection tour of the proposed route, which paralleled that of the existing railroad. While in Panama, de Lesseps assured everyone, "The canal will be made."[24]

In Washington, Hayes had determined that any interoceanic canal would be under United States control. He had not mentioned the de Lesseps project in his recent annual message, but he had anticipated a Nicaraguan canal in the near future, "under the protective auspices of the United States." On 9 January 1880 he ordered two naval vessels to ports in the Chiriqui grant—one on the Caribbean and one on the Pacific coast—to establish naval stations in these harbors, which were strategically located between the proposed Panama and Nicaragua canals.

Hayes knew about the 1861 proposal by Ambrose W. Thompson of Philadelphia to establish a coaling station on the supposedly coal-rich section of the Isthmus of Panama, which was controlled by his Chiriqui Improvement Company. Abraham Lincoln had thought that this territory, if it were developed with a coal-mining industry, would be an ideal place for colonizing free blacks. On 11 September 1862, Thompson and the Lincoln administration had approved a contract providing for a black colony and a coaling station on lands owned by the Chiriqui Company. The project had failed because the coal was inferior and because free blacks did not want to be colonized, but the contract remained. It enabled Hayes to argue that the United States had an interest in the Chiriqui Improvement Company's grant. Alarmed by the threat of the de Lesseps scheme, Hayes planned to use these coaling stations and the presence of United States ships as "a foothold which will be of vast service in controlling the passage from Ocean to Ocean either at Panama or at Nicaragua Lake."[25]

Hayes subsequently asked Congress to appropriate $200,000 for these bases, but the coaling stations were neither pushed by his administration nor approved by Congress. De Lesseps's project, nevertheless, weighed heavily on Hayes's mind. As was his custom when confronted by an important issue, Hayes sorted out his ideas before discussing them with his cabinet. On 7 February he wrote:

> The right of free passage at all times, in peace or war, for the purpose of commerce or for defence the United States deem essential to their safety and prosperity. They wish it to be understood by all concerned that the United States will not consent that any European power shall control the Railroad or Canal across the Isthmus of Central America. With due regard to the rights and wishes of our sister republics in the Isthmus, the United States will insist that this passage way shall always remain under American control.

While adamant that Europe must not control the canal, Hayes was unsure of the role that "sister republics" would play. "The control must be exclusively either in the Country through which it passes," he wrote, "or in the United States, or under the joint control of the American Republics." Then, apparently unaware of a contradiction, he added, "The United States should control this great highway between that part of our Country" on the Atlantic with that on the Pacific; "it must be held and controlled by America—by the American Republics." Hayes apparently thought that the Central American republics would neither wish nor dare to differ with the United States, which in his discussion he sometimes referred to in the singular but more often in the plural. His grammatical inconsistencies suggest that at a time when the nation was being transformed into a modern state, its president thought of it both as a collection of states and as a unified nation. A day later, after stating that "the interest of the U.S. in the . . . interoceanic canal or Railroad does not rest on the Monroe doctrine alone," Hayes emphasized national security more than prosperity, declaring that United States control "is essential for National defense."[26]

Having thought out his views on the canal, Hayes on 10 February laid his "matured distinct and decisive" opinion before his cabinet. To inform all those who were concerned in the construction of the canal "of the principles of the United States on the subject," he told his cabinet that he intended to communicate his views in a special message to Congress. Although no one opposed what Hayes said, Evarts informed the cabinet that he was collecting treaties, correspondence, and other related material. The remainder of the cabinet enthusiastically supported the president. Schurz, who later would be a distinguished anti-imperialist, said, "No European nation under similar circumstances would hesitate an instant to assert its rights in such a case, and to give decided expression of its purpose to maintain them." And with a smile, Secretary of the Navy Thompson said, "You know these have been my views all along."

On 16 February, Trenor W. Park, a Wall Street speculator who was president of the Panama Railroad, gave Hayes an account of the isthmus, of his railroad, of de Lesseps and his surveys, and of the prospects of the enterprise. In the opinion of this far-from-disinterested party (Park had offered the French his 15,000 shares in the railroad at double their market value), a sea-level canal could be built; and although it would not pay as an investment, it would prove useful to the United States. A few days later, Hayes wrote in his diary, "The true policy of the United States as to a canal across any part of the Isthmus is either a canal under American control, or no canal."[27]

Some Americans did not consider the proposed canal to be a threat to either the prosperity or the security of the United States. De Lesseps's company was not connected with the French government, and Americans were free to purchase its stock. George William Curtis, in *Harper's Weekly*, expressed the belief that the de Lesseps's enterprise did not jeopardize American interests, violate the Monroe Doctrine, or concern the American people. "If a private company of Frenchmen can raise the means to open a canal through the Isthmus of Panama," he asked, "why should the government of the United States take action?"

Curtis's attitude, as well as the calm reaction of Evarts and the State Department, disturbed William K. Rogers, Hayes's private secretary, who on 23 February attempted to change Curtis's mind. "Do you not think it will be a mistake for the Weekly to take the side indicated in this way, upon this important matter?'' In his effort to convince Curtis and to drum up public support for Hayes's unannounced position, Rogers stressed that nonpartisan newspaper reaction from all sections was of ''the most pronounced and patriotic character.'' He told Curtis that congressional leaders such as Garfield and William Pierce Frye were disappointed and impatient with the administration for failing to take ''prompt action, called for on the score of national honor, and international fairness'' and that Hayes agreed with them. ''Whatever of hindrance has been interposed,'' Rogers said, ''has come from the Department of State.'' Garfield thought the department feared ''diplomatic complications,'' and he agreed ''that prompt action by the Government is the surest safeguard against such entanglements, and that a firm decided and plainly intelligible announcement of the position which . . . will meet the present occasion as that of Monroe and Adams did the emergency of 1823, is a . . . a plain duty and a necessity, if the expectation of the country is to be responded to.'' The overwhelming reaction of newspapers and public opinion might have been generated in part by the administration. Rogers asked Curtis to write something for the next number of *Harper's Weekly* that would echo the ''admirable editorial in the N.Y. Evening Post, some weeks since under the title— 'The duty of the hour,' urging Congressional and Administrative action.''[28]

Curtis reversed himself gracefully in another editorial entitled ''M. Lesseps and the Monroe Doctrine.'' Curtis acknowledged that de Lesseps's arrival in New York for a tour of the United States had ''greatly stimulated public interest and curiosity'' in his enterprise and conceded ''that trouble may arise from inaction or silence upon the subject, and that no possible harm could arise from a plain statement of the position of the government.'' Curtis, whose rhetorical query two weeks earlier had clearly backed a policy of inaction, now suggested that perhaps de Lesseps was taking the first step in establishing a European foothold and that the Monroe Doctrine would certainly apply to commercial or industrial enterprises projected ''upon this continent under the authority, patronage, control, or protection of European governments.''

Curtis concluded that de Lesseps's enterprise was ''not in itself an infraction of our traditional policy, yet, as involving very serious possibilities, it is a natural public expectation that the attitude of the government toward this new form of the question will be authoritatively defined, without flourish or menace, for the benefit of every interest, domestic and foreign.'' Although Evarts's quip that the Hayes administration had "not been well edited" accurately reflected Democratic hostility, Republican coolness, and the lukewarm nature of reform newspaper support, the administration was certainly supported by George William Curtis. Rogers could not have expected a better response.[29]

De Lesseps's United States tour was both a triumph and a defeat. He was hailed in New York and was feted at a banquet at Delmonico's that was attended by 250 notables. He took pains to disarm hostile Americans by insisting that his venture was a private enterprise and that it in no way contradicted the Monroe Doctrine. He welcomed American investors and would not object to locating his company's headquarters in New York or Washington; but American capitalists did not anticipate success at Panama and therefore did not invest. Although honors and praise were showered upon de Lesseps by the American people, these accolades were more for his achievement at Suez than for his proposed canal at Panama.

On the other hand, there was a chance that he might succeed, and Congress and public opinion shared Hayes's apprehensions concerning an interoceanic canal constructed by foreigners. In Washington, de Lesseps was courteously received by Hayes and by the House Interoceanic Canal Committee, before which he outlined his vision for Panama and incidently heard Eads present his vision of a ship railway across the Isthmus of Tehuantepec. At the very moment that de Lesseps was with the committee, Hayes released the text of a special message to the Senate, accompanied by copies of treaties and correspondence relating to the canal, which it had requested.

The special message of 8 March 1880 unequivocally stated: "The policy of this country is a canal under American control," and it condemned all foreign schemes to connect the Atlantic and Pacific oceans. Hayes anticipated the Theodore Roosevelt Corollary to the Monroe Doctrine by warning foreign investors not to look to their governments for protection: "No European power can intervene for such protection without adopting measures on this continent which the United States would deem wholly inadmissible. If the protection of the United States is relied upon, the United States must exercise such control as will enable this country to protect its national interests and maintain the rights of those whose private capital is embarked in the work."

In an expansive mood, Hayes stressed the value that an interoceanic canal would have for the United States by changing the relationship that the Atlantic and Pacific coasts had to each other. A canal, Hayes proclaimed, "would be the great ocean thoroughfare between our Atlantic and our Pacific shores, and virtually a part of the coast line of the United States. Our merely commercial interest in it is greater than that of all other countries, while its relations to our power and prosperity as a nation, to our means of defense, our unity, peace, and safety, are matters of paramount concern to the people of the United States.'' Evarts's report, which accompanied the documents, also stressed the United States' special interest in the canal, but he rested his case on the 1846 treaty with New Granada (present-day Colombia), rather than on Hayes's broad principles.

De Lesseps refused to be devastated by Hayes's and Evarts's hostility toward his project. He audaciously embraced Hayes's version of the future Roosevelt Corollary, welcomed the protection of the United States, and cabled his son Charles in Paris: ''The message of President Hayes guarantees the political security of the canal.'' Although Hayes's message opposed the construction of a canal by a foreign company, de Lesseps insisted that his project had the support of the United States. With the instincts of a promoter, he took off on a whirlwind transcontinental rail tour, on which he addressed crowds and created headlines all the way to San Francisco and back.[30]

Many Americans thought he was defying the Monroe Doctrine, but de Lesseps maintained that it did not prevent his project. Neither Hayes nor Evarts mentioned the Monroe Doctrine in their communications to Congress, and Hayes realized he had gone beyond that doctrine in stating his position. But Curtis, who was delighted with Hayes's message, stressed that the Monroe Doctrine did apply, because the French might possibly use the canal as an excuse to interfere in Colombian affairs. Curtis chided Professor Theodore Salisbury Woolsey, an international-law specialist at Yale University, for arguing that the Monroe Doctrine had nothing to do with the canal, unless the French government were to use the canal as a pretext for political adventures in the New World. The French quickly assured Hayes that they had no such intent. Two weeks after Hayes had sent his message to Congress, Max Outrey, the French minister to the United States, emphasized that the proposed canal was a private venture and that the French government ''in no way proposed to interfere therein or to give it any support, either direct or indirect.''[31]

Although de Lesseps had triumphed on his tour and had lined up American bankers to market stock in his canal company, he left New York on 1 April 1880 without having persuaded American capitalists to invest in his project. The French people, however, supported him as he plunged ahead, and Hayes was to be plagued by the canal issue for the rest of his term. To attract American investors, de Lesseps formed an

American committee and offered its presidency first to Grant, who wisely rejected it, and then, in a maneuver that was calculated to suggest governmental support for his canal, offered the job to Secretary of the Navy Thompson. When Hayes heard of the offer in late August 1880, he warned Thompson that "of course, you would not think of accepting an employment, or connection with the American Syndicate . . . while you continue in the administration." But the high salary of $25,000 a year tempted Thompson, whose taste for high living could not be satiated by the $8,000 he received as a cabinet officer.

By early December, Thompson had accepted the presidency but, despite Hayes's letter, planned to remain in the cabinet. Having just reiterated his views on the canal in his fourth annual message, Hayes was infuriated that the head of the Navy Department should assume a commanding position in a project that Hayes considered to be a threat to the commerce and security of the United States. Hayes considered Thompson's decision to head the American wing of the de Lesseps organization tantamount to resigning from the cabinet, so Hayes immediately accepted Thompson's resignation. But Hayes did allow Thompson to write a face-saving letter of resignation to hide the fact that he had been fired.[32]

Within days, Thompson ably defended his new employers before the House Foreign Affairs Committee. He claimed that the proposed canal was a private enterprise that posed no threat to "the absolute sovereignty and independence of the South American states," which the Monroe Doctrine protected. Indeed, he insisted that the United States would threaten that sovereignty, if the committee were to adopt the militant resolution it was considering, which invoked the Monroe Doctrine against a foreign-built canal. After Thompson's testimony, the committee recommended a milder resolution, which did not condemn de Lesseps's scheme but did state that any attempt by a European government to build a canal would violate the Monroe Doctrine. The committee avoided the issue that it faced; instead, it made a ringing declaration on a nonexistent problem. The House ignored the committee's recommendations and did not pass any resolution.[33]

Concessions that Colombia made to de Lesseps to build a Panama canal further annoyed Hayes. He argued in his last annual message that the United States' obligations under the 1846 treaty with New Granada, as well as its "interests as the principal commercial power of the Western Hemisphere," required that it approve "so stupendous a change in the region." He also reiterated his statement of March 1880 that the United States must control such a canal in order to "protect our national interest."

The proposed canal widened the global outlook of Hayes. To improve communications and to stimulate shipping and trade, he suggested that Congress subsidize mail steamship lines to Latin America, the Far East, and Australia and also that it subsidize the laying of a telegraph cable from San Francisco to Hawaii and from there to the Far East and Australia. He also suggested that an expanded navy, whose ships would circulate in all quarters of the globe, was necessary both for defense and for the promotion of commerce.

Previously, the small and obsolete navy had not disturbed Hayes. During his administration, Americans were not threatened by other powers and therefore were willing to tolerate a weak navy. Any rationale for replacing rotten and rusted vessels with modern ships had to stress international commerce, rather than national defense. In this last annual message, Hayes called for more ships when he discussed ways of encouraging American trade, but not during his discussion of Navy Department needs. Even the steps that his administration had taken to establish coaling stations in the Chiriqui grant on the Isthmus of Panama were, Hayes explained, to meet the requirements of the nation's growing commercial relations with Central and South America. Of course, this sudden interest in commerce on the isthmus was prompted by the projected de Lesseps canal, and Hayes's primary concern in Panama was, not trade with Latin America, but the control of a vital sea link between the East and West coasts of the United States.[34]

When his administration ended, Hayes had failed to stop the canal, but his aggressive stand had produced a quick denial of interest by France. Hayes also had laid down a line of thought that was, in his view, quite distinct from the Monroe Doctrine. Theodore Roosevelt would later claim that line of thought as a corollary of the Monroe Doctrine.

9

★ ★ ★ ★ ★

THE POLITICS OF SUCCESSION

During the last year and a half that Hayes was president, attention focused on nominating and electing his successor. The maneuvering of candidates to secure the nation's most prized office has always produced speculation and excitement, but the fight for the Republican nomination in 1880 was spectacular. Because Hayes refused to reconsider his pledge that he would serve only one term, the struggle was among two seriously flawed yet extremely popular candidates, Grant and Blaine, and a third candidate, Sherman, whose inside track gave him an outside chance.

With most Americans entranced by the fascinating battle, Hayes continued to administer his office. Contemporaries and historians have usually focused on the politicking that led to winning the prize in 1876/77 and again in 1880, rather than on how the prize was used. In those years, winning at politics depended more on the building of an organization or machine than on the exploitation of issues. The big issue was the survival of the machine, which depended on the power to appoint political supporters to office. With the stress on political organization, rather than on policies or programs, winning was everything. In contrast to machine politicians of his era, Hayes tried to develop a politically neutral civil service and to identify himself with issues. Even when the currency issue was quiescent, Hayes, against conventional political advice, tried to reopen it by asking Congress, in his annual message of December 1879, to stop coining silver at the current ratio and to start retiring greenbacks.[1]

After that message to Congress, campaign politics dominated the attention of Hayes and his colleagues. Blaine, whom Hayes thought had been needlessly hostile during the first year of his administration, made peaceful overtures, and Hayes agreed that there was no good reason why he and Blaine should not be friendly. Blaine's efforts were hardly necessary, for Hayes was not vindictive, except perhaps with Conkling. Besides, despite his closeness to Sherman, Hayes did not actively support or oppose anyone for the nomination. On 17 December the Republican National Committee made its first official move in the presidential campaign by meeting in Washington.[2]

Sherman's supporters, Hayes thought, held the balance of power on the committee, which was about equally divided between Grant and Blaine. While Hayes wished the country to be spared another Grant administration and feared that another term would further diminish Grant's reputation, he was genuinely fond of Grant. The day after Christmas, Hayes journeyed to Philadelphia and spent two hours in a private conversation with him, trying unsuccessfully to dissuade Grant from seeking the Republican nomination. While Hayes was in Phila- delphia, Sherman urged his followers to head off Grant by stressing the nation's hostility to a third term. Sherman added: "The real contest will be between Blaine and me. If Ohio is solid for me I have every reasonable assurance of success."[3]

Despite Hayes's commitment to civil-service reform, Sherman utilized the enormous patronage of the Treasury Department to line up delegates who would support his candidacy. From New Orleans, he heard on 3 January 1880 that "a slight effort" by federal employees, especially those in the customhouse, was needed in order to secure him a favorable delegation from Louisiana to the Republican National Convention in Chicago. Sherman's informant had been told that the present incumbents "are not only inefficient as officers but are opposed to you and divided in their preferences between Grant & Blaine." It was further alleged that William Pitt Kellogg, Louisiana's Republican sen- ator, was Sherman's "stout enemy."

Uncertain about whom to support, Sherman sent William Henry Smith, Hayes's friend and the collector of the port of Chicago, to New Orleans. In asking Smith to secure reliable information on Republican politics in Louisiana, Sherman was violating both the spirit and the letter of Hayes's celebrated 22 June 1877 order prohibiting the manage- ment of political campaigns by officeholders. On 9 February, Smith enumerated those who were "reliable Sherman men in the Government service," before he returned to Chicago a few days later, "sick of a fever" and with little hope for Sherman. Smith predicted that Sherman,

Blaine, and Grant would fail and that the prize would probably be won by a dark horse.[4]

As spring approached, Sherman stepped up his campaign. He relied particularly on his brother-in-law Col. C. W. Moulton of Cincinnati. "He has had great experience," Garfield had noted a few months earlier, "in working up" Sherman's senatorial campaigns in the Ohio legislature. In early March 1880, Sherman sent Moulton to Kentucky. "I think you had better go to Louisville and see Mr. J. E. Hetherington, an Assistant of [S. A.] Whitfield in the Internal Revenue service, and ascertain what movements have been made to promote the election of James Buckner as a delegate to the Convention and what is the position of the Collector of Internal Revenue of that District." Sherman believed that the appointment of storekeepers in the Fifth District, where Lewis Buckner was deputy collector, were being made to secure Grant delegates. "If this be true," Sherman added, "I wish to know it." When Moulton confirmed Sherman's suspicions, the treasury secretary refused to sign the papers of Buckner's appointees and in effect fired the newly appointed pro-Grant gaugers and storekeepers. Sherman also fired Buckner, proving that Treasury Department workers opposed Sherman's candidacy at their peril.[5]

With Treasury Department patronage keeping his candidacy alive, Sherman continued to hope. He wrote to Moulton: "I think you had better go to Chicago as proposed. I know no one to whom I would be more willing to leave the details of organization, quarters and meeting than to you. We have got to raise in some way a general fund to meet expenses, although I suppose the great body of them will be met by the delegates, etc." Three weeks later, Sherman thought "that $2,000 or $3,000 would be sufficient for that purpose," but he confessed that "all plans to raise any considerable sums to aid me in this contest seem to have failed." Although Sherman professed to be pleased with the result of the Ohio convention, its delegation was not unanimous in his support. "If Ohio will stand by me firmly with substantial unanimity," he reiterated, "with such support as I will certainly have from other States, whenever the break between Grant and Blaine comes, I can be nominated."[6]

Just as Sherman's attempt to recruit convention delegates was part of the 1880 presidential campaign, so was the renewed Democratic effort to cripple the election laws. House Democrats attached a rider to an $8-million deficiency-appropriations bill, which on 29 April 1880 passed both houses. The new rider took the power to appoint special deputy marshals away from the district marshal and gave it to the federal circuit court or, if it were not in session, to the district court. The object was to divide and undermine the authority, responsibility, and effectiveness of federal officers who supervised elections.

Although Hayes was willing to "sign an *efficient* measure containing suitable provisions if its only object is to secure non partisan Deputies," he vetoed and killed the bill on 4 May. Rather than discuss his objections to the rider, he took the high ground that general and permanent legislation should not be tacked onto an appropriations bill. Since the appropriations were needed to carry on governmental operations, the rider was, Hayes noted in his diary, a thinly disguised "measure of coercion." Once again beaten back, the Democratic Congress then passed a deficiency-appropriations bill that contained neither the rider nor compensation for the services that deputy marshals rendered at elections. Although deputy marshals would not get $5 a day from the federal government, Hayes approved the bill because the government would continue to operate and the election laws were left intact.[7]

Rallying once more, the Democrats pushed through a bill that was almost identical to the recent rider: the courts would appoint deputy marshals over whom district marshals would have no control. The Democrats made clear their aim to undermine the federal supervision of elections. They rejected a Republican amendment that would allow the courts to appoint deputy marshals but would clothe them with the powers named in the existing election laws and place them, "like other deputy marshals, under the orders and control of the marshal of the district."

Hayes again thwarted a Democratic attack on the election laws. His veto message on 15 June did not object to court appointed deputies to supervise elections, but it did object to divorcing those deputies from existing election laws, which had been enacted to prevent fraud and bloodshed. To buttress his position, Hayes quoted extensively from the recent Maryland election case—*Ex Parte Siebold,* 1879—in which the Supreme Court held that the election laws were constitutional. The majority opinion of Justice Bradley emphasized that "violence, fraud, corruption, and irregularity . . . have frequently prevailed" at recent elections for members of the House of Representatives. He asserted the supremacy of the federal Constitution and federal laws over state laws. The national government "must necessarily have power to command obedience, preserve order, and keep the peace," or, he maintained, "it is no government," and "no person or power in this land has the right to resist or question its authority so long as it keeps within the bounds of its jurisdiction." Under this new bill, Hayes argued, the marshal could not appoint, remove, or control deputy marshals at elections; and the proposed deputy marshals, who would have no powers under the election laws, would not be able to ensure "peaceable, orderly, and lawful elections." By discriminating against the authority of the United States, specifically "the powers of the United States officers at national elections," Hayes concluded that the proposed bill "violates the true principles of the Constitution."[8]

This last veto in defense of the election laws was obscured by the struggle for the Republican presidential nomination, which preceded it. In May, before the Chicago convention opened, Grant had led the field. While his backers were publicly exuding confidence, some of them were doubting privately that their man could be nominated. In Illinois, for example, "the energy of John A. Logan and the devotion of the machine at his back" appeared, "through sharp practice," to be able to make that state's delegation practically solid for Grant. Yet William Henry Smith, who had several interviews with Logan, reported to Hayes that Logan "has hardly any hope of Grant's nomination, and is really fighting for his own political existence." Logan's "high handed proceedings" at the convention in Illinois had appalled Sherman. "The methods by which the wishes of the minority, and in some cases, the majority, have been suppressed by Gen. Grant's followers will make it suicidal to press his nomination." Sherman began "to think they are utterly reckless and would prefer defeat with Grant to success with anyone else."[9]

Sherman's prediction that the methods of Grant's supporters would backfire was correct. They failed to secure a majority of delegates for Grant, and given Grant's record as president and their behavior at state conventions, they were unable to attract new adherents. Weakened by Hayes's civil-service policies and challenged by reformers and by Blaine's people, Grant supporters hatched a desperate plan to force Grant's nomination by having James Donald Cameron, chairman of the Republican National Committee, apply the unit rule to votes from the moment that he called the convention to order on 2 June 1880. This unprecedented rule would have required that the entire vote of a state delegation be cast as a unit for the candidate of the majority of its delegates. It would have enabled Conkling, Cameron, and Logan to ignore the opposition within their New York, Pennsylvania, and Illinois delegations and thus give Grant the unanimous support of those states.

The plan failed even before the convention opened. Grant's opponents on the National Committee forced Cameron to nominate an enemy of the unit rule, Senator George Frisbie Hoar, for the position of temporary chairman. With Hoar in the chair, Grant's strength was soon tested and found wanting. The convention ousted some Grant delegates from Illinois, who had been the beneficiaries of Logan's high-handedness, and sat Blaine men in their places.

Before the balloting had begun, Hayes also thought it was impossible to nominate Grant. He felt that Blaine's chances were good but that Sherman or a fourth candidate might win. "The defeat of Grant is due to the unpopularity of the managers of his canvass, and of their methods. . . . The immediately valuable result is the condemnation of the machine as organized & managed by Conkling and Cameron. The latter is in all respects a failure as a politician. The final overthrow of the Unit rule is a solid achievement." Hayes regretted that "our first soldier and a man of many sterling qualities should be so humiliated and degraded as he has been by his unprincipled supporters." Grant's experience confirmed for Hayes the wisdom of limiting presidents to a single six-year term.

The supporters of Grant could not muster the 378 votes to win his nomination, but they were fanatically loyal to him. On the first ballot, he received 304 votes, and on the thirty-sixth and last ballot, he had 306 votes. The supporters of the other candidates were also disciplined. Blaine had 284 votes on the first ballot and 275 on the thirty-fourth; whereas Sherman started with 93, advanced to 120 on the thirtieth, and still had 99 on the thirty-fifth ballot.

On 8 June the break finally came on the thirty-fourth ballot. James A. Garfield, who was managing the Sherman forces at the convention, was embarrassed and flattered to receive one or two votes between the second and the thirty-third ballot, and on the next ballot his total jumped to 17. The anti-Grant forces had found the candidate on whom they could unite. On the thirty-fifth ballot, most of Blaine's supporters went over to Garfield, and on the thirty-sixth ballot, virtually all of Sherman's men shifted to give Garfield the nomination. To placate Conkling and to win New York's crucial electoral vote in the ensuing campaign, the convention nominated for vice-president Chester A. Arthur, the man whom the Hayes administration had considered unworthy to be collector of the port of New York.[10]

Although Hayes was close to Sherman, he called Garfield's nomination "the best that was possible." Hayes was delighted with the convention and was not even annoyed by Arthur's candidacy. He confessed:

There is much personal gratification in it. The defeat of those who have been bitter against me. The success of one who has uniformly been friendly. Ohio to the front also and again! The endorsement of me and my Administration. The endorsement of Civil Service reform. The sop thrown to Conkling in the nomination of Arthur, only serves to emphasis the completeness of his defeat. He was so crushed that it was from sheer sympathy that this bone was thrown to him.

Hayes thought Garfield was "the ideal candidate," having risen from poverty and obscurity, from the boy on the canal towpath to scholar, major general, statesman, and presidential candidate. Carried away by his enthusiasm, Hayes exclaimed: "The truth is no man ever started so low that accomplished so much in all our history. Not Franklin or Lincoln even."[11]

Sherman was not so enthusiastic, but considering his disappointment, he behaved well. While awaiting Moulton's "theory of the why and wherefore," Sherman professed to be "content with Garfield's nomination unless" he "was the victim of treachery by Friends." Moulton's analysis proved somewhat reassuring, and Sherman was "becoming satisfied that while Garfield had the hope that he would be the dark horse that he faithfully and loyally gave me the benefit of his support until the general break."

In addition to the annoyance of his defeat, Sherman reported to Moulton that the campaign had cost "more than you think" at the very time when he had committed himself to build a home in Washington. His forces spent $1,300 on their headquarters at the Grand Pacific Hotel, another $1,300 for the expenses of Sherman delegates from North and South Carolina and Mississippi, and $200 on cigars and extras. But Sherman's manager in Chicago refused to pay these bills, arguing that since Sherman was not nominated, Garfield's friends must pay them.[12]

Garfield and his friends, who did pay the bills, feared Sherman's reaction; but Hayes assured Garfield that Sherman did not feel betrayed. Garfield wanted neither to be thought guilty of duplicity nor to forego the Treasury Department patronage in the ensuing campaign.

Hayes spelled out three campaign issues for Garfield. With the battle of the riders fresh in his mind, Hayes stressed the attempt by the Democrats "to reestablish the States Rights doctrine of Calhoun and the Rebellion, and the resistance to these reactionary movements by the Republican party." Hayes also wished to advertise the "prosperous condition of the Government and the People by reason of Republican measures & administration." Although he did not elaborate, he obviously thought that his policies in regard to specie resumption and civil-service reform had benefited the economy and the government. The third issue that Hayes wanted his party to exploit was quite predictable, considering his initial reaction to the convention. He wanted to stress: "The character, life, and Services of Gen. Garfield."[13]

Garfield's nomination was the beginning of the end of the Hayes administration. Although Hayes would be president for nine more months, he became more reflective about the accomplishments of his administration and less concerned with its present or future policies. No longer at the center of the vortex of politics, he became an observer at its edge. The nation focused its attention on the campaign and then on the president-elect. After listing possible issues for Garfield, Hayes had nothing to do with the campaign, beyond responding to Garfield's requests. These requests were, not for advice on issues, but for a timely appointment or reappointment that would help to heal party strife and to ensure a Republican triumph in November.

The customhouse in Portland, Oregon, and the post office in Philadelphia concerned Garfield. On 16 June, the day after Hayes had discussed the convention and the campaign with him, Garfield referred to the president a telegram from Portland, claiming that John Kelly "should be reappointed Collector at this port" since "any change now would endanger the success of the republican party here in November." Two weeks later, after claiming to be unwilling to annoy Hayes "with letters in reference to removals or appointments," Garfield repeated warnings from Oregon and elsewhere that Kelly's removal would "seriously affect our prospects." Secretary of the Navy Thompson, through the unlikely medium of Schurz, urged Hayes to retain Kelly or at least to postpone action until Thompson could personally investigate, during his forthcoming trip to the West Coast. Hayes told Thompson he *"probably"* would postpone action until he could report, but he warned Thompson to "hear fully *both* sides—the Kelly men and his opponents."[14]

Garfield also wished to use the Philadelphia postmastership "to heal the dissensions which the contest in Chicago has produced." Since Hayes planned to move former governor John F. Hartranft from the post office to the customhouse, Garfield, after consulting "several prominent Pennsylvania gentlemen," told Hayes he would prefer the new postmaster to be Peter A. B. Widener, a traction magnate and former city treasurer. "He is said to be a man of wealth and influence and not politically obnoxious to either wing of the party & I believe his appointment will greatly aid in the Campaign."

After receiving a second anxious letter, Hayes reassured Garfield: "The Philadelphia Post Office is still in the hands of Gen. Hartranft.

When he leaves it, if he does leave it, I will look carefully into the case. I am doing nothing to hurt the cause if I can avoid it. You will of course be appealed to by all sorts of people and will be perfectly free to make known to me whatever you wish me to know. My purpose is to allow no danger to come through me." Garfield got the point. "I want you," he responded, "to give me credit for many requests I do not make—or rather—for not making very many of those which I am asked to do."[15]

While Hayes wished to cooperate, he followed, as always, his own counsel. He realized that there were "oceans of requests" that Garfield did not transmit to him, and he reassured Garfield, "do not hesitate to refer communications, or make requests." Yet Hayes's next sentence denied Garfield's most recent request:

> I named Gen. [Henry Shippen] Huidekoper for Post Master of Philadelphia. He commanded the Bucktails and lost an arm at Gettysburg—is a man of education and social standing. Any other appointment, which has been strongly urged, would have offended some powerful faction. This will not specially offend anybody, and will be very popular with the whole soldier element of Pennsylvania. He will be an excellent officer, and this in the long run is the consideration which does and should win.

Out on the West Coast, Thompson discovered that the customhouse controversy in Portland was mainly a factional struggle over patronage and that Kelly's reappointment or nonreappointment would not jeopardize Republican control of Oregon.[16]

Although Hayes ardently wanted Garfield to win, Garfield disappointed Hayes as a candidate. Garfield's letter of acceptance seemed to abandon what Hayes had won in his struggle with Conkling over senatorial courtesy, and it ignored the successful application of an appointments policy based on open competitive examinations in the New York Customhouse. Garfield said he would seek and receive guidance from Congress in making appointments. "The first great step in the reform," Hayes wrote upon seeing Garfield's letter, "is to abolish Congressional patronage—to restore to the Executive the appointing power which has been usurped by Congress, and especially by the Senate." Hayes took that step and was "filling the important places of Collector of the Ports, and Post Master at Philadelphia almost without a suggestion even from Senators or Representatives!" Aware that most of his reform accomplishments could disappear, Hayes was disturbed by Garfield's attempt "to be politic—to trim—to talk so equivocally as to have the benefit of opposing no body." Garfield aroused fears among reformers, which were expressed by Curtis, that if elected, he would follow no firm civil-service policy since his "fibre" was not "steel."[17]

Hayes's fiber was steel, and he carefully differentiated between consultation and dictation. No one dictated appointments to Hayes, but his cabinet members regularly consulted with friendly congressmen, such as Garfield, about appointments in their districts. Garfield, in turn, consulted with Charles E. Henry, the special agent of the Post Office Department, who managed the political affairs of Garfield in the Nineteenth Ohio Congressional District. In the three-way relationship between the civil servant, his congressional patron, and his administrative chief, Henry owed most of his allegiance to Garfield. Together, they supported appointees who they thought would make good civil servants and who would work to advance Garfield's political career. It was always possible that disappointed office seekers would turn on Garfield, but that risk was outweighed by the devotion of successful nominees. With Henry running things back home, the congressional control of local patronage had worked well for Garfield, and he failed to see the danger that Hayes insisted was there.[18]

Even though reformers were vexed by the actions of Garfield, they continued to support him. They realized that the Democrats and their nominee, Gen. Winfield Scott Hancock, were less inclined than Garfield to reform the civil service. Hayes continued to give Garfield encouragement and advice. After Garfield had impetuously responded to a hostile letter, Hayes told him that a candidate must be absolutely divorced from his inkstand. He should write *"NO letters to strangers, or to anybody else on politics."*

Garfield's most questionable move was his trip to New York to conciliate Conkling. Because Hayes had won the 1876 election with 19 electoral votes from southern states that the Republicans no longer had any chance of winning, Garfield had to gain an equal number of votes from states that Tilden had carried. New York (35 votes), Indiana (15), and Connecticut (6) were all possibilities. To win the necessary votes, Garfield needed organization, money, and hard work, but Hayes's civil-service policies threatened to wither political organizations and to choke off party revenues from assessments on officeholders. In contrast, the spoilsmen were adept at extracting cash from civil servants, and the Conkling machine, if its members worked, could wrest New York from the Democrats.[19]

With the reform vote still safe, Garfield wrote to tell Hayes that he was going to New York to promote party peace. When the Republican National Committee had asked Garfield to come, he had insisted that

"Sherman & leading men of all shades of Republicanism" be invited. To reassure Hayes, Garfield added, "If any part of the purpose of this meeting is to secure any concessions to the New York men who are sulking—they will find no help in me beyond what I would give to any Republican." To placate the reformers, Garfield also planned to see George William Curtis in New York.

The 5 August meeting of Republican notables at the Fifth Avenue Hotel included Sherman, who thought Garfield should not have attended "a mere political meeting," and Blaine, but not Conkling, who was enjoying the sea breezes at Coney Island. Several of Conkling's lieutenants did attend, however; they claimed that Garfield, who was conciliatory and ambiguous, had promised them the spoils of New York. Accepting his lieutenants' version of what had transpired, Conkling ceased his sulking, took to the stump, worked effectively for the Republican party, but avoided mentioning Garfield in any generous way.[20]

Although Garfield activated the Conkling organization, he had his doubts about the New York meeting. His diary reveals that he felt "no serious mistake had been made and probably much good had been done. No trades, no shackles, and as well fitted for defeat or victory as ever." Garfield said essentially the same thing to Curtis. "I had an exceedingly interesting talk with Garfield in New York," Curtis reported to Hayes, "and I was very glad to know that if elected, he will come in perfectly independent."

Yet Garfield, an introspective man, must have realized that he had led the Conkling men to expect more than he planned to give and that his ambiguity, born of the twin desires to win the election and to please everybody, would later plague him. He confided to Hayes: "If I finished the New York trip without mistakes, I shall be glad. I think some good was done." Schurz thought no good had been done; he wrote to Garfield that his trip was a "mistake, for it was certain that under existing circumstances you could not make it without giving color to rumors of concession, surrender, promises etc., impairing the strength of your legislative record."[21]

Although Hayes acted very presidentially and did not campaign, he followed his advice to Garfield "to drop a good seed at every available point" when he addressed soldier reunions and toured the Far West. Hayes thought that an effective speech on Garfield's behalf would contrast the fifth plank of the Democratic platform, which insisted that a free ballot must "be maintained in every part of the United States," with what Democrats had done "in South Carolina, Mississippi, Louisiana and other States" to disfranchise blacks and to deprive Republicans of a majority in both houses of Congress.

Hayes was certain that white southerners and the Democratic party had injured the South profoundly by failing "to faithfully observe the 15*th* amendment." He continued: "[It] is the cause of the failure of all efforts towards complete pacification. It is on this hook that the bloody shirt now hangs. This causes the immigrant to avoid the South" and explains why "only one city out of the *twenty* which now have a population exceeding one hundred thousand is a Southern City." Hayes had lost all hope that a conciliatory policy would attract moderate southerners to the Republican party.

While planning his remarks to the Union veterans, Hayes decided that he would tell them that they had served the right side of a good cause:

> It is now true that this is God's Country, if equal rights—a fair start and an equal chance in the race of life are every where secured to all. . . . What we fought for was to make us one people—a free people. . . .
>
> Just in proportion as the results and true principles of that combat have been fully and cheerfully accepted, just in that proportion is our Country in its several parts prosperous and happy.

For Hayes, freedom, political equality, and equality of economic opportunity were more than constitutional principles; they were the moral ideals, the secular religious doctrines (more important than Christian dogma) on which "God's Country" had been founded.[22]

Hayes was circumspect, as custom demanded, in his speech at Columbus on 11 August, where he shared the platform with General William T. Sherman, who made his immortal remark, "war . . . is all hell." Neither at Columbus nor at Canton, where on 1 September he spoke at the reunion of his Twenty-third Ohio Regiment, did Hayes attack the Democratic party. He did allude to equal rights, and he conceded that there had been some progress in the South, but he emphasized that though the war had destroyed slavery, "its evils live after it, and deprive many parts of the South of that intelligent self-government without which, in America at least, great and permanent prosperity is impossible." While Hayes believed that the Democrats were responsible for inequality in the South, he realized that even a Republican victory in 1880 could not achieve equality for blacks. Equal rights would be won ultimately through education. "My hobby," he wrote while preparing for his speech at Columbus, "more and more is likely to be Common School Education, or universal education."

Hayes had faith that free schools for the children of all races would eliminate "ignorant voters" who were "powder and ball for the demagogues" and would, as Lincoln wished, give everyone "an unfettered start and a fair chance in the race of life." Hayes was concerned that the political and economic well-being of the country required that all be educated; and this universal education could not be accomplished without federal aid, because southern states and western territories were too impoverished to educate all of their children. Federal subsidies, in the form either of land grants—for which there were ample precedents—or direct appropriations from the United States Treasury, had to be made whenever local systems were inadequate. Wherever the work of the schoolmaster "shall be well done, in all our borders," Hayes predicted at Columbus, "it will be found that there, also, the principles of the Declaration of Independence will be cherished, the sentiment of nationality will prevail, the equal rights amendments will be cheerfully obeyed, and there will be 'the home of freedom and the refuge of the oppressed of every race and of every clime.'"[23]

Hayes's point—that an educated electorate is more difficult for a demagogue to manipulate—was well taken, but as he knew, the problem for southern blacks was not demagogues who deceived them but bulldozers who beat them. Education would improve the economic status of impoverished blacks and whites, and educated blacks would protest their disfranchisement more vigorously than would ignorant blacks, but education alone could not secure equal rights. To achieve them, the federal government would have to enforce the Fourteenth and Fifteenth amendments.

During Hayes's administration, Democratic strength in Congress and apathy among Republicans made enforcing those amendments impossible. Hayes managed to keep the Force Acts (i.e., election laws) on the books, but they were not enforced in the South. After his administration, Republican apathy increased, and ultimately, in 1894 under Grover Cleveland, the Democrats swept away the Enforcement Acts, and virtually all southern blacks became disfranchised. Realizing that there was little chance that the election laws would give blacks the vote, Hayes pinned his hopes on education, which would enable blacks to win the vote. Even this dream was not to be. The Blair bill, which embodied Hayes's ideas on federal aid to education, never passed Congress.[24]

Although Hayes remained aloof from Garfield's campaign, members of his administration became involved in it. He had prohibited political assessments in June 1877, but by early 1878 he had explained that he did not object to officeholders making voluntary contributions. While Hayes insisted that no one would be dismissed for refusing to contribute, civil servants were apprehensive when they received printed circulars stipulating the exact amount they were expected to give. As a congressman, Garfield had condemned political assessments, but as a presidential candidate he knew how badly money was needed for campaign documents, speakers, and meetings. Far from stopping political assessments, he rallied those who collected them. "Old boy," he told a collector, "do all you can to raise the *sinews of war*." About the only civil servants who were safe from these ubiquitous collectors, armed with lists of names specifying expected contributions, were in Schurz's Interior Department and in Silas W. Burt's New York Naval Office.

Sherman insisted that all Treasury Department employees contribute, while local political leaders, such as Chester Arthur in New York, canvassed field offices. Garfield wrote the chief assessor in Washington: "Please say to Brady that I hope he will give us all the assistance he can. I think he can help effectually. Please tell me how the Departments generally are doing." Thomas J. Brady, Hayes's second assistant postmaster general, was busily engaged not only in assessing officeholders but also, unbeknownst to Garfield and Hayes, in defrauding the Post Office Department of large sums of money that was earmarked for its star routes in sparsely populated areas. Assessments were systematically levied during the campaign, and if an officeholder failed to contribute voluntarily, he was sent a reminder. In Pennsylvania, recalcitrant officeholders were warned by a third notice: "At the close of the campaign we shall place a list of those who have not paid in the hands of the Department you are in."[25]

The star-route frauds, for which Brady was primarily responsible, also helped to finance Garfield's campaign. These special postal routes—which were designated on lists by three stars for "certainty, celerity, and security"—were primarily in the West. They depended upon "stagecoach, buckboard and saddle horse" for transportation. Marauders, topography, and climate made them difficult and dangerous. There were 9,225 star routes, some of them handling only three letters a week, for which $5.9 million was appropriated in 1878. Between 1878 and 1880, Second Assistant Postmaster General Brady and his accomplices furnished sham petitions requesting that service be expedited on ninety-three of these star routes. When Congress responded to the petitions and expedited service, the annual operating costs of those routes jumped from $727,119 to $2,802,214, which required a deficiency appropriation that aroused suspicions in Congress and in Hayes's own mind. Although Congress investigated and uneasily sustained Brady, Hayes insisted that no more liabilities be incurred or increased by new contracts until there had been a full consideration by the postmaster general and a presentation to the cabinet and the president.[26]

Hayes's move came too late. He had been out of office only two months when the scandal broke and the connection between the star-route frauds and the 1880 election, in which Garfield triumphed, became apparent. Stephen W. Dorsey, a former carpetbag senator from Arkansas, was secretary of the Republican National Committee. Along with Marshall Jewell, Dorsey had run Garfield's campaign, and he had worked his greatest miracle in Indiana. In February 1881, a tipsy Vice-President-elect Chester Arthur had praised Dorsey at a lavish testimonial dinner at Delmonico's, which was presided over by the Reverend Henry Ward Beecher and General Grant. ''Indiana was really, I suppose, a Democratic State. It had been put down on the books always as a State that might be carried by close and perfect organization and a great deal of——[mingled cries of ''soap'' and laughter]. I see the reporters are present, therefore I will simply say that everybody showed a great deal of interest in the occasion and distributed tracts and political documents all through the State.''

Arthur obviously was referring to money, and the question of where Dorsey got the money for the Indiana campaign was answered by the exposure of the star-route frauds. Among the star-route contractors were Dorsey's brother, his brother-in-law, and a former partner. These three men controlled twenty-four contracts that originally had been worth $55,246, but had been increased in value to $501,072, thus leaving a balance of $445,826. A small part of the increase went for some improvement in service; the rest was put to private and political use. Dorsey later claimed that he had spent $400,000 on the campaign in Indiana. That, no doubt, was an exaggeration, but the expenditure must have been considerable. Hayes, however, was unaware of the extent to which the post office was being plundered or the civil service was being assessed to keep the Republican party in power.[27]

As the campaign geared up, Hayes underscored his semidetachment from politics by a patriotic act and by a journey to the Far West. On 7 August 1880, Hayes participated in the ceremony laying the first stone since 1855 on the Washington Monument. Chagrined that the country had only completed a quarter of the monument that had been started in 1848 to honor its first president, Hayes made finishing it his "study" and "hobby." He decided that the monument "should overtop all other tall structures," and he enlisted the help of Gen. Thomas L. Casey, who devised a plan to strengthen its foundation. To arrive at a proper height for the monument, Hayes consulted George Perkins Marsh, the United States minister to Italy, who was considered a universal genius. Marsh declared "that there was a rule which determined the height of an obelisk by reference to the dimension of its base." According to this rule, the Washington Monument should be 555 feet high. Its builders made it 5⅛ inches higher. When, thanks to Hayes, it was completed in 1884, the Washington Monument was the world's tallest spire. It is still the highest masonry structure.[28]

Almost carefree, Hayes left "dull" Washington on the evening of 26 August for a trip to the West Coast; he was absent during the height of the campaign, when civil servants were pressed most severely to pay political assessments. Coming just before the election of his successor, this pleasant trip was like taking a bow for a job well done, with people thronging to applaud him everywhere he went. The Hayes family left Washington on 26 August. At home in Spiegel Grove, they celebrated Lucy's forty-ninth birthday and rested for nearly a week. On 1 September, having addressed his Twenty-third Ohio Infantry in Canton, Hayes left by train for California. He was accompanied by Lucy, their sons Birchard and Rutherford, Gen. William T. Sherman and his daughter Rachel, and a few other intimate friends. After a nonstop ride to Salt Lake City, Utah, they proceeded to Virginia City, Nevada, crossed Lake Tahoe and the "notable" Sierra Nevada, and arrived at San Francisco, where Hayes became the first president to visit the West Coast while in office.

In California, Hayes pleased crowds by speaking often during a continuous round of "parades, receptions, balls, banquets, and sight-seeing expeditions." He was impressed by the climate, the mountain scenery, the enormous resources, the enterprising people of the Pacific slope, and their fine homes. On 22 September he made his most elaborate speech, while standing on the steps of the California state Capitol in Sacramento. After referring to the mines of California and the commerce of San Francisco, "the Queen City of the Pacific," Hayes predicted that California, Oregon, and the territories of Washington and Alaska, with their population of one to one-and-a-half million, would someday support fifty million people. He alluded to the hostility that Californians had shown toward Asian laborers. "Whatever difficulties you have here," he assured his hearers, "will all work out right if the

Anglo-Saxon race will stand on that great principle of equal rights of all men." Then he added, "With equal rights and universal education, every community is safe." Declaring that they had "reached the margin" at the end of civilization's westward march, Hayes insisted, "now it is for you . . . to see that . . . American institutions and the American name shall lose nothing at your hands."[29]

From Sacramento, the president's party journeyed north and entered Oregon by stagecoach. In a letter to her "little darling" Fanny, Lucy Hayes exclaimed, "What a beautiful country we have passed through—what magnificent scenery, grand majestic trees and of fruits the most luscious I ever tasted." Traveling by steamboat and railroad up the Columbia River, the members of the party went as far as Walla Walla, Washington, whose size and wealth surprised them. After visiting Puget Sound, which with "Mount Rainier . . . and the Olympic Mountains in sight" was most impressive, Hayes and his traveling companions returned to San Francisco by sea. As they left Astoria, Oregon, at the mouth of the Columbia River, their steamer overhauled "a beautiful Ship, the Valiant from Boston," Hayes recorded. "Her flags were all up in honor of the President, and when we were nearest to her she gave us three rousing cheers. She turned northward towards Puget Sound, and we headed Southward for the golden gate! It impressed me deeply."

Arriving back in San Francisco on 18 October, Hayes and his party visited Yosemite and Los Angeles before returning home by way of Tucson, Santa Fe, Topeka, and Chicago. It was 1 November when they arrived at Fremont. Blessed by superb weather, good health, and no accidents, they had traveled by rail, steamship, and stagecoach; and they had enjoyed sumptuous accommodations and had endured primitive ones. The grand sights they had seen, Hayes confessed, left him and Lucy "with a certain incapacity to tell the exact truth."[30]

Hayes arrived home in Fremont in time to vote. He rejoiced in Garfield's victory and was grateful that it was too decisive to be disputed. In addition, he thought Garfield would uphold "the supremacy of the general Government," would foster prosperity through sound money, would not turn the civil service over to the spoilsmen, and would generally continue Hayes's policies. Garfield's victory was particularly gratifying to Hayes, who believed that his own administration had contributed to the victory and had been vindicated by it.

Earlier in August, George William Curtis, while congratulating Hayes on his admirable speech to the soldiers at Columbus, had added, "It will tend, I am sure, to deepen the feeling of sincere regret that your administration draws to an end,—an administration which has constantly commanded, more & more, the confidence of the country, and which to a large class of the best citizens is the strongest argument for the success of General Garfield, as promising a continuance of its general character.''

Three days after the election, the Republican Business Men's Club of Cleveland also maintained that Hayes's record was what had made possible Garfield's victory. Grateful for what he termed the rather extravagant compliment, Hayes responded: ''It has been my firm purpose to do that which appeared to me for the good of the whole country and that of each and all of its inhabitants,'' and in so doing, ''I have to some extent promoted the success of the Republican party.'' Garfield's election proved to Hayes's satisfaction that the most memorable words in his Inaugural Address—indeed the most enduring words that Hayes ever uttered—were true: ''He serves his party best who serves the country best.''[31]

10

★ ★ ★ ★ ★

THE END
OF AN ADMINISTRATION

Buoyed by his "most delightful & instructive" West Coast trip and by the election results, Hayes returned to Washington on 6 November. After an absence of seventy-one days, he was ready to enjoy his four months as a lame duck. His most pressing task was to prepare his fourth and final annual message, which he sent to Congress on 6 December 1880.[1]

For special discussion, Hayes singled out civil rights for blacks, civil-service reform, and polygamy in Utah. In "several of the late slave holding States" during the recent election, he declared, blacks were deprived of the right to vote. They were kept from voting more by fraud than by violence or intimidation. There were frauds in connection with the ballots, with the places and manner of voting, and with the counting, returning, and canvassing of the votes cast. Sectionalism in politics, Hayes predicted, would prevail as long as either of the equal-rights amendments was "flagrantly violated or disregarded." Bygones would not be bygones until every qualified American citizen could freely cast a vote and have it honestly counted. He urged the House and the Senate to investigate violations of the Fifteenth Amendment and to appropriate funds for the executive to prosecute those who deprived any citizens of their constitutional rights. Traversing much of the ground that he had covered in his August speeches, Hayes again asked Congress to supplement local educational funds in states that had inadequate public-school systems.

Once more, Hayes called for civil-service reform. His experience as president strengthened his conviction that appointments for partisan considerations endangered the stability of the government. Regulations that had been designed to secure and retain the best-qualified civil servants had proved most satisfactory, he declared. When he claimed that competitive examinations were in place in several executive departments and in the large customhouses and post offices, Hayes was exaggerating, but he was not exaggerating when he stressed that these examinations had been applied during the past two years to over two thousand positions in the New York Customhouse and Post Office. In those offices, he correctly reported, ''All are subjected to the same tests, and the result is free from prejudice by personal favor or partisan influence.'' Hayes asked Congress for a $25,000 appropriation to enable the president to appoint a commission to devise and supervise a system of competitive examinations for use throughout the civil service. Hayes argued that there should also be legislation to protect governmental workers from political assessments.

Recalling his struggle with Conkling, Hayes said that the most serious obstacle to improving the civil service was the spoils system, which he defined as the encroachment upon the appointing power by members of Congress. ''The first step in the reform of the civil service must be a complete divorce between Congress and the Executive in the matter of appointments,'' he declared. The Senate should advise and consent in regard to major appointments, and the House should accuse and prosecute before the Senate those who have proved faithless, but ''judges and accusers, should not dictate appointments to office.'' Hayes recommended that Congress define the relationship of its members to presidential appointments. He also called for the repeal of the Tenure of Office Act of 2 March 1867, which required that the Senate approve the removal of appointees whom it had confirmed.

Seeing Salt Lake City on his western journey had not reconciled Hayes to polygamy or to the Mormon sect, which dominated political power in Utah Territory. He observed that ''polygamy will not be abolished if the enforcement of the law depends on those who practice and uphold the crime. It can only be suppressed by taking away the political power of the sect which encourages and sustains it.'' To uphold monogamy as well as religious liberty and the separation of church and state, Hayes urged that the government of Utah be reorganized to break sectarian political power. Taking an idea from the Northwest Ordinance of 1787, he recommended that Utah be governed by a governor and judges or commissioners, appointed by the president and confirmed by the Senate. If Congress should balk at depriving Utah of its local government, Hayes suggested that "the right to vote, hold office, and sit on juries in the Territory of Utah be confined to those who neither practice nor uphold polygamy."[2]

Apart from his concern over de Lesseps's proposed Panama Canal, the remainder of Hayes's fourth annual message was routine. He was pleased that with the return of prosperity the federal government's income of $333.5 million during the fiscal year ending 30 June 1880 represented an increase of 22 percent and exceeded its expenditures by $65.9 million. The chief sources of revenue were tariffs ($186.5 million) and excise taxes ($124.0 million), and the major expenditures were for interest on the public debt ($95.8 million); for pensions ($56.8 million); for the army, including river and harbor projects by army engineers ($38.1 million); for public buildings, collecting the revenue, and miscellaneous expenses ($34.5 million); for civil expenses ($15.7 million); for the navy ($13.5 million); and for Native Americans ($5.9 million).

Despite prosperity, Hayes repeated his attack on greenbacks and silver dollars, which were being minted under the Bland-Allison Act. Hayes also urged Congress to improve the army and the navy and to provide for additional circuit-court judges to ease the burden on the existing judicial system. (In 1891, legislation embodying most of Hayes's recommendations to increase the number of judges was finally passed.) Hayes anticipated a demand of the Populist party in 1892 by calling for a system of postal savings, and he anticipated the demands of later conservationists by favoring the orderly but not wasteful utilization of the nation's natural resources. He urged Congress to codify the land laws, to expand the Geological Survey to cover the whole country, and to prevent the "rapid and indiscriminate destruction" of public timber lands."[3]

While the problem of the Poncas pressed Hayes during his last months in office, other problems also vied for his attention. "A perpetual stream, growing too, of matters that must be attended to is pouring in upon me," he complained, "and I haven't time to eat or sleep." Friends, such as William Henry Smith, whom Hayes obliged "if right and practicable," continued to ask for appointments while he remained in office; and Hayes still had to resolve patronage disputes. There was the postmastership at Urbana, Illinois, to which Richard C. McCormick, the secretary of the Republican National Committee in 1876, wanted a Mrs. Whitcomb appointed, but to which Congressman Joseph G. Cannon, in whose district Urbana was located and whose wishes therefore prevailed, wanted the assistant postmaster promoted.

The Richmond Post Office presented a less routine, more delicate, and more significant problem. Marshall Jewell, chairman of the Republican National Committee, and Joseph Jorgensen, a Republican congressman from Virginia, wanted Hayes to pay off a political debt by appointing "Mr. Pelouze of Richmond" as postmaster. The Republicans had nominated Pelouze for Congress, but their strategists "desired him to get off the ticket" so that they could throw their support to the Readjuster party of Democratic dissidents, led by Senator William Mahone of Virginia, whom the Republicans hoped would help them to organize the next Senate. Hayes did not appoint Pelouze. By January 1881 the degree of support that would be given to Virginia Republicans or to Readjusters was up to Garfield.[4]

Hayes also concentrated on easing Garfield's transition into the presidency. Helpful and generous, Hayes made suggestions and offered to make personnel moves to shield Garfield from adverse reactions. Hayes's cabinet suggestions included Horace Davis, a businessman and congressman from California who was the nephew of the historian George Bancroft. Hayes thought that making Davis secretary of the interior would "represent well the Pacific Coast." He also told Garfield that former Governor Elisha M. Pease of Texas—a "noble man,"—a Unionist, a post–Civil War Republican, and Hayes's collector of customs at Galveston—"would be a wise, safe and popular Southern member" in his cabinet.

Hayes also passed on plugs for both Sherman and Blaine. He relayed to Garfield Vice-President Wheeler's view "that it will be regarded as ungenerous in you and a disregard of the public interests if Sherman is not retained" in the Treasury Department. Hayes added: "Blaine is favorably spoken of for Secretary of State in all quarters—but probably he wouldn't accept. Why not offer it?" A month later, when it appeared that Hayes had miscalculated and that Blaine would be in the State Department, Hayes wrote, "it is deemed fortunate and wise" and then warned, "The saving clause in the whole business, is *the faith that you will be president.*"

After it was apparent that Garfield did not want Sherman in his cabinet, Hayes mentioned that Senator William Windom of Minnesota was a favorite for the Treasury Department. Among the names that Hayes had mentioned, only Windom and Blaine, for whom Hayes lacked the enthusiasm that most Republicans possessed, made Garfield's cabinet. Unlike Hayes, Garfield was willing to sacrifice some executive independence in cabinet making in order to secure good relations with Congress. Explaining his decision not to appoint Davis, he said to Hayes, ''I like Horace Davis—and I wish he had the support of his delegation, but fear he has not.''[5]

Military retirements and promotions were particularly prickly, and Garfield hoped that Hayes would settle these nettlesome problems. Garfield requested that his Civil War army aide and crony Maj. David G. Swaim be made judge advocate general, so that he would be near Garfield in Washington. Swaim had lent Garfield $6,500 for his Washington home—about half its cost—and had served him in the recent campaign. Garfield loved to play cards and billiards with Swaim and found peace in his cigar-smoking, hedonistic presence. Garfield explained to Hayes: ''There may be difficulties in the way of detailing, even temporarily, an army officer, to act as my private secretary—I know there were many heart burnings in the army and among civilians growing out of Grant's course on that subject. If therefore you find it convenient to retire the Judge Advocate General, and appoint Major Swaim, I shall be very glad to have you do so. . . . I fear, that should I call him away from his strictly professional duties, antagonisms might be created which would make his promotion more difficult.'' Hayes obliged Garfield, by making Swaim judge advocate general, and noted, ''I would like to have him near me in Washington my last month to help manage matters so they will dovetail with your purposes.'' In addition, Hayes promoted to brigadier general two of Garfield's close friends, Nelson A. Miles and William B. Hazen.

Adding to the army's retired list was a troublesome question. ''I shall look with interest,'' Garfield wrote to Hayes, ''upon the retirement of Army officers & hope you may be well through it before I go in.'' Many army officers fought to avoid retirement at three-quarters pay. When Hayes retired Gen. Edward O. C. Ord, who was stationed in Texas, it was in spite of the support that Ord had mustered from Collis P. Huntington of the Central Pacific Railroad, Thomas A. Scott of the Texas & Pacific and Pennsylvania railroads, and William T. Sherman, the commanding general of the army.[6]

Doing the dirty work to make Garfield's beginning easier created problems for Hayes. Even though William T. Sherman had traveled with Hayes to the West Coast, Hayes noted in January: ''I have for the present lost the friendship of Gen Sherman. Several things have occurred to which this may be attributed. 1. I recommended the promotion of Gen Grant to a Captain Generalcy. 2. I retired certain officers, notably Gen Ord, against his advice and wish. 3. I promoted Gens Hazen and Miles against his wish.''

Although unyielding in his respect for Grant, Sherman had opposed special legislation to create a new title for him and felt that his position had been "misunderstood in high circles." Sherman maintained that "all should be treated alike," that Grant's special treatment might "prejudice the interest and harmony of the Service," and that Grant should be retired at three-fourths pay, like other officers, rather than be given a salary increase by promoting him to a new rank. Sherman's opposition to the promotion of Miles, who had married Sherman's niece, is difficult to understand, but Sherman may have been prejudiced against him because Miles was not a West Pointer. Miles had learned his profession by fighting in every important battle that had involved the Army of the Potomac except for one, had distinguished himself against the Sioux and the Nez Perces, and was helping Hayes to solve the Ponca problem. Sherman's annoyance at Hazen's promotion is more understandable. Through his Garfield connection, Hazen was an early and effective "whistle blower," but he had not endeared himself to his colleagues by helping to expose the corrupt post-trader system in Grant's War Department.[7]

Hayes even wished to collaborate with Garfield on a last-minute cabinet appointment. After firing Secretary of the Navy Thompson for his involvement with de Lesseps's Panama Canal project, Hayes was willing for Garfield to select Thompson's replacement, but Garfield had not as yet decided on that cabinet appointment. Hayes asked Nathan Goff, a district attorney in West Virginia, to complete Thompson's term, with the understanding that when Garfield took office, he would reappoint Goff to his old post.[8]

Hayes and Garfield also collaborated to fill a Supreme Court vacancy. The Massachusetts congressional delegation recommended Attorney General Charles Devens for the post with a delicacy that bordered on hypocrisy. While Senators Dawes and Hoar tried to influence Hayes, they avoided the appearance of such behavior. With Senator Dawes verbally concurring, Senator Hoar wrote the letter recommending Devens for the Court, but neither senator signed it, lest it become a formal recommendation. These maneuverings were futile, for Hayes and Garfield had agreed that Stanley Matthews, Hayes's old friend and Garfield's rival for the Senate in 1877, would get the appointment. But Matthews, who was reputed to be close to railroad and corporate interests and was instrumental in resolving the crisis of 1877, was not confirmed by the Senate. In part, it was felt that his nomination was a reward for services to Hayes. Garfield later renewed the nomination, and Matthews became a member of the Supreme Court by the grace of one vote.

Hayes and Garfield wanted the nominations on which they had

collaborated to be confirmed quickly, so they would not go over into Garfield's administration. The problem, Hayes noted, was that "so many are interested in particular cases, in rejections, that by combining all such opposers into a general opposition it is possible that postponement will result." Undaunted, he continued his efforts to appoint those whom Garfield wished to have in office at the start of his administration.[9]

Although some of Garfield's actions made Hayes apprehensive, their correspondence continued to be cordial during this transitional period. Aware that Garfield could not afford equipage appropriate for his new office, Hayes left his horses and carriage for Garfield's immediate use. Hayes obviously liked Garfield, but he shared with many of his contemporaries the fear that Garfield lacked backbone. Vice-President Wheeler, while chatting with Hayes about Garfield, remarked: "I have said forty times, if he had one tenth of your amiable obstinacy and independence he would be a great success," and Hayes thought the comparison was worth preserving in his diary. Garfield's plan to "restore wine and liquor to the White House," Hayes believed, was evidence that he "lacks the grit to face fashionable ridicule." Garfield, no doubt, had heard Evarts and others quip that water flowed like wine in the Hayes White House.[10]

Despite his placid nature, Hayes was sufficiently agitated to prepare for Garfield a memorandum on temperance in the White House. Whatever may be true of Europeans, Hayes declared, "the American who drinks wine is in danger of becoming the victim of drunkenness, licentiousness and gambling." He believed that Garfield would "grievously disappoint thousands of the best people who supported" him if he were to bring wine and liquor back into the White House, and Hayes warned Garfield that it would "revive the Temperance party, which has now dropped almost out of sight, and give it votes enough to put in jeopardy the republican ascendancy/supremacy in Maine, New Hampshire, Connecticut, New York, Ohio, Indiana and in perhaps thirty Northern Congressional districts," and would "seriously damage your personal reputation and your political prospects" for reelection.

This analysis was uncannily prophetic. In 1880 the Prohibitionists won only 1,517 votes in New York State, but in 1884 they piled up 25,016 votes. The Republicans lost New York by 1,149 votes, and by losing New York, they lost the national election. Perhaps recalling his own reaction in January 1880 to "a state dinner at the President's . . . wet down with coffee and cold water," Garfield was unimpressed by Hayes's argument.[11]

Temperance did not dampen the genial social temperaments of Hayes and Lucy. Departing from their custom, they dined out a number of times during their last winter in Washington. Dinner with the historian George Bancroft was enjoyable, not only for his "conversation and vigor" while telling stories about John C. Calhoun and Henry Clay, but also for the guests, who included Caroline Edgar Bonaparte, Daniel Webster's granddaughter, who told about his midnight-to-dawn preparation for his reply to Robert Y. Hayne; and Henry Adams, who characteristically and undiplomatically declared, "Our system of Government has failed utterly in many respects."

Often dinners, according to the custom of the day, were all-male affairs. When Evarts gave a dinner for the cabinet, all its members were there, with the exception of Postmaster General Horace Maynard. Both Secretary of the Navy Thompson and Assistant Secretary of State John Hay regaled the gathering. The president recorded: "Mr Hay tells anecdotes capitally. He is timely and apt in using them and his fund is prodigious." At yet another bachelor dinner—one in honor of Grant—Senator George F. Edmunds, Hayes noted, told "good anecdotes, and is *both* witty and humorous—a rare combination."[12]

While Hayes was comfortable at formal affairs, Lucy was ill at ease, and both preferred informality. "Lucy," Hayes remarked, "is well enough in all respects in the duties of a State dinner, but she feels unequal to them, and therefore hates State dinners." The state dinner for Grant that provoked these remarks actually "passed off in good style." Hayes was also pleased that the annual New Year's ceremonies were noted in newspapers for their "unwonted brilliancy" and that Lucy kept her 8 January reception from being formal and stiff "by ornamenting the rooms with flags and flowers, and by gathering a number of her most entertaining friends, young and old, to assist her . . . in making it an enjoyable social reunion." At their diplomatic reception on 24 February, the Hayeses entertained between two and three thousand guests, including all the cabinet, members of the diplomatic corps, most of the Supreme Court, many senators, and fifteen representatives who skipped a night session until they were forced to return to the House for a vote. The president and his wife shook hands for two hours and were pleased that the "entertainment in both dining rooms was unusually well done."[13]

Lucy may have been an uneasy hostess at formal events, but she put her guests at ease. People liked her, and Hayes was gratified by "the heartiness and warmth of friendship for Lucy." He was pleased when newspapers unfriendly to him paid compliments to her graciousness. Her dark hair and the light in her eyes made her resemble the Madonna, particularly when the young faces of Fanny and Scott framed her portrait, and the simple elegance of her dress for state affairs made her stand out in an extravagant era. Hayes was proud that she remained beautiful as she grew older and was pleased that her happy spirit permeated the White House. To better impart warmth and cheerfulness to the hundreds of White House guests, without resorting to alcoholic beverages, Lucy sent to Ohio for young reinforcements. A host of young relatives and friends spent weeks or even months at the White House during the winter social season.[14]

Except for the state dinners and receptions, whose formality Lucy tried to mitigate, life at the Hayes White House was unpretentious and lively and centered about family and friends. Hayes, who found that nothing in life equaled family ties and affections, was buoyed in the White House by the obvious delight that his family took in their surroundings. Among relatives and friends in Ohio, Lucy's name was synonymous with "happy, hilarious times," and she filled her children's Washington days with fun.

Holidays were given over to the younger children, Fanny and Scott, who were often surrounded by "a merry crowd of little folks." At the sounding of a bell on Christmas, they raced to bring presents from the Red Room to the library, where family, servants, and friends waited expectantly. Whether sledding after a winter's snow, taking "lessons at the swimming school," or attending their dancing master's costume ball as Martha Washington and an orderly sergeant of their father's Twenty-third Regiment, Fanny and Scott loved each other's company. And Hayes loved watching them at play. While a "noisy happy party of thirty" played "blindman's buff and other sports in the East room and halls" during Scott's seventh-birthday celebration, the president stood nearby, talking "country and religion" with a governor, a general, and a bishop.[15]

Hayes was proud and understanding of his children, but he seldom overrated them. He noted how his "Little Fanny in the presence of strangers spoke lightly" of the death of Old Whitey, his war horse, and then went off alone for "a good cry." Although Webb lacked the scholarship that Hayes wished he might have had, he was "full of social and friendly qualities" and at twenty was his father's stand-by and unofficial secretary. He was the only one of the older children—a trio of boys—to live with his parents in the White House. His older brother Birchard, "conscientious, scholarly, but not so practical," was studying law at Harvard and then practicing it in Toledo; and Ruddy, the family's third son, was at Cornell, studying natural sciences, an area in which he was "quick," though he was "slow in others." On the few occasions when the president's family circle was complete, these young men and their friends made White House dinners "unusually chatty and lively."[16]

These young people were joined by older Ohio relatives and friends, who, along with the entire White House staff, took part on 30 December 1877 in the grandest family celebration that was held during the Hayes White House years. In their unabashed love for each other, Rutherford and Lucy Hayes reenacted their wedding on its silver anniversary. The original minister and attendants repeated their parts, while Lucy was "as merry as a girl" in her twenty-five-year-old wedding garments. The ceremony in the Blue Room was followed by the reading of commemorative poems and congratulatory letters and the christening of the First Lady's namesake Lucy Hayes Herron, followed by that of Fanny and Scott. Lucy's favorite present was an ebony-framed silver tablet engraved "To 'the Mother of Ours'" from the Twenty-third Regiment of Ohio Volunteers. It pictured the log cabin that Lucy and her sons had occupied while visiting Hayes in camp during the Civil War.[17]

Although the Hayeses entertained lavishly, his annual salary of $50,000 easily covered their expenditures. Yearly White House expenses, he estimated, were a bit under $25,000, and in addition, Hayes spent from $6,000 to $7,000 annually "for the advantage of the Republican cause." He told Garfield that he could probably save $20,000 a year while president, although Hayes had "not quite" saved that amount. In debt when he became president, Hayes paid off some of his debts during his White House years but noted: "I shall leave here in debt from twenty thousand to twenty-five thousand dollars, but with a good credit, plenty of property, and in no sense needing pecuniary aid or sympathy. If the times continue good a few years longer, I am sure of a competency—a happy independence." Five months later, Hayes sought a low-interest loan for between $25,000 and $30,000. "It *will be my only debt*," he confided, and "I am always punctual in interest &c." He estimated that at current prices, his property was worth between $200,000 and $300,000.[18]

Hayes and Lucy never regretted the decision to serve only one term. Although William Henry Smith tried to shake his resolve, Hayes remained adamant and at times appeared even anxious to leave. "Well," Elinor (Mrs. William Dean) Howells said to him in May 1880, "you will soon be out of it," to which he replied, "Yes, out of a scrape, out of a scrape." In January 1881, Hayes elaborated on the *New York Daily Graphic*'s comment that he would go out of office "with more peace and blessing than any President in fifty six years," and its question, "Who since Monroe has gone out both *willingly* and regretted?" Suggesting that "gladly" might be truthfully substituted for "willingly," Hayes said:

> We have upon the whole enjoyed our four years here. But the responsibility, the embarrassments, the heart breaking sufferings which we cant relieve, the ever present danger of scandals and crimes among those we are compelled to trust, and a thousand other draw backs to our satisfaction and enjoyment by which we are constantly surrounded leave us no place for regret upon retiring . . . to the freedom independence and safety of our obscure and happy home in the pleasant grove at Fremont.[19]

Although eager to return to Spiegel Grove, Hayes was confident that he had been a good president. He contrasted his arrival in Washington with his withdrawal:

> Coming in, I was denounced as a fraud by all the extreme men of the opposing party and as an ingrate and a traitor by the same class of men in my own party. Going out, I have the good will, blessing and approval of the best people of all parties and sections. . . . I had a strong and comforting faith that I should be able to organize and conduct an administration which would satisfy and win the Country. This faith never deserted me. I had it before either the election or the nomination. Doubtless it was founded on my experience. I have often said that I never fail to gain the confidence and friendship of those I wish to win if I have time and an opportunity to do so.

As he was poised to leave Washington, Hayes remarked: "My closing days are full of satisfaction. I have shaken hands with five hundred today. Many clergymen congratulate me. The burden of the talk on all sides is a clean, honest, independent and successful Administration. Mr. [Alexander H.] Stephens of Georgia says he never saw an Administration go out so well spoken of. Senators, Representatives and Citizens say the same."[20]

On the evening of 3 March the Hayeses entertained his cabinet and the Garfield family. At the inaugural the next day, Hayes, according to George W. Julian, an old abolitionist who had supported Tilden, "looked as sweet & lamblike as possible, but Garfield's face looked worn." After the inauguration, the Hayeses gave the Garfields lunch and, with their personal belongings ready to be shipped to Ohio, left the

White House, spending the night with John and Margaret Sherman and leaving the next morning for Fremont.[21]

The future posed no problem for Hayes. At Fremont, he told the enthusiastic crowd that welcomed him and Lucy that a retired president should, "like every other good American citizen, be willing and prompt to bear his part in every useful work that will promote the welfare and happiness of his family, his town, his State, and his country."

At Spiegel Grove, Hayes and Lucy resumed the quiet life that they had enjoyed before his 1875 nomination for governor. To be sure, the house had been enlarged during his presidency, and distinguished visitors called more frequently and stayed longer than in the past. Hayes managed his real-estate holdings, collected books for his new library, read extensively, and monitored public events, on which he frequently commented in his voluminous correspondence and diary. Out of power and without responsibility, his views were consistent with those he had expressed while in office but were often more pointed. His denunciation of giant monopolistic corporations and his support of federal railroad regulation in 1887, when Congress passed the Interstate Commerce Act, reflected a change, not in his principles, but in an economy that was being reshaped by combinations; not in his beliefs, but in the intensity with which they were felt.[22]

Hayes participated in the life of Fremont. He joined the local post of the Grand Army of the Republic, rejoined—after a thirty-three-year lapse of membership—the International Order of Odd Fellows, and assumed again a major responsibility in directing the Birchard Library, a gift to the community from his uncle. The Hayeses generously supported the local Methodist church, to which Lucy belonged, and occasionally contributed to other churches, including a Roman Catholic one.

Hayes's philanthropic activities fulfilled his vows to promote welfare and happiness and specifically to make universal education his "hobby." Even when president, he was a conscientious trustee of the Peabody Fund, which helped to educate both blacks and whites in the South, and he also worked diligently to educate blacks as president of the board of trustees of the Slater Fund from its creation in 1882. Not only did Hayes attend all meetings of these organizations, he also wrote numerous letters in support of them, made inspection tours, and continued to urge the federal government to underwrite the education of poor children. Hayes served as well on the boards of trustees of Ohio State, Western Reserve, and Ohio Wesleyan universities. On all of these boards, he argued that in addition to traditional disciplines, practical courses and curriculums in manual training and the mechanical arts should be given from primary school through college.[23]

In keeping with his faith that education and training could cure social ills, Hayes in 1883 accepted the presidency of the National Prison Association. In 1870, when governor, he had presided over the first National Prison Congress, which was held in Cincinnati. He had long corresponded with prison reformers, and his interest in that cause had been heightened by his experience, both as a criminal lawyer and as an executive armed with the power to pardon. For the remainder of his life, Hayes remained president of that association and worked for a penal system that would be just, rational, and humane.[24]

In all of these activities, Lucy Hayes staunchly supported her husband. Indeed, whether the issue was abolition or temperance, she was more ardently committed to reform than was Hayes. In June 1889, while he was at Columbus on business for Ohio State University, a stroke rendered Lucy speechless. He rushed to her bedside and felt that she knew him, but she drifted into a coma and died two days later.

Her death was a severe blow for Hayes. Although he attended meetings of the boards of the Peabody and Slater funds, the Prison Association, and the universities, usually accompanied by Fanny, and although he continued to work for the causes that these organizations represented, he was ready to follow Lucy. A few months after his seventieth birthday, an attack of angina pectoris felled him in Cleveland, where he had attended to some business for Western Reserve University. Although Hayes acknowledged that the pain was like that in his wound at South Mountain, he insisted on returning home, after his son Webb gave him some brandy. "I would rather die at Spiegel Grove than to live anywhere else," he said. Three days later, on 17 January 1893, his wish was granted.[25]

Hayes was both a good man and an able president. His administration of that office contradicts the widely held view that he was an inept politician and an ineffective leader. Other chief executives have confronted greater crises upon entering office, but no other president began his term with a vast segment of the population convinced that he had been elected by fraud and that despite the actions of Congress, he was not legally entitled to reside in the White House. In addition to that severe handicap, Hayes had to govern with the opposing Democratic party in control of the House of Representatives and, after the midterm election of 1878, in control of both houses of Congress.

Hampered by a hostile Congress, Hayes faced serious problems. During the Grant administration, northern support for Radical Reconstruction had eroded, while southern opposition to it had grown violent. When Hayes took office, Radical Reconstruction in the South had virtually ended, with Republican governments remaining only in Louisiana and South Carolina, where they were challenged by rival Democratic governments. Hayes had to determine quickly whether he could or should support these Republican governments.

In addition, many citizens urgently demanded civil-service reform to eliminate the corruption that seemed to permeate the federal government under Grant. But most Republican politicians were convinced that reform would destroy party organization, so they were hostile to the reformers, who they thought were impractical, and their program, which they thought was visionary.

Further problems were engendered by the severe economic depression that followed the panic of 1873 and enveloped Americans from coast to coast. For those who suffered from the depression, Reconstruction and corruption were issues of little importance. Besides hurting the Republican party, which was in power when it occurred, the panic led to the Great Strike of 1877, to increased agitation against Chinese laborers in California, and to strident demands for expansion of the currency.

In dealing with these problems, Hayes was principled but practical, cautious yet courageous, open to the advice of cabinet members and friends but decisive. Diligent, conscientious, consistent, and steady, he did not panic under stress, bore criticism and hostility with little complaint, was slow to anger, and bore few grudges. He was a patient reformer, confident that ultimately his modest goals would be attained.

Hayes was as successful in handling these problems as the circumstances of his presidency would allow. Against great odds, he defended the prerogatives of his office and enhanced its power and prestige. He defeated congressional attempts to force him to make appointments and to approve legislation against his will. He fought the Senate over the issue of senatorial courtesy, and by the end of his administration, senators, as well as anyone else, could suggest appointments to Hayes, but no one could dictate them.

Hayes fought hard and successfully to keep the election laws. Sensing correctly that northern public opinion would rally to support the federal supervision of congressional elections, he forced the Democratic Congress to back down. He courageously vetoed appropriation bills containing riders that would destroy laws that enforced voting rights under the Fourteenth and Fifteenth amendments; and ultimately

Congress, under the lash of public opinion, passed the money bills without the obnoxious riders.

Hayes also courageously vetoed popular legislation that would have expanded the currency and that would have excluded Chinese laborers from the migrants who were allowed into the United States. Congress overrode his veto of the Bland-Allison silver-coinage bill, but Hayes minimized its inflationary effect. Near the end of his administration, he claimed that his currency policies—his hard-money stance and especially the resumption of specie payments—had restored the confidence of investors in particular and the business community in general. With abundant capital and low interest rates, industries were thriving, railroads were expanding, and foreign trade was increasing.

The business cycle was primarily responsible for the economic boom, but it had not been hampered by Hayes's policies. Even though his inflationist opponents were closer to the twentieth-century concept of a managed currency than was Hayes, with his almost mystical faith in the gold standard, the fact remains that his notions in regard to the currency prevailed during a stunning business revival. One may quarrel with his monetary theory, but it is difficult to dispute its success.

Hayes was also a man of moderation, as well as a man of principle. His restrained, legalistic response to the Great Strike saved both lives and property. Although railroad and business leaders demanded that he call up volunteers to suppress the strike, Hayes withstood the pressure and did not take an action that might have provoked a revolution. By using small detachments of the regular army wisely and by not operating the railroads, he avoided a confrontation between strikers and federal forces.

Hayes was also a moderate civil-service reformer. His modest efforts dissatisfied both spoils politicians and ardent reformers, but he did not destroy party organization, and he did not attempt the impossible task of reforming the entire civil service. Instead, he supported the merit system in the New York Customhouse and Post Office, where it achieved excellent results. The much-advertised New York experiments caused the public to perceive civil-service reform, not as the hobby of impractical visionaries, but as a necessity demanded by the growing complexity of the nation's bureaucracy. The Civil Service Reform Act passed in 1883, not only because reformers exploited the circumstances of Garfield's assassination but also because the Hayes administration had demonstrated the value of the merit system.

Hayes's decision to withdraw federal support from Republican governments in Louisiana and South Carolina was based on harsh political realities. These governments could only be maintained by a military force, and the Democratic House of Representatives would not appropriate money for such a force, and northern public opinion would not sustain such a policy. Hayes was naïve, however, when he believed that Louisiana and South Carolina officials would keep their promises to respect the civil rights of blacks.

Although Hayes had to abandon these Republican governments, he did not abandon his commitment to civil rights and to equal educational and economic opportunities for all. And he remained conscientious, humane, fair, and just, whether he used the pardoning power, sought justice for Native Americans, or promoted education for all poor children.

Hayes was able and lucky. Although he ignored and offended many party leaders, he was a shrewd judge of what rank-and-file Republicans thought, and his policies attracted the voters. Prosperity returned to the nation; and the Republican party, with its tarnished image newly polished by Hayes, triumphed in 1880 with a Hayes lieutenant at its head. If a politician is to be judged by his victories at the polls, Hayes was phenomenally successful.

Hayes's political genius lay in his moderation, in combining old virtues with new ideas, in mixing sensible proportions of principle and pragmatism. By exploiting issues and by appealing to a broad range of public opinion, rather than by relying on state and local political organizations led by senators and congressmen, Hayes embraced the politics of reform and took a modest step on the path that would be followed by the great presidential leaders of the twentieth century. Yet his honesty, simplicity, and decency echoed the pristine values of the early American Republic.

Mark Twain, who captured the essence of the Gilded Age, grasped the importance of the presidency of Rutherford Birchard Hayes. A year after Hayes had retired, Twain, his wife, Olivia Langdon Clemens, and a few friends, while discussing the Hayes administration, "arrived at the verdict that its quiet & unostentatious, but real & substantial greatness, would steadily rise into higher & higher prominence, as time & distance give it a right perspective, until at last it would stand out against the horizon of history in its true proportions."[26]

NOTES

These acronyms are used throughout the notes:

HPC   Rutherford B. Hayes Presidential Center, Spiegel Grove, Fremont, Ohio

LC   Library of Congress

RBH   Hayes Papers at the Rutherford B. Hayes Presidential Center

CHAPTER 1
THE CAMPAIGN OF 1876

1. Statistics in this paragraph and in the following pages are from U.S., Bureau of the Census, *Historical Statistics of the United States, Colonial Times to 1957* (Washington, D.C.: Government Printing Office, 1960).

2. U.S., Senate, Committee on Education and Labor, *The Relations between Labor and Capital* . . . , 4 vols. (Washington, D.C., 1885), 4:737.

3. On the Centennial Exhibition see Dee Brown, *The Year of the Century: 1876* (New York: Charles Scribner's Sons, 1966), pp. 112–37.

4. Ibid., pp. 165–66.

5. Keith Ian Polakoff, *The Politics of Inertia: The Election of 1876 and the End of Reconstruction* (Baton Rouge: Louisiana State University Press, 1973), pp. 178–80.

6. Henry Adams, *The Education of Henry Adams* (New York: Modern Library, 1931), p. 266. Allan Nevins, in *Hamilton Fish: The Inner History of the Grant Administration* (New York: Dodd, Mead, 1937), pp. 762–837, covers the dismal last days of the Grant administration.

7. *Nation*, 28 Oct. and 25 Nov. 1875, pp. 269, 331.

8. Ari Hoogenboom, "Did Gilded Age Scandals Bring Reform?" in *Before Watergate: Problems of Corruption in American Society,* ed. Abraham S. Eisenstadt, Ari Hoogenboom, and Hans L. Trefousse (Brooklyn: Brooklyn College Press, 1978), pp. 125-31.

9. On Hayes's career see Harry Barnard, *Rutherford B. Hayes and His America* (Indianapolis, Ind.: Bobbs-Merrill, 1954); Charles Richard Williams, *The Life of Rutherford Birchard Hayes: Nineteenth President of the United States,* 2 vols. (Columbus: Ohio State Archaeological and Historical Society, 1928); Arthur Bishop, ed., *Rutherford B. Hayes, 1822-1893: Chronology, Documents, Bibliographical Aids* (Dobbs Ferry, N.Y.: Oceana Publications, 1969); *Diary and Letters of Rutherford Birchard Hayes: Nineteenth President of the United States,* ed. Charles Richard Williams, 5 vols. (Columbus Ohio State Archaeological and Historical Society, 1922-26; hereafter cited as Hayes, *Diary and Letters*); T. Harry Williams, *Hayes of the Twenty-third: The Civil War Volunteer Officer* (New York: Alfred A. Knopf, 1965).

10. Hayes to Oliver Wendell Holmes, 21 Nov. 1885, Holmes Papers, LC, copy at HPC; Hayes to Webb C. Hayes, 1 Mar. 1875, in Hayes, *Diary and Letters,* 3:267.

11. Hayes, *Diary and Letters,* 27 Jan. and 15 May 1861, 2:4, 17.

12. David Donald, *The Politics of Reconstruction, 1863-1867* (Baton Rouge: Louisiana State University Press, 1965), p. 100; Hayes to John Sherman, 18 Nov. 1871, letterbook 2:247, RBH.

13. Hayes to Charles Nordhoff, 5 Apr. 1870, in Hayes, *Diary and Letters,* 3:94; 10 Jan. 1872, ibid., p. 193.

14. Sherman to Hayes, 26 Mar. 1873, Hayes to Sherman, 2 Apr. 1873, Hayes to Grant, 1 May 1873, RBH; Barnard, *Rutherford B. Hayes,* p. 261.

15. Hayes, *Diary and Letters,* 13 Aug., 20 Nov., and 1 Dec. 1874, 3:257, 260-61; T. Harry Williams, ed., *Hayes: The Diary of a President, 1875-1881* (New York: David McKay, 1964), 28 Mar. 1875, pp. 1-2 (hereafter cited as Hayes, *Diary*); Hayes to Rutherford Platt Hayes, 21 Mar. 1875, RBH.

16. H. J. Eckenrode, *Rutherford B. Hayes: Statesman of Reunion* (New York: Dodd, Mead, 1930), p. 98; Hayes to Austin Birchard, 21 Apr. 1874, Hayes to Manning F. Force, 27 Apr. 1874, in Hayes, *Diary and Letters,* 3:255-56; Hayes, *Diary,* 28 Mar. 1875, p. 2.

17. Hayes, *Diary,* 14 and 18 Apr., 31 May, and 3 June 1875, pp. 3-4; Hayes to Laura Mitchell, 1 Apr. 1875, Hayes to W. B. Bickham, 14 Apr. 1875, Hayes to William S. Furay, 5 June 1875, RBH.

18. Hayes, *Diary,* 4 June 1875, pp. 5-6, 8; Hayes to R. M. Stimson, 6 June 1875, Hayes to Clarke Waggoner, 22 July 1875, RBH; Hayes to W. D. Bickham, 10 July 1875, in C. R. Williams, *Life of Rutherford Birchard Hayes,* 1:391.

19. C. R. Williams, *Life of Rutherford Birchard Hayes,* 1:405-6; Hayes, *Diary,* 12 and 17 Oct. 1875, pp. 10-11.

20. Charles Nordhoff to Hayes, 11 Jan. 1876, William Henry Smith to Hayes, 26 Jan., 15 and 21 Feb. 1876, Sherman to A. M. Burns, 21 Jan. 1876, RBH; Hayes to William H. Smith, 29 Jan. 1876, Hayes to Lucy Hayes, 30 Jan. 1876, in

Hayes, *Diary and Letters*, 3:300–301; Hayes, *Diary*, 15 Feb. and 21 Mar. 1876, pp. 15–18.

21. Hayes to Birchard Hayes, 2 Apr. 1876, Hayes to Mrs. Eliza G. Davis, 18 Apr. 1876, RBH; Hayes to Lucy Hayes, 30 Jan. 1876, in Hayes, *Diary and Letters*, 3:300–301; Hayes, *Diary*, 2 and 11 Apr. 1876, pp. 18–20.

22. Dickson to Hayes, 27 Apr. 1876, Dickson to Curtis, 27 Apr. 1876, RBH; Hayes to Dickson, 3 May 1876, in Hayes, *Diary and Letters*, 3:317.

23. Hayes to Blaine, 12 June 1876, Hayes to Ralph P. Buckland, 14 June 1876, RBH; David M. Jordan, *Roscoe Conkling of New York: Voice in the Senate* (Ithaca, N.Y.: Cornell University Press, 1971), p. 80. Polakoff, in *Politics of Inertia*, pp. 44–52, unravels the complicated tale of Blaine's involvement with the Union Pacific and the Little Rock & Fort Smith railroads.

24. C. R. Williams, *Life of Rutherford Birchard Hayes*, 1:446–48; William Henry Smith to Hayes, 21 June 1876, RBH.

25. Polakoff, *Politics of Inertia*, pp. 62–65; C. R. Williams, *Life of Rutherford Birchard Hayes*, 1:448–50; Edward McPherson, *A Hand-book of Politics for 1876* . . . , reprint (New York: Da Capo Press, 1972), pp. 209–12.

26. C. R. Williams, *Life of Rutherford Birchard Hayes*, 1:450–52; Hayes to Birchard Hayes, 15 and 16 June 1876, Hayes to Blaine, 16 June 1876, Newspaper clipping file, RBH.

27. Curtis to Hayes, 22 June 1876, RBH; Hayes to Edwards Pierrepont, 20 June 1876, Rare Book Department, Free Library of Philadelphia, copy at HPC.

28. McPherson, *Hand-book . . . 1876*, pp. 214–17; Smith to Hayes, 1 July 1876, RBH.

29. For the letters of acceptance see McPherson, *Hand-book . . . 1876*, pp. 212–13, 217–22; Hayes to Curtis, 22 and 30 June and 10 July 1876, Sherman to Hayes, 26 June 1876, Foster to Hayes, 29 June 1876, William Dennison (quoting Bristow) to Hayes, 30 June 1876, Garfield to Hayes, 1 July 1876, RBH; Hayes to Sherman, 23 June 1876, Collection of Sherman Descendants, Mansfield, Ohio, copy at HPC; Schurz to Hayes, 21 June 1876, in *Speeches, Correspondence and Political Papers of Carl Schurz*, ed. Frederic Bancroft, 6 vols. (New York: G. P. Putnam's Sons, 1913), 3:250–51 (hereafter cited as Schurz, *Speeches*).

30. Smith to Hayes, 1 July 1876, A. C. Botkin to Smith, Aug. 1876, Curtis to Hayes, 13 July 1876, RBH; "The One-Term Guarantee," *Nation*, 3 Aug. 1876, p. 68.

31. Polakoff, *Politics of Inertia*, pp. 113–16; C. R. Williams, *Life of Rutherford Birchard Hayes*, 1:470; Hayes to Howells, 23 July, 5 and 24 Aug. 1876, Hayes-Howells Correspondence, Harvard University, Cambridge, Mass., copy at HPC; list of diaries, scrapbooks, letters, etc., sent to W. D. Howells [Aug. 1876], Howells to Hayes, 13 Aug. 1876, RBH; Hayes to Garfield, 27 July 1876, Garfield Papers, LC, copy at HPC.

32. Polakoff, *Politics of Inertia*, pp. 94–95; Hayes to E. D. Morgan, 10 July 1876, Morgan Papers, New York State Library, Albany, copy at HPC; Richard C. McCormick to Hayes, 26 July 1876, RBH; C. R. Williams, *Life of Rutherford Birchard Hayes*, 1:471.

33. C. R. Williams, *Life of Rutherford Birchard Hayes*, 1:472; Barnard, *Rutherford B. Hayes*, p. 308; Matthews to Hayes, 24 June 1876, RBH. For perhaps the only example of Zach Chandler's writing to Hayes see Chandler to Hayes, 13 Oct. 1876, RBH. On Chandler's shortcomings see Richard C. McCormick to Hayes, 28 and 29 Aug. and 3 Sept. 1876, RBH. On the difficulty of raising money see McCormick to Hayes, 25 and 28 Aug. and 14 Sept. 1876, RBH. Years later, in 1905 and 1917, William E. Chandler estimated that the committee raised roughly the same amount ($200,000) in 1868, 1872, and 1876. Leon Burr Richardson, *William E. Chandler: Republican* (New York: Dodd, Mead, 1940), pp. 145, 180. On assessments see Hayes to Schurz, 18 Aug. 1876, Hayes to William Henry Smith, 10 Aug. 1876, Schurz to Hayes, 3 and 5 Sept. 1876, Hayes to McCormick, 8 Sept. 1876, McCormick to Hayes, 11 and 14 Sept. and 13 Oct. 1876, RBH; Schurz to Hayes, 14 July and 14 Aug. 1876, Hayes to Schurz, 15 Sept. 1876, in Schurz, *Speeches*, 3:260–61, 285–86, 338–39.

34. Hayes to Garfield, 6 and 12 Aug. 1876, Garfield Papers, copy at HPC; Hayes to Schurz, 9 Aug. 1876, in Schurz, *Speeches*, 3:284–85; Hayes to Sherman, 2 Aug. 1876, Hayes to W. K. Rogers, 13 Aug. 1876, RBH.

35. Nordhoff to Hayes, 22 and 28 June 1876, RBH.

36. Schurz to Hayes, 14 Aug. 1876, in Schurz, *Speeches*, 3:286–87; Curtis to Hayes, 31 Aug. 1876, Hayes to Curtis, 4 Sept. 1876, RBH; *Nation*, 28 Sept. 1876, p. 187; "The Fundamental Reform," *New York Times*, 30 Sept. 1876; Norton to Curtis, 3 Oct. 1876, Norton Papers, Harvard University.

37. Polakoff, *Politics of Inertia*, pp. 178–79, 195. Hayes consistently stressed that cheerful obedience to all of the amendments was the basis on which the South should be pacified; see Hayes to Guy M. Bryan, 30 Sept. 1876, Bryan Papers, University of Texas, Austin, copy at HPC.

38. Polakoff, *Politics of Inertia*, pp. 187–94.

39. Ibid., pp. 181–85; Kellogg to McCormick, 16 Oct. 1876, RBH.

40. Polakoff, *Politics of Inertia*, pp. 185–87.

41. Ibid., p. 141–42; Hayes, *Diary*, 13 Aug. and 18 Sept. 1876, pp. 28–29, 37–38; Hayes to McCormick, 14 Oct. 1876, ibid. pp. 41–42.

42. Nordhoff to Hayes, 15 Oct. 1876, RBH; Polakoff, *Politics of Inertia*, pp. 157–58, 194–95.

43. On Tilden's organization see Polakoff, *Politics of Inertia*, pp. 129–31, 161–62, 164–67.

44. Hayes to Conkling, 15 Aug. 1876, in Hayes, *Diary and Letters*, 3:347; Polakoff, *Politics of Inertia*, p. 161.

45. Polakoff, *Politics of Inertia*, pp. 142–44, 170.

46. On Davenport see ibid., pp. 168–71, which digests Albie Burke, "Federal Regulation of Congressional Elections in Northern Cities, 1871–1894" (Ph.D. diss., University of Chicago, 1968), pp. 180–89. Republicans in Chicago tried to adopt Davenport's system "where practicable"; see Smith to Hayes, 30 Oct. 1876, RBH.

47. Hayes, *Diary*, 22 Oct. and 7 Nov. 1876, pp. 44–47.

48. Ibid., 11 Nov. 1876, pp. 47–48. On the day after the election, Hayes, in defeat, wrote to his son Ruddy: "It would have been a great gratification to try to establish Civil Service reform, and to do a good work for the South. But it is decreed otherwise and I bow cheerfully to the result"; see Hayes to Rutherford Platt Hayes, 8 Nov. 1876, RBH.

CHAPTER 2
THE DISPUTED ELECTION

1. Keith Ian Polakoff, *The Politics of Inertia: The Election of 1876 and the End of Reconstruction* (Baton Rouge: Louisiana State University Press, 1973), pp. 199–202; Jerome L. Sternstein, ed., "The Sickles Memorandum: Another Look at the Hayes-Tilden Election-Night Conspiracy," *Journal of Southern History* 32 (1966): 342–57.

2. Sternstein, "Sickles Memorandum," pp. 342–45; Alexander Clarence Flick, *Samuel Jones Tilden: A Study in Political Sagacity* (New York: Dodd, Mead, 1939), pp. 324–25; H. J. Eckenrode, *Rutherford B. Hayes: Statesman of Reunion* (New York: Dodd, Mead, 1930), pp. 178–84; Polakoff, *Politics of Inertia*, pp. 202–4. For Reid's story see *New York Times*, 11 and 15 June 1887. Reid disparages the role of William E. Chandler, while emphasizing that played by the *New York Times* and Zachariah Chandler.

3. W. E. Chandler to Hayes, 9 Nov. 1876, RBH; Sternstein, "Sickles Memorandum," p. 346; Flick, *Samuel Jones Tilden*, p. 326; James Ford Rhodes, *History of the United States: From the Compromise of 1850 to the End of the Roosevelt Administration*, 9 vols. (New York: Macmillan, 1928), 7:292 n. 2.

4. T. Harry Williams, ed., *Hayes: The Diary of a President, 1875–1881* (New York: David McKay, 1964), 11 and 12 Nov. 1876, pp. 47–50 (hereafter cited as Hayes, *Diary*); Polakoff, *Politics of Inertia*, pp. 206–7; Flick, *Samuel Jones Tilden*, pp. 327–33.

5. Sherman to Col. J. C. Audenreid (aide-de-camp), 18 Nov. 1876, William T. Sherman Papers, HPC.

6. W. E. Chandler to Hayes, 9 Nov. 1876, William Henry Smith to Hayes, 10 Nov. 1876, Grant to John Sherman, 11 Nov. 1876, RBH; Flick, *Samuel Jones Tilden*, p. 328; Polakoff, *Politics of Inertia*, pp. 207–10.

7. James N. Tyner to J. M. Comly, 14 Nov. 1876, RBH; Polakoff, *Politics of Inertia*, pp. 214–20.

8. Polakoff, *Politics of Inertia*, pp. 210–12; Sherman to I. Scott, 12 Nov. 1876, Sherman to Margaret Sherman, 20 and 29 Nov. 1876, John Sherman Papers, HPC; Sherman to Hayes, 23 Nov. 1876, RBH; Hayes to Sherman, 27 Nov. 1876, Sherman Papers, LC, copy at HPC.

9. Polakoff, *Politics of Inertia*, pp. 219–20.

10. Rhodes, *History of the United States*, 7:295, 301; Polakoff, *Politics of Inertia*, pp. 210–14; Smith to Hayes, 5 Dec. 1877, RBH.

11. Polakoff, *Politics of Inertia*, pp. 217–19.

12. Ibid., pp. 225–27.

13. Ibid., pp. 227–31.

14. Memorandum of Hayes Conversation (12 Dec. 1876), RBH.

15. Polakoff, *Politics of Inertia*, pp. 220–23, 234–40; Flick, *Samuel Jones Tilden*, pp. 330–32, 351.

16. Tyner to J. M. Comly, 16 Nov. 1876, RBH; Hayes, *Diary*, 17 Dec. 1876, p. 58; Hayes to Shellabarger, 29 Dec. 1876, ibid. pp. 60–61; Polakoff, *Politics of Inertia*, pp. 234–40.

17. Polakoff, *Politics of Inertia*, p. 259.

18. Hayes, *Diary*, 5 and 17 Dec. 1876, pp. 54, 58–59; Sherman to Hayes, 12 Dec. 1876, Albert D. Shaw to Hayes, 22 and 28 Dec. 1876, Hayes to Shaw, 25 and 31 Dec. 1876, RBH; Hayes to Sherman, 17 Dec. 1876, Sherman Papers, LC, copy at HPC. On Hayes's resolution to be "wholly uncommitted as to persons and policy" see Hayes to W. K. Rogers, 17 Dec. 1876, Hayes papers, LC, and Hayes to Richard Henry Dana, Jr., 18 Dec. 1876, Dana Papers, Massachusetts Historical Society, Boston, copies at HPC.

19. Polakoff, *Politics of Inertia*, pp. 222–23, 244–46; Hayes, *Diary*, 1 Dec. 1876, pp. 52–53; Edward McPherson, *A Hand-book of Politics . . . 1876 . . .*, reprint (New York: Da Capo Press, 1972), p. 213; C. Vann Woodward, *Reunion and Reaction: The Compromise of 1877 and the End of Reconstruction*, 2d ed. (Garden City, N.Y.: Doubleday, 1956), pp. 26–27; Charles Richard Williams, *The Life of Rutherford Birchard Hayes: Nineteenth President of the United States*, 2 vols. (Columbus: Ohio State Archaeological and Historical Society, 1928), 1:504–6; Harry Barnard, *Rutherford B. Hayes and His America* (Indianapolis, Ind.: Bobbs-Merrill, 1954), pp. 357–58.

20. William Henry Smith to Hayes, 7 and 14 Dec. 1876, Hayes to William Henry Smith, 16 Dec. 1876, RBH.

21. Garfield to Hayes, 12 Dec. 1876, Dennison to Hayes, 13 Dec. 1876, RBH; *The Diary of James A. Garfield*, ed. Harry James Brown and Frederick D. Williams, 4 vols. (East Lansing: Michigan State University Press, 1967–81), 11, 12 and 13 Dec. 1876, 3:394–95 (hereafter cited as Garfield, *Diary*); Polakoff, *Politics of Inertia*, pp. 246–47; Woodward, *Reunion and Reaction*, pp. 23–24; Hayes to Sherman, 25 Dec. 1876, Sherman papers, LC, copy at HPC.

22. Boynton to William Henry Smith, morning of 20 Dec. 1876, RBH; Garfield, *Diary*, 18 and 20 Dec. 1876, 3:397–99.

23. Boynton to Smith, evening of 20 Dec. 1876, Smith Papers, Indiana Historical Society, Indianapolis, copy at HPC; Smith to Hayes, 22 Dec. 1876, RBH.

24. Boynton to Smith, 26 Dec. 1876, Smith Papers, copy at HPC.

25. Garfield, *Diary*, 21, 22, and 30 Dec. 1876 and 3 Jan. 1877, 3:400, 404, 409; Comly to Hayes, 8 Jan. 1877, RBH.

26. Hayes to Smith, 3 Jan. 1877, Smith to Hayes, 5 Jan. 1877, RBH; Hayes, *Diary*, 5 Jan. 1877, p. 68; Hayes to Schurz, 4 Jan. 1877, in *Speeches, Correspondence and Political Papers of Carl Schurz*, ed. Frederic Bancroft, 6 vols. (New York: G. P. Putnam's Sons, 1913), 3:355 (hereafter cited as Schurz, *Speeches*).

27. Tyner to Comly, 23 Dec. 1876, Comly to Hayes, 8 Jan. 1877, Samuel Shellabarger to Hayes, 8 Jan. 1877, Sherman to Hayes, 8 Jan. 1877, W. E. Chandler to Hayes, 13 and 16 Jan. 1877, Chandler to ———, 14 and 18 Jan. 1877, R. C. McCormick to W. K. Rogers, 21 Dec. 1876, RBH; Polakoff, *Politics of Inertia,* pp. 261, 264–65.

28. Schurz to Hayes, 4, 5, and 8 Dec. 1876, RBH; Hayes to Schurz, 6 and 7 Dec. 1876, Schurz Papers, LC, copies at HPC; Schurz to Cox, 28 Dec. 1876, in Schurz, *Speeches,* 3:351–54; Polakoff, *Politics of Inertia,* pp. 265–66.

29. Sherman to Hayes, 22 Dec. 1876, Comly to Hayes, 8 Jan. 1877, RBH; Polakoff, *Politics of Inertia,* pp. 261–64.

30. Garfield, *Diary,* 5, 8 and 14 Jan. 1877, 3:411–13, 415; Polakoff, *Politics of Inertia,* pp. 268–69.

31. C. R. Williams, *Life of Rutherford Birchard Hayes,* 1:518; Polakoff, *Politics of Inertia,* pp. 269–71; William Henry Smith to John Sherman, 8 Dec. 1876 and 3 Jan. 1877, John Sherman Papers, HPC; Sherman to Hayes, 3 Jan. 1877, Comly to Hayes, 8 Jan. 1877, RBH; Garfield, *Diary,* 4 Jan. 1877, 3:410.

32. Hayes to Sherman, 16 Jan. 1877, RBH; Polakoff, *Politics of Inertia,* pp. 271–76.

33. Garfield, *Diary,* 19 Jan. 1877, 3:420; Michael Les Benedict, "Southern Democrats in the Crisis of 1876–1877: A Reconsideration of *Reunion and Reaction,*" *Journal of Southern History* 46 (1980): 509–10. Dennison claimed that prominent businessmen opposed the measure, but he probably was indulging in wishful thinking; see Dennison to Hayes, 22 Jan. 1877, RBH.

34. Hayes, *Diary,* 21 Jan. 1877, pp. 69–70; Garfield, *Diary,* 18 and 24 Jan. 1877, 3:418–19, 423; Smith to Hayes, 23 Jan. 1877, RBH. John Sherman opposed the bill; he also called it "the surrender of a certainty for an uncertainty," which was obviously the favorite phrase in the Hayes camp; see Sherman to Hayes, 26 Jan. 1877, in C. R. Williams, *Life of Rutherford Birchard Hayes,* 1:526 n. 1; see also Dennison to Hayes, 20 Jan. 1877, ibid., p. 529 n. 1, and Boynton to Comly, 25 Jan. 1877, RBH.

35. Foster to Hayes, 21 Jan. 1877, RBH; Hayes, *Diary,* 26 Jan. 1877, pp. 70–71.

36. Sherman to Hayes, 26 Jan. 1877, W. E. Chandler to ———, 29 Jan. 1877, RBH; Garfield, *Diary,* 29 Jan. 1877, 3:426; Hayes, *Diary,* 31 Jan. 1877, p. 71; Polakoff, *Politics of Inertia,* pp. 279–85.

37. Polakoff, *Politics of Inertia,* pp. 230–31, 286. Rhodes, in *History of the United States,* 7:329–37, gives a full account of the commission's decision on Florida.

38. Garfield, *Diary,* 7 Feb. 1877, 3:435; Hayes, *Diary,* 8 and 9 Feb. 1877, pp. 73–74; Chandler to Hayes, 9 Feb. 1877, RBH; Polakoff, *Politics of Inertia,* p. 290.

39. Polakoff, *Politics of Inertia,* pp. 290–92; Boynton to Smith, 11 Feb. 1877, Smith Papers, copy at HPC.

40. Garfield, *Diary,* 12–16 Feb. 1877, 3:438–42; Rhodes, *History of the United States,* 7:338–39; Polakoff, *Politics of Inertia,* pp. 300–301. Had Davis been on the commission, the result might not have been different. William Henry Smith

reported to Hayes from Chicago: "Judge David Davis . . . spending three days in this city . . . most heartily approves the action of Judge Bradley. He says no good lawyer, not a strict partizan, could decide otherwise." Of course, the peculiar circumstances of his election—specifically the scheme of Tilden's nephew—could have affected Davis's judgment; see Smith to Hayes, 17 Feb. 1877, RBH.

41. Hayes, *Diary*, 17–18 Feb. 1877, pp. 74–75; Hayes to Shellabarger, 18 Feb. 1877, in Hayes, *Diary and Letters*, 3:417; Boynton to Smith, 18 Feb. 1877, Kellar to Smith, 17 Feb. 1877, Smith Papers, copies at HPC; Woodward, *Reunion and Reaction*, pp. 192–93; Polakoff, *Politics of Inertia*, pp. 301–3. On delays see Garfield, *Diary*, 17 Feb. 1877, 3:442–43.

42. Nordhoff to Foster, 15 Feb. 1877, enclosed in Foster to Hayes, 16 Feb. 1877, RBH. Nordhoff had written Hayes in a similar vein during the recent campaign; Nordhoff to Hayes, 22 and 28 June 1876, RBH.

43. Dodge to Hayes, 15 Feb. 1877, RBH.

44. William Henry Smith to Richard Smith, 19 Feb. 1877, Foster to Hayes, 16 Feb. 1877, Sherman to Hayes, 18 Feb. 1877, RBH.

45. Polakoff, *Politics of Inertia*, pp. 303–4; Woodward, *Reunion and Reaction*, p. 175.

46. Kellar to Smith, 20 Feb. 1877, Smith Papers, copy at HPC; Smith to Hayes, 21 Feb. 1877, Foster to Hayes, 21 Feb. 1877, RBH; Polakoff, *Politics of Inertia*, pp. 304–5; Woodward, *Reunion and Reaction*, pp. 194–96.

47. Boynton to Smith, 22 Feb. 1877, Smith Papers, copy at HPC; Garfield, *Diary*, 17–23 Feb. 1877, 3:442–47; Rhodes, *History of the United States*, 7:350.

48. Shellabarger to Hayes, 23 Feb. 1877, Matthews, Foster, and Dennison to Comly, 23 Feb. 1877, RBH; Polakoff, *Politics of Inertia*, p. 308; Woodward, *Reunion and Reaction*, pp. 201–5.

49. Garfield, *Diary*, 24 and 25 Feb. 1877, 3:447–48; Sherman to Hayes, 24 and 25 Feb. 1877, RBH; Woodward, *Reunion and Reaction*, pp. 195, 210; Polakoff, *Politics of Inertia*, pp. 306–9.

50. Polakoff, *Politics of Inertia*, pp. 309–10; Woodward, *Reunion and Reaction*, pp. 210–12.

51. Garfield, *Diary*, 26 Feb. 1877, 3:448–50; Boynton to Smith, 26 Feb. 1877, Smith Papers, copy at HPC; Polakoff, *Politics of Inertia*, pp. 310–11; Woodward, *Reunion and Reaction*, pp. 212–15.

52. Benedict, "Southern Democrats in the Crisis of 1876–1877," pp. 512–18; George Rable, "Southern Interests and the Election of 1876: A Reappraisal," *Civil War History* 26 (1980): 347–61.

53. Garfield, *Diary*, 27 Feb. 1877, 3:450; Matthews and Foster to Gordon and Brown, 27 Feb. 1877, Hayes Scrapbook, 35:16–18, Boynton to Smith, 27 Feb. 1877, RBH; Barnard, *Rutherford B. Hayes*, pp. 389–91; Woodward, *Reunion and Reaction*, pp. 213–15; Polakoff, *Politics of Inertia*, pp. 311–12.

54. Garfield, *Diary*, 28 Feb. 1877, 3:451; Barnard, *Rutherford B. Hayes*, pp. 391–92; Woodward, *Reunion and Reaction*, p. 216; Polakoff, *Politics of Inertia*, p. 312.

55. Garfield, *Diary*, 1 Mar. 1877, 3:452; Polakoff, *Politics of Inertia*, p. 312; Woodward, *Reunion and Reaction*, pp. 216–18; Barnard, *Rutherford B. Hayes*, pp. 392–95.

CHAPTER 3
A NEW SOUTHERN POLICY

1. T. Harry Williams, ed., *Hayes: The Diary of a President, 1875–1881* (New York: David McKay, 1964), 14 Mar. 1877, pp. 79–80 (hereafter cited as Hayes, *Diary*).

2. Ibid., 5 and 17 Jan. 1877, pp. 68–69.

3. Hayes to Sherman, 15 and 16 Feb. 1877, Sherman to Hayes, 17 and 18 Feb. 1877, W. K. Rogers to John Sherman, 28 Feb. 1877, Hayes to Evarts, 19 Feb. 1877, Dodge to Hayes, 15 Feb. 1877, Dickson to Hayes, 19 Feb. 1877, RBH; Hayes, *Diary*, 17, 19, and 27 Feb. 1877, pp. 74–75, 78–79; Hayes to Schurz, 17 and 29 Jan. and 25 and 27 Feb. 1877, Schurz to Hayes, 30 Jan. and 26 Feb. 1877, Murat Halstead to Schurz, 16 and 20 Feb. 1877, in *Speeches, Correspondence and Political Papers of Carl Schurz*, ed. Frederic Bancroft, 6 vols. (New York: G. P. Putnam's Sons, 1913), 3:361–62, 376–83, 388–89, 402–6 (hereafter cited as Schurz, *Speeches*); Charles Richard Williams, *The Life of Rutherford Birchard Hayes: Nineteenth President of the United States*, 2 vols. (Columbus: Ohio State Archaeological and Historical Society, 1928), 2:20.

4. Smith to Hayes, 17 Feb. and (3 Mar.) 1877, Dickson to Hayes, 19 Feb. 1877, RBH; C. R. Williams, *Life of Rutherford Birchard Hayes*, 2:20–24; Hayes, *Diary*, 27 Feb. and 14 Mar. 1877, pp. 78–80; *The Diary of James A. Garfield*, ed. Harry James Brown and Frederick D. Williams, 4 vols. (East Lansing: Michigan State University Press, 1967–81), 4 Mar. 1877, 3:453.

5. C. R. Williams, *Life of Rutherford Birchard Hayes*, 2:22–24.

6. For the Inaugural Address see James D. Richardson, comp., *A Compilation of the Messages and Papers of the Presidents*, 20 vols. (New York: Bureau of National Literature, 1897–1918), 10:4394–99.

7. Ibid.; C. R. Williams, *Life of Rutherford Birchard Hayes*, 2:15.

8. Schurz to Hayes, 25 Jan. and 2 Feb. 1877, in Schurz, *Speeches*, 3:366–76, 384–87. When Hayes recollected a few years later how he had composed the most quotable line in his Inaugural Address, he forgot about Schurz's suggestion. It, he recalled, "occurred to me as I was walking east on the North side of Broad Street in Columbus with a small party of friends in February 1877." Hayes gave four less felicitous versions of the same thought, none in the form in which it had occurred to Schurz; see Hayes, *Diary*, 3 Aug. 1880, p. 290. The *Indianapolis* (Ind.) *Journal* suggested that Alexander Pope's translation of Homer's *Iliad* was the source of the idea. In the tenth book, Nestor awakens Diomed, one of his captains, saying, "He serves me most who serves my country best"; see C. R. Williams, *Life of Rutherford Birchard Hayes*, 2:13 n. 1.

9. Garfield, *Diary,* 5 Mar. 1877, 3:454; C. R. Williams, *Life of Rutherford Birchard Hayes,* 2:6 n. 3; Kenneth E. Davison, *The Presidency of Rutherford B. Hayes* (Westport, Conn.: Greenwood Press, 1972), p. 53.

10. C. R. Williams, *Life of Rutherford Birchard Hayes,* 2:16–17, 25–26; Hayes, *Diary,* 14 Mar. 1877, pp. 80–81; Garfield, *Diary,* 7 Mar. 1877, 3:455.

11. Sherman to Hayes, (Mar. 1877), Pierce to William Dennison, 10 Mar. 1877, RBH; George W. Childs, proprietor of the *Philadelphia Public Ledger,* to Evarts, 9 and 12 Mar. 1877, Ebenezer Rockwood Hoar to Evarts, 12 Mar. 1877, Evarts Papers, HPC; Garfield, *Diary,* 8 Mar. 1877, 3:455; C. R. Williams, *Life of Rutherford Birchard Hayes,* 2:27–29.

12. Garfield, *Diary,* 14 Mar. 1877, 3:458.

13. Ibid., 11 Mar. 1877, 3:457; Hayes, *Diary,* 14 and 16 Mar. 1877, pp. 81, 83; William Gillette, *Retreat from Reconstruction, 1869–1879* (Baton Rouge: Louisiana State Univeristy Press, 1979), pp. 338–39; C. Vann Woodward, *Reunion and Reaction: The Compromise of 1877 and the End of Reconstruction,* 2d ed. (Garden City, N.Y.: Doubleday, 1956), pp. 218–19; Hayes, memorandum (Mar. 1877), Joseph H. Oglesby to Sherman, 12 Mar. 1877, O. M. Conover to Matthews, 13 Mar. 1877, RBH.

14. Harry Barnard, *Rutherford B. Hayes and His America* (Indianapolis, Ind.: Bobbs-Merrill, 1954), p. 405; Hayes, *Diary,* 5 Aug. 1880, p. 291; Davison, *Presidency of Rutherford B. Hayes,* pp. 92–95.

15. On the Whig party see Thomas Brown, *Politics and Statesmanship: Essays on the American Whig Party* (New York: Columbia University Press, 1985); on Lincoln see David Donald, "Abraham Lincoln: Whig in the White House," in *Lincoln Reconsidered: Essays on the Civil War Era,* 2d ed. (New York: Vintage Books, 1961), pp. 187–208; on Hayes see Harry Barnard's perceptive chapter "Un-Whiggish Old Whig" in his *Rutherford B. Hayes,* pp. 450–64. One of the few books that Hayes found time to read while president was the *Diary* of John Quincy Adams; see Hayes, *Diary,* 15 Mar. and 27 Dec. 1878, pp. 128, 178.

16. Davison, *Presidency of Rutherford B. Hayes,* pp. 97–114.

17. Hayes, *Diary,* 20 and 23 Mar. 1877, pp. 84–85; Gillette, *Retreat from Reconstruction,* pp. 340–41.

18. In addition to the arguments of Henry Boynton, Andrew Kellar, William Henry Smith, and Charles Nordhoff, Hayes also received advice to abandon the carpetbaggers from Jacob Dolson Cox and William Johnston; see Cox to Hayes, 31 Jan. 1877, Johnston to Hayes, 19 Feb. 1877, RBH.

19. Hayes to Cox, 2 Feb. 1877, Cox Papers, Oberlin College, Oberlin, Ohio, copy at HPC; Hayes, *Diary,* 4 Oct. 1876, p. 39. T. Harry Williams incorrectly ascribes MacVeagh's views to Blaine.

20. S. Straight to Matthews, 8 Mar. 1877, C. W. McIntyre to Hayes, 14 Mar. 1877, Stuart to Richard W. Thompson, 15 Mar. 1877, John J. McCook to William Dennison, 23 Mar. 1877, RBH; Hayes to Garfield, 10 Mar. 1877, Garfield Papers, LC, copy at HPC. On business hostility to carpetbag regimes see Stanley P. Hirshson, *Farewell to the Bloody Shirt: Northern Republicans and the Southern Negro, 1877–1893* (Bloomington: Indiana University Press, 1962), pp. 29–32.

21. Robert Bolling to David M. Key, 17 Mar. 1877, Lawrence S. Marye to Key, 17 Mar., 14 Apr., and 1 May 1877, RBH.

22. Dickson to Hayes, 20 Mar. 1877, RBH.

23. Hayes, *Diary*, 20 Mar. 1877, p. 84; Foster to Hayes, 21 Mar. 1877, RBH; Gillette, *Retreat from Reconstruction*, p. 341.

24. Kellar to Medill, 20 Mar. 1877, Kellar to Smith, 29 Mar. 1877, William Henry Smith Papers, Indiana Historical Society, Indianapolis, copies at HPC; Hill to Thompson, 23 Mar. 1877, Smith to Hayes, 22 Mar. 1877, RBH.

25. Foster to Hayes, 21 Mar. 1877, RBH; Hayes, *Diary*, 28 Mar. 1877, p. 86; Garfield, *Diary*, 29 and 31 Mar. and 4 Apr. 1877, 3:465, 467, 469; C. R. Williams, *Life of Rutherford Birchard Hayes*, 2:49–53; Gillette, *Retreat from Reconstruction*, pp. 341–44.

26. Smith to Hayes, 22 Mar. 1877, RBH.

27. Hayes, *Diary*, 4 Oct. 1876, p. 39; C. R. Williams, *Life of Rutherford Birchard Hayes*, 2:54.

28. Evarts to Lawrence et al., 2 Apr. 1877, RBH.

29. Evarts to Lawrence, ''Second Instructions to Louisiana Commssion, (Apr.) 1877,'' RBH.

30. C. R. Williams, *Life of Rutherford Birchard Hayes*, 2:56–58; Gillette, *Retreat from Reconstruction*, p. 344. Williams says the commission arrived on 6 Apr., while Gillette says 5 Apr.

31. C. R. Williams, *Life of Rutherford Birchard Hayes*, 2:57–59; Gillette, *Retreat from Reconstruction*, pp. 344, 430 n. 31.

32. Kellar to Smith, 12 Apr. 1877, Smith Papers, copy at HPC; Kellar to Key, 14 Apr. 1877, RBH. The administration did not follow Kellar's advice. Absalom S. Badger, not Phelps, whom Kellar suggested, was named collector of New Orleans.

33. Kellar to Webb Hayes, 16 Apr. 1877, RBH.

34. Hayes to McCrary, 20 Apr. 1877, McCrary to W. T. Sherman, 20 Apr. 1877, RBH; C. R. Williams, *Life of Rutherford Birchard Hayes*, 2:59–64; Gillette, *Retreat from Reconstruction*, p. 345.

35. Kellar to Key, 19 Apr. 1877, Smith to Hayes, 19 Apr. 1877, RBH; C. R. Williams, *Life of Rutherford Birchard Hayes*, 2:65; Gillette, *Retreat from Reconstruction*, pp. 345–46; Hirshson, *Farewell to the Bloody Shirt*, pp. 33–34.

36. M. F. Force to Hayes, 10 Apr. 1877, Charles Foster to Hayes, 27 Apr. 1877, RBH; Garfield, *Diary*, 6 Apr. 1877, 3:471. Hirshson, in *Farewell to the Bloody Shirt*, pp. 34–35, says that few Republicans supported the administration. Gillette, in *Retreat from Reconstruction*, pp. 346–47, attacks Hayes's policy as appeasement.

37. Kellar to Hayes, 20 Apr. 1877, RBH; Hayes, *Diary*, 22 Apr. 1877, pp. 86–87.

38. Hayes to Holmes, 2 July 1877, Holmes Papers, LC, copy at HPC; C. R. Williams, *Life of Rutherford Birchard Hayes*, 2:241–53; Hayes, *Diary*, 26 Aug. and 4 Oct. 1877, pp. 94–95, 97.

39. C. R. Williams, *Life of Rutherford Birchard Hayes,* 2:351ff.; Hayes, *Diary,* 25 Sept., 7 Oct., and 3 Nov. 1877, pp. 96–97, 101.

40. William Henry Smith agreed that the trip South was the "greatest success"; see Smith to Hayes, 27 Sept. 1877, RBH.

41. Garfield, *Diary,* 8, 14, 15, and 19 October 1877, 3:526–27, 529–30, 532; James M. Comly to Hayes, 11 May 1877, RBH. David M. Abshire, in *The South Rejects a Prophet: The Life of Senator D. M. Key, 1824–1900* (New York: Frederick A. Praeger, 1967), pp. 160–64, claims that moderate southern Democrats did not join the Republican party because Hayes procrastinated before removing troops from South Carolina and Louisiana. He argues, unconvincingly, that Andrew Kellar's strategy would have worked if Hayes had acted immediately after his inauguration.

42. Sherman to Hayes, 9 Feb. 1878, RBH.

43. Hayes to Devens, 9 Feb. 1878, RBH; Hayes, *Diary,* 15 Feb. and 21 Mar. 1878, pp. 116, 132.

44. C. R. Williams, *Life of Rutherford Birchard Hayes,* 2:150–55; Edward McPherson, *A Hand-book of Politics for 1878 . . . ,* reprint (New York: Da Capo Press, 1972), pp. 186–91; Hayes, *Diary,* 14, 19, and 31 May 1878, pp. 141–43; Smith to Hayes, 27 Sept. and 5 Dec. 1877, Smith to Webb Hayes, 4 June 1878, Dickson to Hayes, 1 June 1878, RBH; Smith to Kellar, 3 Nov. 1877, Smith to Richard Smith, 19 Nov. 1877, Smith letterbook, pp. 310, 316, Ohio Historical Society, Columbus, copies at HPC; Kellar to Smith, 8 Nov. 1877, Smith Papers, copy at HPC.

45. C. R. Williams, *Life of Rutherford Birchard Hayes,* 2:153–59; McPherson, *Hand-book . . . 1878,* pp. 192–94; Sherman to Charles F. Conant, 26 June 1878, Sherman Papers, HPC.

46. Hayes, *Diary,* 5 Oct. and 12 Nov. 1878, pp. 164, 170; I. R. Burns (assistant U.S. attorney) to Sherman, 19 Nov. 1878, Key to Hayes, 15 Aug. 1878, RBH; Hirshson, *Farewell to the Bloody Shirt,* pp. 45–50.

47. Richardson, *Messages,* 10:4445–47; Hayes, *Diary,* 25 Dec. 1878, p. 178; Hirshson, *Farewell to the Bloody Shirt,* pp. 50–54.

48. C. R. Williams, *Life of Rutherford Birchard Hayes,* 2:160–69.

49. Edward McPherson, *A Hand-book of Politics for 1880 . . . ,* reprint (New York: Da Capo Press, 1972), pp. 55–64.

50. Johnston to Hayes, 15 May 1879, in C. R. Williams, *Life of Rutherford Birchard Hayes,* 2:172 n. 1; Hayes, *Diary,* 9 Mar. 1879, p. 192. In 1868, Grant lost New York by 10,000 out of 850,000 votes cast. Republicans, including Hayes, believed that frauds in New York City were responsible for the loss; see ibid., 23 Mar. 1879, p. 199.

51. Hayes, *Diary,* 26, 27, and 28 Apr. 1879, pp. 216–17; Sherman to Hayes, 3 May 1879, Smith to Hayes, 10 May 1879, RBH. For Hayes's veto message see Richardson, *Messages,* 10:4475–84; McPherson, *Hand-book . . . 1880,* p. 107. Judge William Johnston of Cincinnati influenced this veto message; see Johnston to Hayes, 29 Mar. 1879, Hayes to Johnston, 31 Mar. 1879, RBH.

52. McPherson, *Hand-book . . . 1880*, pp. 107–9; Garfield to Hayes, 12 May 1879, RBH. For Hayes's veto message see Richardson, *Messages*, 10:4484–88. The opinion of Samuel Shellabarger helped Hayes to shape his veto message; see Shellabarger to Hayes, (May 1879), RBH.

53. Hayes, *Diary*, 27 Apr. and 15, 18, and 25 May 1879, pp. 216–17, 219–21. For this veto message see Richardson, *Messages*, 10:4488–93; McPherson, *Hand-book . . . 1880*, p. 121.

54. Dickson to Hayes, 20 May 1879, RBH.

55. Hayes, *Diary*, 2, 4, and 20 June 1879, pp. 224–26, 230–31; C. R. Williams, *Life of Rutherford Birchard Hayes*, 2:199–200; Richardson, *Messages*, 10:4493–96; McPherson, *Hand-book . . . 1880*, pp. 112–13, 122–26, 128.

56. Hayes, *Diary*, 25 and 27 June 1879, pp. 232–33; Richardson, *Messages*, 10:4497–99; McPherson, *Hand-book . . . 1880*, pp. 128–31.

57. Hayes, *Diary*, 3 July 1879, pp. 233–34.

CHAPTER 4
LABOR AND CURRENCY PROBLEMS

1. Robert V. Bruce, *1877: Year of Violence* (Indianapolis, Ind.: Bobbs-Merrill, 1959), pp. 33–34, 40–42, 47–48, 50–55.

2. Ibid., pp. 63–65, 75–85.

3. Hayes to Sheriff of Stark County (14 Apr. 1876), letterbook, 3:52, Hayes to Allen T. Wikoff, 16 Apr. 1876, Hayes, "Governor's Proclamation," 19 Apr. 1876, RBH; Hayes to Garfield, 7 and 17 May 1876, Garfield Papers, LC, copies in HPC; Charles Richard Williams, *The Life of Rutherford Birchard Hayes: Nineteenth President of the United States*, 2 vols. (Columbus: Ohio State Archaeological and Historical Society, 1928), 1:439–40.

4. Bruce, *1877*, p. 87; Hayes to M. F. Force, 22 Oct. 1871, RBH; Rutherford B. Hayes, *Annual Message of the Governor of Ohio, to the Sixtieth General Assembly, at the Regular Session, Commencing Jan. 1, 1872* (Columbus, Ohio: Nevins & Myers, 1872), pp. 7–8.

5. Bruce, *1877*, pp. 85–94. These were the men whom Sherman had diverted from New York to Washington to prevent violence over the disputed election.

6. Ibid., pp. 94–114, 209–10.

7. For the story of the Great Strike in Pittsburgh as given here and in the following paragraphs see ibid., pp. 115–83 passim.

8. Ibid., pp. 195, 209–18.

9. Ibid., pp. 220–22.

10. Ibid., pp. 188–96; McCrary to Stokley, 23 July 1877, Executive Mansion Telegrams, 1:237, RBH.

11. Bruce, *1877*, pp. 196–208, 222–23; T. Harry Williams, ed., *Hayes: The Diary of a President, 1875–1881* (New York: David McKay, 1964), 24 July 1877, pp. 87–88 (hereafter cited as Hayes, *Diary*).

12. Bruce, *1877*, pp. 218–20.

13. Ibid., pp. 223–29.

14. Ibid., pp. 233–53 passim.

15. Ibid., pp. 253–60, 273–76, 281–82.

16. Ibid., pp. 270–71, 278–80. See S. D. Morgan to Key, 24 July 1877, RBH, for a plea to "keep the soldiers away" from the strikers.

17. Bruce, *1877*, pp. 285–91.

18. Ibid., pp. 287–90, 308–9; Hayes, *Diary*, 26 July 1877, pp. 89–90; Gerald G. Eggert, *Railroad Labor Disputes: The Beginnings of Federal Strike Policy* (Ann Arbor: University of Michigan Press, 1967), pp. 34–41; McCrary to Hancock, 27 July 1877, RBH.

19. Bruce, *1877*, pp. 310–15; Hayes, *Diary*, 31 July 1877, pp. 91–92; Dickson to Hayes, 29 July 1877, RBH.

20. Bruce, *1877*, pp. 300–304.

21. Hayes, *Diary*, 5 Aug. 1877, p. 93; Evarts to Hayes, 6 Aug. 1877, William Henry Smith to Hayes, 8 Aug. 1877, Sherman to Hayes, 12 Aug. 1877, Hayes to Smith, 11 Aug. 1877, McCrary to F. L. Wood, 13 Aug. 1877, RBH.

22. C. R. Williams, *Life of Rutherford Birchard Hayes*, 2:382–84.

23. Edwin J. Perkins, "Monetary Policies," *Encyclopedia of American Political History*, ed. Jack P. Greene, 3 vols. (New York: Charles Scribner's Sons, 1984), 2:834, 838–39; Allen Weinstein, *Prelude to Populism: Origins of the Silver Issue, 1867–1878* (New Haven, Conn.: Yale University Press, 1970), pp. 8–32; Irwin Unger, *The Greenback Era: A Social and Political History of American Finance, 1865–1879* (Princeton, N.J.: Princeton University Press, 1964), passim.

24. C. R. Williams, *Life of Rutherford Birchard Hayes*, 2:112–13; Unger, *Greenback Era*, pp. 336–53; Weinstein, *Prelude to Populism*, pp. 205–8; John Sherman, *Recollections of Forty Years in the House, Senate and Cabinet: An Autobiography*, 2 vols. (Chicago: Werner, 1895), 1:583.

25. Edward McPherson, *A Hand-book of Politics for 1878* . . . , reprint (New York: Da Capo Press, 1972), pp. 128–29, 145–47; Unger, *Greenback Era*, pp. 353–55.

26. James D. Richardson, comp., *A Compilation of the Messages and Papers of the Presidents*, 20 vols. (New York: Bureau of National Literature, 1897–1918), 10:4413–17, 4422–23; Weinstein, *Prelude to Populism*, pp. 239–40.

27. Charles Conant to Sherman, 3 Jan. 1878, H. C. Fahnestock to Sherman, 1 Feb. 1878, RBH; Unger, *Greenback Era*, pp. 357–58, 360–61.

28. Hayes, *Diary*, 3 and 6 Feb. 1878, pp. 115–16; Henry C. Lea to Schurz, 22 Feb. 1878, RBH.

29. Hayes, *Diary*, 17, 23, and 26 Feb. 1878, pp. 117–18, 121–22; McPherson, *Hand-book* . . . *1878*, pp. 129–34.

30. Hayes to Smith, 6 Mar. 1878, M. Halstead & Co. to Matthews, 25 Feb. 1878, RBH; Medill to Hayes, 25 and 27 Feb. 1878, in C. R. Williams, *Life of Rutherford Birchard Hayes*, 2:122–23; Unger, *Greenback Era*, pp. 362–63; Richardson, *Messages*, 10:4438–40.

31. McPherson, *Hand-book* . . . *1878*, pp. 127–28; Hayes, *Diary,* 1 Mar. and 13 and 14 Apr. 1878, pp. 122–23, 139; Weinstein, *Prelude to Populism,* pp. 345–49; Unger, *Greenback Era,* pp. 364–73, 401–2; Sherman, *Recollections,* 2:629–46; Sherman to Hayes, 9 Apr. 1878, RBH.

32. Richardson, *Messages,* 10:4450–51, 4510–11; Unger, *Greenback Era,* pp. 372–73; Edward C. Kirkland, *Industry Comes of Age: Business, Labor, and Public Policy, 1860–1897* (New York: Holt, Rinehart & Winston, 1961), pp. 279–80.

33. Richardson, *Messages,* 10:4567–69.

CHAPTER 5

THE FEDERAL BUREAUCRACY

1. Ari Hoogenboom, "The Pendleton Act and the Civil Service," *American Historical Review* 64 (1959): 301–3.

2. *Congressional Globe,* 39th Cong., 2d sess., p. 1036; Ari Hoogenboom, *Outlawing the Spoils: A History of the Civil Service Reform Movement, 1865–1883* (Urbana: University of Illinois Press, 1961), pp. 13–134 passim.

3. *The Diary of James A. Garfield,* ed. Harry James Brown and Frederick D. Williams, 4 vols. (East Lansing: Michigan State University Press, 1967–81), 5 Apr. 1877, 3:470.

4. U.S. Bureau of the Census, *Historical Statistics of the United States, Colonial Times to 1957* (Washington, D.C.: Government Printing Office, 1960), p. 710. Civil-service statistics are frequently contradictory and must be used with caution; see Paul P. Van Riper, *History of the United States Civil Service* (Evanston, Ill.: Row, Peterson, 1958), pp. 56–59. Data on civil servants in this chapter is based on U.S., *Register of Officers and Agents . . . for 1877, 1879, 1881, . . .* (Washington, D.C., 1878, 1880, 1882).

5. On the Liverpool consul see Sam Ross, *The Empty Sleeve: A Biography of Lucius Fairchild* (Madison: State Historical Society of Wisconsin, 1964), p. 164. In 1900, however, the Liverpool consulate was worth $60,000 per annum; see Richard Hume Werking, *The Master Architects: Building the United States Foreign Service, 1890–1913* (Lexington: University Press of Kentucky, 1977), p. 5.

6. Allan Nevins, *Hamilton Fish: The Inner History of the Grant Adminstration* (New York: Dodd, Mead, 1937), p. 863.

7. *Dictionary of American Biography* (hereafter cited as *DAB*), s.v. "Adee, Alvey Augustus."

8. Nevins, *Hamilton Fish,* p. 864; Werking, *Master Architects,* pp. 15–19.

9. *DAB,* s.vv. all those mentioned in this paragraph except Comly.

10. Edward Younger, *John A. Kasson: Politics and Diplomacy from Lincoln to McKinley* (Iowa City: State Historical Society of Iowa, 1955), pp. 197–98, 276–77.

11. *DAB,* s.v. "Welsh, John."

12. Dana to Evarts, 30 Mar. 1877, Evarts papers, HPC.

13. On the status of women in the Washington offices of the government see Cindy Sondik Aron, *Ladies and Gentlemen of the Civil Service: Middle-Class*

Workers in Victorian America (New York: Oxford University Press, 1987), pp. 40–290; *DAB*, s.v. "Sherman, John."

14. *DAB*, s.vv. "McCormick, Richard Cunningham," "French, William Merchant Richardson," "French, Daniel Chester." French's position in the Treasury Department was no handicap for his sculptor son. Young French's next major commission was a sculptural group for the new St. Louis Customhouse (1877).

15. *DAB*, s.v. "McPherson, Edward."

16. Allen Weinstein, *Prelude to Populism: Origins of the Silver Issue, 1867–1878* (New Haven, Conn.: Yale University Press, 1970), pp. 8–32.

17. *DAB*, s.v. "Knox, John Jay"; Ross M. Robertson, *The Comptroller and Bank Inspection: A Historical Appraisal* (Washington, D.C.: Office of the Comptroller of the Currency, 1968), pp. 45–47, 61, 72.

18. *DAB*, s.v. "Morrill, Lot Myrick."

19. Hoogenboom, *Outlawing the Spoils*, pp. 130–31, 156, 254.

20. Leonard D. White, *The Republican Era, 1869–1901: A Study in Administrative History* (New York: Macmillan, 1958), pp. 113–14. Massive changes were made in 1885, 1889, 1893, and 1897 with the alternation of party control; see ibid.

21. *DAB*, s.v. "Kimball, Sumner Increase."

22. T. Harry Williams, ed., *Hayes: The Diary of a President, 1875–1881* (New York: David McKay, 1964), 24 Mar. 1877, p. 85 (hereafter cited as Hayes, *Diary*); Emily Apt Geer, *First Lady: The Life of Lucy Webb Hayes* (Kent, Ohio: Kent State University Press, 1984), pp. 145–46.

23. *DAB*, s.vv. "Peirce, Benjamin," "Peirce, Charles Sanders," "Hilgard, Julius Erasmus."

24. Richard Hofstadter, *Social Darwinism in American Thought* (Boston, Mass.: Beacon Press, 1955), pp. 67–84.

25. *DAB*, s.v. "Newcomb, Simon."

26. White, *Republican Era*, pp. 222–30.

27. Ibid., pp. 208–21; Margaret Susan Thompson, *The "Spider Web": Congress and Lobbying in the Age of Grant* (Ithaca, N.Y.: Cornell University Press, 1985), pp. 261–62. Schurz pioneered in the use of a quantitative-rating system, but Bentley could make only limited use of it, because the variety of tasks his clerks performed made statistical comparisons difficult, if not impossible; see Aron, *Ladies and Gentlemen of the Civil Service*, pp. 126–27.

28. "Report of the Commissioner of the General Land Office," *House Executive Documents*, 45th Cong., 2d sess., 1877, no. 1, pt. 5, Interior, 1:1–2; ibid., 46th Cong., 3d sess., 1880, no. 1, pt. 5, Interior, 1:414–17; White, *Republican Era*, pp. 196–203.

29. White, *Republican Era*, pp. 186–87.

30. *DAB*, s.vv. "Eaton, John," "Blair, Henry William."

31. *DAB*, s.v. "Baird, Spencer Fullerton."

32. *DAB*, s.vv. "King, Clarence," "Hayden, Ferdinand Vandiveer," "Powell, John Wesley."

33. *DAB*, s.v. "Walker, Francis Amasa"; White, *Republican Era*, pp. 193–94.

34. *DAB*, s.v. "Waring, George Edwin"; Hans L. Trefousse, *Carl Schurz: A Biography* (Knoxville: University of Tennessee Press, 1982), p. 247.

35. Trefousse, *Carl Schurz*, p. 339 n. 33.

36. *DAB*, s.v. "Brumidi, Constantino."

37. *DAB*, s.v. "LeDuc, William Gates."

38. *DAB*, s.vv. "Comstock, Anthony," "Heywood, Ezra Hervey"; Hayes, *Diary*, 30 Dec. 1877 and 10 Jan. 1879, pp. 108–11, 183–84; Hayes to Rev. Dr. R. M. Hatfield, 21 Feb. 1879, ibid., p. 188; Charles Richard Williams, *The Life of Rutherford Birchard Hayes: Nineteenth President of the United States*, 2 vols. (Columbus: Ohio State Archaeological and Historical Society, 1928), 2:318–19.

39. *DAB*, s.v. "Bennett, De Robigne Mortimer"; Hayes, *Diary*, 10 and 19 July 1879, pp. 237, 240; *Diary and Letters of Rutherford Birchard Hayes: Nineteenth President of the United States*, ed. Charles Richard Williams, 5 vols. (Columbus: Ohio State Archaeological and Historical Society, 1922–26), 27 Mar. 1892, 5:67–68.

CHAPTER 6
CIVIL-SERVICE REFORM

1. T. Harry Williams, ed., *Hayes: The Diary of a President, 1875–1881* (New York: David McKay, 1964), 22 Apr. 1877, p. 87 (hereafter cited as Hayes, *Diary*); William J. Hartman, "Politics and Patronage: The New York Custom House, 1852–1902" (Ph.D. diss., Columbia University, 1952), p. 202; Venila Lovina Shores, *The Hayes-Conkling Controversy, 1877–1879* (Northampton, Mass.: Smith College Studies in History, 1919), pp. 228–30.

2. *The Diary of James A. Garfield*, ed. Harry James Brown and Frederick D. Williams, 4 vols. (East Lansing: Michigan State University Press, 1967–81), 14 Mar. 1877, 3:458 (hereafter cited as Garfield, *Diary*); John C. Hopper to Schurz, 14 Mar. 1877, William Endicott, Jr., to Schurz, 22 Mar. 1877, William Welsh to Schurz, 24 Mar. 1877, Schurz Papers, LC.

3. "Systematic Reform," "Civil Service Reform in England," "Blackboard Examination," *New York Times*, 21, 22, and 26 Mar. 1877. George Jones, the proprietor of the *New York Times*, had pledged to Jacob Dolson Cox his emphatic support of an "earnest" attempt by the administration to reform the civil service; see Cox to Hayes, 20 Feb. 1877, RBH; Grosvenor to Schurz, 26 Mar. 1877, M. Ralph Thayer to Schurz, 11 Apr. 1877, Schurz Papers; Schurz to Grosvenor, 29 Mar. 1877, in *Speeches, Correspondence and Political Papers of Carl Schurz*, ed. Frederic Bancroft, 6 vols. (New York: G. P. Putnam's Sons, 1913), 3:410 (hereafter cited as Schurz, *Speeches*); *Nation*, 31 May 1877, p. 313.

4. "The Civil Service," *New York Times*, 6 Apr. 1877; P. O. to editor, ibid., 9 and 16 Apr. 1877; *Nation*, 12 Apr. and 10 May 1877, pp. 213, 271; Horace White to Schurz, 10 Apr. 1877, Hawley to Schurz, 3 May 1877, Schurz Papers.

5. Reid to Schurz, 10 June 1877, Schurz Papers; John Cochrane to Schurz, 16 June 1877, Cochrane to Hayes, 18 June 1877, RBH.

6. "Commissions to Examine Certain Custom-Houses of the United States," *House Executive Documents,* 45th Cong., 1st sess., 1877, vol. 1, no. 8, pp. 14–16.

7. Sherman to Hayes, 26 May 1877, RBH; Hayes to Sherman, 26 May 1877, in Charles Richard Williams, *The Life of Rutherford Birchard Hayes: Nineteenth President of the United States,* 2 vols. (Columbus: Ohio State Archaeological and Historical Society, 1928), 2:77.

8. Sherman to Arthur, 28 May 1877, in "Commissions to Examine Certain Custom-Houses," pp. 18–20; "The Prospects of Reform," *Harper's Weekly,* 7 July 1877, p. 518.

9. White to Schurz, 14 June 1877, Schurz Papers; see also Henry Cabot Lodge to Schurz, 6 June 1877, Samuel Bowles to Schurz, 13 June 1877, ibid.

10. See Schurz's undated memo on the political activities of officeholders, RBH; James D. Richardson, comp., *A Compilation of the Messages and Papers of the Presidents,* 20 vols. (New York: Bureau of National Literature, 1897–1918), 10:4402–3; *Nation,* 28 June 1877, p. 373; Bowles to Schurz, 3 July 1877, in Schurz, *Speeches,* 3:414.

11. Sherman to Hayes, 5 July 1877, Dickson to Hayes, 8 July 1877, Bickham to Hayes, 15 July 1877, RBH.

12. Norton to Hayes, 22 July 1877, RBH.

13. Grosvenor to Schurz (15 July 1877), E. L. Godkin to Schurz, 15 July 1877, Charles Nordhoff to Schurz, 16 July 1877, Schurz to Grosvenor, 17 July 1877, Wells to Schurz, 1 Sept. 1877, Schurz Papers; *Nation,* 19 July and 6 and 13 Sept. 1877, pp. 33, 143, 159, 162. Arthur claimed that his removals were based on evidence the Jay Commission had collected; see Hartman, "Politics and Patronage," p. 206.

14. Shores, *Hayes-Conkling Controversy,* p. 235. Perhaps the Jay Commission was just repeating the 25 percent estimate of loss that originally had been made by Revenue Commissioner David A. Wells in 1866 and that had been utilized by Curtis in 1871, when he was chairman of the Grant Civil Service Commission; see Ari Hoogenboom, *Outlawing the Spoils: A History of the Civil Service Reform Movement, 1865–1883* (Urbana: University of Illinois Press, 1961), pp. 117–18.

15. Hoogenboom, *Outlawing the Spoils,* pp. 155–56; Sherman to Hayes, 12 Dec. 1876, 5 July 1877, and 8 Mar. 1881, RBH.

16. "Original Draft of the Famous *Substitute Resolution* . . . ," 26 Sept. 1877, Rochester Historical Society, Rochester, N.Y., copy at HPC; David M. Jordan, *Roscoe Conkling of New York; Voice in the Senate* (Ithaca, N.Y.: Cornell University Press, 1971), pp. 277–79; Sessions to Charles Foster, 29 Sept. 1877, RBH; Curtis to Norton, 30 Sept. 1877, Curtis Papers, Harvard University, Cambridge, Mass.; *Nation,* 4 Oct. 1877, p. 203; Samuel Ward to Evarts, 28 Sept. 1877, Evarts papers, HPC.

17. Hayes, *Diary,* 4 and 18 Oct. 1877, pp. 96–98; Hoogenboom, *Outlawing the Spoils,* pp. 160–61; Shores, *Hayes-Conkling Controversy,* p. 239; Charles Nordhoff to Schurz, 6 July 1877, Dorman B. Eaton to Schurz, 8 July 1877, Wells to Schurz, 9 July 1877, Schurz Papers; Curtis to Hayes, 14 Mar., 2 Aug., and 25

Oct. 1877, abstracts in "Letters Received by the President of the United States, 1877–1881," 2:180, RBH; Curtis to Burt, 22 Oct. 1877, Burt Collection, New-York Historical Society, New York, N.Y.; Evarts to Curtis, 24 Oct. 1877, Curtis Papers, Harvard University. Curtis requested Evarts to destroy his letters attacking Prince, but Curtis saved Evarts's letter reporting that the letters had been destroyed.

18. Garfield, *Diary*, 13 Oct. 1877, 3:529; Hayes, *Diary*, 24 Oct. 1877, pp. 100–101; Schurz to Henry Cabot Lodge, 1 Dec. 1877, Schurz Papers; Shores, *Hayes-Conkling Controversy*, pp. 236–37.

19. Samuel Ward to Evarts, 4 Nov. 1877, Evarts Papers; Devens to J. E. Sanford, 24 Oct. 1877, in *Boston Journal*, 29 Oct. 1877, Hayes to A. H. Rice, 7 Nov. 1877, ibid., 12 Nov. 1877, copies in RBH; Hoogenboom, *Outlawing the Spoils*, pp. 163–64.

20. "The President's Present Position as Described by Himself," *Nation*, 6 Dec. 1877, p. 342; Stanley P. Hirshson, *Farewell to the Bloody Shirt: Northern Republicans and the Southern Negro, 1877–1893* (Bloomington: Indiana University Press, 1962), pp. 40–41; Hayes to Smith, 8 Dec. 1877, RBH; Hayes, *Diary*, 9 Dec. 1877, pp. 106–7.

21. *Nation*, 13 and 20 Dec. 1877, pp. 357, 373; Dana to Hayes, 14 Dec. 1877, RBH.

22. Horace White, "The Civil-Service Issue in the Senate," *Nation*, 20 Dec. 1877, p. 376; Pierce to Schurz, 27 Dec. 1877, Lodge to Schurz, 20 Jan. 1878, Schurz Papers; "The New Year in Politics," *Harper's Weekly*, 12 Jan. 1878, p. 26.

23. Hayes, *Diary*, 13 Dec 1877, p. 107.

24. Ibid., 6 Dec. 1877, p. 106; Smith to Hayes, 13 Dec. 1877, Hayes to Smith, 16 Dec. 1877, Hayes to Curtis, 31 Dec. 1877, in *Diary and Letters of Rutherford Birchard Hayes: Nineteenth President of the United States*, ed. Charles Richard Williams, 5 vols, (Columbus: Ohio State Archaeological and Historical Society, 1922–26), 3:454–57 (hereafter cited as Hayes, *Diary and Letters*); Curtis to Hayes, 26 Dec. 1877, 2 and 9 Jan. 1878, Edmunds to Hayes, 29 Dec. 1877, W. P. Rogers to George W. McCrary, 7 Jan. 1878, RBH.

25. "The Republican Senators and 'Harmony,'" *Nation*, 10 and 17 Jan. 1878, pp. 20, 34; Hayes, *Diary*, 29 Jan. 1878, p. 115.

26. Hayes, *Diary*, 24 Mar. 1877, 1 and 12 Mar. 1878, pp. 85, 122–23, 126–27.

27. Ibid., 12 Mar. 1878, pp. 125–26; James Freeman Clarke to Schurz, 1 July 1878, in Schurz, *Speeches*, 3:421; Reid to William Henry Smith, 7 Mar. 1878, RBH.

28. Hayes, *Diary*, 25 and 26 Mar. and 13 Apr. 1878, pp. 133, 136–39; E. L. Godkin, "The Senatorial Attack on the Administration," *Nation*, 4 Apr. 1878, p. 222; ibid., 18 Apr. 1878, p. 253; Schurz to Lodge, 6 Apr. 1878, Schurz Papers.

29. MacVeagh to Norton, 13 Apr. 1878, Norton Papers, Harvard University; Hayes to Curtis, 2 May 1878, Curtis Papers, Harvard University; Curtis to Cox, 3 May 1878, Cox Papers, Oberlin College, Oberlin, Ohio; *Nation*, 2 May 1878, p. 285.

30. George C. Gorham to ———, 27 May 1878, Curtis Papers, HPC; Schurz to ———, 12 June 1878, in Schurz, *Speeches*, 3:420–21; *Nation*, 27 June 1878, p. 412.

31. "The Democratic Designs," *Nation*, 4 July 1878, pp. 4–5; "Illustrations of 'Reform,'" *New York Times*, 8 July 1878, p. 4.

32. Hayes to Curtis, 31 July 1878, Curtis Papers, Harvard University.

33. Sherman to Hayes, 10 July 1878, RBH; Weed to Henry L. Dawes, 12 Dec. 1881, Dawes Papers, LC; Norton to George William Curtis, July 1878, Norton Papers.

34. Evarts to Hayes, 13 July and 14 Aug. 1878, Curtis to George Edward Hall, 17 and 25 July 1878, Curtis to Hayes, 17 July and 20 Aug. 1878, RBH; *Nation*, 18 July 1878, p. 33. Graham was backed by Congressman Anson G. McCook; see Webb C. Hayes to McCook, 19 July 1878, Webb C. Hayes Papers, HPC.

35. Hayes to Curtis, 31 July 1878, Curtis Papers, Harvard University; Hayes to Curtis, 22 Aug. 1878, James to Curtis, 11 July and 23 Sept. 1878, Curtis to Hayes, 20 Aug. and 30 Sept. 1878, Anson G. McCook to Hayes, 23 Aug. 1878, RBH.

36. McCook to Hayes, 28 Sept. 1878, McCook to Sherman, 14 Nov. 1878, Smith to Hayes, 27 June 1878, RBH.

37. Hayes to Curtis, 22 Aug. 1878, Smith to Hayes, 3, 16, and 30 Oct. 1878, Key to Hayes, 15 Aug. 1878, Smith to Webb Hayes, 17 Oct. 1878, RBH; Hayes to Schurz, 4 Sept. 1878, Schurz Papers.

38. Hayes, *Diary*, 16 Dec. 1878, pp. 176–77; Hayes to Curtis, 16 Dec. 1878, Curtis to Hayes, 18 Dec. 1878, RBH; "Civil Service Reform," *New York Times*, 31 Jan. 1879.

39. *Nation*, 23 Jan. 1879, p. 60; Horace White, "Reform within the Party," ibid., 30 Jan. 1879, p. 78; Jordan, *Roscoe Conkling*, pp. 297–98; Shores, *Hayes-Conkling Controversy*, pp. 257–62; Hayes to the Senate of the United States, 31 Jan. 1879, in Richardson, *Messages*, 10:4463–64; Hayes, *Diary*, 2 Feb. 1879, p. 185.

40. *Journal of the Executive Proceedings of the Senate of the United States of America* (Washington, D.C.: Government Printing Office, 1828–1948), 21:501–4; *New York Times*, 4 Feb. 1879; *Nation*, 6 Feb. 1879, p. 93; "Who Is Responsible for the Custom-House?" ibid., pp. 96–97.

41. *Nation*, 12 Sept. 1878, p. 154; Hayes to Schurz, 4 Sept. 1878, Schurz Papers; Schurz to Hayes, 13 Sept. 1878, Hayes to Sherman, 4 Dec. 1878, RBH.

42. Hayes to Merritt, 4 Feb. 1879, RBH; Hayes to Burt, 6 Feb. 1879, in Hayes, *Diary and Letters*, 3:520–21; *Nation*, 20 Feb. and 13 Mar. 1879, pp. 127, 174.

43. Silas Wright Burt, "A Brief History of the Civil Service Reform Movement in the United States," pp. K–L, Burt Writings, New York Public Library. Internal evidence suggests that this manuscript was written in 1906 and revised in 1908.

44. For Merritt's lukewarm attitude see Merritt to Curtis, 13 June 1879, Curtis Collection, Staten Island Institute of Arts and Sciences, Staten Island, N.Y.; Curtis to Hayes, 28 June 1879, RBH; "The Civil Service Reform in the

Custom-House," *New York Times,* 9 July 1879; Curtis to Burt, 18 Aug. 1879, Burt Collection.

45. William Henry Smith to Rogers, 26 Apr. 1879, Rogers Papers, HPC; W. K. Rogers to Smith, 23 Apr. 1879, Smith to Hayes, 9 July and 7 Nov. 1879, Smith, "Personal Memoranda," 11 Sept. 1879, D. V. Bell to Sherman, 5, 13, and 24 May 1879, RBH. Postmaster George C. Codd of Detroit reiterated Bell's argument that the rules were admirable for a large office but not for his office, which had only forty clerks; see Codd to Key, 27 June 1879, RBH. For an example of modifying the rules out of existence see T. B. Shannon to Sherman, 26 Nov. 1879, RBH.

46. Tyler to Sherman, 17 May 1879, with notation by Lamphere, Tyler to Sherman, 25 June 1879, Tobey to Key, 19 May 1879, Curtis to Hayes, 28 June 1879, RBH.

47. Curtis to Hayes, 28 June 1879, Hayes to Sherman, 30 June 1879, RBH. Grace had been pardoned and had seen Sherman and Hayes in a successful attempt to collect his back pay; see *New York Times,* 21 July, 14, 21, 22, and 25 Sept., 29 Nov. 18 and 19 Dec. 1877.

48. Hayes to Evarts, 22 Aug. 1879, Curtis to Hayes, 24 Aug. and 5 Sept. 1879, Hayes to Curtis, 30 Aug. 1879, William Henry Smith, "Personal Memoranda," 11 Sept. 1879, RBH.

49. Sherman to Hayes, 4 Oct. 1879, Schurz to Hayes, 25 Oct. 1879, RBH; *Nation,* 30 Oct. 1879, p. 283.

50. Hayes to MacVeagh, 30 Oct. 1879, MacVeagh Papers, Historical Society of Pennsylvania, Philadelphia, copy at HPC; Wendell Phillips Garrison, "Disappearance of the Reform Administration," *Nation,* 20 Nov. 1879, pp. 339–40; Cary to Silas W. Burt, 3 Dec. 1879, Burt Collection.

51. Richardson *Messages,* 10:4512–18.

52. Hayes to Curtis, 15 Jan. 1880, Curtis to Hayes, 20 Jan. 1880, RBH.

53. Dorman B. Eaton, *The "Spoils" System and Civil Service Reform in the Custom-House and Post-Office at New York* (New York: G. P. Putnam's Sons, 1881), pp. vi, 62–82.

CHAPTER 7
THE NATIVE AMERICANS

1. Leonard D. White, *The Republican Era, 1869–1901: A Study in Administrative History* (New York: Macmillan, 1958), pp. 182–85, 187; Hans L. Trefousse, *Carl Schurz: A Biography* (Knoxville: University of Tennessee Press, 1982), p. 244; Wilcomb E. Washburn, *The Indian in America* (New York: Harper & Row, 1975), pp. 207–8.

2. White, *Republican Era,* pp. 187–92. White gives the number of Indian commissioners as ten, but he may have included the board's secretary and assistant secretary in his tally.

3. Details on the Nez Perce War come almost entirely from Alvin M. Josephy, Jr., *The Nez Perce Indians and the Opening of the Northwest* (New Haven, Conn.: Yale University Press, 1965), pp. 445–643.

4. Ibid., p. 491; Schurz to John D. Long, 9 Dec. 1880, in *Speeches, Correspondence and Political Papers of Carl Schurz*, ed. Frederic Bancroft, 6 vols. (New York: G. P. Putnam's Sons, 1913), 4:55 (hereafter cited as Schurz, *Speeches*).

5. Josephy, *Nez Perce Indians*, p. 531.

6. Ibid., p. 543.

7. Russell F. Weigley, *History of the United States Army* (New York: Macmillan, 1967), p. 269; T. Harry Williams, ed., *Hayes: The Diary of a President, 1875–1881* (New York: David McKay, 1964), 27 July 1877, p. 91 (hereafter cited as Hayes, *Diary*).

8. Hayes to Schurz (1877–81), no. 8978, Schurz Papers, LC, copy in HPC. These notes probably, but not positively, refer to the Nez Perce War. In any event, they do reveal Hayes's attitudes.

9. Josephy, *Nez Perce Indians*, p. 630.

10. John B. Wolff to Schurz, 6 Aug. 1877, RBH. Wolff, a Washington attorney, drafted a bill to "regulate Indian Affairs" and published his "Thorough Digest of the Indian Question . . . ," a copy of which is in RBH.

11. Hans L. Trefousse, "Carl Schurz and the Indians," *Great Plains Quarterly* 4 (Spring 1984): 111–13; Trefousse, *Carl Schurz*, p. 243; *The Diary of James A. Garfield*, ed. Harry James Brown and Frederick D. Williams, 4 vols. (East Lansing: Michigan State University Press, 1967–81), 17 and 19 Jan. 1878, 4:8–10; Bristow to Schurz, 6 Feb. 1878, in Schurz, *Speeches*, 3:418–19; *Nation*, 10 and 17 Jan. 1878, pp. 18, 34; John Q. Smith to Schurz, 8 Jan. 1878, Schurz to Hayes, 11 Feb. 1878, RBH.

12. William T. Hagan, *Indian Police and Judges: Experiments in Acculturation and Control* (New Haven, Conn.: Yale University Press, 1966), pp. 39–43, 69–70, 154, 169–70.

13. Hayes, *Diary*, 1 and 7 July 1878, pp. 147–49.

14. Hayes's Proclamation, 26 Apr. 1879, in James D. Richardson, comp., *A Compilation of the Messages and Papers of the Presidents*, 20 vols. (New York: Bureau of National Literature, 1897–1918), 10:4499–4500; Hayt to Schurz, 16 Aug. and 23 Oct. 1879, copies in RBH.

15. On the persistency of the trespassers see E. J. Brooks to Schurz, 31 Jan., 9 Feb., and 9 Mar. 1880, Alexander Ramsey to Schurz, 14 and 20 Feb., 2 and 10 Mar., and 15 July 1880, copies in RBH; Richardson, *Messages*, pp. 4550–51; Richard N. Ellis, *General Pope and U.S. Indian Policy* (Albuquerque: University of New Mexico Press, 1970), pp. 219–22.

16. Richardson, *Messages*, 10:4575–76; Lucy Hayes to Fanny Hayes, 3 Oct. 1880, RBH.

17. Hayes, *Diary*, 8 Dec. 1880, p. 301; Hoar to Hayes, 20 Nov. 1880, Hayes to Hoar, 24 Nov. 1880, Hayes to Dawes, 27 Nov. 1880, in *Diary and Letters of Rutherford Birchard Hayes: Nineteenth President of the United States*, ed. Charles

Richard Williams, 5 vols. (Columbus: Ohio State Archaeological and Historical Society, 1922–26), 3:626 (hereafter cited as Hayes, *Diary and Letters*).

18. Trefousse, *Carl Schurz*, pp. 242–45.

19. Schurz to John D. Long, 9 Dec. 1880, in Schurz, *Speeches*, 4:50–67; Trefousse, *Carl Schurz*, pp. 245–47; Hayes, "Special Message to Congress," 1 Feb. 1888, in Richardson, *Messages*, 10:4584.

20. *Dictionary of American Biography* (hereafter cited as *DAB*), s.vv. "Tibbles, Thomas Henry," "Bright Eyes"; Trefousse, *Carl Schurz*, p. 246; Richardson, *Messages*, 10:4584.

21. Schurz to Long, 9 Dec. 1880, in Schurz, *Speeches*, 4:65–74. The petition dated 25 Oct. 1880 was regarded by the friends of Bright Eyes and Tibbles as having been obtained by fraud, bribery, or cajolery; but there is little doubt that it represented a genuine sentiment among the Poncas. Among the twenty signers was Frank La Flesche. If this signature did belong to Francis, Bright Eyes's brother, they were on opposite sides of this issue.

22. Richardson, *Messages*, 10:4582, 4585; Trefousse, *Carl Schurz*, pp. 246–47; Hayes to Hoar, 16 Dec. 1880, in Hayes, *Diary and Letters*, 3:631. Hayes, in his methodical way, had already made inquiries about Allen; see Hayes to William Dean Howells, 8 Aug. 1879, Hayes-Howells Correspondence, Harvard University, Cambridge, Mass., copy at HPC. Hayes rejected the first man that the Boston committee named because he was "bitterly hostile" to the Interior Department; see Hayes to Walter Allen, 18 Dec. 1880, RBH.

23. Schurz, "Draft of a Message on the Ponca Commission," Jan. 1881, RBH; "Report of the Secretary of the Interior," *House Executive Documents*, 46th Cong., 3d sess., 1880, no. 1, pt. 5, Interior, vol. 1, pp. 3–4; Richardson, *Messages*, 10:4585–86.

24. Richardson, *Messages*, 10:4585–86; Dawes to Hayes, 1 Feb. 1881, in Hayes, *Diary and Letters*, 3:629 n; Trefousse, *Carl Schurz*, p. 247.

CHAPTER 8
FOREIGN AFFAIRS

1. T. Harry Williams, ed., *Hayes, The Diary of a President, 1875–1881* (New York: David McKay, 1964), 25 May 1879, pp. 221–22 (hereafter cited as Hayes, *Diary*).

2. Hayes to Garfield, 16 Dec. 1880, Garfield to Hayes, 14 Jan. 1881, Garfield Papers, LC, copies at HPC; Garfield to Hayes, 1 Dec. 1880, William Henry Smith Papers, Indiana Historical Society, Indianapolis, copy at HPC; Allan Peskin, *Garfield: A Biography* (Kent, Ohio: Kent State University Press, 1978), pp. 146, 305–6, 488; Thompson to Hayes, 22 Sept. 1879, RBH.

3. Harry Barnard, *Rutherford B. Hayes and His America* (Indianapolis, Ind.: Bobbs-Merrill, 1954), pp. 443–44; Charles Richard Williams, *The Life of Rutherford Birchard Hayes: Nineteenth President of the United States*, 2 vols. (Columbus: Ohio State Archaeological and Historical Society, 1928), 2:208–10. Much of this

account is based on Claude G. Bowers and Helen Dwight Reid, "William M. Evarts," in *The American Secretaries of State and Their Diplomacy,* ed. Samuel Flagg Bemis, 10 vols. (New York: Alfred A. Knopf, 1928), 7:239–44; Brainerd Dyer, *The Public Career of William M. Evarts* (Berkeley: University of California Press, 1933), pp. 193–203; Chester Leonard Barrows, *William M. Evarts: Lawyer, Diplomat, Statesman* (Chapel Hill: University of North Carolina Press, 1941), pp. 350–61.

4. Rosecrans to Matthews, 13 July 1877, enclosed in Matthews to Hayes, 6 Aug. 1877, RBH. On Rosecrans's railroad career in Mexico see David M. Pletcher, *Rails, Mines, and Progress: Seven American Promoters in Mexico, 1867–1911* (Ithaca, N.Y.: Cornell University Press, 1958), pp. 34–71.

5. Hayes, *Diary,* 24 and 31 July 1877, pp. 87, 92, 104–5 n. 5; Bowers and Reid, "William M. Evarts," pp. 239–44.

6. James D. Richardson, comp., *A Compilation of the Messages and Papers of the Presidents,* 20 vols. (New York: Bureau of National Literature, 1897–1918), 10:4561–62; Charles S. Campbell, *The Transformation of American Foreign Relations, 1865–1900* (New York: Harper & Row, 1976), pp. 87–91; Pletcher, *Rails, Mines, and Progress,* pp. 24–25.

7. Richardson, *Messages,* 10:4448; Allan Nevins, *Hamilton Fish: The Inner History of the Grant Administration* (New York: Dodd, Mead, 1937), p. 479; Edward McPherson, *A Hand-book of Politics for 1878 . . . ,* reprint (New York: Da Capo Press, 1972), pp. 212–13; idem, *A Hand-book of Politics for 1880 . . . ,* reprint (New York: Da Capo Press, 1972), pp. 67–68; Evarts to Hayes, 26 Aug. 1878, John Welsh to Evarts, Cipher Telegrams 1 and 2, 8 Nov. 1878, copies, Evarts to Hayes, 21 Nov. 1878, RBH.

8. Alexander Saxton, *The Indispensable Enemy: Labor and the Anti-Chinese Movement in California* (Berkeley: University of California Press, 1971), pp. 3–8; Henry Pelling, *American Labor* (Chicago: University of Chicago Press, 1960), p. 67.

9. Saxton, *Indispensable Enemy,* pp. 5–7, 76–77.

10. Ibid., pp. 104–5, 109–10, 132.

11. Ibid., pp. 118–20, 128–29; 132–33; McPherson, *Hand-book . . . 1880,* pp. 39–41.

12. Saxton, *Indispensable Enemy,* pp. 134–35; Curtis to Hayes, 21 Feb. 1879, RBH; Beecher to Evarts, no day and 26 Feb. 1879, Evarts Papers, HPC.

13. Saxton, *Indispensable Enemy,* pp. 136–37; Hayes, *Diary,* 23 Feb. 1879, p. 190.

14. Hayes, *Diary,* 28 Feb. 1879, p. 192; Richardson, *Messages,* 10:4466–72; C. R. Williams, *Life of Rutherford Birchard Hayes,* 2:214–15; Barrows, *William M. Evarts,* pp. 383–84.

15. Hayes, *Diary,* 20 and 23 Feb. 1879, pp. 187–88, 190.

16. Ibid., 28 Feb. 1879, p. 192; see also Hayes to Beecher, 1 Mar. 1879, RBH.

17. *Congressional Record,* 45th Cong., 3d sess., pp. 1770, 2141, 2384–85; *Dictionary of American Biography* (hereafter cited as *DAB*), s.v. "Seward, George Frederick."

18. George F. Seward, "Memorandum on the Chinese Question handed by Minister Seward to Mr. Evarts," 25 Mar. 1879, RBH.

19. George F. Kennan, e.g., flatly states that Hay "knew little if anything about China" and that the Open Door, though an old British policy, "was not an American policy." Foster Rhea Dulles, however, observes that the roots of the Open Door notes extend back to the mid nineteenth century, though the notes themselves reflected America's expansion into East Asia; see George F. Kennan, *American Diplomacy, 1900–1950* (Chicago: University of Chicago Press, 1951), pp. 27, 36; Foster Rhea Dulles, *1898–1954: America's Rise to World Power* (New York: Harper & Row, 1955), pp. 62–63.

20. Bowers and Reid, "William M. Evarts," pp. 254–55; Barrows, *William M. Evarts*, pp. 384–85; *Congressional Record*, 45th Cong., 3d sess., pp. 1774–75; *DAB*, s.v. "Seward, George Frederick."

21. Hayes, *Diary*, 14 July 1880, p. 287; *DAB*, s.vv. "Angell, James Burrill," "Swift, John Franklin," "Trescot, William Henry"; Bowers and Reid, "William M. Evarts," pp. 255–56; Charles I. Bevans, ed., *Treaties and Other International Agreements of the United States of America, 1776–1949*, 13 vols. (Washington, D.C.: Government Printing Office, 1968–76), 6:685–90. President Chester Arthur vetoed the twenty-year suspension as an "unreasonable" restriction.

22. Jose S. Decond to Evarts, 1 Aug. 1879, RBH.

23. David McCullough, *The Path between the Seas: The Creation of the Panama Canal, 1870–1914* (New York: Simon & Schuster, 1977), pp. 70–86. Hayes had insisted that the United States delegation be in full accord with Ammen; see Hayes to Thompson, 26 Mar. 1879, George N. Meissner Collection, Washington University, St. Louis, Mo., copy at HPC.

24. McCullough, *Path between the Seas*, pp. 67–68, 85–86, 104.

25. Richardson, *Messages*, 10:4521–22; Dexter Perkins, *The Monroe Doctrine, 1867–1907* (Baltimore, Md.: Johns Hopkins Press, 1937), pp. 74–75; Hayes, *Diary*, 13 Jan. 1880, p. 258. On the Chiriqui grant see *The Collected Works of Abraham Lincoln*, ed. Roy P. Basler, 9 vols. (New Brunswick, N.J.: Rutgers University Press, 1953–55), 4:561–62, 5:414, 418–19, 434, 561–62; J. G. Randall, *Lincoln the President: Springfield to Gettysburg*, 2 vols. (New York: Dodd, Mead, 1946), 2:137–40; John G. Nicolay and John Hay, *Abraham Lincoln: A History*, 10 vols. (New York: Century, 1890), 6:357–59.

26. Hayes, *Diary*, 7 and 8 Feb. 1880, pp. 261–63; news clippings, Hayes administration, 1877–81, vol. 85, p. 19, RBH.

27. Hayes, *Diary*, 11, 17, and 20 Feb. 1880, pp. 263–65.

28. "M. Lesseps and the Monroe Doctrine," *Harper's Weekly*, 28 Feb. 1880, p. 131; Rogers to Curtis, 23 Feb. 1880, Rogers Papers, HPC.

29. *Harper's Weekly*, 13 Mar. 1880, pp. 162–63; Hayes, *Diary*, 11 Apr. 1880, p. 273.

30. McCullough, *Path between the Seas*, pp. 118–22; Perkins, *Monroe Doctrine*, pp. 71–77; Richardson, *Messages*, 10:4537–38.

31. "The United States and the Lesseps Canal," *Harper's Weekly*, 27 Mar. 1880, p. 195. Perkins agrees with Woolsey, who should not be confused with his

father, President Theodore Dwight Woolsey of Yale, who was, like his son, an authority on international law; see Perkins, *Monroe Doctrine*, pp. 86–88; *DAB*, s.vv. "Woolsey, Theodore Salisbury" and "Woolsey, Theodore Dwight"; McCullough, *Path between the Seas*, p. 122.

32. McCullough, *Path between the Seas*, pp. 122–27; Thompson to Hayes, 18 and 26 Aug. 1880, RBH; Hayes to Thompson, 28 Aug. 1880, Lincoln National Life Foundation, copy at HPC; C. R. Williams, *Life of Rutherford Birchard Hayes*, 2:223–24.

33. Perkins, *Monroe Doctrine*, pp. 78–86.

34. Richardson, *Messages*, 10:4562–63, 4565–66, 4573.

CHAPTER 9
THE POLITICS OF SUCCESSION

1. William Henry Smith, "Personal Memoranda," 23 Nov. 1879, RBH; T. Harry Williams, ed., *Hayes: The Diary of a President, 1875–1881* (New York: David McKay, 1964), 26 Nov. 1879, p. 253 (hereafter cited as Hayes, *Diary*); James D. Richardson, comp., *A Compilation of the Messages and Papers of the Presidents*, 20 vols. (New York: Bureau of National Literature, 1897–1918), 10:4510–11.

2. Hayes to William Walter Phelps, 7 Dec. 1879, in Hayes, *Diary*, p. 255.

3. Ibid., 18 Dec. 1879, pp. 256–57; Sherman to R. M. Stimson, 27 Dec. 1879, Sherman Papers, HPC. Hayes left no record of the conversation with Grant beyond that they "had a nice quiet time" and that Grant "looks well and is in excellent spirits"; see Hayes to Lucy Hayes, 27 Dec. 1879, in *Diary and Letters of Rutherford Birchard Hayes: Nineteenth President of the United States*, ed. Charles Richard Williams, 5 vols. (Columbus: Ohio State Archaeological and Historical Society, 1922–26), 3:583 (hereafter cited as Hayes, *Diary and Letters*).

4. S. Peyton to Sherman, 3 Jan. 1880, Smith to Sherman, 9 Feb. 1880, Smith to Webb C. Hayes, 17 Feb. 1880, RBH.

5. Garfield to Charles E. Henry, 24 Nov. 1879, in James D. Norris and Arthur H. Shaffer, eds., *Politics and Patronage in the Gilded Age: The Correspondence of James A. Garfield and Charles E. Henry* (Madison: State Historical Society of Wisconsin, 1970), pp. 251–52; Sherman to Moulton, 6 and 20 Mar. 1880, Sherman Papers, HPC.

6. Sherman to Moulton, 1 and 21 May 1880, Sherman to S. S. Warner, 15 May 1880, Sherman Papers, HPC.

7. Hayes, *Diary*, 20 Mar. and 8 May 1880, pp. 267–68, 276; Richardson, *Messages*, 10:4543–44; Edward McPherson, *A Hand-book of Politics for 1880 . . .*, reprint (New York: Da Capo Press, 1972), pp. 131–34.

8. McPherson, *Hand-book . . . 1880*, pp. 135–40, 143–45; Richardson, *Messages*, 10:4544–50.

9. Smith to Hayes, 5 and 15 May 1880, RBH; Sherman to Moulton, 21 May 1880, Sherman Papers, HPC. On the desperate mood of Grant's supporters see

Robert D. Marcus, *Grand Old Party: Political Structure in the Gilded Age, 1880-1896* (New York: Oxford University Press, 1971), pp. 29–36.

10. McPherson, *Hand-book . . . 1880*, pp. 188–92; Marcus, *Grand Old Party*, pp. 30, 34–35; Hayes, *Diary*, 5 June 1880, pp. 277–78.

11. Hayes, *Diary*, 11 June 1880, pp. 278–79. Evidence that Hayes included Blaine among those who were bitter against him may be found in Lucy Hayes's comment, "We are happy in the general's [Garfield's] nomination, and the escape from James G. B[laine]"; see Lucy Hayes to Elinor Gertrude Mead [Mrs. William Dean] Howells, quoted without place or date in Hayes, *Diary and Letters*, 3:606 n.

12. Sherman to Moulton, 9 and 13 June 1880, Sherman Papers, HPC; Foster to S. T. Everett, 12 June 1880, letterpress copy, letterbook 1880–82, pp. 237, 238, 240, 241, Foster Papers, Ohio Historical Society, Columbus, copy at HPC; Foster to Sherman, 23 June 1880, ibid., pp. 247–54; Foster to Sherman, 7 July 1880, ibid., pp. 266–68.

13. Hayes, *Diary*, 15 June 1880, p. 279; Hayes, "*The Issues:* Notes by Pres. Hayes June 16, 1880," Garfield Papers, LC, copy at HPC.

14. E. L. Applegate to Garfield, 16 June 1880, Garfield to Hayes, 30 June 1880, R. W. Thompson to Schurz, 30 June 1880, Hayes to Thompson, 7 July 1880, RBH.

15. Garfield to Hayes, 21 June, 5 and 19 July 1880, William Henry Smith Papers, Indiana Historical Society, Indianapolis, copies at HPC; Hayes to Garfield, 8 July 1880, Garfield Papers, copy at HPC.

16. Hayes to Garfield, 23 July 1880, Garfield Papers, copy at HPC; R. W. Thompson to Hayes, 27 July and 18 Aug. 1880, RBH.

17. McPherson, *Hand-book . . . 1880*, pp. 192–94; Allan Peskin, *Garfield: A Biography* (Kent, Ohio: Kent State University Press, 1978), p. 484; Curtis to Burt, 22 July 1880, Burt Collection, New-York Historical Society, New York, N.Y.; Hayes, *Diary*, 13, 14, and 19 July 1880, pp. 285–88.

18. Norris and Shaffer, *Politics and Patronage*, passim.

19. Hayes to Garfield, 26 July 1880, Garfield Papers, copy at HPC. Peskin, in *Garfield*, p. 484, clearly explains the simple arithmetic that compelled Garfield to appease the Stalwarts.

20. Garfield to Hayes, 31 July 1880, Smith Papers, copy at HPC; Sherman to Moulton, 2 Aug. 1880, Sherman Papers, HPC; Peskin, *Garfield*, pp. 487–91.

21. *The Diary of James A. Garfield*, ed. Harry James Brown and Frederick D. Williams, 4 vols. (East Lansing: Michigan State University Press, 1967–81), 9 Aug. 1880, 4:439; Curtis to Hayes, 15 Aug. 1880, RBH; Garfield to Hayes, 18 Aug. 1880, Smith Papers, copy at HPC; Schurz to Garfield, 22 Sept. 1880, in *Speeches, Correspondence and Political Papers of Carl Schurz*, ed. Frederic Bancroft, 6 vols. (New York: G. P. Putnam's Sons, 1913), 4:48.

22. Hayes to Garfield, 5 Aug. 1880, Garfield Papers, copy at HPC; Hayes, *Diary*, 21 and 25 July 1880, pp. 288–89; McPherson, *Hand-book . . . 1880*, p. 195.

23. Charles Richard Williams, *The Life of Rutherford Birchard Hayes: Nineteenth President of the United States*, 2 vols. (Columbus: Ohio State Archaeological

and Historical Society, 1928), 2:290–92; Hayes, *Diary*, 5 Aug. 1880, p. 291. Hayes slightly misquoted Abraham Lincoln's "Special Session Message, July 4, 1861." Lincoln's exact words were; "To afford all an unfettered start and a fair chance in the race of life."

24. Edward McPherson, *A Hand-book of Politics for 1894* . . . , reprint (New York: Da Capo Press, 1972), pp. 131–42; Stanley P. Hirshson, *Farewell to the Bloody Shirt: Northern Republicans and the Southern Negro, 1877–1893* (Bloomington: Indiana University Press, 1962), pp. 192–200. As a private citizen, Hayes continued to drum up support for the Blair bill for southern education; see Hayes to J. M. Comly, 27 Mar. 1886, RBH; Hayes to Comly, 2 Apr. 1886, Comly Papers, Ohio Historical Society, copy at HPC.

25. Peskin, *Garfield*, pp. 495–96; Garfield to Jay Hubbell, 22 Aug. 1880, Garfield Papers, copy at HPC; Edw. M. Johnson to S. B. Curtis, 23 Oct. 1880, George William Curtis Papers, HPC. Johnson was secretary of the New York State Republican Committee, and S. B. Curtis was a customhouse employee. John Cessna to (officeholder), 25 Oct. 1880, copy, ibid. Cessna was chairman of the Pennsylvania State Republican Committee.

26. *Nation*, 28 Apr. 1881, p. 287; Ellis Paxson Oberholtzer, *A History of the United States since the Civil War*, 5 vols. (New York: Macmillan, 1917–37), 4:116–17; Leonard D. White, *The Republican Era, 1869–1901: A Study in Administrative History* (New York: Macmillan, 1958), pp. 376–78; Hayes, *Diary and Letters*, 28 Apr. and 3 May 1881, 4:10, 13.

27. *Nation*, 24 Feb. and 28 Apr. 1881, pp. 122, 287; Peskin, *Garfield*, pp. 504, 579. Peskin estimates Republican expenditures in Indiana at $70,000; see ibid., p. 504.

28. C. R. Williams, *Life of Rutherford Birchard Hayes*, 2:225–26; *Dictionary of American Biography*, s.v. "Marsh, George Perkins"; Hayes, *Diary*, 14 June 1879, 12 July and 8 Aug. 1880, pp. 230, 283, 291; Washington Metropolitan Chapter of the American Institute of Architects, *A Guide to the Architecture of Washington, D.C.* (New York: Frederick A. Praeger, 1965), pp. 39–40.

29. Hayes, *Diary*, 19, 24, and 28 Aug. 1880, pp. 293–95; C. R. Williams, *Life of Rutherford Birchard Hayes*, 2:293–96; Hayes to William Henry Smith, 19 Aug. 1880, in Hayes, *Diary and Letters*, 3:622; Hayes to Fanny Hayes, 18 Sept. and 17 Oct. 1880, RBH.

30. Lucy Hayes to Fanny Hayes, 3 Oct. 1880, Hayes to Fanny Hayes, 3, 6, and 17 Oct. 1880, Hayes to Mrs. E. J. Davis, 1 Dec. 1880, RBH; Hayes, *Diary*, 7 Nov. 1880 and 2 Jan. 1881, pp. 297–98, 304.

31. C. R. Williams, *Life of Rutherford Birchard Hayes*, 2:297–98; Curtis to Hayes, 15 Aug. 1880, RBH. "Our strength in this campaign," John Sherman wrote Hayes, "has been in the success of your administration. This is universally conceded by all intelligent men. No one has ignored it but Conkling and he has done it in the most offensive way possible"; see Sherman to Hayes, 1 Nov. 1880, RBH; see also Charles Francis Adams, Jr., to Schurz, 3 Nov. 1880, and William Henry Smith to Hayes, 8 Nov. 1880, RBH.

CHAPTER 10
THE END OF AN ADMINISTRATION

1. Hayes to Garfield, 30 Oct. 1880, Garfield Papers, LC, copy at HPC.

2. James D. Richardson, comp., *A Compilation of the Messages and Papers of the Presidents*, 20 vols. (New York: Bureau of National Literature, 1897–1918), 10:4553–58.

3. Ibid., pp. 4566–77; Carl Brent Swisher, *American Constitutional Development* (Boston, Mass.: Houghton Mifflin, 1943), pp. 495–97.

4. Hayes to Smith, 3 Jan. 1881, in *Diary and Letters of Rutherford Birchard Hayes: Nineteenth President of the United States*, ed. Charles Richard Williams, 5 vols. (Columbus: Ohio State Archaeological and Historical Society, 1922–26), 3:634–35 (hereafter cited as Hayes, *Diary and Letters*); James N. Tyner to McCormick, 7 and 11 Dec. 1880; Jewell to Tyner, 3 Jan. 1881, Tyner to Hayes, 6 Jan. 1881, RBH. On 1 July 1881, G. K. Gilmer, not Pelouze, was postmaster of Richmond.

5. Hayes to Garfield, 29 Nov. and 4 Dec. 1880, 8 and 28 Jan. 1881, Garfield to Hayes, 17 Feb. 1881, Garfield Papers, copies at HPC.

6. Hayes to Garfield, 16 Dec. 1880, Garfield to Hayes, 14 Jan. 1881, Garfield Papers, copies at HPC; Garfield to Hayes, 1 Dec. 1880, William Henry Smith Papers, Indiana Historical Society, Indianapolis, copy at HPC; Allan Peskin, *Garfield: A Biography* (Kent, Ohio: Kent State University Press, 1978), pp. 146, 305–6, 488; Huntington to John Sherman, 6 July 1880, personal file of Gen. E. O. C. Ord, National Archives, copy at HPC; Scott to Garfield, 29 Nov. 1880, RBH.

7. T. Harry Williams, *Hayes: The Diary of a President, 1875–1881* (New York: David McKay, 1964), 23 Jan. 1881, p. 307 (hereafter cited as Hayes, *Diary*); William T. Sherman to John Sherman, 31 Jan. 1881, William T. Sherman Papers, HPC; *Dictionary of American Biography* (hereafter cited as *DAB*), s.vv. "Miles, Nelson Appleton" and "Hazen, William Babcock."

8. Hayes to Garfield, 16 Dec. 1880 and 8 Jan. 1881, Garfield to Hayes, 14 Jan. 1881, Garfield Papers, copies at HPC.

9. Leopold Morse et al. to Hayes, 10 Dec. 1880, RBH; Hayes to Garfield, 11 Feb. 1881, Garfield Papers, copy at HPC; *DAB*, s.v. "Matthews, Stanley."

10. Garfield to Hayes, 7 Feb. 1881, Garfield Papers, copy at HPC; Hayes, *Diary*, 14 Dec. 1880 and 16 Jan. 1881, pp. 302, 305–6.

11. Hayes, Memorandum for Garfield, 17 Jan. 1881, RBH; *The Diary of James A. Garfield*, ed. Harry James Brown and Frederick D. Williams, 4 vols. (East Lansing: Michigan State University Press, 1967–81), 8 Jan. 1880, 4:348 (hereafter cited as Garfield, *Diary*); Edward McPherson, *A Hand-book of Politics for 1886* . . . , reprint (New York: Da Capo Press, 1972), p. 236.

12. Hayes to Frederick T. Frelinghuysen, 2 Apr. 1877, RBH; Hayes, *Diary*, 4 and 17 Dec. 1880, 2 Jan. and 5 and 11 Feb. 1881, pp. 300, 302–3, 304, 307–9.

13. Hayes, *Diary*, 15 and 16 Dec. 1880, 2 and 9 Jan., and 25 Feb. 1881, pp. 302, 304, 305, 311.

14. Ibid., 28 Mar. 1875 and 28 May 1879, pp. 1–2, 222; Charles Richard Williams, *The Life of Rutherford Birchard Hayes: Nineteenth President of the United States*, 2 vols. (Columbus: Ohio State Archaeological and Historical Society, 1928), 2:299–301; Harry Barnard, *Rutherford B. Hayes and His America* (Indianapolis, Ind.: Bobbs-Merrill, 1954), p. 404.

15. Hayes, *Diary*, 8 Feb. 1878, 13 June and 25 Dec. 1879, 13 Mar. and 25 Dec. 1880, pp. 116, 230, 257–58, 266–67, 303; C. R. Williams, *Life of Rutherford Birchard Hayes*, 1:82; Barnard, *Rutherford B. Hayes*, p. 185.

16. Hayes, *Diary*, 1 Jan. and 4 Oct. 1877, 21 and 31 Mar. and 14 June 1879, pp. 65, 96, 196, 208, 230.

17. Ibid., 30 Dec. 1877, pp. 108–12; C. R. Williams, *Life of Rutherford Birchard Hayes*, 2:318–19.

18. Hayes to Murat Halstead, 26 Nov. 1880, Halstead papers, Cincinnati Historical Society, copy at HPC; Hayes to William Henry Smith, 3 Jan. 1881, in Hayes, *Diary and Letters*, 3:635; Hayes to John Sherman, 3 May 1881, RBH.

19. Barnard, *Rutherford B. Hayes*, p. 496; Hayes, *Diary*, 16 Jan. 1881, p. 305.

20. Hayes, *Diary*, 23 Jan. and 2 Mar. 1881, pp. 307, 313.

21. Barnard, *Rutherford B. Hayes*, p. 500; Peskin, *Garfield*, p. 540; Garfield, *Diary*, 3 and 4 Mar. 1881, 4:552–53.

22. C. R. Williams, *Life of Rutherford Birchard Hayes*, 2:335; Barnard, *Rutherford B. Hayes*, pp. 513–18.

23. C. R. Williams, *Life of Rutherford Birchard Hayes*, 2:335–39, 349–57.

24. Ibid., pp. 346–48, 392 n. 3, 394.

25. Ibid., pp. 386–98; Barnard, *Rutherford B. Hayes*, pp. 509–12, 521–22.

26. Samuel Langhorne Clemens to Hayes, 10 Apr. 1882, RBH.

BIBLIOGRAPHICAL ESSAY

This study is based primarily on the Hayes Papers (abbreviated as RBH in the notes) at the Rutherford B. Hayes Presidential Center, Spiegel Grove, Fremont, Ohio (HPC). The Hayes Papers are voluminous and are available on microfilm. In addition, the Hayes Presidential Center has acquired, from other collections, copies of correspondence between Hayes and members of his administration and has assembled this material and copies of many of its own holdings in easy-to-read typewritten loose-leaf books. Hayes also kept a diary, which, while it is neither complete nor written with a literary flair, is a valuable contemporary record of his thoughts. It has been published, with a generous selection of his correspondence, in *Diary and Letters of Rutherford Birchard Hayes: Nineteenth President of the United States*, edited by Charles Richard Williams, 5 vols. (Columbus: Ohio State Archaeological and Historical Society, 1922–26); it covers the years 1830 to 1892. Williams wrote out abbreviations, corrected errors in spelling, and supplied punctuation in this edition. In contrast, T. Harry Williams scrupulously edited *Hayes: The Diary of a President, 1875–1881, Covering the Disputed Election, the End of Reconstruction, and the Beginning of Civil Service* (New York: David McKay, 1964) to reveal the original manuscript, including occasional minor errors and crossed-out words.

Besides editing the *Diary and Letters*, Charles Richard Williams wrote *The Life of Rutherford Birchard Hayes: Nineteenth President of the United States*, 2 vols. (Columbus: Ohio State Archaeological and Historical Society, 1914, reprint 1928), which, though laudatory in spirit, is crammed with information and quotes extensively from difficult-to-find speeches, letters, and newspapers. While the Williams biography is in the life-and-letters-of-a-public-figure tradition, Harry Barnard's *Rutherford B. Hayes and His America* (Indianapolis, Ind.: Bobbs-Merrill, 1954) is more concerned with Hayes the man than with Hayes the president and is more interested in the development of his character and personality than in how he functioned as a political leader. Although super-seded by Barnard's book, H. J. Eckenrode's *Rutherford B. Hayes: Statesman of Reunion* (New York: Dodd, Mead, 1930) is still useful, and the salient events of Hayes's career may be conveniently found in Arthur Bishop, ed., *Rutherford B. Hayes, 1822–1893: Chronology, Documents, Bibliographical Aids* (Dobbs Ferry, N.Y.: Oceana Publications, 1969). John W. Burgess's *The Administration of President Hayes* (New York: Charles Scribner's Sons, 1916), though by a distinguished scholar, is uncritical, thin and dated; but Kenneth E. Davison's *The Presidency of Rutherford B. Hayes* (Westport, Conn.: Greenwood Press, 1972) is useful.

On Lucy Hayes, a spirited, compassionate advocate of abolition and temperance and a devoted Methodist who influenced her husband, despite his moderate, rational, and secular outlook on life, see Emily Apt Geer, *First Lady: The Life of Lucy Webb Hayes* (Kent, Ohio: Kent State University Press, 1984).

Among his cabinet members, Hayes depended heavily on William M. Evarts, John Sherman, and Carl Schurz. The selections by editor Frederic Bancroft, in *Speeches, Correspondence and Political Papers of Carl Schurz*, 6 vols. (New York: G. P. Putnam's Sons, 1913), are particularly useful for the presiden-tial campaign of 1876 and for Indian affairs. Hans L. Trefousse, in *Carl Schurz: A Biography* (Knoxville: University of Tennessee Press, 1982), while illustrating that Schurz was a practitioner of ethnic politics, also analyzes his performance as secretary of the interior. Winfield S. Kerr, in *John Sherman: His Life and Public Service*, 2 vols. (Boston, Mass.: Sherman, French, 1908), supplements Jeannette P. Nichols's sketch of John Sherman in *The Dictionary of American Biography*, edited by Allen Johnson and Dumas Malone, 20 vols. (New York: Charles Scribner's Sons, 1928–37). Sherman's own *Recollections of Forty Years in the House, Senate and Cabinet: An Autobiography*, 2 vols. (Chicago: Werner, 1895) is lucid and detailed on financial affairs. Brainerd Dyer's *The Public Career of William M. Evarts* (Berkeley: University of California Press, 1933) is useful, but Chester Leonard Barrows's *William M. Evarts: Lawyer, Diplomat, Statesman* (Chapel Hill: University of North Carolina Press, 1941) is more detailed on Evarts's tenure as secretary of state. Claude G. Bowers and Helen Dwight Reid, in "William M. Evarts," in *The American Secretaries of State and Their Diplomacy*, edited by Samuel Flagg Bemis, 10 vols. (New York: Alfred A. Knopf, 1928), 7:215–59, discuss the foreign policy of the Hayes administration. On the southern member in the cabinet, who personified Hayes's efforts to garner support for the Republican party from the ashes of southern Whigs, see David M. Abshire, *The South Rejects a Prophet: The Life of Senator D. M. Key, 1824–1900* (New York: Frederick A. Praeger, 1967).

Two repositories of primary source materials that were indispensable for this study are James D. Richardson's, *A Compilation of the Messages and Papers of the Presidents*, 20 vols. (New York: Bureau of National Literature, 1897–1918), 10:4391–4592, and the biennial collection of documents by the head of Hayes's Bureau of Printing and Engraving, Edward McPherson, under the title of *Hand-book of Politics* (1872–94). This collection has been reissued in four volumes (New York: Da Capo Press, 1972), with an introduction by Harold M. Hyman and

Hans L. Trefousse. Two old but valuable general works are James Ford Rhodes, *History of the United States: From the Compromise of 1850 to the End of the Roosevelt Administration,* 9 vols. (New York: Macmillan, 1928), volumes 7 and 8, which were first published in 1906 and 1919 respectively, and Ellis Paxson Oberholtzer, *A History of the United States since the Civil War,* 5 vols. (New York: Macmillan, 1917–37), volumes 3 and 4.

Secretary of State Evarts quipped that the Hayes administration was not well edited, and Hayes remarked that it had no organ. The Democratic press—for example, the *New York World*—was hostile to Hayes and continued to question his right to the presidency; partisan Republican papers—for example, the *New York Tribune*—were hostile to his notions of civil-service reform; and the independent or Republican reform papers—for example, the *New York Times*—were often angry because his reform notions were not sweeping enough. *Harper's Weekly,* edited by George William Curtis, was consistently friendly to the Hayes administration; whereas the independent *Nation,* under Edwin L. Godkin, uncompromisingly backed reform and was, more often than not, critical of Hayes, even while recognizing that he was as much of a reformer as was likely to occupy the White House. The *Nation* is an incomparable source of important information and of intelligent, although biased, commentary.

The perspective of political leaders outside of the Hayes administration was helpful for this study. *The Diary of James A. Garfield,* edited by Harry James Brown and Frederick D. Williams, 4 vols. (East Lansing: Michigan State University Press, 1967–81), is the most valuable record left by any of these men. Garfield, who was friendly to Hayes but critical of him, records the hostile views of several Republican politicians. Garfield's diary should be supplemented by Allan Peskin's excellent *Garfield: A Biography* (Kent, Ohio: Kent State University Press, 1978). In contrast to Garfield, both Arthur and Conkling, who were hostile to Hayes, left few papers. Tracking down Arthur materials enabled Thomas C. Reeves to write the informative and appreciative *Gentleman Boss: The Life of Chester Alan Arthur* (New York: Alfred A. Knopf, 1975); but because Conkling did a more thorough job of destroying his literary remains, David M. Jordan, in *Roscoe Conkling of New York: Voice in the Senate* (Ithaca, N.Y.: Cornell University Press, 1971), often surmises but does not know, describes but does not explain actions, raises but does not settle questions. Nevertheless, it is the best Conkling biography to date. For another biography of a Republican who was hostile to Hayes see Leon Burr Richardson's *William E. Chandler: Republican* (New York: Dodd, Mead, 1940), which is detailed and an excellent source of information. For the point of view of the Democratic candidate in 1876, who also had his papers destroyed, see Alexander Clarence Flick, *Samuel Jones Tilden: A Study in Political Sagacity* (New York: Dodd, Mead, 1939); but for more critical appraisals of Tilden see Mark D. Hirsch, "Samuel J. Tilden: The Story of a Lost Opportunity," *American Historical Review* 56 (1951): 788–802, and Robert Kelley, "The Thought and Character of Samuel J. Tilden: The Democrat as Inheritor," *Historian* 26 (1964): 176–205. For authoritative biographies of innumerable persons connected with the Hayes administration, *The Dictionary of American Biography* has been indispensable.

The best book on the 1876 presidential campaign, the dispute over its outcome, and its resolution is Keith Ian Polakoff's *The Politics of Inertia: The Election of 1876 and the End of Reconstruction* (Baton Rouge: Louisiana State University Press, 1973). The most provocative and most influential book on the settlement of that dispute is still C. Vann Woodward's *Reunion and Reaction: The Compromise of 1877 and the End of Reconstruction* (Boston: Little, Brown, 1951; 2d ed., Garden City, N.Y.: Doubleday, 1956), with its hypothesis that northern Republicans and southern Democrats of Whig extraction, moved primarily by economic concerns, united to give the election to Hayes. No one denies that there were negotiations along these lines, but Polakoff, as well as Allan Peskin, in "Was There a Compromise of 1877?" *Journal of American History* 60 (1973): 63–75, Michael Les Benedict, in "Southern Democrats in the Crisis of 1876–1877: A Reconsideration of *Reunion and Reaction,*" *Journal of Southern History* 46 (1980): 489–524, and George Rable, in "Southern Interests and the Election of 1876: A Reappraisal," *Civil War History* 26 (1980): 347–61, agree that Woodward exaggerates the importance of those negotiations and that they did not affect Hayes's victory.

For Hayes's southern policy see William Gillette, *Retreat from Reconstruction, 1869–1879* (Baton Rouge: Louisiana State University Press, 1979), and Stanley P. Hirshson, *Farewell to the Bloody Shirt: Northern Republicans and the Southern Negro, 1877–1893* (Bloomington: Indiana University Press, 1962). Hirshson discusses the Republican party's reaction to Hayes's southern policy and emphasizes that political calculations, rather than moral considerations, inspired the party leaders, whether they embraced or rejected the bloody shirt.

Two issues of great concern to Hayes were civil-service reform and hard money. On the American bureaucracy in the late nineteenth century see the classic work by Leonard D. White, *The Republican Era, 1869–1901: A Study in Administrative History* (New York: Macmillan, 1958), and peruse the United States, *Register of Officers and Agents*, for *1877, 1879, 1881*, etc. (Washington, D.C., 1878, 1880, 1882), for the size, organization, and complexity of the civil service during the Hayes administration. Cindy Sondik Aron, in *Ladies and Gentlemen of the Civil Service: Middle-Class Workers in Victorian America* (New York: Oxford University Press, 1987), discusses how male and female civil servants functioned and interacted with each other in the large departmental offices in Washington. On the symbiotic relationship of the civil service with the political parties and on the difficulties involved in divorcing the two see Ari Hoogenboom, *Outlawing the Spoils: A History of the Civil Service Reform Movement, 1865–1883* (Urbana: University of Illinois Press, 1961). The New York Customhouse has received deserved attention by William J. Hartman, in "Politics and Patronage: The New York Custom House, 1852–1901" (Ph.D. diss., Columbia University, 1952); by Dorman B. Eaton, in *The "Spoils" System and Civil Service Reform in the Custom-House and Post-Office at New York* (New York: G. P. Putnam's Sons, 1881); and by Venila Lovina Shores, *The Hayes-Conkling*

Controversy, 1877–1879 (Northampton, Mass.: Smith College Studies in History, 1919). The last two are reprinted in *The Spoils System in New York* (New York: Arno Press, 1974). Irwin Unger's *The Greenback Era: A Social and Political History of American Finance, 1865–1879* (Princeton, N.J.: Princeton University Press, 1964) details the Hayes administration's preparations for specie resumption and its reaction to the Bland-Allison Act. Hayes's attitudes emphasize Unger's perception that the struggle between the soft-money and the hard-money interests was more than an economic division, since it also reflected clashing intellectual and ethical systems. Allen Weinstein's *Prelude to Populism: Origins of the Silver Issue, 1867–1878* (New Haven, Conn.: Yale University Press, 1970) comes to grips with the economic complexity of the silver movement up to the passage of the Bland-Allison Act.

Hayes had scarcely taken office before a violent strike and a tragic war broke out. Robert V. Bruce, *1877: Year of Violence* (Indianapolis, Ind.: Bobbs-Merrill, 1959) is graphic, readable, and scholarly. Although the Great Strike is usually seen as disastrous for workers, Bruce argues that the fight they made was worthwhile, since the railroad management became frightened, ceased to cut wages, and within a few years restored the earlier wage cuts. On the role of the federal courts during the Great Strike see Gerald G. Eggert, *Railroad Labor Disputes: The Beginnings of Federal Strike Policy* (Ann Arbor: University of Michigan Press, 1967). Both the Nez Perce tribe and its war with the United States are covered eloquently and exhaustively in Alvin M. Josephy, Jr., *The Nez Perce Indians and the Opening of the Northwest* (New Haven, Conn.: Yale University Press, 1965). An evaluation of an attempt by reformers to integrate Native Americans into the larger society is found in William T. Hagan, *Indian Police and Judges: Experiments in Acculturation and Control* (New Haven, Conn.: Yale University Press, 1966). For a discussion of the United States Army, upon which frequent calls were made during the summer of 1877, see Russell F. Weigley, *History of the United States Army* (New York: Macmillan, 1967).

Two vexing foreign-policy issues that arose during the Hayes administration were the demand that the Burlingame Treaty with China be abrogated and the attempt by Ferdinand de Lesseps to dig a canal in Panama. The prejudice against Chinese laborers is discussed by Alexander Saxton in *The Indispensable Enemy: Labor and the Anti-Chinese Movement in California* (Berkeley: University of California Press, 1971). On the canal in Panama see David McCullough's fascinating book *The Path between the Seas: The Creation of the Panama Canal, 1870–1914* (New York: Simon & Schuster, 1977), and for the proposed canal's implications on what was already a traditional policy see Dexter Perkins, *The Monroe Doctrine, 1867–1907* (Baltimore, Md.: Johns Hopkins Press, 1937). For a balanced overview of late-nineteenth-century foreign relations see Charles S. Campbell, *The Transformation of American Foreign Relations, 1865–1900* (New York: Harper & Row, 1976).

Three other works that are instructive on politics in this period are Margaret Susan Thompson, *The "Spider Web": Congress and Lobbying in the Age of Grant* (Ithaca, N.Y.: Cornell University Press, 1985); James D. Norris and Arthur H.

Shaffer, eds., *Politics and Patronage in the Gilded Age: The Correspondence of James A. Garfield and Charles E. Henry* (Madison: State Historical Society of Wisconsin, 1970); and Robert D. Marcus, *Grand Old Party: Political Structure in the Gilded Age, 1880–1896* (New York: Oxford University Press, 1971).

INDEX

Adams, Henry, 218
Adams, John Quincy, 59, 137, 144
Addee, Alvey A., 105
Adjutant general, office of, 115
Advisors of RBH, 58
Agriculture, 1, 2; department of, 123
Akerman, Amos T., 68
Allen, Walter, 169
Allen, William, 11, 12
Allison, William B., 94, 96; and Bland-
   Allison (silver-coinage) Act, 96–98, 110,
   137, 213, 225
American Ephemeris and Nautical Almanac,
   116
American Indians. *See* Native Americans
Ames, Adelbert, 5
Ammen, Daniel, 185
Anderson, Thomas C., 71
Angell, James B., 183–84
*Annual Reports on the Internal Commerce of
   the United States*, 114
Anthony, Susan B., 5
Appointments to civil service
—of Garfield, suggestions of RBH on,
   214–15
—investigation and reform of, 127–51
—of RBH, 57, 133–135, 137; to cabinet,
   51–53, 56, 134; in collaboration with
   Garfield, 200–1, 215–17; conflict with

Congress over, 58–59, 134, 135, 136,
   137, 201, 212, 224; Potter investigation
   of, 139; in N.Y. Customhouse, 133–36,
   139–40, 141, 142–44; in post offices, 142,
   145; to Supreme Court, 137, 216
Appropriations bills, 74, 75–76, 77–78,
   195–97; for army, 76, 77, 82, 94, 173; for
   civil-service reform, 102; for restitution
   to Ponca Indians, 167, 171; vetoed by
   RBH, 224–25; weakening election laws,
   195–97
Argentina, and RBH, 184
Army, U.S., 82, 115, 174, 215–16; appropriations for, 76, 77, 82, 94, 173;
   enforcing election laws, 74, 75, 76, 78;
   expansion of, RBH supporting, 213;
   maintaining governments in southern
   states, 20, 57, 58, 60, 62, 63, 64, 65, 67,
   69; in Mexican border dispute, 174; and
   Native Americans, 153–54, 162, 163,
   165, 168; in Nez Perce War, 82, 155,
   156–59; pension payments to veterans,
   117–18
Arrears Act (1879), 117
Arthur, Chester A., 139, 149, 198, 206,
   207; in N.Y. Customhouse, 111–12,
   129–30, 131–32, 135, 136, 139, 140, 142
Assassinations, fear of, 55
Assessments on wages of civil servants, 7,

RBH refers to Rutherford B. Hayes.